COMPLIANCE
JURISDICTIONALISATION

Previously published in the *Compliance & Regulation* Serie:

M.-A. Frison-Roche (ed.), *Compliance Monumental Goals*, 2023.
M.-A. Frison-Roche (ed.), *Compliance Tools*, 2021.

COMPLIANCE JURISDICTIONALISATION

Edited by
Marie-Anne Frison-Roche

Journal of Regulation & Compliance

Journal of Regulation & Compliance (JoRC)

BRUYLANT

For information on the Journal of Regulation & Compliance (JoRC) activities and publications, go to www.thejournalofregulation.com.

FSC
www.fsc.org
MIX
Paper from responsible sources
FSC® C008551

For all information the Larcier's funds and new products in your area of specialisation, please consult our websites via www.larcier-intersentia.com.

Printed in Belgium

Legal deposit:
National Library, Paris: January 2024
Royal Library of Belgium, Brussels: 2024/0023/006

ISBN : 978-2-8027-7074-9

Summary

INTRODUCTION

Main Aspects of the Book
Compliance Jurisdictionalisation

Marie-Anne Frison-Roche

Agrégée des Facultés de droit

Professor of Regulatory Law and Compliance Law

Director of the *Journal of Regulation & Compliance (JoRC)*

Director of the *European School of Regulation and Compliance Law*

This book, *Compliance Jurisdictionalisation*, takes up a challenge: how can we understand, make coherent and anticipate the evolution of Compliance Law that is characterised as a set of mechanisms that are developed within companies, *ex ante*, with the effect, or even the purpose, of avoiding the judge, while we are constantly reading new court decisions on the subject day after day? Sanctions, controls, appeals, settlements: judges and lawyers are everywhere in compliance mechanisms, creating new situations, sometimes with no solution yet available. Even though compliance tools were designed to avoid the judge and produce security by avoiding conflict.

Is it a sign of failure or of the maturity of this new branch of Law? This present book shows that if we do not see compliance as a mindless mechanism for automatically applying regulations, but as a system whose spirit and normativity are rooted in the Monumental Goals towards which all are converging, then the *jurisdictionalisation of compliance* is, on the contrary, a sign of its maturity. The challenge taken up by this book is to demonstrate this, despite the many technical difficulties, and to anticipate the future of Compliance Law, in which judges and judicial officers will, on the contrary, be at the centre. In this respect, it is closely linked to the previous book on *Compliance Monumental Goals* since it is to achieve these goals that public authorities, companies and judges form an alliance, just as it is closely linked to the two books that will follow, firstly *Compliance Obligation*, because the enforcement of this obligation, legal, or contractual, or issued by self-regulation is made also by the judge, and secondly *Compliance Evidence System*, because proof, demonstrated notably before the judge, is in fact the primary challenge of Compliance, not only in legal terms but also in financial, managerial and societal terms.

This is why the book opens with a general article written by Marie-Anne Frison-Roche: *Reinforce the Judge and the Lawyer to impose Compliance Law as a characteristic of the Rule of Law.* It shows that it is understandable that compliance mechanisms are perceived by many with hostility, because they seem designed to distance the judge, whereas there can be no Rule of Law system without a judge. It is true that there are solid arguments that present compliance techniques as converging towards the uselessness of the judge, and the first part of this article sets out the solidity of these arguments. Admittedly, there are judges of all kinds, and some very powerful ones, but this may be a sign of imperfection: once the *ex ante* logic has been deployed to its full efficacy, the judge would no longer be needed… and the lawyer would disappear with him. This prospect of a world without judges, without lawyers and ultimately without Law, a world where algorithms could use multiple *ex ante* processes to organise the "conformity" of all our behaviour with all the regulations applying to us; this vision presupposes that we define this new branch of Law as the concentration of processes that gives full effectiveness to all the rules, regardless of their content. Assuming that this engineer's dream is even feasible, even in this very mechanical conception, we cannot do without judges and lawyers.

Therefore, the second part of the article shows that it is imperative to recognise their contributions to Compliance Law, contributions linked and invaluable. Firstly, because there has never been a purely *ex ante* legal system, and even in the days of the Chinese legists, there was still a need for people to interpret regulations, because a legal system must always be interpreted *ex post* by the person who must in any case answer the questions asked to him or her by the subjects of Law, as soon as the political system accepts that they have the right to bring claims before a judge. Then there is the lawyer, whose role, although linked to that of the judge, is distinct from the latter, both more limited and broader, since he or she must appear in all cases where the jurisdictional figure is established. However, Compliance Law has increased the number of such cases since not only does it extend Regulation Law by conferring numerous powers on the administrative authorities, but it also turns companies into judges, which is what lawyers have to deal with. What's more, Compliance Law only makes sense in terms of the Monumental Goals it serves. It is in this way that this branch of Law preserves the freedom of human beings, particularly in the digital world where compliance techniques protect them from the power of companies through the use that Law forces these companies to make of this very power. Firstly, however, it is the judges who, in their diversity, impose the protection of human beings as a benchmark, either as a limit to the power of compliance tools or as their very purpose. Secondly, the lawyer, once again distinguishing himself or herself from the judge, reminds us that all the parties whose interests are involved must be taken into consideration. In an increasingly flexible and dialogical legal system, each party presents oneself as the "advocate" of this or that monumental goal: the lawyer is entitled to be the first to occupy this position.

From there, the book unfolds into 4 chapters. The Chapter I is devoted to what is specific to Compliance Law: the transformation of companies into prosecutors and judges of themselves, and even of others, the very title of this chapter illustrating the oxymoron: *The Company established Prosecutor and Judge of itself by Compliance Law*. Since the figure of the judge is thus present, the procedure is bound to make its appearance, willingly or by force.

This is why the aim of the Chapter II is to study the interferences that are developing between General Procedural Law and compliance techniques: *Procedural Law in Compliance Law*.

Building on the previous chapters, the Chapter III can broaden the spectrum of analysis on a topic that is not only topical but also, and above all, has a great future: the *Articulation between Compliance Law and International Arbitration*. This chapter measures the influence of the reasoning and requirements of Compliance Law in methods of dispute resolution where it has not, with a few exceptions, been present, but where it has a great future.

This allows the Chapter IV to return in a loop to what began the book: *The Judge in Compliance Law*. Because trials and judgements are indissociable, because legal techniques and the Rule of Law must not be dissociated, but because compliance techniques could paradoxically be used to dissociate them, because the power to judge and the procedures surrounding it must not be dissociated, because compliance and the Rule of

Law must be conceived and then practised, the rise of one must be the sign of the rise of the other, and not the price of the weakening of the Rule of Law, which implies not only thinking about the place of the various judges but also adjusting their role to what is required, by Compliance Law, of companies and public authorities.

CHAPTER I. THE COMPANY ESTABLISHED PROSECUTOR AND JUDGE OF ITSELF BY COMPLIANCE LAW

Marie-Anne Frison-Roche deals directly with the oxymoron imposed on companies by Compliance Law: *the "judge-judged"*, the challenge being to *articulate Words and Things in the face of Conflicts of Interest.* Before even tackling the situation of the company, thus placed as "judge-judged" by Compliance Law, because the issue is first and foremost that of the appropriate qualification, the article begins by stating that three principles must be borne in mind: what Law is in its correlation with reality, entrusting it with the task of maintaining, even in relation to its own power, a minimal link with reality or of restoring the link between words and things, thanks to qualification; what the activity of "judging" is and its corollary, procedure, obliging Law, through what the courts say, to qualify as a "judge" the person who judges in order to better constrain him or her by General Procedural Law; what legal personality is, a concept that allows the enterprise to split into two and thus seems very convenient for sanctioning an employee, or even a corporate officer, but which runs counter to the systemic hostility of Compliance Law towards this concept. With this in mind, the article begins by showing how Law "unmasks" companies that judge and punish by pretending not to do so, a judicial qualification imposed in order to force companies to respect general procedural principles for the benefit of those they prosecute or judge. This becomes acrobatic when the legal entity sues itself, not only in application of legal principles, but also, for example, in the name of the contract or in the name of ethics or *raison d'être.* Nevertheless, judges do so, Compliance Law taking up all the solutions that case law has developed in Regulatory Law concerning administrative regulatory authorities, according to a functional reasoning, to be repeated here, Compliance Law once again extending Regulatory Law. This transposition makes it possible to justify the accumulation of powers by companies which, having to admit the extent of these powers exercised, must therefore organise themselves so that the structural conflicts of interest they engender are nevertheless resolved. To this end, Impartiality is both a central and sufficient concept.

The second part of the article looks at how companies can sue and judge themselves, albeit impartially. If we consider that ethical heroism, which consists of punishing oneself impartially so that interests other than one's own prevail, is not enough to build a system and sustain it over time, then it is all a question of the art of distance, which must be reconstituted within the "judging-judged" company itself. To avoid sacrificing the coherence of Compliance Law, which can no longer give force to personality, the company must organise distances between who judges and who is judged without resorting to legal personality. If we do not believe that "impartial machines," as promised by the proponents of artificial intelligence, can be a consistent prospect, we need to look more closely at prospects such as internal mediation structures, or even external structures, of which Meta's *Oversight Board* is one experiment. The richest perspective remains that of recourse to human third parties, distinguishing between the different, even divergent, interests involved in the implementation of compliance tools, such as internal investigations, with each of these interests being defended by its own counsel, in particular a lawyer.

Taking a more upstream approach, Cécile Granier leads a *Reflection on the existence of companies' jurisprudence through Compliance.*

Because it overturns established frameworks, Compliance forces us to look at certain concepts in a new light. This is particularly true of case law. Recent developments in compliance raise the question of whether there might not be a body of "case law" produced by companies when they implement compliance procedures. At first glance, the concept of "corporate case law" may seem unnatural, given that case law is traditionally seen as the fruit of the office of the judge and, more particularly, of the State judge. However, the observation that a company can position itself as a judge in relation to itself and others in the context of implementing compliance legitimately raises the question of whether it can produce jurisprudence. The example of Meta's Oversight Board and the first decisions handed down by this body increase the legitimacy of this question.

Thinking about the concept of "company jurisprudence" involves comparing the process of emergence of the jurisprudential norm emanating from the judge with the process of emergence of a "jurisprudential norm" that would be produced by companies in the course of their "jurisdictional" functions. In material terms, an analogy between State case law and company case law seems conceivable. An organic obstacle then remains to be overcome: can an institution other than the judge be understood as producing case law? In the light of contemporary developments in Law and the practical interest that exists in devising a body of case law for companies, it seems appropriate to adopt a broader vision of case law, one that is detached from the traditional organic criterion. It therefore seems that it is possible, but above all necessary, to consider the concept of "corporate jurisprudence," in order to highlight a new facet of the normative power of companies in the context of compliance, particularly with a view to its supervision.

This power of the operators, stemming in particular from the digital space that they themselves have designed and built, is also the starting point for Luc-Marie Augagneur's examination of *The jurisdictionalisation of reputation by platforms*. He shows that the major platforms are the arbiters of the reputation economy (referencing, notoriety) in which they themselves operate. Although the stakes are usually low on a unit basis, the jurisdictional nature of reputation represents a significant aggregate stake. Platforms are thus required to detect and assess reputation manipulation (by users: SEO, fake reviews, fake followers; or by the platforms themselves, as highlighted by the *Google Shopping* case) which is implemented on a large scale using algorithmic tools. The identification and processing of manipulations are themselves only possible using artificial intelligence tools, of which the article gives many examples. However, this jurisdictionality of reputation has little in common with procedure as defined by Law, which is characterised more by the absence of transparency of the rules and by a probabilistic inductive model based on the identification of abnormal behaviour in relation to centroids, with the *Rule of Law* giving way to *Data is Law*, i.e. a "governance by numbers." In addition, collective jurisdiction is being established, with sanctions stemming from a computational apprehension of the phenomena of the multitude and not from an individual assessment, in man-machine cooperation. To date, the framework for these processes has been based essentially on the mechanisms required by successive laws on transparency, limited adversarial requirements and the availability of appeal procedures, but this remains fairly limited. The author believes that the most efficient forms of this jurisdictionality ultimately come from the role played by third parties in a form of participative dispute resolution, such as trusted flaggers, who identify illegal content on platforms.

In this context, the author believes that this singular jurisdictional configuration (judge and party platform, massive situations, algorithmic systems for handling manipulations) leads us to reconsider the grammar of the jurisdictional process and its characteristics. If Law is a language, it offers a new grammatical form that would be that of the middle voice (*mésotès*) described by Benveniste. Between the active voice and the passive voice lies a voice in which the subject performs an action in which it includes himself or herself. Now, it is the very nature of this jurisdictionality of compliance to make laws by including oneself in them (*nomos tithestai*). In this respect, the arrival of artificial intelligence in this jurisdictional process is an undeniable proof of the renewal of the language of Law.

To illustrate this in a much older activity, Alain Bruneau shows how *The company judges itself* with *the Compliance function in the bank*. He begins by pointing out that the compliance function originated in finance, and that as it developed, it evolved to accompany the transition from Regulatory Law to Compliance Law. Through these changes, compliance has evolved from an *ex post* control function to an *ex ante* enforcement function. The Libor crisis provides an imperfect illustration of the primacy of this transition. The evolution of this role is illustrated by concrete examples.

The article begins by examining the management of reputational risk, a fundamental element for a company prosecutor and judge of itself. Reputational risk is a significant factor for a financial institution, as it can have a negative impact on its capitalisation and even culminate in a systemic crisis. Avoiding a major financial crisis is also one of the Compliance Monumental Goals. In order to avoid complex and inopportune scenarios, Compliance Law intervenes as far upstream as possible and identifies issues likely to have an impact on reputation. Regulations require certain measures to be put in place *ex ante*. The French so-called "Sapin 2" law requires the introduction of tools that concern all companies (and not just banks). In addition to reputational risk, it is essential to consider the risk of corruption. Consideration of reputational risk may justify refusal to carry out certain transactions. From this point of view, compliance must assess the potential consequences of entering into a relationship with a new customer beforehand, so that the provision of services can sometimes be refused. In this way, the compliance function unilaterally assesses the relationship with a view to managing its reputational risk.

Secondly, the internal sanction mechanism instituted by Compliance Law is also discussed, in particular the internal sanctions adopted by compliance in a financial institution. Compliance can oblige the bank to act as a prosecutor *via* committees set up within the business lines. Compliance can also determine and apply sanctions against employees. In this way, we see a dual role of prosecutor and judge for the compliance function within the framework of an extraordinary system of ordinary Law. Finally, the analysis deals with the case of the "judge-judged": following a decision by the bank, the Regulator may take a position that is all the stricter because it considers that the bank is applying its guidelines incorrectly. In this way, Compliance Law, which is established within the banking company, finds itself under the judgement of its own Regulator. The company finds itself on trial and is called upon to be the prosecutor and judge not only of itself, but also of its customers.

Jean-Marc Coulon adopts the same vision, which is both very broad and very concrete, with regard to another sector, when he discusses the way in which companies operate to give concrete form to *Compliance Law in the construction industry and the contradictions, impossibilities and deadlocks that companies face*. He points out that the construction industry is not a regulated sector. Its market is made up of a superimposition of territorial strata which are as many relevant markets, to each of which corresponds a specific microcosm of companies. Finally, the temporary association between companies for the purposes of carrying out a project or work is consubstantial with this sector. The author stresses that the penetration of compliance in this sector is inevitably very heterogeneous and is the result of both exogenous factors (other partners within temporary associations, influence of economic operators from other sectors of activity, investors and financial backers, encouragement from professional organisations) and endogenous factors (such as the submission to a regulator due to recourse to public offerings, the French laws on the duty of Vigilance or the French so-called "Sapin 2" law). For example, subject to all these factors combined, the Bouygues group is particularly permeable to compliance.

Not only is the Bouygues Group an internal "legislator," it is also a "prosecutor and judge," both of itself and of others. In fact, by conducting an investigation, lodging a complaint, triggering an ethics alert or making use of the leniency programme, it is nothing more than an auxiliary to the public prosecutor. Moreover, by scrutinising its stakeholders, sanctioning its employees, resorting to the *convention judiciaire d'intérêt public* (Judicial Public Interest Agreement) or negotiating its sanction within the framework of a procedure instituted by a multilateral bank, it fulfils the function of a judge. As legislator, prosecutor and judge, the Bouygues group is faced with a paradox: in a way it is encouraged to exercise "sovereignty," yet it enjoys neither the attributes that go with it nor the unfailing support of the competent public authorities.

Christophe Lapp builds on the previous article to analyse *Compliance in companies: the statutes of the process.* He concludes from the previous article that companies are caught in the pincers of Compliance Law, the jaws of which are those of the incentives and sanctions that they must apply to ensure the effectiveness of their processes, for which they are themselves answerable. The first result is that the company has been delegated the task of manufacturing the reprehensible rules that it must apply to itself and to third parties with whom it has dealings. To this end, the company puts in place "processes," i.e. verification and prevention procedures, to ensure that the offences it is likely to commit are not committed. The processes thus constitute a standard of behaviour to prevent and avoid the offences themselves being committed. They are thus one of the elements of the legal rule of civil liability in its preventive or remedial purposes.

Secondly, the author points out that the repression of non-compliance with processes presents companies with two pitfalls. The first pitfall requires the company to define processes *for* its employees and partners that also constitute a quasi-jurisdictional settlement of non-compliance, the company having to reconcile the sanction it imposes with the fundamental principles of traditional Criminal Law, constitutional principles and all substantive rights. Processes thus become the procedural rule. By reversing the burden of proof, the company is then required to prove that its processes are at least as effective as the measures defined by laws and regulations, the *Agence française anticorruption – AFA* (French Anti-Corruption Agency), European directives and various communications on tools for combating breaches of probity, environmental offences and current social concerns. Processes then become the constitutive element, *per se*, of the offence. In seeking to strike a balance between prevention and the sanctions to which it is itself subject, will the company not be tempted to prefer the orthodoxy of its processes to the expectations of the *AFA*, regulators and judges, to the detriment of their effectiveness? In so doing, are we not moving towards instrumental and conformist compliance, which paradoxically disempowers Compliance Monumental Goals? The author concludes with a series of questions about the future.

This questioning mode is shared by Jérémy Heymann, who wonders what *The Legal Nature of the Facebook "Supreme Court"* is. Seeking to make words and things coincide, his reflection concerns the nature of the so-called "Supreme Court" set up by the Meta group to hear appeals against decisions relating to content on the digital social networks Facebook and Instagram. Is it really a Supreme Court, responsible for "judging" the Meta group? A close look at the *Oversight Board* set up by Meta reveals that, in addition to its title, it can claim to exercise a form of jurisdictional activity in addition to its "advisory" role (which consists of issuing "consultative opinions on Facebook's and Instagram's content policies"). This is essentially conceived in terms of verifying that content published on the Facebook or Instagram social networks complies with the standards issued by these two companies, and that decisions – to moderate or assess this moderation – comply with Law. However, the legal framework of reference is vague, and also seems to have the particularity of evolving according to the geographical context in which the case is examined. It would therefore appear that the *Oversight Board* has a jurisdictional role, even if its role is limited and can only be exercised within a restricted framework.

The author therefore proposes that the nature of the *Oversight Board* should be that of a preventive dispute settlement body – the objective being to avoid referral to state courts by ruling prior to a judicial decision. Various questions must subsequently be raised, both in terms of the legitimacy and the authority of such an *Oversight Board*. But whatever the answers to these questions, the fact remains that the creation of an *Oversight Board* by a company governed by Private Law already reveals the liveliness of contemporary legal pluralism.

This liveliness of practice, which is difficult for Law to put into words, is particularly remarkable in the *Internal investigations within companies*, described by Daphné Latour. She shows that internal investigations, particularly in Labour Law, are not new, but that in compliance their exponential growth is relatively recent, having been accelerated by the French so-called "Sapin 2" law of 2016 and the resulting introduction into the French legal system of the transactional tool represented by the *convention judiciaire d'intérêt public – CJIP* (Judicial Public Interest Agreement). Even if an internal investigation is not, strictly speaking, a legal condition for opening a *CJIP*, the fact remains that the negotiation of a *CJIP* requires a form of in-depth investigation or audit since the public prosecutor, in order to open discussions, expects the beneficiary company to cooperate actively in uncovering the truth about the offences covered by the negotiation. However, despite the infatuation, albeit sometimes forced, of companies with this new tool, the internal investigation, and the stakes and risks it entails, the author considers that the French legislator has not yet given sufficient consideration to its framework, since there is currently no specific and uniform legal provision governing its use in French Law. This leads companies and their advisers to draw inspiration for their investigation procedures from the relevant Anglo-Saxon Law, the fundamental rights enshrined in particular in the European Convention for the Protection of Human Rights and Fundamental Freedoms (ECHR), French Criminal Law and Procedure, as well as from Labour Law and the sometimes contradictory case law it gives rise to in terms of defending employees' rights.

This legal insecurity, resulting from the uncertainty and unpredictability of the applicable rule, is all the more prejudicial given that, at the same time, companies are now being asked to take ever greater responsibility for their own behaviour and that of their employees, and to "self-regulate," thereby assuming certain sovereign functions. Private companies seem to be seen as omniscient and capable of preventing crimes from being committed within their walls, even though modern technological tools make it easier to commit them. Failing that, and *a posteriori,* it is required to detect these offences and/or breaches and prevent their recurrence, in particular through internal investigations.

The increasingly important role that these compliance tools are playing in companies is also illustrated by the French Judicial Public Interest Agreement, as shown by Alexis Bavitot, who describes the *Shaping* of *the company through negotiated Criminal Justice Agreements* in a *French perspective*. The author points out that negotiated justice is "the situation in which the criminal conflict is the object of a trade in the etymological sense of the term *negotio*, that is to say, of a debate between the parties in order to reach an agreement." He wonders whether the French legislator has not succumbed to globalised mimicry by creating the *CJIP* in matters of probity, and then environment, and questions the wider nature of this "convention." Validated by a court order, it does not entail any declaration of guilt, has neither the nature nor the effects of a conviction, and is not entered in the criminal record. The *CJIP* can be used at both the investigation and pre-trial stages, and is unique in that it avoids either prosecution by the public prosecutor or the wrath of the judge.

A detailed study of the agreements signed shows that, in order to negotiate in the best possible way, the company can and must *shape* itself. The company will shape the facts of its agreement, shape its accusation and, finally, shape its penalty. The article offers a concrete analysis of these three dimensions of the shaping of the company in order to better understand the legal nature of negotiated criminal justice agreements.

But while it is true that the very physiognomy of the company is changing as a result of these new activities, Samir Merabet takes a closer look at the duty of *Vigilance* to see a particular situation with the company *being a judge and not judge.* He believes that Vigilance presents two diametrically opposed dangers. The company is caught in the crossfire. On the one hand, there is the risk that it will perform its role at a minimum, so that the obligations imposed on it are ineffective, thereby taking the risk of incurring its own liability. On the other hand, there is a danger that the company will exceed its role and take the place of the judge. Does Vigilance always present the same dangers? Does it systematically imply the same role for the company? Does being vigilant mean passing judgement? The answer to these questions depends on the content of the obligations that Vigilance entails. Today, these obligations seem to be very diverse.

How can we distinguish between the various due diligence obligations? A first approach might be to consider a formal identification that leads to a distinction being drawn between Vigilance in the *strict sense*, as envisaged by the French so-called "Sapin 2" law and identified as such, and obligations that are similar to it, for example the duty of moderation of companies on social networks, which, although not called a duty of vigilance, is nonetheless close to it. The extension of Compliance Obligations leads to a blurring of the boundaries between what exactly constitutes due diligence and what does not. A more substantive approach is needed to consider the degree of control exercised by the company. On this basis, two categories can be distinguished: negative vigilance, which implies the identification of a risk, and positive vigilance, which implies even more the neutralisation of the risk. The former presupposes a limited role for the company, while the latter encourages it to act positively, even before an authority has taken a decision. This time, the company's role is closer to that of the judge. It is clear that not all due diligence obligations can be approached in a uniform manner.

Since the company is led – if not to substitute itself for the judge – to act even before the latter has had the opportunity to give a ruling, it seems legitimate to frame the implementation of the company's duty of vigilance by a form of proceduralisation of compliance. Both the company and its employees or partners would benefit from greater supervision of Vigilance. Insofar as not all due diligence obligations call for the same role on the part of the company, it is advisable to envisage guiding principles for due diligence, more or less intense depending on whether positive or negative due diligence is involved.

This first chapter has shown what happens in companies that are called upon to prosecute, investigate, listen and judge. It is therefore desirable, and fortunately inevitable, that General Procedural Law penetrates Compliance Law, which is the subject of the chapter II.

CHAPTER II. PROCEDURAL LAW IN COMPLIANCE LAW

Nicolas Cayrol opens this chapter by looking at the *Procedural principles in Compliance Law*. It would certainly be sufficient to examine the reception of General Procedural Law principles in contentious compliance cases and the distortion that compliance techniques justify in procedural mechanisms. But the innovation represented by this emerging branch of Law, Compliance Law, justifies going further. From this perspective, we must ask ourselves what is the very legitimacy of the general procedural principles in this branch of Law, in that General Procedural Law is built on the notion of "litigation," whereas Compliance Law deals with such enormous situations, concerning the fate of the planet for example, that this notion seems inadequate, and that General Procedural Law would therefore be outdated.

If, however, we maintain this perspective of Compliance Law confronting the greatest challenges of our time from an almost warlike point of view, the relevance of General Procedural Law requires us to rethink the very definition of litigation. Compliance proceedings call into question the future of systems and it is in this capacity that they call to account the entities at the heart of these systems. This is why liability proceedings are more like "accountability" proceedings, enabling the judge to demand action for the future, proceedings in which commitments are made and the "intentions" of those involved are tested.

From the same highly innovative perspective, François Ancel raises a question, which is like a proposal: *Compliance Law, a New Guiding Principle for the Trial?* The aim is to elevate the principle of compliance to the status of a guiding principle of litigation. To support this, in the first part of his article, the author emphasises the convergence of the goals of compliance and the purpose of litigation. Indeed, recalling that Compliance Law does not oust either the State or the judge, from the moment compliance means that the person must respect his commitments and that the trial is also based on the principle that the parties must comply with the principles and their own "discourse," compliance thus becomes a guiding principle of the trial. In the second part of the article, the author illustrates his point in very concrete terms. Firstly, the procedural protocols drawn up by the courts and bar associations are commitments that should justify a form of constraint which, while it does not need to be of the same form and nature as that of the laws, must nonetheless have consequences when a party fails to comply, for example with regard to article 700 of the *Code de procédure civile* (French Civil Procedure Code). Secondly, based on French case law which has sanctioned a party who had accepted the principle of arbitration and then systematically obstructed its implementation, the author suggests that the principle of compliance could encompass the currently scattered notions of the principles of loyalty, consistency (estoppel) and effectiveness. In this way, practice would already validate this theoretical proposal exposed in the first part.

In any case, these new types of lawsuits will certainly be influenced by the American conception of the lawsuit and the role of judges and prosecutors. At the very least, it is important to take into account the way they operate in order to understand how Compliance Law, which is often global in scope (finance, digital, climate), works. Bryan Sillaman proposes *Taking the Compliance U.S. Procedural Experience globally* and apply it to a key practical issue: professional secrecy and cooperation. He points out that the French legal system is evolving, organising interactions between lawyers, regulators and prosecutors, particularly in investigations into corruption or corporate misconduct, adopting American methods of resolution, as exemplified by the *Convention judiciaire d'intéret public – CJIP* (French Judicial Public Interest Agreement) which encourages "collaboration" between them. The author describes the evolution of American institutional doctrine and describes the evolution of French legal system, inspired by the American procedural experience from which this mechanism originates. The DOJ has published several memorandums on the subject of "collaboration," according to which professional secrecy must remain intact when the information is not merely "factual," in order to maintain trust between prosecutors, regulators and lawyers.

The French authorities had not followed this path, but the very recent law recognises a sort of solicitor-client privilege *à la française*, particularly useful when they are involved in internal investigations within companies.

However, the perspective of the authorities issuing injunctions or sanctions must also be taken into account, as their normative framework has evolved more in the subsequent phase of the procedure. Alexandre Linden, for example, studies the rules governing the *Motivation and publicity of the decisions of the Restricted formation of the* French Data Protection Authority *(Commission nationale de l'informatique et des libertés – CNIL) in a Compliance Perspective*. He points out that in the event of a breach of the rules on the protection of personal data, the *CNIL*'s Restricted formation issues fines, compliance orders or reminders. It may order the publication of these measures, which may be challenged before the *Conseil d'État* (French Council of State). It is essential that reasons are given for these decisions, not only to comply with the Rule of Law, but also to ensure that the public concerned, which is very heterogeneous, understands them, as the *CNIL*'s educational role also applies.

The principle of publicity is handled with nuance, as data controllers often request closed hearings and very few members of the public attending it. Conversely, publicising decisions is in itself a sanction. Moreover, publication may not be total, or may only be for a limited period of time. Anonymisation often allows a balance to be struck between the need to educate and the need to protect interests, and the *CNIL* pays close attention to the actual methods of publication, even though it cannot control the circulation and media use that is subsequently made of the information.

Lawyers take a more radical view of the place that should be given to the rights of individuals, particularly the rights of the defence, at all stages of the process. Sophie Scemla and Diane Paillot set out what they describe as *The difficulty for Compliance Enforcement Authorities to comprehend the Rights of the Defence in compliance matters*. They point out that since December 2016, the French so-called "Sapin 2" law has required French companies falling within its scope to put in place eight highly restrictive anti-corruption measures, such as risk mapping, an alert system and a procedure for evaluating third parties. In order to ensure that these obligations are implemented, the "Sapin 2" law created the *Agence française anticorruption – AFA* (French Anti-Corruption Agency) which has three missions: firstly, to help anyone prevent and detect corruption; secondly, to monitor the quality and effectiveness of the anti-corruption programmes deployed; and thirdly, to impose sanctions, via its Sanctions Committee, for any breaches found.

However, as the *Conseil d'État* (French Council of State) has pointed out, the powers given to administrations have become stratified and multiplied. While the Council of State is proposing to improve the conduct and effectiveness of administrative controls by harmonising practices and simplifying their powers and responsibilities, we also feel that there is an urgent need to remedy the many procedural shortcomings that are highly prejudicial to the rights of the defence. During its inspections, the *AFA* assumes various powers, some of which are not provided for by law and most of which infringe fundamental rights and freedoms, foremost among which are the principle of adversarial proceedings and the right not to incriminate oneself. For example, the *AFA* does not consider it necessary to draw up minutes of the hearings of the individuals it hears, depriving them of the possibility of defending themselves against statements that would be reported by the supervisory authority to the Sanctions Committee.

More structurally, the scope of *AFA*'s mission is extremely broad, as the law allows it to demand that it be provided with "*tout document professionnel ou toute information utile*" ("any professional document or any useful information"), without further specifying the notion of usefulness. The *AFA* also considers that professional secrecy cannot be invoked against it and that the voluntary and unconditional handing over of documents means that the entity waives its right to invoke professional secrecy. Apart from the potentially serious consequences if proceedings were also initiated by a foreign authority, the concept of "voluntary surrender" in no way reflects the reality of these controls. Audited entities cooperate under the threat of prosecution for the offence of obstruction, which forces them to disclose documents at the risk of contributing to their own incrimination.

This is undoubtedly all the more reason not to pit General Procedural Law and Compliance Law against each other. Marie-Anne Frison-Roche's article, *Adjusting General Procedural Law to Compliance Law by the Nature of Things,* attempts to find a better link between the two. The article begins by pointing out that Geneal Procedural Law is an invention, essentially due to Professor Motulsky, which goes far beyond the benefits of comparing different types of procedures. As he said, there is a sort of natural Law in General Procedural Law, in that, as soon as there is a Rule of Law, cannot be excluded, whatever the "procedure," or even the "process," a particular way of doing things: for example, of deciding, of referring the matter to the person who decides, of listening before deciding, of challenging the person who decides.

The first part of the article draws the conclusions from the fact that General Procedural Law is based on the nature of things, but Compliance Law organises things in a new way. Therefore, the simple and ironclad principles of General Procedural Law find their way into places where they are not at first sight expected, notably because there is no judge, the figure around whom procedures are usually organised. They are particularly prevalent in companies. Even if the regulations say nothing about it, it is up to the judges, and in particular the Supreme Courts, to recognise this nature of things, because it is on this effect of nature that General Procedural Law is built: when compliance mechanisms oblige companies to strike, General Procedural Law must oblige, even in the silence of the texts, to arm those who may be struck, or even stand up against systems that would too easily rule out these defences, which are considered to be contrary to effectiveness.

In the second part, the article shows that, because it is a question of making room for that nature of things which the Rule of Law entrusts the care to the judge and the lawyer, General Procedural Law must also adjust to what the extraordinary Compliance Law is. Indeed, Compliance Law is extraordinary in that it expresses the political claim to act now to ensure that the future shall be not catastrophic, in particular by detecting and preventing the occurrence of systemic risks, or even that it shall be better, in particular by building effective equality or genuine concern for others. Because it is the issue at stake that defines this new branch of Law, a disputed systemic issue, possibly disputed by several parties before a judge, the general procedural principles must be considerably broadened: they must then include civil society and the future. General Procedural Law thus naturally acquires an even more important place than in the traditional branches of Law since on the one hand it imposes itself outside legal proceedings, particularly in companies, and on the other hand before the courts it involves people who had little say in the matter and who enter into the "compliance cases" now debated before the judge.

These "compliance cases" are "systemic cases" and will increasingly be brought before all kinds of judges, judges that everyone will look at because the cases will involve more and more people, and judges that are increasingly global because the issues themselves will be increasingly global. Therefore, international arbitration, which is by nature a global jurisdiction, is destined to play a major role in Compliance Law in the future. The following chapter is devoted to this specific dimension.

CHAPTER III. ARTICULATION BETWEEN COMPLIANCE LAW AND INTERNATIONAL ARBITRATION

Jean-Baptiste Racine raises the issue of the relationship between *Compliance and arbitration* and makes *an attempt at problematisation*. He points out that the arbitrator is a judge, indeed the natural judge of international trade. Arbitration is therefore naturally destined to encounter compliance, which transforms corporate action in an international context. However, the links between compliance and arbitration are not obvious. The aim here is not to provide firm and definitive answers, but rather, and above all, to ask questions. We are in the early stages of reflection on this subject, which explains why there is, for the time being, little legal literature on the relationship between compliance and arbitration. This is not to say that there are no connections. Quite simply, these relationships may not have come to light, or they may be in the making. We need to look at the existing or potential bridges between two worlds that have long gravitated separately: compliance on the one hand and arbitration on the other. The author thus formulates what seems to him to be the central question: is or can the arbitrator be a compliance judge and, if so, how?

In all cases, arbitrators come into contact with matters that require compliance methods, tools and logic. In addition to the prevention and repression of corruption, three examples can be given. Firstly, arbitration has for several years been faced with economic sanctions (embargos in particular). The link with compliance is obvious, insofar as texts providing for economic sanctions are often accompanied by compliance measures, as in the United States. Arbitrators are concerned by the way in which they deal with economic sanctions in disputes. Secondly, Competition Law is a subject that has come into contact with Arbitration since the late 1980s. The arbitrability of this type of dispute has now been established and arbitrators regularly apply it. At the same time, compliance has also made its entry into Competition Law, albeit more vigorously in the United States than in France. The existence, absence or inadequacy of a compliance programme designed to prevent breaches of the competition rules are thus circumstances likely to help the arbitrator in assessing anti-competitive behaviour. Thirdly, Environmental Law is also concerned. There is such a thing as Environmental Compliance, with regard, for example, to the French law of 27 March 2017 on the duty of Vigilance. Companies are thus responsible for helping to protect the environment, by internalising these concerns in their internal and external operations (within their sphere of influence). As soon as an arbitrator is tasked with settling a dispute relating to Environmental Law, the question of the relationship with compliance, from this angle, naturally arises. The author concludes that the multiple interactions between compliance and arbitration, both actual and potential, are thus opened up.

Eduardo Silva-Romero and Raphaëlle Legru illustrate this general proposition by asking: *What place is there for compliance in investment arbitration?* The authors emphasise the new and growing role of compliance in international arbitration, particularly in terms of the need to respect ethical values, since arbitrators can introduce a moral code that is sometimes lacking in international trade, and should only use their power in the service of law-abiding investors.

In this way, compliance is achieved through the traditional review by arbitrators of the legality of the investment, which applies both to the establishment of the treaty itself and to the investor. More recently, arbitrators can exercise control over an investor's "social licence to operate," a concept linked to corporate social responsibility that has emerged in particular for the protection of indigenous peoples. Moreover, compliance may justify a substantial assessment by the arbitrator of the effective respect of human rights and the environment through an investment treaty, with the State party being able to act to ensure the effectiveness of these rights.

The chapter continues with a more technical breakdown of international arbitration, starting with its main player. Mathias Audit examines *The arbitrator's position on compliance.* For an arbitrator to intervene in compliance matters, there must be an "obligation to comply." Identifying such a duty is tricky because it cannot generally be identified *per se*, if it is only understood in terms of Criminal Law, which does not directly fall within the scope of arbitration, which has developed an independent concept of acts, particularly corruption, that are otherwise punishable under Criminal Law. But, because the Compliance Obligation is itself autonomous since it involves detecting and preventing various offences and breaches, arbitrators rely on detection and prevention mechanisms as such, distinct from the possible commission of acts that were not intended to occur.

But the question of the source of this Compliance Obligation is central because it must originate in a standard that can lead to arbitration. This could be a contract, for example an intermediary contract, which not only prohibits all corrupt practices but also provides for audit or control, or a national law, in particular the U.K. Bribery Act or the French so-called "Sapin 2" law, or even decisions imposing compliance programmes or the uncoerced adoption of such programmes by the company. Depending on the source, the arbitrator will take it into account. If a compliance obligation, having a source that gives it scope in arbitration proceedings, is considered by the arbitrator to have been disregarded, the consequences often depend on the source. The solution is classic if it concerns the *lex contractus*, but more difficult if it is a law that has inserted the obligation into the *lex societatis*, as compliance requirements are generally considered to be mandatory provisions. If arbitrators are unable to apply the sanctions imposed by Criminal Law, they may base their decision on the breach found to assess the lawfulness of conduct or the validity of a contract, using the *ICC Rules on Combating Corruption* as a guide.

Keeping pace with arbitration and the strategies of legislators, contracting parties and litigants, Elie Kleiman analyses *The objectives of compliance confronted with the actors of arbitration*. He reminds us that International Arbitration, which remains the preferred method of settling disputes arising from international commercial relations, is being overtaken by compliance, the manifestations of which are everywhere: arbitration centres, arbitrators and courts reviewing the international legality of awards are regularly called upon to take into account the rules of compliance.

The author notes that compliance has undeniably taken hold of those involved in arbitration. As players in an unregulated activity, arbitration institutions and arbitrators must generate trust; their ability to regulate themselves effectively is a prerequisite for the success of arbitration, and this requires transparency and exemplarity. This self-imposed compliance is today consubstantial with arbitration and is illustrated in particular in the traditional areas of preventing conflicts of interest and monitoring the availability of arbitrators, but also in the newer areas of parity and diversity, and reducing the carbon footprint. Furthermore, arbitration activity, and in particular the monitoring of the international legality of awards, is not exempt from the *ex post* application of compliance criteria, particularly in the fight against corruption and money laundering. There is therefore room for debate, particularly in France, due to the porosity of the boundaries between the methods specific to mandatory compliance rules intended to prevent the most serious offences and those specific to the establishment of the constituent elements of such offences in criminal matters. This is an important issue, especially as the increasing imperative nature of climate change and human rights requirements will extend the scope of these overlaps between compliance methods and the review of arbitration awards.

But arbitration is also taking over compliance. Arbitrators are called upon to rule on controversies arising from economic activities that have their origins in compliance: contracts relating to the implementation of anti-corruption and anti-money laundering measures, such as due diligence obligations, transactions relating to the reduction of the carbon footprint and climate change, and so on. In addition, compliance is also a subject that can be arbitrated, with arbitrators having to apply or take into consideration compliance rules in the settlement of commercial or investment disputes, particularly in view of the consequences that can be drawn from ignoring or observing them.

CHAPTER IV. THE JUDGE IN COMPLIANCE LAW

On the contrary, the judge is the link between the company and the compliance obligations that it takes on, by order of the legislators or because it shares their desire to serve common interests, this link being tested and reinforced through legal proceedings. Therefore, as Compliance Law matures, it will leave an increasingly limited role to the criminal courts, in favour of a more general conception of the role of the ordinary courts, which are themselves renewed by Compliance Law in that they will be more in *ex ante*, particularly in digital and climate-related matters.

With this in mind, Marie-Anne Frison-Roche opens this final Chapter by examining *The Judge, the Compliance Obligation and the Company: the Compliance Evidence System*. Before the courts, the company must prove that it has implemented its compliance obligation, the proof thus establishes the link between the company in its relationship with the compliance obligations it assumes and the judges to whom it is accountable in this respect: this link is established through the use of evidence. The evidentiary system has yet to be developed, and this contribution sets out the prolegomena. To this end, the article begins with a description of what is referred to as the "evidence square" in an "evidence system" that is superimposed on the system of rules of substantive Law. This is all the more important as compliance seems to be in head-on collision in its very principles with the general principles of the evidentiary system, in particular because it seems that the company must prove the existence of the legal rules or that it must definitively bear the burden of proving the absence of a violation, which seems contrary not only to the presumption of innocence but also to the principle of freedom of action and enterprise. In order to re-articulate Compliance Law and the compliance obligations that legitimately fall on companies, it is necessary to revisit the evidentiary system specific to compliance, so that it remains within the Rule of Law. This presupposes that we adopt a substantive definition of compliance, that is not simply a conformity with the rules, which is only a minimal dimension, but require the definition of Compliance Law by the Monumental Goals for which, in a substantive way, the public authorities and companies form an alliance. The general evidentiary system brings into play its four cornerstones: the burden of proof, the object of proof, the means of proof and their admissibility. Compliance Law is not outside this evidence square, marking its full membership of the Rule of Law and laying the foundations for the evidentiary system specific to Compliance Law. The first part of the article sets out the specific evidentiary requirements of Compliance Law, distinguishing between structural measures and expected behaviour. The first involves proving that the structures required to achieve the monumental goals of compliance have actually been put in place. The object of proof is then the effectiveness of this implementation, which presents the effectiveness of the system. As far as behavioural obligations are concerned, the object of proof is the efforts made by the company to obtain these behaviours, the principle of proportionality governing the establishment of this proof, while the systemic efficiency of the whole reinforces the evidentiary system. But for the company, even though the principle remains that of freedom of proof, the wisdom of proof consists in establishing the effectiveness, efficacy and efficiency of the system as a whole, independently of the burden of proof.

The second part of the article focuses on those who bear the burden of proof under Compliance Law. As a matter of principle, Compliance Law places this burden on the company, in terms of its legal obligations. This burden stems from the legal origin of the obligations, which blocks the "round of the burden of proof." But in the interplay of the different vertices of the evidentiary square, the issue becomes more delicate when it comes to determining the contours of the compliance obligations that the company must fulfil. Moreover, the burden of proof may itself be the object of proof, just as the company's performance of its legal obligations may also be the object of contracts, which brings us back into the system of proof ordinarily applicable to contractual obligations. The situation is different when it comes to a "compliance contract" or when it comes to one or more "compliance clauses," concepts that have not yet been fully developed in Contract Law. Furthermore, as all branches of Law belong to a legal system governed by the principle of the Rule of Law, other branches of Law interfere and modify evidentiary methods and solutions. This is the case when the fact, which is the object of proof, may give rise to a penalty, Repressive Law imposing its own solutions in terms of the burden of proof.

The third part of the article examines the relevant means of proof in Compliance Law, used because Compliance Law is above all a branch of Law whose object is on the one hand Information and on the other hand the Future. Open questions remain, such as whether companies could be forced by the courts to develop technologies to invent new means of proof in order to show that they are actually achieving the Monumental Goals with which they are charged. The fourth part shows the vital nature of the pre-construction of Evidence, which reflects the *ex ante* nature of Compliance Law: evidence must be pre-constructed in order to avert the very prospect of having to use it, by finding every means of establishing the effectiveness, efficacy and even efficiency of the various Compliance tools. If companies do all this methodically, the Compliance Evidence System will be established, in harmony with the General Evidence System, Compliance Law and the Rule of Law.

Juliette Morel-Maroger shows the role played by Judges in making compliance an integral part of the Rule of Law, particularly in Europe, by studying *The application of compliance standards by European Union judges*. She shows that, intended to pursue objectives of general interest – or Monumental Goals – compliance standards are in principle aimed at modifying and guiding the behaviour of economic operators. To achieve these objectives, compliance uses the full range of the normative spectrum. What is and should be the role of the judges of the European Union in the face of the development of compliance standards? As in domestic Law, the very legality of the compliance standards drawn up by the regulatory authorities is being challenged.

Beginning by analysing the control exercised by the judges of the European Union in this respect, the question arising here is essentially on rules of soft Law which can be challenged in two ways: by way of an action for annulment and, by way of exception, by a reference for a preliminary ruling. But beyond the control of the legality of compliance standards exercised by European judges, they also contribute to their application. The effectiveness of compliance depends first and foremost on the support of those to whom it is addressed, and economic operators are undoubtedly the key players in its success. However, the judges of the European Union, who have jurisdiction to settle disputes between Member States, European institutions and individual claimants concerning the application of European Union Law, may be called upon to ensure the effectiveness of European compliance standards and to interpret them.

Jurisdictional efficiency also depends on simplicity. With this in mind, Sophie Schiller talks about *A single judge in the event of an international breach of compliance obligations*. She stresses that, given the highly international nature of the issues involved, the players involved and therefore the litigation in compliance matters, it is essential to know whether a person can be accused before several judges, attached to different states, or even whether they can be condemned by several jurisdictions. The answer is provided by the *ne bis in idem* principle, which is the subject of a wealth of case law based on Article 4 of Protocol No. 7 to the ECHR, which is clearly inapplicable to courts in different countries. In order to assess whether breaches of compliance obligations may be subject to multiple sanctions in different states, it will first be necessary to ascertain whether there are any textual grounds on which they can be invoked. At European level, Article 50 of the Charter of Fundamental Rights now allows the *ne bis in idem* principle to be invoked. Applicable to all areas of compliance, it provides very strong protection covering not only convictions but also prosecutions. Like its effects, the scope of Article 50 is very broad. The proceedings concerned are those of a repressive nature, over and above those handed down by criminal courts in the strict sense, which makes it possible to cover decisions handed down by one of the many regulatory authorities competent in compliance matters. Internationally, the situation is less clear. Article 14-7 of the International Covenant on Civil and Political Rights can be invoked, provided that a number of obstacles are overcome, including the Human Rights Committee's decision of 2 November 1987, which restricted its application to the domestic context, i.e. the case of a double conviction by the same State.

Even if the bases are applicable, two specific features of compliance situations risk hindering their application, the first relating to the applicable procedural rules, in particular the rules of jurisdiction, and the second relating to the specific features of the situations. The application of the *ne bis in idem* rule is formally accepted only in relation to universal jurisdiction and personal jurisdiction, i.e. extraterritorial jurisdiction, which is only one part of jurisdiction. The *Cour de cassation* (French Court of cassation) confirmed this in the famous "Oil for Food" ruling of 14 March 2018. The refusal to recognise this principle as universal, whatever the jurisdictional rule in question, deprives French companies of a means of defence. In addition, violations of compliance rules are increasingly being dealt with through settlement mechanisms. These do not always fall within the scope of the European and international rules laying down the *ne bis in idem* principle, as they are sometimes not qualified as a "final judgment" under the terms of Article 50 of the Charter of Fundamental Rights and Article 14-7 of the International Covenant on Civil and Political Rights.

Compliance breaches are often based on multiple acts. This results in statutes of limitations whose starting point is postponed until the last event to occur and makes it easier for French courts to assume jurisdiction if only one of the constituent acts is recorded in France. In terms of compliance, the *ne bis in idem* principle does not generally protect companies and does not prevent them from being sued in the courts of two different countries for the same matter. It does, however, afford them some additional protection, by requiring foreign decisions to be taken into account when determining the amount of the penalty. The penalty imposed on *Airbus SE* in the *convention judiciaire d'intérêt public – CJIP* (French Judicial Public Interest Agreement) of 29 January 2020 is a perfect illustration of this.

The supreme courts, or the "judge of the Law," who exist more in the civil Law systems than in the common Law ones, cannot be absent from this general movement. It is this judge that Olivier Douvreleur examines in this new comparison: *Compliance and Judge of the Law*. The author admits that compliance has a complex relationship with the Judge, and even more so with the Judges of the Law, who, as a matter of principle and for example the *Cour de cassation* (French Court of cassation) in the French judicial system, have no knowledge of the facts and leave them to the sovereign judgement of the judges of the merits. At first sight, compliance is a technique that is internalised in companies, and the place occupied by negotiated justice techniques calls for little intervention by the judge of the Law.

However, the role of the judge of the Law is destined to develop, particularly in relation to the duty of vigilance or in the articulation between branches of Law when compliance meets Labour Law, or in the adjustment between American Law and the other legal systems. The way in which the principle of proportionality takes its place in Compliance Law is also a major challenge for the judges of Law.

To integrate so many different perspectives, the judge must use new methods, of which soft Law is a central element. Fabien Raynaud studies *The Administrative Judge and Compliance*. He highlights the close relationship between compliance and soft Law, as introduced by the French administrative courts in their case law. This was particularly the case with the *Conseil d'État* (French Council of State) 2016 judgements on Regulatory Law, which Compliance Law extends. This consist of internalising in companies what the public authorities want, method that the French Council of State, in small steps from 2010, has been continually taking in account and fleshed out in 2016. This is particularly the case when the documents issued are "likely to produce 'significant effects,' particularly of an economic nature, or are intended to have a significant influence on the behaviour of the persons to whom they are addressed," which is directly related to compliance issues. The new approach adopted by the French Council of State has led it to review numerous "positions," "recommendations," "guidelines," etc., adopted by various authorities, in particular to protect the persons on whom these acts have a "significant effect," sometimes even censuring the issuing body. The soft Law on banking compliance, more specifically the one issued by the EBA, has given the administrative courts the opportunity to adjust their review to that exercised by the Court of Justice of the European Union in response to a reference for a preliminary ruling.

Thus, through its jurisprudence on the justiciability of soft Law acts, the French Council of State is asserting itself as a player in the compliance field by allowing the entities targeted by these acts and subject to a compliance obligation to bring an action for annulment of these acts before the administrative judge, so that they can be subject to a legality review and, where appropriate, annulled. But the case still has to be referred to the administrative court. This may be the case in new areas, such as climate change, as was the so-called *Grande Synthe* case. With its decisions, the French Council of State thus goes to the logical end of the mechanism put in place by the legislator and the regulatory authority to implement the Paris agreements, which are based on a form of compliance on a global scale, with each signatory State committing, in a way, to do what is necessary to achieve a common objective by a given date, with each State being responsible for organising itself to achieve it. In the absence of an international judge capable of verifying compliance with these commitments, the national judge seems the most natural to agree to verify, when a dispute is referred to him or her, that these commitments do not remain a dead letter.

Finally, which is logical since Compliance Law is defined by its Monumental Goals, which may themselves be found in the ambition to protect the individual, Erik Wennerström concludes this book with *Some Reflections on Compliance and the European Court of Human Rights*. The author points out that the development of the case law of the European Court of Human Rights, contributing to European integration, has incorporated the substantial idea of "compliance," which goes beyond the idea of legality, in relation to which companies remain passive, and promotes legal systems as interacting with one another. The author develops the spirit and scope of Protocol 15, which sets out both the principle of subsidiarity and the margins for manoeuvre of the signatory states to the Convention, mechanisms informed by the principle of proportionality. Subsidiarity implies that States are in the best position to devise the most appropriate application of the Convention, with close links between States enabling it to be applied effectively. In addition, the advisory opinion procedure, which enables a national court to obtain the non-binding opinion of the ECHR on a pending case, ensures that compliance is more effective in terms of the objectives of the Convention.

The Court's case law takes up this substantive requirement through its doctrine, particularly as set out in the *Bosphorus* case, emphasising that a State's European Union membership presumes its compliance with the obligations arising from the ECHR, by implementing European Union Law, even if this presumption may be rebutted if the protection is manifestly deficient, which has been accepted in several cases, particularly concerning the right to an impartial tribunal in matters of economic regulation. The different legal orders are thus articulated. The author concludes that the European Court of Human Rights, like the Court of Justice of the European Union, contributes to the construction of Compliance Law in Europe, from an *ex ante* perspective favouring opinions rather than *ex post* sanctions, and creating, notably through the *Bosphorus* doctrine, elements of security and confidence for European integration around values common to the different legal systems articulated and leaving the States adequate margins to favour this integration.

This is the conclusion of this book that shows not only the extent of the *Jurisdictionalisation of Compliance*, but also the benefits that the *Rule of Law* will have to draw from it in the future, so that Compliance does not mean blind obedience to so many regulations, which is the hallmark of totalitarian systems, but rather tends, in an alliance between public authorities and crucial economic operators, towards the achievement of Monumental Goals, of which the protection of the individual is at the heart, the hallmark of democracies.

This is also the global challenge of Compliance Law.

Reinforce the Judge and the Lawyer to Impose Compliance Law as a characteristic of the Rule of Law*

Marie-Anne Frison-Roche

Agrégée des Facultés de droit

Professor of Regulatory Law and Compliance Law

Director of the *Journal of Regulation & Compliance (JoRC)*

Director of the *European School of Regulation and Compliance Law*

There is no Rule of Law without a judge. It is therefore understandable that compliance mechanisms are presented with hostility if they appear to be designed to remove the judge. There are sound arguments for considering compliance techniques as converging towards the idea, or even the ideal, of an unnecessary judge (I). In practice, it is true that in compliance situations everyone sees many judges, of all kinds and very powerful ones, but this would be seen as a sign of imperfection: once the *ex ante* logic of Compliance has been deployed in all its effectiveness within companies, the judge would no longer be required… And the lawyer, especially the attorney, would disappear with him…

* This article is based on a bilingual working paper, along with additional developments, numerous technical references and hypertext links. It is accessible at the following address: https://mafr.fr/en/article/conforter-le-juge-et-lavocat-pour-conforter-le-dro/.

This prospect of a world without judges, without lawyers, and ultimately without Law deserving of its capital letter, reduced to a mass of regulations, a regulatory system where algorithms could use multiple *ex ante processes*, sufficient to organise the "conformity" of all our behaviour with the whole mass of technical texts applicable to us, requires to reconsider the definition of this new branch of Law, often presented as the concentration of *processes* that gives full effectiveness to all the legal rules, which then only deserve lower case letters, regardless of the content of all these rules.

Even supposing that this engineer's dream is achievable, we cannot do without judges and lawyers. It is even imperative to recognise the contributions of the Judge and the Lawyer to Compliance Law: their contribution is invaluable and linked to the very definition of Compliance Law (II).

Firstly, because a pure *ex ante* has never existed. Even in the days of the Legists, (1) humans were still needed to interpret regulations, because a prescription must always be interpreted in *ex post* by a person who must in any case answer questions, whether they are formulated by the Despot-regulator himself or by the subjects of Law, as soon as the political system admits of attributing to the latter the right to construct claims before the Judge. (2)

The role of the lawyer, although linked to the judge's role, is distinct from it. It is both narrower and broader since the lawyer must appear in all cases where the jurisdictional figure is established. Like in Regulation Law, Compliance Law confers numerous jurisdictional powers on administrative authorities, but it is in a specific and spectacular way that it transforms companies into judges. Lawyers have to deal with this, both internally and externally.

Moreover, Compliance Law only takes on its full meaning from the Monumental Goals it serves. (3) It is in this way that this branch of Law safeguards the freedom of human beings, particularly in the digital space

(1) The Chinese Empire apparently never appreciated judges, making room for them only as pure servants of the State, whether as investigators, punishers or guardians of public policy. On this particularly bloody period for *legal scholars*, when the principle of the "certainty" of legislation was carried to its nines, see J. Escarra, *Chinese law: conception and evolution, legislative and judicial institutions, science and teaching*, translated by G.R. Browne, Harvard, Harvard University Press, 1961.

(2) N. Borga, J.-Cl. Marin and J.-Chr. Roda (eds), *Compliance: l'entreprise, le régulateur et le juge*, "Régulations & Compliance" Serie, Paris, Dalloz, 2018.

(3) M.-A. Frison-Roche (ed.), *Compliance Monumental Goals*, "Compliance & Regulation" Serie, Brussels, Journal of Regulation & Compliance (JoRC)/Bruylant, 2023.

where compliance techniques protect them from the power of companies by forcing these companies to use this power to protect individuals, particularly in the handling of data.

Firstly, however, it is the Judges who, in their diversity,(4) impose the protection of human beings as a reference point, either as a limit to the power of compliance instruments or as their very purpose. Secondly, the Lawyer, once again distinguishing himself from the Judge, reminds us, if need be, that all the parties whose interests are involved must be taken into consideration. In an increasingly soft and dialogical Law, everyone presents themselves as the "advocate" of some monumental goal or other: the Lawyer is legitimate to be the first to occupy this position.

I. COMPLIANCE: A *TOOLBOX* TO MAKE JUDGES UNNECESSARY?

Compliance mechanisms seem to have been invented so that companies can finally stop having to deal with judges. Indeed, if compliance tools, which are *ex ante*, work well, then recourse to the judge would become, *ex post*, unnecessary (A), the desired disappearance of the judge bringing with it that of the lawyer. This project is driven in particular by what is known as "artificial intelligence" (B).

A. The Judge and the Lawyer, by their very nature, useless in a well-done Compliance?

It could be argued that the judge is unnecessary, or even incongruous, in compliance mechanisms for the simplest of reasons: the judge is an *ex post* character, whereas the tools of Compliance are *ex ante*.

If Compliance Law is defined as requiring companies to show everyone at all times that their structures and the behaviours of the people for whom they are accountable are conform with the regulations applicable to them,(5) a definition quite common,(6) this requirement takes the form

(4) This is a general article. For a more analytical study, see M.-A. Frison-Roche, "Adjusting General Procedural Law to Compliance Law by the Nature of Things", *this book*.

(5) On the definition of Compliance Law, see more developments in M.-A. Frison-Roche (ed.), *Compliance Monumental Goals*, *op. cit.*, esp. "Compliance Monumental Goals, Beating Heart of Compliance Law", pp. 33-58.

(6) M.-A. Frison-Roche, "Compliance Law", 2016, https://mafr.fr/en/article/le-droit-de-la-compliance/.

of several techniques: risk mapping, commitments, drawing up plans and standards of behaviour covered by framework documents and charters, all of which link companies to the external regulations affecting them.

These compliance tools (7) have a wide range of applications and a very variation of enforcement. Indeed, Compliance may be so soft that in its definition itself it is possible to associate it with soft Law. In fact, sometimes compliance mechanisms have a purely incentive effect, and are often presented as being ethical in nature (driven in particular by moral concern for others) and can therefore have a "community" influence. This community of people, such as investors or Internet users, may be based on a shared culture that transcends legal boundaries, as in the case of "community standards," (8) which are common in the digital environment. The soft norm of compliance then affects people all over the world, making Compliance more powerful than State laws and regulations, which "only" have an *erga omnes* effect on a limited territory. (9) This global compliance perspective may also be due to the fact that the compliance norm is based on long-term calculations, for example in financial or energy matters. (10) When compliance obligations take the form of contractual clauses, particularly in economic supply chains, they are imbued with the binding force of the contract. (11) The notion of "contract of compliance" and "compliance clauses" is emerging. (12) However, these provisions take on a more binding scope when they are formulated by laws, (13) which is so often the case: in France, who is unaware of the existence of the

(7) M.-A. Frison-Roche (ed.), *Compliance Tools*, "Compliance & Regulation" Serie, Brussels, Journal of Regulation & Compliance (JoRC)/Bruylant, 2021.

(8) For example, the "community standards" of the global company *Meta*, on the basis of which disputes are settled and sanctions are imposed by a body set up by the group itself, the *Oversight Board*, which has jurisdiction over all the companies within the group.

(9) On the renewal of sovereignty in spaces over which borders have little control, such as the digital space, see M.-A. Frison-Roche, "The Principle of Active Systemic Proximity: Corollary of the Renewal of the Principle of Sovereignty by Compliance Law", *in* M.-A. Frison-Roche (ed.), *Compliance Monumental Goals*, *op. cit.*, pp. 487-508.

(10) L. Benzoni, "International Trade, Competitivity and Sovereignty: Towards a Political Economy of Compliance", *in* M.-A. Frison-Roche (ed.), *Compliance Monumental Goals*, *op. cit.*, pp. 447-458.

(11) M.-A. Frison-Roche (ed.), *Compliance Obligation, to be published*.

(12) M.-A. Frison-Roche, "Compliance contract, Compliance clauses", 2022, https://mafr.fr/en/article/contrat-de-compliance-clauses-de-compliance/; id., "Laws, Compliance, Contracts, and Judges: places and alliances", 2023, https://mafr.fr/en/article/la-loi-la-compliance-le-contrat-et-le-juge-places-/.

(13) All these sources are cumulative and interrelated. In financial matters in particular, see O. Boulon, "Compliance et régulation financière : le rôle de l'Autorité des marchés financiers", *in* N. Borga, J.-Cl. Marin and J.-Chr. Roda (eds), *Compliance: l'entreprise, le régulateur et le juge*, *op. cit.*, pp. 167-192.

so-called "Sapin 2" law, which seems to be the starting point for learning about Compliance? In the US, who is unaware of the FCPA? In the UK, who is unaware of the *Bribery Act*? And so on…

In this range of mechanisms, all these tools are always *ex ante*, and if they work well, the judge would not be useful… It is not true. It has always been known that even in *ex ante* cases the judge's subsequent view will come into play, and it has always also been known that case law is, in its creative force, retroactive. We also know that in contracts, the judge is virtually present, the potential presence of the judge sanctioning the contractual inexecution increasing the certainty of execution. We also know that Criminal Law is inseparable from Criminal Procedural Law, which only have meaning in relation to the judge. Therefore, the famous French so-called "Sapin 2" law being in the hands of the Public Prosecutor, a magistrate who only appears in criminal proceedings. More generally, the American DPA, model for the others, is within the hands of the DOJ.

Every lawyer knows that. But Compliance system is not just a matter for lawyers. Because Compliance Law is a very new branch of Law and its tools are often rightly designed by specialists in other disciplines, such as finance, engineering or *data science*, compliance tools are conceived as a means, sometimes presented as infallible, of securing a company so that it can always "be conform", offering permanent proof of that, and thereby evading the person who sanctions breaches and deals with disputes: the judge.

This systemic conception of a company that "always complies" and always shows its "compliance" would therefore render the judge useless.

This is what many companies aspire to, all the more so as academic doctrine presented them the criminal courts as the only judge concerned by the matter… It is precisely because Compliance Law is presented to them in this way that they very logically perceive the intervention of a judge as a "nightmare,"(14) or at the very least as an intrusion. Therefore, the performance of algorithms should protect them from this by compliance by design.

(14) M.-A. Frison-Roche, "The Dreamed Compliance Law", 2020, https://mafr.fr/en/article/le-droit-reve-de-la-compliance/.

B. Compliance by design: the dream of the useless Judge?

It is often explained that the ability of algorithms would ensure not only the detection and prevention of non-compliance but also a company's compliance with regulations (1). This would render the judge and the lawyer unnecessary, implying that their very presence would be a sign of dysfunctional compliance (2).

1. A presentation of the ability of the algorithms to be sufficient to ensure compliance by the company and by the people for whom it is accountable to the applicable regulations

Compliance by design is sometimes referred to as *Automated Compliance*: the benefit lies in the automation that makes it possible to eliminate the sort of "hazard" that is the human being, the "legal hazard" being just one illustration particularly feared by companies in the repertoire of risks to be identified, assessed and minimised. (15)

The technological performance of algorithms could lead to this reduction. It is described in three stages. There are now algorithms that are so well adapted and scalable that they could *accumulate* all the legal information available, known as "regulatory data" (first stage), *arrange* each regulatory data in relation to each other (second stage) in order to automatically *detect* non-coincidences between this "regulation" and the behaviour of the people for whom the company is accountable (third stage).

This learning process enables the algorithm to move on to the fourth stage: *taking action*. This action itself takes place in two stages. The first consists of *alerting the system* to non-conformities. The algorithm can in fact "learn" as it goes along from all the cases that arise, learning from successive adjustments to texts and decisions, to automatically produce alerts when situations in which the company and the people for whom the company is personally responsible are prohibited by the "regulations": this is the red flags tool.

As all the specialists always remind us that machines are only tools, it may happen that the combination and comparison between the stock of "learned" situations, the stock of "rules" retained and the situation identified does not result in a proven non-coincidence but in a "risk of

(15) M.-A. Frison-Roche, "Drawing up Risk Maps as an Obligation and the Paradox of 'Conformity Risks'", *in* M.-A. Frison-Roche (ed.), *Compliance Tools*, *op. cit.*, pp. 61-71.

non-conformity."(16) In this case, the algorithm does not signal an actual or future breach, but a risk of breach, through the orange flag, implying human beings then assess the risk: this is the role of compliance officers.(17) Managers, who decide on the "compliance strategy" on the advice of their chief compliance officer, usually give instructions either not to take such a risk or to report it to the relevant public authorities (for instance regulatory authorities or prosecutor), so as not to incur any penalties. In this mechanical approach, the challenge for the company is to avoid incurring sanctions.

This latter treatment of information is all the more logical given that these public authorities themselves claim to come in *ex ante*, to be the "advocate" of the rules with which compliance is required and present themselves as being "in support" of companies(18) so that they do not incur sanctions; the Authorities finding this way more effective than being in ambush to impose sanctions. This is what states the *Autorité de la concurrence* (French Competition Authority) in its Framework Document of 23 May 2022 *on competition compliance programmes*(19) and the *Agence française anticorruption – AFA* (French Anti-Corruption Agency), which publishes numerous guides to help companies, expressly linking these guides to its support function, to which a specific department of the Agency is dedicated.

As a result of this "learning" process, algorithms, these "intelligences without intelligence," provide companies with information about their "risks of non-conformity," to which they mechanically submit in order to avoid being sanctioned, with the help of the public authority endowed with the power to sanction them.

(16) On the legal nonsense of the very notion of "compliance risk", as referred to in the risk mapping technique, see M.-A. Frison-Roche, "Drawing up Risk Maps as an Obligation and the Paradox of the 'Conformity Risks'", *op. cit.*

(17) On the role of compliance officers through active use of the principle of proportionality, see the remarkable forward-looking article by L. Rapp, "Compliance, Proportionality and Normativity", *in* M.-A. Frison-Roche (ed.), *Compliance Monumental Goals, op. cit.*, pp. 189-212.

(18) See European Commission, Directorate-General for Competition, *Compliance matters – What companies can do better to respect EU competition rules*, Publications Office, 2012, https://data.europa.eu/doi/10.2763/60132.

(19) In this text of soft law, the Authority presents itself, together with the *Direction générale de la concurrence, de la consommation et de la répression des fraudes – DGCCRF* (French Directorate General for Competition Policy, Consumer Affairs and Fraud Control), as "partner institutions" of the company (No. 48 *et seq.*), playing a "role in facilitating a culture of compliance" (No. 48). This takes the form of the decisions themselves insofar as they constitute a reference system, the form of their consultative practice, and various "compliance tools" of a mainly educational nature (see in this dimension of an Authority that is above all a teacher, M.-A. Frison-Roche, "Training: Content and Container of Compliance", *in* M.-A. Frison-Roche (ed.), *Compliance Tools, op. cit.*, pp. 245-264, esp. the conclusion, p. 263.

Such "efficacy" encourages companies to want to go further in the mechanical action of algorithms. Indeed, algorithms can produce knowledge not only about "non-conformity" but also about "positive conformity," the appearance of *green flags* having already reassured the company that it is conform with its "regulatory environment." Going a step further, the algorithms can readjust a "non-conform" company to its legal environment so that it becomes "conform", or build the company and its future links with suppliers, investors, employees, etc. so that they are "always conform." To achieve this, the algorithms that detect "conformity" and "non-conformity" can be combined with others to generate smart contracts. (20)

Contractual clauses that "comply with all applicable regulations" are then written by algorithms with the same automaticity and indifference to content, and contracts may finally be "certified" as complying with regulatory requirements, whereas stipulations in projects, or even in simple exchanges, such as e-mails or recorded telephone discussions, may be detected as "non-conform" and lead to the company's intervention before any possible exchange of consents between the parties; the behaviours detected as non-conform with a clause recorded as "compliant" may ultimately be sanctioned by the company, for example by disciplinary action.

By moving from the algorithmic ability to identify "non-conformity" in structural arrangements and behaviours to the algorithmic ability to impose conformity in structures and behaviour by a kind of *by-design* machinery since the writing of secondary standards (corporate structures or contracts) can ensure the conformity with the regulations, (21) technological performance and neutrality offer to the company the assurance of being "conform with the regulations." There would be no more breaches. No more judges. A wonderful dream. For that, companies agree to pay a lot.

---

(20) On the general phenomenon of *smart contracts*, since the less human intelligence there is and the more that vocabulary is used, whereas there is very little intelligence and very little contractuality in this method of managing transactions, see in particular UK Law Commission, *Smart legal contracts – Advice to Government*, November 2021, https://www.lawcom.gov.uk/project/smart-contracts/; A. Rocher, "Considération d'épistémologie juridique sur les *legaltechs*", *RTD com.*, 2022, pp. 13 *et seq.*; A. Bulmer, "Smart contracts: what are they and what should you look out for?", *Ent. L.R.*, 2022, Vol. 33, No. 5, pp. 172-177; L. Procopie, "Are smart contracts actually contracts? How smart contracts can work globally", *JIBLR*, 2021, Vol. 36, No. 1, pp. 25-30; Cl. Leveneur, *Les smart contracts. Étude de droit des contrats à l'aune de la blockchain*, "Nouvelle Bibliothèque de thèses" Serie, Paris, Dalloz, 2024.

(21) On the illusory distinction between primary standards, where there would be "meaning," housed in the legislator, and secondary standards, where there would only be the neutral application of the former, with algorithms taking on this sort of stewardship, see C. Granier, "The Normative Originality of Compliance by Design", *in* M.-A. Frison-Roche (ed.), *Compliance Tools*, *op. cit.*, pp. 287-298.

But of course, this presupposes two things. Firstly, it assumes that artificial intelligence can achieve the feat of grasping the meaning of "regulations," this term that is always used to designate the Law in almost all presentations on artificial intelligence, and in particular the meaning that the Judge will give to these legal rules. Secondly, it assumes that Compliance Law is defined as the fact that a company complies with regulations.

However, these two very mechanical presuppositions are inaccurate, in that the first sees the Law, which is so alive and changing, as a "regulatory mass," while the second sees Compliance as a "conformity."

The further we go in defining Compliance as "complying in all respects and in advance with all the regulations applicable to us" – a mass of regulations to which the Law is reduced – the more we have to rely on algorithms. However, according to Yann Le Cun, a theoretical and practical reference in the field of artificial intelligence, for algorithms to become truly "intelligent," i.e. to acquire "common sense," they would need to make radical advances in deep learning, which they have not managed to do, and perhaps will never be able to do, unless the mathematicians who develop them change their concept (22) and adopt a new one that has yet to be developed.

Furthermore, if we distinguish the regulatory mass from the Law, the "common sense" of the Law is what we might call the "sense of Justice." Regulations may not need it. But that is precisely what makes the difference between a State governed by the Rule of Law and a simple regulatory system neutrally offered to a political power. But of the first, it is the Judge and the Lawyer, each in their own role, who are its guardians.

If we believe that our societies should continue to be governed by the Rule of Law and not by the mass of regulations, and that artificial intelligence is not capable of grasping this sense of justice, then it is the very definition of Compliance (23) that should not be reduced to "compliance with the mass of regulations." The role of algorithms then becomes very limited, not only because new laws prevent an excessive use of this technology, for instance the European *Data Act*, but because A.I. is only a tool of conformity, without purpose, without goals.

(22) Y. Le Cun, "A Path Towards Autonomous Machine Intelligence", *Position Paper*, 27 June 2022.

(23) M.-A. Frison-Roche, "What can Compliance Law build relying on the European Humanist Tradition", 2019, https://mafr.fr/en/article/ce-que-le-droit-de-la-compliance-peut-soffrir-en-p/.

The fact remains that algorithms are very often presented as the *Alpha* and *Omega* of compliance. Compliance is therefore seen as a discipline primarily for mathematicians, in which cultural specificities and depths have been absorbed by this "regulatory mass" which acts like a sponge.

In this widespread view, if there is a judge, it is because something has gone wrong.

It would therefore not be a sign of the system's vitality, but a sign of its weakness.

2. The Judge, presented as a sign of dysfunction in the mechanical Compliance System

From this point of view, the judge should only intervene when the machines have not functioned effectively, i.e. have not detected the non-conformities, have not warned the company of them, have not drafted the contracts described as "intelligent," and have not in advance censured the non-conforming clauses.

The judge would appear to sanction a malfunction. The judge would thus be no more than a sign of the progress that the system still has to make to become perfect, a simple figure of "transition."

In this period of transition towards what would be progress, leading to a world governed by mechanical processes, this conception of the judge, often promoted, has several consequences.

Firstly, it is above all the judge of the sanction who must intervene since the issue is the unilateral relationship between the company and the legal norms that the company need to respect actively. The unilateral relation between companies and laws must be rectified, the sanction itself having a corrective role. The *ex ante* approach continues to prevail, injecting into the company a "lesson" in the primary sense of the term, i.e. information about its past non-conformity so that the firm can organise its future conformity more solidly. In the French legal system, the so specific "*peine de conformité*" that we can translate as "compliance penalty," provided for in article 131-39-2 of the *Code pénal* (French Criminal Code), (24) is an ancillary penalty. It has been criticised in that it could also have been

(24) Free translation: "I. – Where the law so provides in respect of a legal person, an offence may be punished by the obligation to submit, under the supervision of the French Anti-Corruption Agency, for a maximum period of five years, to a compliance programme designed to ensure the existence and implementation within the legal person of the measures and procedures defined in II

designed as an independent penalty since it is more of an educational tool for the future than a penalty for the past, which can be applied as a principal and sufficient penalty. (25)

Secondly, it is a judge who must intervene immediately since the primary aim is to identify a "non-conformity" and impose provisions for the future. But in the American Deferred Prosecution Agreement (DPA) or in the French *Convention judiciaire d'intérêt public – CJIP* (Judicial Public Interest Agreement), the deal is made between the company and the public prosecutor, the intervention of the judge having only a purpose of validation, ultimate example of this way of saving time by eliminating the last step that leads to the courtroom, with this "validation" by the judge merely expressing a light control to ensure that everything goes as quickly as possible. (26)

More generally, it is often said that, if a judge had to intervene, it would be above all the judges of first instance who would be concerned; the supreme courts would not be concerned at all, since there would hardly be any legal principle in these processes of effectiveness of the rules, whose content would not be in question, and since it takes so long to reach them. This is why it is still frequently said that the supreme courts are not the Judges of Compliance. (27)

The lawyers' main task would then no longer be to avoid punishment, but to negotiate the "price" to be paid for past misconducts and to negotiate programmes to build a future of full conformity.

As it will be demonstrated below, this is a complete misrepresentation.

II. – The penalty provided for in I includes the obligation to implement the following measures and procedures: 1° A code of conduct defining and illustrating the different types of behaviour to be prohibited as being likely to constitute corruption or trading in influence; 2° An internal alert system designed to enable the collection of reports from employees concerning the existence of behaviour or situations contrary to the code of conduct of the legal entity; 3° Risk mapping in the form of regularly updated documentation designed to identify, analyse and prioritise the risks of exposure of the legal entity to external solicitations for the purposes of corruption, in particular as a function of the business sectors and geographical areas in which the legal entity operates; 4° Procedures for assessing the situation of customers, first-tier suppliers and intermediaries with regard to risk mapping; 5° Internal or external accounting control procedures designed to ensure that books, registers and accounts are not used to conceal corruption or influence peddling. These controls may be carried out either by the legal entity's own accounting and financial control departments, or by using an external auditor when carrying out the accounts certification audits provided for in Article L. 823-9 of the French Commercial Code; 6° A training system for managers and staff most exposed to the risks of corruption and influence peddling; 7° A disciplinary system enabling the legal entity's employees to be sanctioned in the event of a breach of the legal entity's code of conduct."

(25) J.-M. Brigant, "Les peines complémentaires dans la loi Sapin 2: entre extension et innovation", *Revue Lamy Droit des affaires*, 2017, pp. 45-50.

(26) On the question of the intensity of control, see M.-A. Frison-Roche, "Definition of Proportionality and Definition of Compliance Law", *in* M.-A. Frison-Roche (ed.), *Compliance Monumental Goals*, *op. cit.*, pp. 259-288.

(27) For a demonstration of the contrary, see *supra*.

C. The emergence of the Deferred Prosecution Agreement and the French Judicial Public Interest Agreement, these technical embodiments of the introduction of conformity as a bifurcation in the road before the courts

If the mechanisms of the American Deferred Prosecution Agreement (DPA) and the French Judicial Public Interest Agreement have given rise to numerous studies, (28) which are most often critical, particularly in the European perspective, it is because they present these tools as a sign of the invasion of this exogenous Law which is of an American conception. In France, the criticisms first come from the fact that through these mechanisms we see the profile of the American Judge entering our system and because it illustrates what a principle of expulsion of the Judge would be like (1). However, it is more a question of transforming the Public Prosecutor into a Judge – phenomenon common to both these mechanisms – something over which the Validation Judge exercises only a fairly formal control (2), because of the uncertainties that mark the legal qualifications of the whole. This shows that, for the moment, the Judge has not yet fully found his or her place in Compliance Law.

1. The French *CJIP*, an attempt to expel the Judge, a mechanism that has itself been widely criticised for having been designed for American Prosecutors and Judges, strangers to the continental legal culture

One of the grievances often levelled against Compliance Law is that even if it has given a place to the Judge, it would be to the American Judge, either in person, through the extraterritorial effect of sanctions validated by American courts, as in the *BNP* and *Alstom* cases, (29) or as a model,

(28) Analyses full of interest and in large numbers, compared to other mechanisms. See a comparative analysis of the US DPA, the UK DPA and the French Judicial Public Interest Agreement: R. Burlingame, K. Coppens, N. Power and D. H. Lee, "Anti-Corruption Compliance: Global Dimension of Enforcement and Risk Management", *in* M.-A. Frison-Roche (ed.), *Compliance Tools*, "Compliance & Regulation" Serie, Brussels, Journal of Regulation & Compliance (JoRC)/Bruylant, 2021, pp. 199-208. See also F. Mazzacuva, "Justifications and purposes of negotiated justice for corporate offenders: deferred and non-prosecution agreements in the UK and US systems of criminal justice", *J. Crim. L.*, 2014, Vol. 78, No. 3, pp. 249-262; M. Bisgrove and M. Weekes, "Deferred prosecution agreements: a practical consideration", *Crim. L.R.*, 2014, Vol. 6, pp. 416-438.

(29) J. Morel-Morager, "La compliance financière, les enseignements de l'affaire BNP Paribas", *in* N. Borga, J.-Cl. Marin and J.-Chr. Roda (eds), *Compliance: l'entreprise, le régulateur et le juge, op. cit.*, pp. 69-78; P. Hardouin, "The BNP Paribas 'tour de fraud': extortion, war and justice", *Comp. Law.*, 2014, Vol. 35, No. 12, pp. 367-370; C.M. Swift, "European banks and extraterritorial sanctions: lessons from the BNP Paribas settlement", *Int. T.L.R.*, 2015, Vol. 21, No. 2, pp. 61-64; "Alstom pays USD 772m to settle US bribery allegations", *Compliance & Risk*, 2015, Vol. 4, No. 1, p. 14.

Compliance then being the battering ram of the "Americanisation of Law" in other geographical areas, the French so-called "Sapin 2" law of 2016 being presented by many as nothing more than a kind of translation-collage from the American Foreign Corrupt Practices Act (FCPA). From this critical perspective, the little that the Judge is present in the compliance system should therefore be rejected since it would merely be the gateway to a foreign domination.

Against what would be not only an invasion but also an elimination of the Judge – even more in the recent legal mechanism of the "declination" proposed by the DOJ, which would be a pure contract for the extinction of the legal action of the public prosecutor… (30)– the French Parliament has affirmed in its reports (31) that these judicial apparatus should be rejected, as should everything attached to Compliance Law, as an illegitimate "extraterritorial" arm of American legal system. (32) It is not only because it is not from a real national source that it must be fought, but also because it would invade us with a legal culture that is foreign to us: the culture of the trial, whereas we are built on a culture of the legislation, the general text and not the particular cases, which is disappearing all the more. The same image of the "spectre" is then used, because the "litigious society" is linked to the contractualisation of litigation. This would contribute to the dissolution of the identity of societies with a Romano-Germanic culture (Civil Law), a dissolution in which legal techniques would play a part. (33)

All these works are partly well-founded but draw general conclusions on very specific cases, most often embargoes, which are effectively unjustifiable extraterritorial applications of national policies, and express nostalgia for a kind of golden age without indicating how, here and now, the

(30) U. S. Department of Justice, *9-47.120 – Criminal Division Corporate Enforcement and Voluntary Self-Disclosure Policy*, January 2023; Assistant Attorney General Kenneth A. Polite, Jr., *Remarks on Revisions to the Criminal Division's Corporate Enforcement Policy*, Speech, 17 January 2023.

(31) *Assemblée nationale* (French National Assembly), *Rapport d'information sur l'évaluation de l'impact de la loi n° 2016-1691 du 9 décembre 2016 relative à la transparence, à la lutte contre la corruption et à la modernisation de la vie économique, dite "loi Sapin 2"* (Information Report on assessing the impact of the law No. 2016-1691 of 9 December 2016 on transparency, fight against corruption and modernisation of economic life, known as the "Sapin 2 law"), 2021 (mainly the so-called "Gauvin" report).

(32) French National Assembly, *Rapport sur l'extraterritorialité de la législation américaine* (Report on the extraterritoriality of the US legislation), 2016 (the so-called "Lellouch-Berger" report); *Sénat* (French Senate), *Rapport sur l'extraterritorialité des sanctions américaines* (Report on the extraterritoriality of US sanctions), 2019 (the so-called "Bonnecarrère" report).

(33) On the historical importance of the law, particularly in France, see Carbonnier, who describes the *Code civil* (French Civil Code) as a "*lieu de mémoire*" ("place of me mory"): J. Carbonnier, "Le Code civil", *in* P. Nora (ed.), *Les lieux de mémoire*, III, *La Nation*, 2, *Le territoire, l'État, le patrimoine*, "nrf – Bibliothèque illustrée des histoires", Paris, Gallimard, 1986, pp. 293-315.

global systemic problems addressed by Compliance Law can be tackled by national texts or the traditional branches of Law, whereas the human and climate issues (34) are tackled by judges who rule with decisions of a large scale, the same scale as those of the woes submitted to them. Because these cases are systemic themselves, the Judge works in a new systemic way. (35)

Furthermore, Compliance Law is not limited to the American FCPA or the French law known as "Sapin 2," which deal with the specific subject of corruption and are only one example of Compliance Law. Compliance Law covers a whole range of mechanisms that require companies in a position to do so to fulfil obligations that would have been considered as "public service" obligations in the past, such as personal data protection and circulation; the activities of the data regulatory public bodies are now essentially based on Compliance mechanisms. In the same way, the notion of "vigilance" will be deployed above all to protect human beings and to ensure that something is done effectively and efficiently in the area of climate change, the extraterritorial scope of the measures being welcomed and recognised as consubstantial with the subject, the whole being entrusted to the courts. (36)

Data Protection Law, whether personal or not, was born in Europe and not in the United States. If there is an export, it is not from the U.S. to Europe but from Europe to the U.S., and it is the European judge who has above all conceived and applied it, (37) either to impose the transmission of information or to prohibit it, for example by creating the "right to be forgotten" (38) or by hindering the circulation of information across the Atlantic to protect the people concerned. (39) In the same way, systemic

(34) The two need not be distinguished, as demonstrated by C. Huglo, "Under what Conditions could Climate Law Constitute a Priority Monumental Goal?", *in* M.-A. Frison-Roche (ed.), *Compliance Monumental Goals, op. cit.*, pp. 181-186.

(35) On the notion of "systemic case", M.-A. Frison-Roche, "The hypothesis of the category of systemic cases brought before the judge", 2021, https://mafr.fr/en/article/lhypothese-des-causes-systemiques/.

(36) E. Hannezo, J.-C. Jaïs and C. Cavicchioli, "First decision by French courts on duty of vigilance law: dismissal of claims lodged by six NGOs against TotalEnergies", 1st March 2023, https://sustainablefutures.linklaters.com/post/102i8vw/first-decision-by-french-courts-on-duty-of-vigilance-law-dismissal-of-claims-lod.

(37) As Koen Lenaerts, president of the Court of Justice of the European Union, himself pointed out in his article "Le juge de l'Union européenne dans une Europe de la Compliance" in the opening article of the book *Pour une Europe de la Compliance*, "Régulations & Compliance" Serie, Paris, Dalloz, 2019, pp. 1-12.

(38) CJEU, GC, 13 May 2014, *Google Spain*, case C-131/12.

(39) CJEU, GC, 6 October 2015, *Maximilian Schrems v. Data Protection Commissioner* (*Schrems I*), case C-362/14; CJEU, GC, 16 July 2020, *Maximilian Schrems v. Data Protection Commissioner* (*Schrems II*), case C-311/18.

climate issues are above all protected by the courts. (40) If we are so hostile to the Judges when it comes to international sanctions for money laundering or corruption, or if we see them as being effectively circumvented, it is because we do not yet have a global vision of Compliance Law.

Because the substantial unity of the branch of Law already constituted by Compliance Law is not yet fully perceived, whereas it is unfolding before our eyes, unity constituted by the Monumental Goal of the protection of human beings, (41) a claim expressed by the Political Powers and put into practice by the Crucial Economic Operators (42) in a position to do so, the Judge may therefore be considered unnecessary.

The Judge is indeed useless in a mechanical conception of bringing organisations into compliance with regulations; but he or she is central to a Compliance Law defined by the claim to protect human beings, a major political ambition which he or she shares with the Lawyer and which is the mark, heavy and costly, of States governed by the Rule of Law.

The French Law mechanism of the *Convention judiciaire d'intérêt public – CJIP* (Judicial Public Interest Agreement), modelled on an American legal mechanism, as it is developing, could be called into question if it does not remain within the founding limits of the Rule of Law. Time will tell.

2. A Prosecutor transformed into a Judge and the question of the office of the Validation Judge

French legislation is clear, and the mechanism is often modelled on that of the *composition pénale* (French criminal settlement). Article 41-1-2 of the *Code de procédure pénale* (French Criminal Procedure Code) sets out the procedure for terminating criminal proceedings. It is not, therefore, the exchange of two wills, that of the Public Prosecutor and that of the legal entity (expressed by its corporate officer), that produces the extinction of the public prosecution, but the power of the Public Prosecutor who issues a "proposal" within a framework strictly established by Criminal Law, a proposal that must subsequently be validated by the President

(40) M.-A. Frison-Roche, "Compliance Law and Climate. To prevent Climate Risk and build Climate Balance", 2022, https://mafr.fr/en/article/prevention-et-gestion-du-risque-climatique-par-le-/.

(41) M.-A. Frison-Roche, "Compliance Monumental Goals, Beating Heart of Compliance Law", *in* M.-A. Frison-Roche (ed.), *Compliance Monumental Goals*, "Compliance & Regulation" Serie, Brussels, Journal of Regulation & Compliance (JoRC)/Bruylant, 2023, pp. 33-58.

(42) On the notion of "crucial operator", see M.-A. Frison-Roche, "Proposal for a notion: the 'Crucial Operator'", 2006, https://www.mafr.fr/fr/article/proposal-for-a-notion-the-crucial-operator/.

of the *tribunal judiciaire* (French First Instance Civil Court), even if the entire process is only effective if this proposal receives the pure and simple acceptance of the legal person.

In a visionary article, Jean-Claude Marin, former *Procureur général* (Prosecutor-General) at the *Cour de cassation* (French Court of cassation), describes this agreement as a new expression of the discretionary power to prosecute. (43)

The French Criminal Procedure Code lays down the procedure, which, because the mechanism must be understood as under Criminal Law principles, must be followed to the letter. The process should therefore be interpreted restrictively (*a contrario*) when it is a source of danger for the person who may be punished, and *ad favorem* when it is favourable, because we are dealing with Criminal Law and not Contract Law.

In fact, in Europe as it is in the U.S., the process is done as a contractual one. The proposal is made by the Public Prosecutor, and the company accepts it. The justification is just the freedom for the company to refuse and the efficacity of the result for everyone and for the Public Policy, the company accepting the commitment of a compliance programme. (44)

In this very contractual conception, there is very little room for the Judge. Firstly, he or she only controls the existence of the company's consent. Secondly, the effective person who articulates a "judgment" on the situation, the criminal qualification of what the company has done, the fine to apply and the commitment to impose, is the public prosecutor himself or herself.

In this evolution, which is justified by the effectivity, the efficacy and the efficiency, the problem is: if, in practice, in every legal system the Public Prosecutor acts as a Judge, but the mechanism, for instance the DPA or the *CJIP*, is presented as a sort of "contract", there is no place for the rights of the defence of the "accused" legal person, neither for the managers, neither for the victims.

This raises two questions. The first one is about the object of the judicial validation of the agreement (only a simple formal approval...), and, more crucial, the second question is about the transformation of the Public

(43) J.-Cl. Marin, "Droit pénal et compliance", *in* M.-A. Frison-Roche (ed.), *Régulation, Supervision, Compliance*, "Régulations" Serie, Paris, Dalloz, 2017, pp. 65-72.

(44) R. Burlingame, K. Coppens, N. Power and D. H Lee, "Anti-Corruption Compliance: Global Dimension of Enforcement and Risk Management", *op. cit.*

Prosecutor into a Judge of what is nevertheless presented as an agreement of wills, without necessity of rights of defence in this sort of "contractual process."

While some have argued that the *CJIP*, as the DPA, has "privatised" Criminal Law, (45) it is the rules of Criminal Law that must be preserved, particularly their strict nature. However, as Professor Guillaume Beaussonie points out, (46) because the *CJIP* is perceived more as a contractual tool than as a mechanism for the legal action of the prosecutor, the restrictive interpretation and the control of proportionality hardly seem to be respected.

For example, the French *CJIP* of 26 August 2021 between the *Parquet national financier* (French National Financial Prosecutor's Office) and the bank Morgan Stanley, which intervened at the end of a scheme designed to enable its clients to avoid paying tax immediately, provided for a public interest fine calculated not on the basis of the profits made by the bank, which were small in this case, but on the basis of the profits made by its clients, which were much higher. It is a broad interpretation of the text to impose a penalty which refers not to the profits of the legal person obliged to pay after having accepted the proposal but to the profits of the beneficiaries of its possible failure. Admittedly, the bank agreed to pay such an amount, but the fine is not a price and the bank's consent to pay is not sufficient to transform a fine imposed into a freely negotiated price. The legality of criminal offences and penalties continues to govern the setting of the public interest fine, particularly for the person who sets the amount (the public prosecutor) and, more generally, in the way in which the provision is to be interpreted, i.e. strictly, as the amount is not the result of a free meeting of minds.

More generally, it is a powerful Judge who must be at the centre of Compliance Law, and the Lawyer with him or her. This is because Compliance Law is itself the expression of the Rule of Law, of which the Judge and the Lawyer are inseparable. (47) However, because Compliance Law is a new branch of Law, characterised by the power of companies, the offices of both these actors are transformed.

---

(45) E. Breen, "La 'compliance', une privatisation de la régulation?", *Revue de science criminelle et de droit pénal comparé*, 2019, p. 327.

(46) G. Beaussonie, "Do Criminal Law and Compliance Form a System?", *in* M.-A. Frison-Roche (ed.), *Compliance Monumental Goals*, *op. cit.*, pp. 169-180.

(47) See *supra*.

II. THE LINKED AND INVALUABLE CONTRIBUTION OF JUDGES AND LAWYERS TO COMPLIANCE LAW

The role of the Judge and the Compliance Lawyer is to maintain Compliance Law as a characteristic of States governed by the Rule of Law (A). Because Compliance Law extends beyond States, the jurisdictional figure can take various forms, in particular the company itself transformed into a judging entity, it is essential that the Lawyer retains his classic role: defending (B).

A. The duty of the Judge and the Lawyer to maintain Compliance Law as a characteristic of states governed by the Rule of Law

If it is argued that compliance is simply a process for conforming with regulations at all times, then if it succeeds, there is no need for judges and lawyers. (48) But if Compliance Law is defined by its purpose, by "Monumental Goals," then it is not a way of efficacy that applies to all applicable regulations, but it does live up to the claim expressed by such goals, thus constituting a characteristic of States governed by the Rule of Law (1). Because of this, not only do Judges and Lawyers cease to be absent or the sign of a transitory dysfunction, but even more so: they are the guardians of it (2).

1. Compliance, the hallmark of the Rule of Law

Compliance Law is defined by the Monumental Goals that the political and public Authorities want to achieve (and not by all the various and accumulated regulations). (49)

In a very systemic conception, these political and public Authorities have the claim to modify the future, so that it is preserved from systemic disasters that ravage societies, such as corruption, money laundering, climate imbalance, hatred, misinformation, etc. This "claim" can take on a new dimension when these Monumental Goals are not only "negative" (making sure that it does not happen) but "positive" (making sure that it

---

(48) See the entire first part of this study, on this very definition and what would make it possible to realise this ambition, namely artificial intelligence. This is both technologically illusory and extremely dangerous because it could work to the benefit of any "regulation" that might be harmful to human beings.

(49) M.-A. Frison-Roche (ed.), *Compliance Monumental Goals*, *op. cit.*

does happen). Indeed, this "claim" can take on even greater significance when these Monumental Goals are not just "negative" but "positive," when the aim of compliance techniques is to establish situations for tomorrow that would not otherwise be possible: effective equality between human beings, a principle of respect, probity, and consideration for others. (50)

This concern for others, even in the distant future, of which the duty of vigilance is the most advanced instrument, (51) converges with the classic notion of the common good, as laid down in Ancient Roman legal system through the *res publica*. Compliance Law, therefore, by focusing on companies because they are the entities "in a position" to achieve these monumental goals, whether or not they wish to do so, (52) with Criminal Law providing support, develops this public ambition by giving a new dimension to what is an act of sovereignty, by taking it beyond the borders of the State.

The fact that Compliance Law shows concern for others, even when they are beyond the ordinary reach of States, because they are in a remote territory or are Internet users, (53) is characteristic of the Rule of Law, because it is driven by concern for others

This is why it is essential to distinguish between the submission of each person in advance to regulations, which technically corresponds to conformity as developed in legal systems of submission of individuals, for example in the current Chinese legal system, and the protection of each individual by Compliance Law, which technically corresponds to the systemic conception of Compliance legal mechanisms as developed in States governed by the Rule of Law.

But it is difficult to distinguish between the two, because the instruments are often the same since the aim is always to gather information and "re-educate" people. The rhetoric of concern for others is easily suspected of being nothing more than sophistry.

(50) M.-A. Frison-Roche, "Compliance Monumental Goals, Beating Heart of Compliance Law", *in* M.-A. Frison-Roche (ed.), *Compliance Monumental Goals*, *op. cit.*, and all the contributions in this book.

(51) E. Piana and P. Utho, *L'Epervier Vigilance et le Pays au nom au nom oublié*, "Les Aventures de l'Ogre Compliance" Serie, Journal of Regulation & Compliance (JoRC), 2023.

(52) A.-V. Le Fur, "Interest and '*raison d'être*' of the Company: How Does It Fit Together with the Compliance Monumental Goals?" and A. Le Goff, "Monumental Goals Perceived by the Firm: Serene Business or Business under Pressure?", *in* M.-A. Frison-Roche (ed.), *Compliance Monumental Goals*, *op. cit.*, pp. 69-82 and pp. 83-90.

(53) R.-O. Maistre, "What are the Monumental Goals for the Regulator in a Rapidly Changing Audiovisual and Digital Landscape?", *in* M.-A. Frison-Roche (ed.), *Compliance Monumental Goals*, *op. cit.*, pp. 61-68.

The presence or absence of Judges and Lawyers is the clue, almost the key, to distinguishing between conformity techniques, which are a way of subjecting the individual to any regulation, and Compliance Law, which is a way of protecting individuals in order to build a system in which they remain at the centre, or even more so.

In a conformity system, there are no judges or lawyers. They are unnecessary. In a Compliance Law system, which is defined by Monumental Goals that all express concern for others, they are indispensable and central.

2. Judge and Lawyer, consubstantial guardians of Compliance Law, characteristic of the Rule of Law

As the President of the Court of Justice of the European Union has remarkably demonstrated,(54) the Court of Justice was a driving force in the birth of Compliance Law, because it was concerned to protect a trader whose name appeared in the course of searches that the Google search engine offered to everyone and for all time. In the digital space, there is no statute of limitations, no forgetting: we are indefinitely offered to others.

This limitless space, neither of space nor of time, which ancient wisdom associates with unreason, is hardly a place where classical Law can lay down rules in the ordinary way since it itself moves within a space enclosed by borders and follows the ordinary course of time. Furthermore, digital space feeds all our desires, in particular the pleasure we take in watching the misfortune of others, for example the bankruptcy of that trader for whose protection the Court of Justice invented in 2014 in its *Google Spain* ruling the subjective right to be forgotten,(55) as well as the pleasure we take in hating everyone and everything, the main driving force behind the prosperity of social networks.

Algorithms capture the factual state of limitless spaces, they do not express external principles. Companies can relay principles through technology but, as they are not external to the economic and social system in which they have a direct interest, they are not legitimate in issuing first principles.

---

(54) K. Lenaerts, "Le juge de l'Union européenne dans l'Europe de la compliance", *op. cit.*

(55) CJEU, GC, 13 May 2014, *Google Spain*, case C-131/12, this subjective right to be forgotten goes beyond the right to remove a mention from a file.

If the Rule of Law can resist this technological neutrality, which allows a new corrosion of systems through corruption, money laundering, hate and the denial of truth, it is through the character of the Judge who, as an impartial and disinterested third party, can listen to both sides, the weak and the strong (but also the strong and the weak) being able to be right.

What is more, "regulation" levels out its content, the idea of hierarchy and system, conformity taking texts literally, the notion of principle being unable to emerge in the face of the omnipresence of this single norm: pure obedience. The Rule of Law, however, is based on the opposite principle since it limits power by anchoring the techniques on substantial principles, the application of which can be discussed, and the application of which the Judge, especially the Supreme Courts, has both the custody and the prerogative of deciding on a case-by-case basis to concretise them, without being bound by the use made of them by subjects of Law and Governments.

The memory of the dispute between Kelsen and Schmitt should definitively make us prefer the conception of Compliance Law to the conformity process; this Compliance Law which, through the Monumental Goals, places a limit on the power of the Authorities and companies and which links the exercise of all this power thus given to companies to the protection of human beings, but only for this purpose, (56) under the control of the Judges. Because the Rule of Law is what limits the power of those who make the rules by offering control of their application to an impartial and disinterested third party, it is essential that the Judge is at the heart of Compliance Law, which offers so much power to the players, whether they are public Authorities whose prescriptions have an extraterritorial reach, sovereignty having a new dimension, or whether they are private companies, able to make rules about others. (57)

As Justice Breyer wrote on 29 June 2022 (58) in his letter to the President of the United States when he resigned as a Justice of the Supreme Court of the United States: "It has been my great honor to participate as a judge in the effort to maintain our Constitution and the Rule of Law."

(56) See M.-A. Frison-Roche, "Conceiving power", 2021, https://mafr.fr/en/article/le-pouvoir-pour-mieux-servir/.

(57) With particular reference to the obligation they now have to be "vigilant", M.-A. Frison-Roche, "Thinking and using Vigilance through its Compliance Monumental Goals", 2023, https://mafr.fr/en/article/vigilance-buts-monumentaux-de-la-compliance-et-soc/.

(58) This letter is available on the Supreme Court website.

This letter, which defines the role of the judge, distinguishes between the two: the Constitution and the Rule of Law, and combines them. The Judge must cumulatively uphold the texts and the Rule of Law, ensuring that the two always converge. With this sentence, we might think that Justice Breyer was saying that the judge is failing in his duty when he ensures that the law is "upheld", but that in doing so he is ceasing to protect human beings by freeing the legislature from this task, because he is no longer upholding the Rule of Law, as the Supreme Court did in *Dobbs v. Jackson*, handed down 5 days before, (59) by "upholding" the American Constitution, which is one aspect of its role, but no longer protecting women, which is another aspect of its role, both of which are inseparable from the Rule of Law.

It is essential that this same anchorage be found in Compliance Law: all the power it develops must be anchored in the Monumental Goals, which limit this power and anchor it in the Rule of Law, since it is always a question of protecting human beings. This is what Judges must guard.

No algorithm can fulfil this essential function for the very definition of Compliance Law, a definition which itself constitutes this branch of Law as essential for a civilised conception of our Future.

Because these are political principles that presuppose the realisation of political projects, the Judges must be present to listen to one another, develop case law, and themselves participate directly in the construction of this future, in particular through the handling of Tort Law. (60)

The first role of the Lawyer is to take part in the debate, because in a State governed by the Rule of Law, until the judge puts a "stop" to it, everything can be debated: the facts, the qualifications and the meaning of the Law, as everyone is defensible, even and especially the culprits. (61)

---

(59) By asserting that women's right to voluntary termination of pregnancy is not a right protected by the US Constitution.

(60) Tort Law being an essential branch of the Law in the use that the Judge must make of it to respond to the demands of the litigants, in particular to resolve questions about the future, which supposes that the Judges elaborate an "*Ex Ante* Responsibility", but also conceive an *ex ante* office, and adjust the procedure accordingly, in particular by the admission of the parties involved, or even of *amici curiae*. See M.-A. Frison-Roche, "*Ex Ante* Responsibility", 2021, https://mafr.fr/en/article/la-responsabilite-ex-ante/; "The hypothesis of the category of systemic cases brought before the judge", 2021, https://mafr.fr/en/article/lhypothese-des-causes-systemiques/.

(61) M.-A. Frison-Roche, "Adjusting General Procedural Law to Compliance Law by the Nature of Things", *this book*.

Where there is a Judge, there must be a Lawyer, who both are the troublemakers of conformity, who both are the characters at the heart of Compliance Law.

B. The specific role of the Lawyer

The role of the Lawyer, although linked to that of the Judge, can also be deployed in a distinct manner, outside the intervention of the Judge. The Lawyer's role is both narrower and broader because the Lawyer must appear in all cases where the jurisdictional figure is established. As in regulatory matters, Compliance confers numerous jurisdictional powers to administrative authorities, but it is in a unique and spectacular way that it transforms companies into judges. (62) Lawyers have to deal with this, particularly internally (1), the balance being struck, as the Court of Justice of the European Union has pointed out, from the perspective of sanctions, which refers to a burden of proof that has yet to be refined (2).

1. The Lawyer, present in the Compliance mechanisms which transform the company into a Judge

Whether the company likes it or not, the firm must prevent, detect and punish behaviours that are against the Compliance Monumental Goals, such as corruption. To this end, the company draws up plans, gathers information, carries out compliance audits, (63) takes responsibility for projecting into the future so that third parties are protected from the risks to which they are exposed or, as they are part of the value chain, contribute to these actions, either passively (through the supervision to which they are subject) or actively.

In so doing, the company evaluates past, present and future situations, both internal and external to the company, making "judgements" in the intellectual sense of this term. What is missing, therefore, is what leads to the legal definition of a judgement, i.e. the articulation of this first intellectual phase of the judgement with a second phase, which is the adoption of

(62) M.-A. Frison-Roche, "The "Judge-Judged". Articulating Words and Things in the face of Conflicts of Interest", *this book*.

(63) On the concept of a compliance audit, see N. Guillaume, "Compliance Risk Mapping: First Insight into the Challenges, Limits and Best Practices", *in* M.-A. Frison-Roche (ed.), *Compliance Tools*, "Compliance & Regulation" Serie, Brussels, Journal of Regulation & Compliance (JoRC)/Bruylant, pp. 73-79.

a decision concerning the person involved in the situation being assessed, a decision against which that person has a grievance and which is taken in application of the Rule of Law, for instance the Due Process. (64)

Firstly, whether it likes it or not, the company gathers information about people, or even from them, in application of legal rules, those of Compliance Law, which will subsequently form the basis of decisions, for example dismissal or transmission of these facts to a judge, a public prosecutor or an administrative authority. Consequently, the person from whom information is requested in such a context must be offered the assistance of a lawyer.

Secondly, and this was rightly criticised, because the mechanism of the DPA or of the Judicial Public Interest Agreement only keeps the Judge away for the benefit of the legal entity and not the corporate officer. As soon as the facts are qualified by both Compliance Law and Criminal Law, the information collected by the company under Compliance which keeps the Judge away, on the other hand, brings the corporate officer before the Judge to whom is offered a probationary gift made up without the intervention of a lawyer.

2. The Lawyer, present to ensure that the rights of the defence are respected, and not just the adversarial principle, when the gathering of information potentially leads to the imposition of a penalty

Furthermore, investigations are often initiated not only by companies but also by public authorities. This may involve the Public Prosecutor, who, in discussions with a view to obtaining a deal, requests an internal investigation and asks to be given the results, or a regulatory and supervisory authority, which enters the company to carry out an internal investigation for which it asks for "full cooperation."

These investigations are sometimes presented as controls in themselves, carried out as part of the supervisory process made by the administrative bodies, for instance the Financial Markets Authorities.

(64) There are many works on the definition of what a judgment is in the legal sense and its structure. For instance, H. Motulsky, *Principes d'une réalisation méthodique du droit privé. La théorie des éléments générateurs des droits subjectifs*, preface by P. Roubier, Paris, Sirey, 1948, republished with a foreword by M.-A. Frison-Roche, "Bibliothèque Dalloz" Serie, Paris, Dalloz, 1992, the foreword of M.-A. Frison-Roche, which summarises the substance of the book, is available in English at the following address: https://mafr.fr/en/article/avant-propos-a-la-reimpression-de-louvrage-dhenri-/.

The legal system then seems to break down. Indeed, the Rule of Law requires that the person questioned should have the fundamental right not to cooperate, a right that a lawyer must enable him or her to assert in the face of a principle of efficiency in which the extraction of information seems to predominate, whereas the inspection is often no more than a preliminary to a notification of complaint. (65)

The two principles were remarkably articulated by the Court of Justice of the European Union in its judgment of 2 February 2021, *Consob*. Basing itself on the Charter of Fundamental Rights, to which it linked Article 6 of the ECHR, the Court ruled that in the context of an investigation by the financial regulator, in this case *Consob*, (66) its investigative powers were intended to bolster its power to supervise operators (which does indeed refer autonomously to the function of Supervision), the rights of the defence, in particular the right to remain silent, which are at the heart of the latter, applied. The Court points out that "the right to silence cannot reasonably be confined to statements of admission of wrongdoing or to remarks which directly incriminate the person questioned, but rather also covers information on questions of fact which may subsequently be used in support of the prosecution and may thus have a bearing on the conviction or the penalty imposed on that person." (67)

This key judgment has found the right balance between the obligation to cooperate, which is at the centre of the compliance system, and the right to remain silent, i.e. to not cooperate, which is at the centre of the rights of the defence.

The Court respects the Compliance Law principles that stems from the European Union Law on which the Supervisory Authorities rightly rely and which entities conducting internal investigations could undoubtedly rely on in the name of the principle of effectiveness that justifies investigations, including those conducted by a company that must "detect and prevent" behaviour that may be criminally reprehensible.

The Court did not ignore this principle. Indeed, it concluded that the right to silence must be effective when it is exercised by a person who may suffer the consequences of his or her collaboration, but it stated that the

(65) *Autorité des marchés financiers – AMF* (French Financial Markets Authority), *AMF Investigation Guide*, September 2021, that states: "The evidence obtained through this process may establish that a breach of obligations has occurred" (p. 6).

(66) CJEU, GC, 2 February 2021, *DB v. Consob*, case C-481/19.

(67) *Ibid.*, pt 40.

rights of the defence, including at its core the right to silence, do not justify the refusal of all collaboration in all matters and by all persons.

It is not acceptable for a legitimate refusal to degenerate into illegitimate obstruction. As the Court states: "That right precludes, *inter alia*, penalties being imposed on such persons for refusing to provide the competent authority under Directive 2003/6 or Regulation No 596/2014 with answers which might establish their liability for an offence that is punishable by administrative sanctions of a criminal nature, or their criminal liability."

This judgment has often been presented by companies as giving a right not to cooperate, which is excessive (and contrary to Compliance Law), and presented by the authorities as underlining the Court's adoption of the general obligation to cooperate laid down in European texts by diminishing the central place recognised to the rights of the defence, which is also excessive because the refusal to speak is a major right.

If we follow more closely this clear ruling, which sets out the procedure to be followed and is based on the case law of the ECHR and the texts of the European Union, two principles must be articulated: the search for information, which is fully deployed in the surveillance function when it is directed at people against whom it will not be used, and the rights of defence, which will diminish this effectiveness in the opposite case.

This must apply not only to the right to silence, which is at the heart of the rights of defence, but also to all the other rights of defence, and it is the Lawyer who is the guardian of these rights. This applies not only to investigations carried out within companies by the public supervisory authorities, but also to investigations carried out by the companies themselves.

The courts, which are equally committed to the rights of the defence and the adversarial principle, will undoubtedly sanction a failure to respect other rights of the defence of which a person has been deprived, provided that he or she has not acted in total obstruction.

But companies and their lawyers must be careful not to believe that they are entitled to refuse everything and to shut themselves off, thinking that the rights of the defence entitle them to do so.

The limit is fully justified because a person who completely evades the supervisory power of a public authority blocks the very principle of Compliance, i.e. the penetration of the Authority that is the bearer of a systemic concern into the company that must implement the Monumental Goal, for example the integrity of the markets and their protection against systemic risks. And it is inconceivable that a hypothetical prospect of conviction could be used as an abstract reason to close the door on an Authority, when Compliance is associated with the principle of transparency, even if it is not a regulated sector. It is therefore necessary for the person concerned to give the *first indications* that this surveillance investigation could result in a conviction, for the rights of defence to be triggered and for collaboration to cease.

It may be thought that proof of these initial indications will have to be provided by the person who will subsequently have to justify his failure to cooperate, but this will only be a burden of probability. (68)

This transition from the general principle of collaboration to the general principle of the rights of the defence will have to be proven by the individual, on the basis of facts and presumptions. But the evidentiary game, essential in Compliance Law because Judge and Lawyer are at the centre, is another story... (69)

In conclusion, in a Compliance Law which must not be mechanical but must, on the contrary, be understood and accepted for the specific purposes it serves, everyone wants to be the "advocate" of the rules in question, with the Regulator as the primary advocate. It would be paradoxical if the lawyer were to be excluded from this branch of Law, even though he is the surest indicator of the luxury that we will enjoy and in which we want to remain anchored in the future: the Rule of Law.

(68) M.-A. Frison-Roche, "The Judge, the Compliance Obligation and the Company. The Compliance Evidence System", *this book*.

(69) *Ibid*.

CHAPTER I
THE COMPANY ESTABLISHED PROSECUTOR AND JUDGE OF ITSELF BY COMPLIANCE LAW

The "Judge-Judged." Articulating Words and Things in the face of Conflicts of Interest*

Marie-Anne Frison-Roche

Agrégée des Facultés de droit

Professor of Regulatory Law and Compliance Law

Director of the *Journal of Regulation & Compliance (JoRC)*

Director of the *European School of Regulation and Compliance Law*

1. Underneath the mass of regulations and technical difficulties, keeping the foundations intact so that Democratic Systems can endure. In order to understand the situation of companies which, under Compliance Law, have to prosecute and judge the natural and legal persons responsible for carrying out the requirements of regulations, we need to readjust what we observe and how this is described, either in the texts or in the practice of the companies themselves. Companies take action to prosecute and judge persons by a variety of means, such as internal investigations, through various structures, in particular some sort of internal tribunals that examine the actions of people working in the company but also of people from outside the company, in the light of standards that are external to the company but also decreed by it.

* This article is based on a bilingual working paper, along with additional developments, numerous technical references and hypertext links. It is accessible at the following address: https://mafr.fr/en/article/le-jugeant-juge-le-pourchassant-pourchasse-le-scru/.

The range of words used can be correct, exact, right, when the words correspond to what is done, (1) for example when the person who "judges" is called a "judge." The relation ceases to be accurate if the words *go beyond* this, for example when the person who is called a "judge" hardly judges at all and the jurisdictional function, which would be required, is therefore not actually carried out, this emptiness going unnoticed thanks to this judicial vocabulary used in excess. The relation also ceases to be accurate if the words are used *in excess*, for example when the person who prosecutes is not designated to everyone as such and thus evades the regime attached to this power, because this power is hidden.

For words and things to be right, for this relation between them to be fair, we must bear in mind three elements that must not be deviated from. Unless we change our legal system, based on the Rule of Law. (2)

2. Three pillars that Compliance Law could compromise or, on the contrary, promote: Law, Judge and Procedure. However, the accumulation of texts, hard and soft, and the speed with which various cases arise and need to be resolved, mean that the three pillars which are Law, Judge and Procedure, and their simplicity, are disappearing, with legal skill concentrating above all on one or two paragraphs of the latest guidelines issued or on the most recent dispute brought before a court and reported by the media. These principles have almost been forgotten, yet it is on the basis of these principles that concrete and practical solutions must be found, firstly because this makes it possible to give coherence to all this jumble (3) and to anticipate future texts and solutions, and secondly out of attachment to the Rule of Law. (4) Losing sight of these three pillars is one of the greatest dangers facing our democratic systems, and

(1) The relationship that human beings have with the world through the mechanism of language is the subject of an immense body of philosophical, sociological and literary work, if only because *logos* is itself often equated with reason itself. For a more restricted perspective, the vocabulary used here refers to Michel Foucault's *The Order of Things: An Archaeology of the Human Sciences* (translation of *Les mots et les choses. Une archéologie des sciences humaines*), Vintage, 2012. Even more important is Foucault's inaugural lecture at the *Collège de France* in 1970, *L'ordre du discours*, "blanche" Serie, Paris, Gallimard, 1971, in which he argues that science seeks to correlate words and things because it seeks truth, whereas Law, allied with politics to govern the city, does not. The historical dimension of all these works is sometimes obscured by an excessively sociological reading.

(2) For developments on the relation between Compliance Law, Jurisdictionalisation and Rule of Law, M.-A. Frison-Roche, "Reinforce the Judge and the Lawyer to impose Compliance Law as a characteristic of the Rule of Law", *this book*.

(3) Notably with regard to the central object in practice that are the probatory obligations: M.-A. Frison-Roche, "The Judge, the Compliance Obligation and the Company. The Compliance Evidence System", *this book*.

(4) From this perspective, M.-A. Frison-Roche, "Reinforce the Judge and the Lawyer to impose Compliance Law as a characteristic of the Rule of Law", *this book*.

Compliance Law must counter this, even though compliance techniques are often accused of contributing to their downfall, particularly through the role played by artificial intelligence and the role played by private companies, which prosecute, judge, and punish. On the contrary, this is not the case as long as these three pillars are always kept in mind when it comes to making compliance mechanisms work when companies are prosecuting and judging.

PREREQUISITE: BEARING IN MIND THREE PRINCIPLES FOR IMPLEMENTING THE APPROPRIATE LEGAL REGIME FOR THE *JUDGE-JUDGED*

3. Law; Judge and Procedure; the legal personality and the company. The first element relates to what Law is and the need to preserve the very principle of Law itself in the machinery of compliance. This has direct practical effects in that compliance techniques tend to take the form of technologies in which Law seems to have so little place. (5) The next principle takes the form of the couple formed by the office of the Judge office and the Procedure. Even if the practice of prosecution and trial by the company itself can explain, or even justify, many adjustments in the processes, there can be no denaturation by too great a distortion between the activity carried out by the company and the words by which this activity is designated, because it is still the Rule of Law that is at stake, unless we change the legal and political system. The final principle is that of legal personality as it relates to the company. This is more of a reverse situation, since Economic Law has replaced the legal person with the Corporate and Compliance direct duties put on the enterprise itself, but it is still the legal person that makes it possible to distinguish between the "judge" (the enterprise as a legal person) and the "judged" (the enterprise as an organisation and a group of natural persons). Can such a legal artifice be tolerated? How technically can it be tolerated?

4. When examining Compliance techniques making Companies judge and prosecute themselves, the first thing to bear in mind is the definition of Law, so that these Compliance techniques do not evacuate Law in its relationship with reality. The first thing to bear in mind is

(5) On the relationship between Compliance Law and what is commonly referred to as artificial intelligence, M.-A. Frison-Roche, *ibid.*

the definition of Law itself. In a State governed by the Rule of Law, it is the Law that defines words and establishes the link between words and activities; it is not individuals who, at their discretion, have the power to say, for example, "I am a judge" (if they are not) and impose this definitively *erga omnes*, any more than they would have the power to say "I am not a judge" (if they are). Even if the legal system is a system of language, (6) creating a new reality within reality, this does not mean that the reality on which the legal system is based does not exist or no longer exists and that it can dispose of it entirely. Only totalitarian systems can erase the faces in photographs of people they no longer like. In States governed by the Rule of Law, neither the State nor its subjects can erase everything from the reality to which they add the words they print on it. So even if they can, under certain conditions, institute "prosecuting authority" and "judge" for people who have not hitherto had the designation, or even institute themselves as courts, they cannot always do so, and cannot escape the legal regime that the activity of prosecuting and judging triggers, in particular through the protection that the power to judge others justifies. (7) Indeed, companies must not be legally able to deny that they have the power to do so, which means that they must be accountable for it, (8) and that they must submit to certain forms and limits. Compliance Law, insofar as it relies on the power of companies, as a fact and as a tool, (9) also attaches to it the regime that is naturally linked to the exercise of power in a State governed by the Rule of Law. (10)

To achieve this, Law, through case law, gives back to things the words that respect them, in particular by calling "judge" the person who judges, "prosecuting authority" the person who prosecutes. This tautology between reality and Law is sometimes the most difficult to identify, to operate and to impose, yet it allows the legal order to be bearable and sustainable. (11) Of course, we still have to determine what "judging" means... But this is

---

(6) J.L. Austin, *How to do Things with Words*, Oxford, OUP, 1962; B.N. Cardozo, "Law and literature", *Yale Review*, 1925, Vol. 14, pp. 699-718. In a legal perspective, see also A. Supiot, *Homo Juridicus. Essai sur la fonction anthropologique du Droit*, "La couleur des idées" Serie, Paris, Seuil, 2005.

(7) See *infra*, No. 5.

(8) In this sense and more generally, A. Supiot and M. Delmas-Marty (eds), *Prendre la responsabilité au sérieux*, Paris, PUF, 2015.

(9) M.-A. Frison-Roche, "Conceiving Power", 2021, https://mafr.fr/en/article/le-pouvoir-pour-mieux-servir/.

(10) See *infra* and M.-A. Frison-Roche, "Adjusting General Procedural Law to Compliance Law by the Nature of Things", *this book*.

(11) "The mother must be called mother and the son must be called son." On this Confucian conception of order, see in *The Analects of Confucius*: "To each his own role: let the sovereign be the sovereign, the subject a subject, the father a father, and the son a son.".

already an entry point into the following pairs of principles because it is when an "office of the judge" is identified that a judge is discovered, and then, in a second step, procedural principles are attached, by an effect of nature,(12) to his way of doing things.

5. In examining Compliance techniques that make companies the Judge and Prosecutor of themselves, the second thing to bear in mind is the principles governing the role of Judge and the Procedure, so these Compliance techniques do not take Justice out of the equation. From there, we come to what makes a couple: Judge and Procedure. It is only by virtue of an optical effect that the procedure precedes the judge's entry on the scene, even in adversarial civil litigation, which remains governed by the principle of dispositive justice, even if the procedure does not reach the judgment, through mediation for example, and even if the judgment is an act that is intellectually distinct from the procedure that preceded it. The procedure, whether defined as an objective set of principles and mechanisms or as a set of subjective procedural rights, is there because the Judgment is in perspective. This inseparability between procedure and judgement seems self-evident: it is only because there is a prospect of a judgement that a procedure must be organised. But apart from the fact that many compliance tools are designed to avoid the intervention of a judge,(13) the confusion between words and the mechanisation of compliance have led to the introduction of processes that are often called "procedures", which have nothing to do with what defines procedure in Law. While procedure is indeed a "way of doing things," not every process can be equated with the legal concept of Procedure.

Firstly, however, *procedure and the role of the judge are one and the same*. Even when the procedure is interrupted by mediation, for example, it takes place under the control of the judge, who is always the master of the procedure(14). Secondly, the principle of *Impartiality* remains at the heart of all procedural tools, because if the one who benefits of this

(12) M.-A. Frison-Roche, "Adjusting General Procedural Law to Compliance Law by the Nature of Things", *this book*.

(13) On compliance tools as a means of avoiding the judge, in particular the *convention judiciaire d'intérêt public* (Judicial Public Interest Agreement), see M.-A. Frison-Roche, "Reinforce the Judge and the Lawyer to impose Compliance Law as a characteristic of the Rule of Law", *this book*.

(14) When the procedure is inquisitorial, which is characteristic of criminal procedure and administrative litigation, it is the presence of the judge that colors the very definition of this procedure. In civil proceedings, while "*les parties conduisent l'instance*" ("the parties conduct the proceedings") (Article 6 of the *Code de procedure civile* – CPC [French Civil Procedure Code]), "*le juge veille à son bon déroulement*" ("the judge ensures that they run smoothly") (Article 3 CPC).

approach, i.e. the judge,(15) is not impartial, then the procedure loses its very relevance. Conflicts of interest are at the heart of the procedure. This exclusion of conflicts of interest, which is common to both Compliance Law and General Procedural Law because the company is considered from the point of view of the judge's office, gives rise to rules that apply regardless of who is judging, including the company. In the same way Compliance Law excludes conflicts of interest, the company does it because it is also the subject of Compliance Law, just as General Procedural Law excludes conflicts of interest, since the company is the judge and prosecutor for itself and others, regardless of who is being judged, including itself: when it is the same person who is "judge and judged", the bull is in the China shop.

6. In examining Compliance techniques that make the Company the Judge and Prosecutor of itself, the third point to bear in mind is the principle of legal personality, even if it is necessary to replace legal personality by the factual notion of enterprise. However, the situation seems to require fewer adjustments as far as legal personality is concerned. After often wondering whether legal personality was real or fictitious, whether its nature was contractual or institutional, Economic Law has made its relationship with the company particularly translucent, for example in Competition Law, Tax Law or Labour Law. Compliance Law most often sees it as an artifice, aimed more directly at "beneficial owners,"(16) for example, while the new compliance tool of the duty of vigilance leaves this mechanism behind to make a new place for the powerful enterprise in value chains. (17) As a result, the mask of legal personality is most often discarded, and the pragmatism of not being hindered by the artificiality of so many legal persons, so many screens, or even "empty shells," against which Compliance Law fights, is generally welcomed. But here the advantage is reversed, because if there is no longer a separate legal entity to prosecute and judge subsidiaries or corporate officers within

(15) On the idea that the beneficiary of the procedure comes before the judge, see e.g. J.-F. Burgelin, J.-M. Coulon and M.-A. Frison-Roche, "L'office de la procédure", *in Mélanges offerts à Pierre Drai. Le juge entre deux millénaires*, Paris, Dalloz, 2000, pp. 253-267.

(16) M.-A. Frison-Roche, "Compliance & Personality", 2019, https://mafr.fr/en/article/compliance-et-personnalite/.

(17) B. Deffains, "Compliance and International Competitiveness", *in* M.-A. Frison-Roche (ed.), *Compliance Monumental Goals*, "Compliance & Regulation" Serie, Brussels, Journal of Regulation & Compliance (JoRC)/ Bruylant, 2023, pp. 343-354. On the European Regulation, see C. Patz, "The EU's Draft Corporate Sustainability Due Diligence Directive: A First Assessment", *Business and Human Rights Journal*, 2022, Vol. 7, No. 2, pp. 291-297; A. Lafarre, "The proposed Corporate Sustainability Due Diligence Directive: corporate liability design for social harms", *European Business Law Review*, 2023, Vol. 34, No. 2, pp. 213-238.

the same economic and business unit, how can we stand back? When it is the same person who questions, as the representative of the legal entity, and who is questioned, as a corporate officer, one wonders where the hidden camera is, and one says to oneself that the legal entity must be real.

The procedural question of Impartiality, which is defined by the distance between who judges and what, or whom, he or she judges, (18) then comes back as a boomerang. Because if Compliance Law has taken leave of the legal personality, it suddenly needs it when the company becomes the prosecutor and judge of itself. This is a difficulty that needs to be borne in mind in order to resolve or, at the very least, to manage it, because we do not know how to overcome the structural conflict of interest that appears before everyone's eyes, it being understood that, here again, it is in terms of Impartiality that the resolution must be made and that we would have to find a way of being both judge and party if we decided not to believe in the reality of the legal person.

7. Convergence of the three pillars towards Impartiality, keystone of the legal admissibility of the Enterprise, Prosecutor and Judge of itself. It would seem that all of the requirements and difficulties surrounding these three pillars can be summed up in one word: Impartiality. It is this word that both French and European case law have brandished to demand that organisations that claimed not to be courts, because they did not have the title, should nevertheless, because they exercised the office, show everyone their objective Impartiality. This assertion was born of Regulation Law. Insofar as it is an extension of Regulation Law, (19) Compliance Law can only take it up in the same terms, applying it no longer to administrative Authorities but to the company itself. Dissociation is therefore essential.

8. Compel and unify Compliance techniques under the tutelary shadow of these three pillars. Unfolding the practical consequences of these three pillars, the first two of which are defended by Compliance Law (Law and Procedure) while the third (legal personality) is not, leads to unmasking companies that would judge and prosecute while pretending not to do so because they are not called either "judge" or "prosecutor,"

(18) ECHR, GC, 15 December 2005, *Kyprianou v. Cyprus*, No. 73797/01, para. 118 *et seq.*; ECHR, GC, 15 October 2009, *Micallef v. Malta*, No. 17056/06, para. 93 *et seq.*

(19) On this very principle, M.-A. Frison-Roche, "From Regulation Law to Compliance Law", 2017, https://mafr.fr/en/article/du-droit-de-la-regulation-au-droit-de-la-complianc/; for an illustration of this, S. Scemla and D. Paillot, "The difficulty for Compliance Enforcement Authorities to Comprehend the Rights of the Defence in Compliance Matters", *this book*.

in order to force them to act within the constraints that Law imposes on judges and prosecuting authorities (I). Companies cannot escape this, and perhaps they do not want to, because the management of conflicts of interest is common to both General Procedural Law and Compliance Law, since it always expresses the principle of Impartiality. To achieve this, therefore, Law itself must enable companies to set up structures and encourage behaviour so that their impartiality can be seen to be effective, efficient and efficacious, even if the mask of the legal personality is no more active on the firm's reality (II).

I. UNMASKING COMPANIES THAT CLAIM NOT TO BE "PROSECUTORS" OR "JUDGES" AND SUBJECTING THEM TO PROCEDURAL CONSTRAINTS

9. Reveal the power of companies to prosecute and punish themselves and others. Being a "Judge" or "Prosecutor" is therefore a binding qualification. It is both negative and positive: negative in that it prevents an entity that judges or prosecutes from masking this under other words, in order to not be constrained by the regime associated with the activity. This is all the more understandable in the case of a firm because it is Compliance Law that most often requires it to prosecute and then judge, whereas this entity has not chosen to do so and is thus accumulating activities (prosecuting, judging) that it has not itself chosen (A). But the fact that a company has not chosen to prosecute and judge does not mean that it is exempt from the qualifications that General Procedural Law will trigger, in that it belongs to the same legal order as Compliance Law.(20) These required organic qualifications appreciate the company as the "prosecutor" and then the "judge" that it successively is (B), in order in particular to protect the persons who are the subject of the prosecution and judgment activities carried out by the company, the fact that this is done in accordance with the legal Obligations of Compliance being irrelevant.

(20) M.-A. Frison-Roche, "Adjusting General Procedural Law to Compliance Law by the Nature of Things", *this book*.

A. The confusion of roles "imposed" by *Ex-Ante* Compliance Law

10. Confusion arising from the dual source of prosecutions and sanctions imposed by companies. A great deal of uncertainty stems from the fact that compliance processes have been devised and implemented outside Law,(21) for instance the internal investigations, and that, even if the legal nature of compliance is accepted, the jurisdictional nature of many of these mechanisms remains unclear. This is due to Compliance Law itself, which aims to provide Information and requires cooperation, whereas, for example, General Procedural Law sets out the rights of the defence, which are based on secrecy, on the right to not cooperate, etc. In addition, the company may take legal action against a third party. Furthermore, the company can claim that it is merely a subject under constraint, since it is indeed by order of the Law that it performs a series of tasks that Compliance Law itself does not qualify as prosecution and judgment activities (1). The argument is undoubtedly less strong when these activities are carried out of the company's own free will (2).

1. The legal obligation to carry out investigations, risk assessments, reporting and sanctions

11. Powers exercised by order of the Law. The company may argue that it is merely obeying the prescriptions of the legislator itself. Indeed, it is in fact laws that oblige companies to fulfil their general Compliance Obligation,(22) i.e. to detect and prevent systemic risks and to use their strengths and position to achieve the "Monumental Goals" that give substance and meaning to the various compliance tools, to ask people for Information and to hold them to account.

It is also to prevent behaviours that damage economic and social systems that the company will use its sanction's power, through its disciplinary power or by terminating the contracts to which it has committed itself, for example, internally, through employment contracts or, externally, through distribution contracts or supply or subcontracting contracts, with regard to all the people for whom the firm is accountable under

(21) See *supra*, No. 4.

(22) M.-A. Frison-Roche, "The Compliance Obligation, between will and consent: obligation on obligation work", *in* M-A. Frison-Roche (ed.), *Compliance Obligation*, to be published.

Compliance Law.(23) The company that is accountable under Compliance Law for its Compliance Obligations(24) and for what is expected of it by virtue of its power to achieve the Monumental Goals that this new branch of Law aims to achieve,(25) in turn obliges it to hold to account those for whom it is itself accountable, both internally and externally.

12. Obey and be obeyed. So it is because of treaties, laws, and regulations, most often of a public order nature, sometimes overriding mandatory provisions, that companies are obliged not only to prosecute and even punish themselves, but also to prosecute and punish others. The firm is obliged to do this by Compliance Law, which itself takes the form of legislations that attaches criminal penalties to failure to comply with it; laws as the Bribery Act in the U.K. or the so-called "Sapin 2" law in France being just examples of this.

2. The proportion of externally imposed obligations and the proportion of the "responsible" economic operator's own expression of will

13. The will of the company, a source of Compliance Obligations and correlated powers. However, these activities by which the company holds its internal and external employees to account may not only be the result of exogenous regulations, but also of the will of the group of people that makes up the company. The growing importance of the *raison d'être* has shown that companies not only have to "take into account" social and environmental interests, but can also choose to take charge of such interests, by extending them, for example, to the climatic interest,(26) because that is what they want, the adoption of the statutory form of "*entreprise à mission*" ("company with a mission") crystallising this will in the marble of Corporate Law, which then adjoins Compliance Law.(27)

14. The impact of the points of contact between the *raison d'être* and Compliance Law. The company then claims to be "responsible," i.e. to voluntarily assume obligations in order to satisfy collective

(23) M.-A. Frison-Roche, "Compliance contract, Compliance clauses", 2022, https://mafr.fr/en/article/contrat-de-compliance-clauses-de-compliance/.

(24) M.-A. Frison-Roche, "The Compliance Obligation, between Will and Consent: Obligation on Obligation works", *op. cit.*

(25) M.-A. Frison-Roche, "*Ex ante* Responsibility", 2021, https://mafr.fr/en/article/la-responsabilite-ex-ante/.

(26) M.-A. Frison-Roche, "Compliance Law and Climate. To prevent Climate Risk and build Climate Balance", 2022, https://mafr.fr/en/article/prevention-et-gestion-du-risque-climatique-par-le-/.

(27) A.-V. Le Fur, "Interest and '*raison d'être*' of the Company: How Does It Fit Together with the Compliance Monumental Goals?", *in* M.-A. Frison-Roche (ed.), *Compliance Monumental Goals*, *op. cit.*, pp. 69-82.

interests. (28) The French so-called "Pacte" law has many points of contact with Compliance Law, since it aims to develop *ex ante* responsibility with regard to issues that are most often global. This *ex ante* dimension brings together Corporate Law, Compliance Law and Labour Law, with the company at the heart of a concept that rearranges it both in the definition of what a company is, through a rewriting of articles 1832 and following of the *Code civil* (French Civil Code), and what a company is in a competitive market economy.

In such an *ex ante* conception, General Procedural Law does not immediately have an entry point, as it comes into play more in the context of disputes brought before a court when a company is accused of not having properly fulfilled its Compliance Obligations, which is an entirely different matter. (29)

It is therefore *ex post* that the judge will intervene to apply procedural words to the way in which the company, in the ordinary course of business and in the performance of its legal Compliance Obligations, behaves as "prosecutor" and "judge," thus exposing the difficulty that this combination of qualities creates.

B. The *Ex Post* power of qualification by the Courts

15. The practical art of qualification. The judge has the prerogative of putting words on things, i.e. the qualification power (1), making Compliance Law an extension of Regulatory Law (2).

1. The Judge's prerogative in qualification power, control of the relationship between Words and Things

16. Qualification, the art of the Judge. Qualification is the intellectual operation which characterises the art of Law, since it consists for the judge, in a definitive way, whatever the parties or even the legislator may have said, in readjusting words and reality, by bringing situations into the legal category which corresponds to them. Qualification is not only the judge's prerogative, in the sense that no one can deprive him or her of

(28) The so-called "Notat-Senard" report, *L'entreprise, objet d'intérêt collectif*, which served as the basis for the French law *pour la croissance et la transformation des entreprises* (for the growth and transformation of businesses), known as the "Pacte" law, of 22 May 2019.

(29) On this subject, see the remarkable article by Nicolas Cayrol, "Procedural Principles in Compliance Law", *this book*.

this power, except for facts over which the parties exercise such a power of disposition that they can remove them from the evidentiary system by which the facts come to the judge's knowledge. (30)

17. Call "Judge" the person who "judges"; call "Prosecutor" the person who "prosecutes." When a company conducts an internal investigation by requesting information, it is acting like a prosecutor; similarly, when it conducts an investigation at the premises of one of its economic partners, with a view to obtaining evidence because it has detected past, present or future breaches of Compliance Obligations, it is acting like a prosecutor.

18. The irrelevance of sources in the legal exercise of qualifications. Whether this conduct has its source in legislations that oblige the company to detect and prevent behaviour or in soft Law, such as a charter issued by the firm itself, or in contractual stipulations, does not interfere with the only thing that will count in the qualification exercise for which the judge is responsible: the Information that the company collects and the possible use that will be made of it for the people concerned by this information in subsequent decisions that may be prejudicial to them, whether this involves breach of contract, transmission to public authorities, disciplinary action, etc. Because, by acting in this way, even when ordered to do so by Compliance Law, the company is acting like a prosecutor, providing the public authorities with this information, and may even subsequently draw its own conclusions from the information thus obtained, i.e. pass judgement.

Even before examining the fact that the company is thus, by order of Compliance Law, *judge-judged*, it is already *prosecutor-judge*, which is a procedural situation already dealt with by the courts, since its qualification is a pillar of Regulatory Law. It will therefore suffice to borrow from it the solutions that have been developed there.

2. Integration into the jurisdictional model, placing Compliance Law in the continuity of Regulatory Law

19. The effectiveness of the link between Regulatory Law and Compliance Law. This is, in a way, the easiest part of the issue, not in itself but because case law has already been confronted with it and has

(30) On the evidentiary system, itself closely linked to the effectiveness, efficacy and efficiency of compliance obligations, see M.-A. Frison-Roche, "The Judge, the Compliance Obligation and the Company. The Compliance Evidence System", *this book*.

already provided the answer. Indeed, Compliance Law is an extension of Regulatory Law (31) but goes beyond it since it no longer requires the pre-condition of a sector, (32) of which the duty of vigilance, which requires the collection of a great deal of information, is an example.

20. The transposition of General Procedural Regulatory Law. Since Compliance Law is therefore the extension of Regulation Law beyond the borders of sectors, the solutions of the former can, and indeed must, be transposed into the latter. However, the State, being in a conflict of interest since the independent administrative authorities, belonging to it, render administrative decisions, which are certainly subject to appeal before a judge, would entrust the same regulatory body with the task of gathering information, assessing the appropriate use to be made of it, for example entering into sanction proceedings, and then assessing the facts thus gathered in order to sanction, the system being justified in particular by its efficacy.

21. The relevance of converging case law on Regulatory and Supervisory Authorities. In case law about procedural rules which must be followed by independent Regulatory and Supervisory Authorities, many courts consider that the gathering of Information made by the Authority must be qualified as a prosecutorial and investigative activity, whereas the sanction must be qualified as the pronouncement of a penalty. Consequently, the same person cannot objectively be in charge of these various functions, because the person who has gathered the Information and formulated an opinion on whether or not it justifies the prospect of a penalty, a position which constitutes an objective "prejudice," cannot then participate in the objective activity of passing judgment. This case law position is common to national courts and European courts, such as the European Court of Human Rights (*Dubus* ruling of 11 June 2009 (33)), but also to Constitutional Courts, for instance the *Conseil constitutionnel* (French Constitutional Council) (decision *Numéricâble et autres* of 5 July 2013 (34)) and the Court of Justice of the European Union (the *Consob* judgement of 5 February 2022 (35)).

(31) M.-A. Frison-Roche, "From Regulation Law to Compliance Law", 2017, *op. cit.*

(32) M.-A. Frison-Roche, "Compliance Law Loses the Ties of Regulation Law but retains its Principles: Consequences for Companies", 2018, https://mafr.fr/en/article/le-droit-de-la-compliance-lache-les-amarres-du-dro/.

(33) ECHR, 11 June 2009, *Dubus S.A. v. France*, No. 5242/04.

(34) *Conseil constitutionnel* (French Constitutional Council), 5 July 2013, *Société Numéricâble SAS et autre*, No. 2013-331 QPC.

(35) CJEU, Grand Chamber, 2 February 2021, *DB v. Commissione nazionale per le società e la Borsa (Consob)*, case C-481/19.

22. General Procedural Regulatory and Compliance Law: articulating the accumulation of powers thanks to the distinction of functions. The analysis of General Procedural Regulatory Law is very broad and the central idea always emerges that it is Impartiality that must be preserved. It is under this same principle that the reasoning, from Regulatory Law, must move on to Compliance Law *via* the power of qualification held by the Judge. But this does not mean taking away the company's own power to implement its own legal Compliance Obligations! After all, the legal system cannot require companies to prosecute and judge, while at the same time depriving them of the means to do so. On the contrary, when we look at the evolution of Law, efficacy justifies increasingly powerful prosecuting and judging bodies, even inside the firms or in the management's hand of the firms. Thus, whatever the subject, procedures, particularly international ones, are becoming increasingly inquisitorial.

23. The even greater need to combine powers in Compliance Law than in Regulation Law. Examples include the digital space, the environment and climate change. What is more, the adoption and establishment of the European Public Prosecutor's Office will put in place European public prosecutors who will carry out both prosecution activities and the function of investigating judge, particularly in the latter's jurisdictional activity. (36) Therefore, the issue is not to prevent the cumulation of functions, quite the contrary, since cumulation is a guarantee of the system's effectiveness (which the regulatory authorities have always asserted to justify their own operation), but the issue is in the organisation of the procedure.

For example, the ambition to "regulate the Internet," a political ambition that is essential if we pretend that the digital space in which we all live needs to not be left solely to hatred and disinformation, (37) implies that, willingly or by force, the crucial digital firms must control content, prosecute obvious inaccurate or hateful contents and punish their authors, doing so either by applying their own standards or by applying legislation

(36) On the European Public Prosecutor's Office, see M. Zwiers, *The European Public Prosecutor's Office: Analysis of a Multilevel Criminal Justice System*, Intersentia, 2011. and H. Christodoulou, *Le parquet européen : prémices d'une autorité judiciaire de l'Union européenne*, preface by B. de Lamy, "Nouvelle Bibliothèque de Thèses" Serie, Paris, Dalloz, 2021. See also C. Gómez-Jara Díez and E. Herlin-Karnell, "Prosecuting EU Financial Crimes: the European Public Prosecutor's Office in Comparison to the US Federal Regime", *German Law Journal*, October 2018, pp. 1191-1220.

(37) M.-A. Frison-Roche, "Having a good behavior in the digital space", 2019, https://mafr.fr/en/article/se-tenir-bien-dans-lespace-numerique-2/.

with extraterritorial scope, such as the European Union's *Digital Services Act – DSA* commands it. (38) They are therefore the prosecutors and judges of others. In the same way, as we have seen with regard to the duty of vigilance, notably through the European *Corporate Sustainability Due Diligence Directive – CS3D*, the monumental goals of protecting human rights and the environment throughout value chains justify the accumulation of powers for the company, a condition for it to be able to comply with the burden imposed on it by the laws.

24. The remaining issue: combining powers and Impartiality. As soon as we consider that the activity thus imposed, or thus willingly assumed, or even voluntarily chosen by the firm, is indeed an activity calling for the qualification of "prosecution" and "judgment," that the company is indeed, whatever words it may have chosen, a "judge" and a "prosecutor," because the procedure is indissociable from the act of prosecuting and the act of judging, the major challenge is therefore not to hinder it in this continuous activity but rather to organise its Impartiality.

But how can one be impartial not only towards others but also towards oneself? Regulatory Law is not enough to provide the solutions, because Law had entrusted the Regulatory and Supervisory Authorities with the task of prosecuting and judging others, but not with the task of prosecuting and judging themselves. Compliance Law is therefore all alone in enabling companies, which it has obliged to do so, to prosecute and judge themselves impartially.

II. ENABLING COMPANIES TO PROSECUTE AND JUDGE THEMSELVES IMPARTIALLY

25. An impossible obligation? On the face of it, you cannot judge yourself impartially, as common sense would have it, and as the legal system takes up in a more sophisticated way through Constitutional Law, according to which you cannot be "judge and jury." How can we distance ourselves? The temptation then is to resort to Ethics, a solution that solves everything and is often proposed, the superposition of the cold legal techniques of compliance and the warmth of ethical sense making it possible

(38) P. Church and C.N. Pehlivan, "The Digital Services Act (DSA): A New Era for Online Harms and Intermediary Liability", *Global Privacy Law Review*, 2023, Vol. 4, No. 1, pp. 53-59.

to resolve the whole difficulty. But because Law is a practical art that takes human beings as they are, it would be better to abandon this quite easy postulate of ethical heroism, which would lead a person to condemn himself for the good of others.

26. Do not get lost in the perspectives. If we are willing to forego this sublime solution of ethical heroism as a matter of method, we should look for technical solutions that place a legal distance between the person to whom the information is given and the person who could use this information to his or her detriment, because, for this person who therefore risks something, the former is then both a prosecutor and a judge, who destroys Impartiality to his detriment. On a more technical level, the company must put in place all the techniques necessary to create a distance between itself and the person who could suffer the negative consequences of its information-seeking activity, both internally and externally, without resorting to the technique of legal personality (A). To achieve this, it is necessary to organise within the companies themselves the dual handling of opposing interests (B).

Prerequisite: renouncing the only sublime ethical heroism

27. The ever-renewed hope of a common and global ethic in everyone. We can always hope that the sense of duty will be such that the natural persons who, within the company bodies, express the will of the legal entity or who, as managers, direct the company, will impose the sacrifice of the particular and immediate interest of the company, in favour of the reign of Law and the General Interest and long-term reputation of the company.

28. The less sublime legal solution. This moral heroism and sense of responsibility, as expressed by Hans Jonas (39), can work but they are too specific, uncertain and difficult to control to be the sole basis of an *ex ante* compliance system. They should be replaced by mechanisms that distance the company that prosecutes and punishes from the person who may suffer the harmful consequences of this dual activity required by Compliance Law.

---

(39) For this germinal conception, see H. Jonas, *The Imperative of Responsibility. In Search of an Ethics for the Technological Age*, University of Chicago Press, 1985; for the first legal analysis in the same way, see B. Edelman, "La responsabilité pour les générations futures", *in* M. Vacquin (ed.), *La responsabilité*, "Morales" Serie, Paris, Autrement, 1997, pp. 132-144.

A. Putting in place all the legal distances between the judging Company and the Company being judged, without resorting to legal personality

29. From the machine to the structure, to the human beings, without going through the notion of a legal entity. At the end of its own internal investigations, the company will gather Information on the basis of which it will later be judged by the public authorities, which it is obliged to alert and to which it must give access to all this information in informal procedures which are not yet sanctions. In the same way, it will gather information on facts which, at a later date, may be classified as administrative failings or even criminal offences.

The situation seems aporetic. Indeed, from the point of view of General Procedural Law, it seems inconceivable to require a company to judge itself, as one cannot be both judge and party. And yet, from the point of view of Compliance Law, it is effective, and therefore required, that it should be the companies themselves, since they are in the best position to do so, that detect behaviours that contravenes the rules that give concrete form to the Monumental Goals, for example the fight against money laundering or pollution.

But the solution is once again to return to Regulatory Law (1) by putting in place functional solutions without resorting to the concept of legal person, not out of hostility in principle to the latter but because Compliance Law itself seeks to remove the legal personality mask and weakens itself by resorting to it here (2).

1. Importing the solution found in General Procedural Regulatory Law into General Procedural Compliance Law

30. Taking advantage of the development of Regulatory and Supervisory Authorities. The General Procedural Regulatory Law has not drawn as a consequence of the above-mentioned case law(40) the disappearance of the power of repression of administrative regulatory authorities: texts were immediately adopted, in a so-called "functional" perspective, so that all the powers are retained by the authority but their implementation is, as it were, "split up." As a result, the regulatory and

(40) See *supra*, No. 21 *et seq*.

supervisory authorities continue, and increasingly so, to combine all the legal powers: issuing norms, formulating opinions to the political authorities, negotiating commitments, promoting mediation, settling disputes between operators, sanctioning breaches, lodging appeals with the courts, intervening before the courts and themselves making claims before the courts.

31. Law does not reject the accumulation of powers. It can be said that no organisation has more legal powers than the independent Regulators and Supervisors: in France, these administrative authorities are so powerful that the *Sénat* (French Senate) has considered that they would constitute a "State within the State,"(41) the title of this report being in itself a protest. However, this combination of powers is in accordance with the legal system, in particular Constitutional Law,(42) because the different activities, in particular the collection of information, the assessment made of it (the investigation) and the decision taken from it (the judgement) are functionally separate, as the persons carrying out one and the other are not the same, and the opinion of the other being therefore not objectively taken up by the second activity.

32. Regulation – Supervision – Compliance: a profound movement. What results from this long jurisdictional process concerning General Procedural Regulatory Law can be taken up in General Procedural Compliance Law: the company must combine the powers to prosecute and to judge, because Compliance Law requires it to do so insofar as these powers are necessary for it to fulfil its Compliance Obligations,(43) and it must not be deprived of one or the other. This makes it possible to dispense with this principle, which the traditional legal system retains, but Compliance Law tends to deliberately ignore, legal personality.

(41) *Sénat* (French Senate), *Un État dans l'État: canaliser la prolifération des autorités administratives indépendantes pour mieux les contrôler. Rapport sur le bilan et le contrôle de la création, de l'organisation, de l'activité et de la gestion des autorités administratives indépendantes* (A State within the State: channelling the proliferation of independent administrative authorities to control them better. Report on the assessment and control of the creation, organisation, activity and management of independent administrative authorities), Report No. 126, 28 October 2015, free translation of "*État dans l'État.*"

(42) G. Canivet, "Autorités de régulation. Encadrement constitutionnel : le point de vue de juge", *in* M. Bazex, G Eckert, R. Lanneau, Ch. Le Berre, B. du Marais and A. Sée (eds), *Dictionnaire des régulations*, Paris, LexisNexis, 2016, pp. 125-137.

(43) M.-A. Frison-Roche, "Conceiving Power", 2021, https://mafr.fr/en/article/le-pouvoir-pour-mieux-servir/.

2. The need to establish functional autonomy for the prosecution and judgment activities without resorting to the concept of legal personality

33. The false ease of recourse to legal personality. Admittedly, if we keep the concept of the legal person in the game, (44) things are easier. Indeed, it is enough to say that it is the legal person who is responsible for taking legal action and imposing sanctions since it is the subject of Compliance Law, whereas the person to whom the legal person's activity gives rise to grievance, for example the employee or the corporate officer, is therefore another person: there is no longer any *judge-judged*, since there are two different persons, the legal person and the natural person, facing each other. They have opposing interests and while one questions, the other answers. The possible fact that the latter represents the former under Corporate Law is not decisive.

34. The price to be paid: the French mechanism of the Judicial Public Interest Agreement in the middle of the road, only accessible to the legal person. It is on the basis of this consideration, which some would call legal formalism, that the *Convention judiciaire d'intérêt public* (French Judicial Public Interest Agreement), (45) being accessible only to the legal entity, leads to the provision of information to the public prosecutor, a contribution for which in return the legal entity obtains the termination of the action against it. But as the legal entity is distinct from the personality of its corporate officer, the same facts, thus proven, will be used in an action, criminal or civil, against the corporate officer who cannot rely on an agreement that has been concluded for the benefit of another person. This solution is different of the American one, the natural person being able to obtain the same agreement. (46) As the French so-called "Sapin 2" law has not taken over the entire mechanism from American Law, which closes the public prosecution for both the company and its director – the legal personality, which enables the company to

(44) On the importance of this notion and the fact that it must be borne in mind for the subject under discussion, see *supra*.

(45) See the presentation of the technique *supra*, No. 5.

(46) F. Mazzacuva, "Justifications and purposes of negotiated justice for corporate offenders: deferred and non-prosecution agreements in the UK and US systems of criminal justice", *J. Crim. L.*, 2014, Vol. 78, No. 3, pp. 249-262; M. Bisgrove and M. Weekes, "Deferred prosecution agreements: a practical consideration", *Crim. L.R.*, 2014, Vol. 6, pp. 416-438. See also B. Sillaman, "Taking the Compliance U.S. Procedural Experience globally", *this book*.

carry out its role as internal prosecutor, also gives it the possibility of receiving a proposal to close the public prosecution, in particular because of the general information it provides, including information concerning the corporate officer who was nevertheless acting on its behalf – this shows that the autonomy of the legal person is both the remedy and what will produce a greater evil.

35. Finding technical solution about Impartiality without recourse to legal personality would also restore coherence of Compliance Law. Since the concept of "person" was created by Law, not only for the legal personality of organisations but also for the legal personality of human beings, the work of Michel Foucault having established it in a general way (47) as Jean-Paul Baud established it for the legal systems since Roman Law, (48) when Compliance Law resorts to it to establish a convenient distance between the person who prosecutes and the person who is prosecuted, between those who judge and those who are judged, it pays for itself considerably, since the benefits that the legal entity derives from the *convention judiciaire d'intérêt public*, the employees and corporate officers, thus "distanced," cannot benefit from it, even though the evidence collated concerns them directly and the public authorities will use it against them, quite rightly since the legal system allows it. (49) The French legislator should have put the legal mechanisms in order, but he did not.

For lack of a better solution, remembering that General Procedural Law had helped the Public Regulatory Authorities to organise the functional autonomy of the prosecuting, investigating and sanctioning bodies, (50) Law leaves it up to companies to organise this functional autonomy in compliance matters. They must do so under the aegis of the principle of Impartiality, which, as we have seen, encompasses all the others. (51)

(47) See also M. Foucault, *L'herméneutique du sujet : cours au Collège de France (1981-1982)*, Paris, Seuil, 2001.

(48) J.-P. Baud, *Histoire de la main volée. Une histoire juridique du corps*, Paris, Seuil, 1993.

(49) On the *Bolloré* case, see "The Bolloré case and the risks attached to the French Individual Guilty Pleas", *Bastille Day Newsletter 2021*, Enforcement & Court Decisions, 2021, https://navacelle.law/the-bollore-case-and-the-risks-attached-to-the-french-individual-guilty-pleas-2/.

(50) See *supra*, No. 30.

(51) See *supra*, No. 6.

B. Organising the principle of Impartiality within Companies to distance opposing interests when prosecuting and judging at the same time

36. The three perspectives for establishing Impartiality within the Company, supporting the combination of Prosecution and Judgment activities that Compliance Law requires companies to undertake. Since companies are left to their own tools, which also corresponds to the liberal principle that leaves companies free to organise themselves as they wish as long as they effectively fulfil their Compliance Obligations, it has been demonstrated that Impartiality must be the principle and the focus of *ex post* control by the courts. In this respect, there are three perspectives open to them. The first is the mechanical perspective of algorithms (1), the second is the organic perspective of the entities set up externally to carry out these activities (2) and the third is that of the human beings who come to represent each other in the company, because different positions correspond to different interests that need to be defended (3).

1. The mirage of "impartial machines"

37. The dream of machines that prosecute and judge without opinion. The first prospect is that of replacing humans with algorithms that will collect information, correlate data and highlight both what does not correspond, i.e. "non-conformities," and what does correspond, i.e. "conformities." This power of "conformity" scanning machines has been discussed at greater length in this book. (52)

38. The dangers of believing in "impartial algorithms," whose biases could simply be corrected. Here again, compliance by design has a new attraction: that of Impartiality. Assuming we correct the flaws that can affect it, namely the "biases" that human beings have allowed to contaminate the very design of algorithms that "learn," there would therefore be the same "Impartiality" in an algorithm that prosecutes and punishes, or at least no less, than in human organisms. A great deal of work has been done on the ability of algorithms to "judge," the ability to remove from algorithms the biases that human beings had inserted into them, initially or in the course of use or development, making it possible to obtain pure

(52) M.-A. Frison-Roche, "Reinforce the Judge and the Lawyer to impose Compliance Law as a characteristic of the Rule of Law", *this book*.

Impartiality, no longer requiring procedure in the legal sense of Law, the process having thus rendered procedure useless, since the removal of useful intervention would no longer be the problem but the solution... This is criticised in particular in Labour Law. (53) This impartiality of machines is most often denounced either as an illusion, because biases cannot be extracted, or as a great danger in that this Impartiality that would be achieved would be at the price of a dehumanisation of the legal practice, whereas Compliance Law must be seen as something that is substantially aimed at defending human beings and not at mechanically subjecting them to regulations. (54)

2. Modelling internal organisations on the Regulatory Authorities example: creating functionally autonomous bodies

39. The prospect of strengthening the structures of company ombudsmen. Many organisations, whether public, such as the French Ministry of the Economy with its "*médiateur du crédit,*" or the English Financial Ombudsman Service, or the *Autorité des marchés financiers – AMF* (French Financial Markets Authority), with its "AMF Ombudsman" who makes up for the lack of power to settle disputes, or large companies, such as in France the *La Poste* group or the *SNCF*, have assigned people who are seized by those who are having difficulties with others, which is not a dispute in the strict sense but constitutes a bad relation with the entity itself or with other persons or entities over which the organisation has control about a precise fact. If we strengthen, in Law or in fact, the fields of intervention of these structures, which are sometimes built around a physical person, on the model of the ombudsman, which is how the French *Défenseur des droits* (Defender of Rights) (55) got started, who is interfering more and more in Compliance Law, particularly in the whistleblowing mechanism, it then becomes possible for the company, which may be

(53) *Ibid.* See also B. Géniaux, "Quel type de régulation pour l'intelligence artificielle, ou comment justifier l'irrationnel", *in* P. Adam, M. Le Friant and Y. Tarasewicz (eds), *Intelligence artificielle, gestion algorithmique du personnel et droit du travail*, "Thèmes et commentaires" Serie, Paris, Dalloz, 2020, pp. 105-114, in particular insofar as it links, through the GDPR, Compliance Law and "*le droit à l'intervention humaine*" ("the right to human intervention") (pp. 112 *et seq.*).

(54) M.-A. Frison-Roche, "Compliance Monumental Goals, Beating Heart of Compliance Law", *in* M.-A. Frison-Roche (ed.), *Compliance Monumental Goals*, "Compliance & Regulation" Serie, Brussels, Journal of Regulation & Compliance (JoRC)/Bruylant, 2023, pp. 33-58.

(55) See the English website of the French *Défenseur des droits* (Defender of Rights): https://www.defenseurdesdroits.fr/en. See also her guide on the whistleblowing: French Defender of Rights, *Guide – Orientation and protection of whistleblowers*, July 2017.

the entity against which a reproach is made, thus being in the position of the *judged*, to be able, without difficulty, to also be the *judge* because the mediation structure is impartial.

40. Impartiality and Neutrality. The principle of neutrality, which is essential to the ombudsman's role, but which must be combined with the adversarial principle, is linked to the principle of Impartiality, which is the overriding principle of the whole. The development of these internal structures within companies, combining the principles of neutrality and adversarial proceedings, both of which are governed by the primary principle of Impartiality, is certainly a way forward.

41. The prospect of outsourcing a prosecution, investigation and/or judgement structure. A more decisive step can be taken by no longer seeking to develop a structure that already exists within the company, but by creating one on a blank page with no link to the company, on the model of the Regulatory Authorities, which are within the State but independent of it. Compliance Law always benefits from relying on Regulatory Law that preceded it and from which it must import both the spirit and the techniques in the a-sectoral, or even territory-less spaces that it is nevertheless the ambition to regulate. The example of this was given by the Oversight Board set up by Meta, in particular its decision of 5 May 2019 concerning Donald Trump, an example much studied,(56) and most often criticised.

42. The merit of existing. On a more pragmatic note, short of establishing prosecuting authorities with a global reach and global judges to effectively protect people from the global evils that disinformation constitutes, this solution has the merit of existing and of being situated in the relevant segment of time: *ex ante* and not *ex post.* (57) States governed by the Rule of Law make these structural outsourcing initiatives subject, on the one hand, to the condition of an appeal to a State Court (as is the case for decisions taken by Administrative Regulatory Authorities) and, on the other hand, to the existence of permanent supervision by a public authority (as is the case in banking, finance, digital technology, etc.). It is likely that this model, in perfect continuity with Regulatory Law, internalised in companies and freed from the prerequisites of the sector, will develop, within the framework of permanent public supervision and formal *ex post* judicial control.

(56) See in particular. J. Heymann, "The Legal Nature of the Facebook 'Supreme Court'", *this book*.

(57) On the question of relevant time, see M.-A. Frison-Roche, "The Judge, the Compliance Obligation and the Company. The Compliance Evidence System", *this book*.

43. Adjusting Words and Things *Ex Post* or *Ex Ante*. Moreover, as has happened in Regulatory Law, the structures set up in this way, which function like "judges," combining "investigative" functions by gathering information and assessing it, and even prosecutorial functions, will themselves have to function "like" courts. This readjustment of things and words will either be carried out by the courts in their *ex post* review, or will already be carried out by the structure put in place, as was the case in the decision adopted by the Meta Oversight Board concerning Donald Trump, recalling in particular the impossibility of life sentences after having reclassified the closure of a digital account as constituting a sentence. This means exercising the jurisdictional office of requalification oneself, or even more so by the company, which will benefit from establishing all that is necessary for the full effectiveness of the principle of Impartiality, which is important for the principles that States governed by the Rule of Law have established for its effectiveness. To this end, the use of human beings is undoubtedly the most valuable.

3. The prospect of using human third parties: the central role of the Compliance Department and Lawyers

44. Placing third parties in each of the places of the parties involved. The jurisdictional triangle. Motulsky conceived of the trial as a triangle, the base of which is formed by the two parties whose interests diverge and the apex of which is occupied by the judge.(58) One of the solutions is therefore to identify the different interests that are expressed by the situation of the company, which must sue and judge: for example, insofar as it is being *judged*, it has one interest, and insofar as it is *judging*, it has another interest. As this is required by Compliance Law, the efficacy of which presupposes the accumulation of functions to achieve the Monumental Goals that give it its substantial definition, the solution is to entrust these interests to separate persons: thus, a first person must represent the company in its capacity as *judged* and a second person must represent the company in its capacity as *judge*.

45. The pointlessness of dissociating the enterprise from the legal person by multiplying the number of interest representatives according to the multiplicity of interests within the enterprise. If we

(58) On the usefulness of always referring to Motulsky to understand new situations such as this, see also M.-A. Frison-Roche, "Adjusting General Procedural Law to Compliance Law by the Nature of Things", *this book*.

proceed in this way, there is no longer any need to assert that the subject of Law is the individual, which would make it impossible to allow individuals within the company, in particular the directors, to benefit from compliance mechanisms, even though they have negotiated them and, in so doing, have compromised themselves *de facto* but, as the legislation stands, not "*de jure*": we can say that the subject of Law is always the company. This makes it possible to reconcile a major point of Compliance Law, that of its legal subject! Indeed, taking the example of the Vigilance duty, the subject to this legal duty is the firm in the broadest sense of the term. In the French law of 2017, the subject is the "*entreprise donneuse d'ordre*" ("ordering enterprise"), with all the very serious consequences that this has for it since this enterprise becomes responsible *ex ante* for the behaviour of economic operators with whom it may not even have contractual links. This is in coherence with the logic of Compliance Law, which is no limited by the legal personality.

It must be recognised that, when a company, in obeying Compliance Law, prosecutes and punishes itself, and this cannot be justified on ethical grounds alone, the conflicting interests involved must be defended separately. This is why the compliance department, which exists autonomously within the company and acts as an investigation department, often reporting to a structure which decides (and therefore judges) or which decides itself (for example by passing on information to the public authorities), organises the representation of interests whose diversity, or even opposition, must be identified.

46. *Conclusion*. The overall improvement of Compliance Law through the direct representation of the various interests concerned by the company's combined powers of prosecution and judgment over itself and others. These structural and behavioural changes within the company, because it is obliged to do so by Compliance Law, itself borrowing from Regulatory Law, will enable the company to assume these powers that Law imposes on it and which give it a central place, that the new ambition to provide solutions here and now to global issues, particularly digital and climate issues, requires of it.

Reflections on the existence of companies' jurisprudence through Compliance matters

Cécile Granier

Senior Lecturer, Jean Moulin Lyon 3 University

1. Innovative nature of compliance. Compliance (1) is a process whose ability to shake up established frameworks no longer needs to be demonstrated. (2) In the light of this, certain concepts that one might have thought were well understood – because they had been studied extensively – appear in a new light, which suggests that we should consider the question again. This seems to be the case with jurisprudence. Recent developments about compliance (3) lead us to question the possible existence of a "jurisprudence" produced by companies. (4) The establishment of what appears to be close to a "jurisdiction" within the company Facebook (5) – now called Meta – and which constitutes an example likely to spread, contributes in a decisive way to give rise to this question.

(1) Relating the concept of compliance, M.-A. Frison-Roche, "Le droit de la compliance", *D.*, 2016, p. 1871; A. Gaudemet (ed.), *La compliance, un monde nouveau ?*, Paris, Éditions Panthéon-Assas, 2016; M.-E. Bousier, "Qu'est-ce que la *compliance* ? Essai de définition", *D.*, 2020, p. 1419.

(2) The advent of compliance has been accompanied by the rise of obligations with original content weighing on companies and their managers: obligation to set up systems to prevent and detect acts of corruption or influence peddling, the obligation of vigilance or new concepts and tools, such as whistleblowers or risk mapping. Beyond that, the advent of compliance questions the very contours of the legal phenomenon: its characteristic elements such as constraint and its motives, and its actors through the question of the respective roles of States and private actors in the design and application of the law.

(3) If this question is linked here to the compliance process, it is because it is in this context that it appears to have emerged most clearly to date. However, the question of the existence of a jurisprudence produced by companies seems to go beyond the sole field of compliance and can therefore be separated from it.

(4) The notion of company is understood here in its economic dimension and therefore refers to entities carrying out an economic activity in an organised manner, i.e. the production or distribution of goods or services.

(5) On the institution of the Facebook *Oversight Board*: K. Kate, "The Facebook Oversight Board: Creating an Independent Institution to Adjudicate Online Free Expression", *Yale Law Journal*, 2020, Vol. 129, No. 8, pp. 2418-2499; V. Ndior, "Le Conseil de surveillance de Facebook, 'service après-vente' de la liberté d'expression ?", *D.*, 2020, p. 1474; J. Heymann, "The legal nature of the Facebook 'Supreme Court'", *this book*; A. Piper, "Oversight and the Future of Social Media Regulation", 74 N°. 5 *IBA Global Insight* 14.

2. An unnatural idea. At first glance, the idea of a jurisprudence shaped by companies is a challenge, even a shock, to the jurist. Its evocation seems like heresy because it refers to an unnatural association: that of two terms – jurisprudence and company – which appear deeply incompatible. Indeed, jurisprudence is traditionally understood as being the result of the office of the judge and, more precisely, of the State (6) judge. Classically, there is an intrinsic and organic link between judges and jurisprudence: the latter can only emanate from judges and can only be supported by a judgment.

3. Merits of the reflection. The idea of jurisprudence produced by companies seems, however, to be a legitimate one to explore, for several reasons. Firstly, because it would not be the first time that a concept that initially seems counter-intuitive has finally found relevance. If it had been presented to the lawyers of the last century, the concept of "soft law" would surely have generated the same unease because of the unnatural association it carries. However, it is now enjoying undiminished success. (7)

Beyond this, the questioning of the existence of a jurisprudence produced by companies is the logical consequence of the observation that the company or one of its emanations can sometimes place itself in the position of judge, i.e. in a position to settle a dispute with the help of an identified body of rules. For example, Facebook's Oversight Board has the task of confirming or reversing a decision to remove content that is contested by a user of a platform managed by the company. (8) It is therefore a matter of deciding between the company and one of its users regarding the publication of content. (9) From that moment, whether its mission is to settle disputes, does this council not have the function of producing decisions and jurisprudence? In this respect, when consulting the Facebook (10) Supervisory Board's website, the lawyer can only be struck by the formal similarity with a court's website: the decisions rendered are summarised, classified in chronological order and signed, which makes it

(6) Embodied by judges, justice is traditionally conceived as a "state function."

(7) See in particular, Conseil d'État, *Le droit souple*, Doc. fr., 2013.

(8) The definition of the functions of the Oversight Board are defined in its statutes: "The board will review cases where people disagree with the outcome of Facebook's decisions and have exhausted the appeals process with Facebook. The board will also be able to hear cases that have been referred by Facebook. The board will review and decide on content in accordance with Facebook's content policies and values (Oversight Board Bylaws, Article 1, Section 3, October 2021)

(9) On the importance of moderation, K. Langvart, "Regulating Online Content Moderation", *Georgetown Law Journal*, 2018, Vol. 106, No. 5, pp. 1353-1388.

(10) www.oversightboard.com.

possible – like a court decision – to cite them. In such a context, it is the intrinsic link between judge and jurisprudence itself that legitimises the question raised: if companies exercise a judicial function in certain cases and adopt the position of judge, does it not then have the vocation to produce jurisprudence?

Finally, it is the logic behind compliance that makes it legitimate to question the existence of a jurisprudence emanating from companies. Compliance is in fact a process that consists in shifting onto certain companies, and therefore onto private actors, the burden of implementing and enforcing major legal objectives – the "monumental goals" (11) – defined upstream by the public authorities (for example, the fight against corruption, money laundering, environmental protection, etc.), on pain of punishment. To this end, companies are responsible for drawing up rules that they impose on themselves and their partners. (12) To a certain extent, compliance therefore results in the outsourcing to private companies of functions that traditionally fall within the remit of the State: that of enforcing the law but also of devising standards with a view to ensuring compliance with "monumental goals." Also, in this widespread context of outsourcing and privatisation of functions that were initially State functions, could it not be accepted that companies can, like a State judge, interpret and enrich the content of the standards they apply in the course of a dispute, which is precisely what jurisprudence is all about?

4. Reasoning by analogy. Placed in this context, the idea of a companies' jurisprudence no longer seems so incongruous. On the contrary, it even seems legitimate to explore it. In order to foresee or refute the possibility of such a jurisprudence, the starting point of the reasoning can only lie in the notion of jurisprudence as it is commonly understood. (13) It is only on this basis and by developing a reasoning by analogy that the reflection on a possible extension of the concept of jurisprudence seems to be possible. Without insisting too much on a widely studied concept, jurisprudence can schematically be understood as the result of the conjunction of two components. Firstly, jurisprudence refers to a specific technique for creating legal standards. With regard to this first aspect, a comparison can be made between the jurisprudence of judges and that which could

(11) For the use of the expression, *cf.* M.-A. Frison-Roche, "Le droit de la compliance", *op. cit.*

(12) For example, the development of codes of conduct.

(13) This is not easy because jurisprudence is not always understood in a consensual manner by French authors: its status as a "source of law" and the value of the norms produced still sometimes give rise to doctrinal divergences.

be designed by a company. Indeed, it will be shown that there is nothing to prevent the technique of creating the norm that distinguishes this source of law from being used by companies. Functionally, this specific technique is therefore not the prerogative of the judge. On this point, an analogy between the jurisprudence of the judges and that of companies is possible (I). To this first element must be added a second, this time of an organic nature. Jurisprudence then traditionally echoes a set of norms that are produced by judges. (14) With regard to this second component, the analogy between jurisprudence as classically understood and jurisprudence produced by companies is at first glance impossible (II).

I. A POSSIBLE FUNCTIONAL ANALOGY

5. A functional analogy between jurisprudence produced by judges and jurisprudence produced by companies can be identified both with regard to the specific mode of constitution of the jurisprudential norm (A) and with regard to the scope of the rule once it has been created (B).

A. Analogy in the process of rule emergence

6. Singularity of the process of emergence of the jurisprudential rule. Jurisprudence follows a specific mode of elaboration which is fundamentally different from that used by other sources of law, i.e. mainly the legislator or the authorities holding executive powers. Its emergence process is first of all original because of the context in which it takes place. It is also original because of its indirect and incidental nature. Whereas, for example, the direct and principal aim of the legislative procedure is to produce legal norms, jurisprudence only emerges on the occasion of a decision settling a dispute and only thanks to an interpretation that will occasionally be used. The context of rise of a jurisprudential norm will thus necessarily be that of a dispute that an institution will be responsible for resolving by settling opposing claims relating to the application of a rule of law. Obliged to put an end to this dispute, (15) this institution will sometimes be led to interpret the applicable rules and, by this means, to

(14) The term judge is used here in an organic dimension: it refers to State judges sitting in public Courts.

(15) For the judge, this obligation is based for example in France on the Article 4 of the *Code civil* (French Civil Code).

enrich their content, or even sometimes, under cover of this interpretation function, to create new rules which alone will enable it to settle the dispute. If traditionally the person in charge of such mission is a judge, is it conceivable that a company might find itself in a similar situation, for example, when implementing a compliance policy?

7. Process that can be used by a company. The example offered by the former Facebook company provides a positive answer. In the event of a conflict between the latter and one of its users regarding the removal of content from a platform managed by the company (Facebook or Instagram), the Oversight Board is called upon to decide and therefore to settle the dispute between the company and the user using the "Values" and "Community Standards" recognised and endorsed by the company itself. (16) The "decision-making process" to be followed by the Oversight Board is described in the charter governing its operation: "Facebook uses a set of values to guide its content rules and decisions. The Board will review content enforcement decisions and determine whether they are consistent with Facebook's rules and values," (17) which are the so-called "Community Standards." To this end, it is expressly provided that the Board collectively has the authority to "interpret the Facebook Community Standards and other relevant policies (collectively referred to as the 'Content Rules') in light of Facebook's stated values". The resemblance to the situation of a judge when deciding a dispute is striking. This similarity seems to be deliberately maintained by Facebook in both form (18) and substance. (19)

In addition to this first example, which is not a fiction, one could also imagine other configurations in which a company would entrust one of its bodies or one of its emanations with the task of settling a dispute. For example, in the context of a compliance policy, it is conceivable that a company might place itself in a position to settle a dispute with one of its employees or partners concerning its compliance policy as described in a code of conduct or an ethical charter, whatever it may be called. The company or one of its emanations could thus be responsible for deciding between the claims of the employee or partner who considers that he or

(16) For these standards: www.facebook.com/communitystandards/objectionable_content.

(17) Charter of the Oversight Board, section "Competence", point 2, www.oversightboard.com.

(18) In particular, the use of vocabulary related to the lexical field of jurisdictions ("judgment," "appeal procedure," "enforceability," "precedent," etc.) both in the documents governing the Board's operation and on the Board's website.

(19) For example, with a strong reference to the 'independence' of the Board as an inherent feature of Courts.

she has behaved in accordance with the company's compliance policy and the claims of the company who considers the opposite. The body entrusted with such a mission, which is necessarily independent, would then have to interpret the standards contained in the applicable rules in order to reach a decision and could, on this occasion, call for an interpretation.

8. Conclusion: a valid analogy. In the context of their compliance policy, companies may settle a dispute using abstract and pre-existing rules. However, it is precisely in this context that the entity applying the standards may be led to enrich their content or to create new rules to make up for their shortcomings. The fact that a new norm can be created is the consequence of the application of an abstract rule to concrete facts. Thus, this creative dimension is not related to the nature of the rule interpreted (legal or not), nor to the identity of the interpreter (judge or company), it is a consequence of the process of settling a concrete dispute with abstract and pre-existing rules. In the same way that the law cannot anticipate everything, the "Facebook Community Standards" or the codes of conduct drawn up by companies cannot anticipate the multiplicity of factual situations. However, it is precisely in this gap that the institution that applies and interprets the rule gives rise to the jurisprudential norm. Materially, it therefore seems conceivable that a company could create a rule when resolving a dispute that would supplement the rules previously enacted. An analogy between jurisprudence produced by a judge and jurisprudence produced by a company therefore appears possible on this point. This reasoning by analogy must now be continued with regard to the scope of the rule that has been established.

B. Analogy in the scope of the rule

9. Normativity of jurisprudence. If jurisprudence is described as a "source of law," it is because the rule established by a judge in a particular dispute is intended to produce effects beyond this framework alone and to be taken up in other disputes as soon as they concern a similar question. It is this repetition that attests to and underpins the normative effect of the jurisprudence. Is it conceivable that a similar influence could be attached to the decision of a company whose purpose is to settle a dispute and to the rule underlying it? Once again, the answer seems to be positive. It seems possible that the standards established by a company in the context analysed have a scope that goes beyond the case in point. Nevertheless, like the "classic" jurisprudential norm – the one produced by judges – the sources of this influence may be twofold: it may be imposed or, it may not be imposed, and result from the *de facto* influence exercised by the decision.

10. Imposed normativity of the jurisprudential rule produced by a company. The Facebook Oversight Board is a good example of a configuration in which the decisions rendered by a company on the occasion of a dispute are binding on their author for future decisions. The documents organising the functioning of this Board have framed the scope of the solutions rendered. The charter governing its operation specifies that "For each decision, the Board's previous decisions will have precedent value and must be considered highly persuasive when the facts, applicable rules and other elements are substantially identical." (20) The reference to "precedent" is particularly significant and should be understood as referring to "binding precedent." The Oversight Board therefore seems to have no option but to adopt the decision and thus the standard set in another case if a similar configuration arises. Only a difference in context would justify the Oversight Board's departure from a rule that it had, through an interpretation of the "Community Standards," identified in a previous case. The consistency of its "jurisprudence" seems assured. With the aforementioned provision, Facebook has ensured the transposition before the Oversight Board of the rule of binding precedent, so characteristic of the jurisprudence in Anglo-Saxon systems. This mimicry is hardly surprising given that the company – of American origin – is familiar with the rule of *stare decisis* and, above all, that the very objective of the creation of this Board is to adopt decisions to create rules to guide the company's action in its moderation activities, in order to give predictability to its users and guarantees of surveillance and control to the public authorities.

11. *De facto* normativity of jurisprudence produced by a company. The configuration illustrated by the Facebook Oversight Board does not seem to be the only one imaginable. As with the normativity of jurisprudence in civil law systems, (21) the influence of a rule created by a company on the occasion of litigation may be based on levers other than the

(20) Article "Competence", point 2, para. 2, of the Charter of the Facebook Oversight Board, *supra*. A similar reference to "precedents" is found in the Oversight Board's Articles of Association regarding the selection of cases by the Board (see point 1.2.1 *Case Selection Committee*).

(21) In these systems, jurisprudence only has a *de facto* authority, see P. Deumier, "La jurisprudence", *op. cit.*, No. 90.

textual obligation to adopt it. Even in the absence of binding precedents, the likelihood that the precedent and the rule created on the occasion of litigation will have an impact beyond the case in point is high. There are several reasons for this. Some of these have already been identified in relation to jurisprudence as traditionally understood. In this respect, the need for consistency in jurisprudence and the correlative need for certainty on the part of those to whom it is addressed justify the fact that the decisions and the rules on which they are based are mostly repeated in future decisions. This consideration seems to prevail as regards both "jurisprudence of judges" and the "jurisprudence of companies". Without consistency, the credibility and legitimacy of the decision-making institutions would be greatly diminished.

Other levers of influence then appear to be specific to a possible "company jurisprudence." This is particularly true of the unity of the company and therefore of the likely unity of the body entrusted with the task of settling disputes involving it. For example, within the company Facebook, the Oversight Board is the only body entrusted with this task. This unity of the decision-making body – which contrasts with the diversity of the public Courts – is clearly such as to encourage it to adopt the decisions and rules reached in a previous decision, if only because of a desire not to be overruled. Here again, what credibility would an institution have if its position changed too much with each case? Changes in jurisprudence are possible, but they must necessarily remain exceptional. Finally, it is the very purpose of the process of setting up a body within a company whose purpose is to settle disputes to which it is a party that justifies the *de facto* authority attached to previously rendered decisions: for the company, it is a question of giving reliable guidelines for taking certain decisions to the potential recipients of its decisions, but also to the public authorities, if one is to follow a compliance logic. A lack of consideration of precedents would then contradict this objective. In this respect, it should be noted that the configuration appears to be different for state Courts: the performance of such a function, which can be described as "normative," appears to be secondary because their primary function is to settle disputes with a view to seeking social appeasement. The order of priorities seems to us to be reversed with regard to "private courts": the identification of operating rules seems to be the primary objective, while the resolution of the dispute only appears secondary: it constitutes a context and a pretext for their normative function.

12. Conclusion: a valid analogy. Whether or not the influence of the standard created by a company in a decision ruling on a dispute is imposed, the possibility of such influence beyond the dispute alone appears real. This observation reinforces the validity of an analogy between jurisprudence of judges and jurisprudence of companies concerning the scope of the rule created and ends up convincing us of a possible functional analogy between these two "jurisprudences." It now remains to confront the organic criterion of jurisprudence which, for its part, seems to make any attempt at analogy between jurisprudence as commonly understood and a jurisprudence of companies impossible.

II. AN IMPOSSIBLE ORGANIC ANALOGY

13. Organic obstacle. In addition to its original methods of creation, the jurisprudential norm is classically characterised by the singular identity of its creator: it is the State(22) judge when he or she sits within the Courts and adopts judicial decisions. This organic component of the notion of jurisprudence seems to stop short of an analogy between jurisprudence as classically understood and companies' jurisprudence. Indeed, it necessarily leads to a positive answer to the following question: can only a judge produce jurisprudence? However, if the answer is positive and jurisprudence is understood as being the result of the judge's office, this initial assumption prevents any possibility of conceiving companies' jurisprudence. While a company may functionally exercise a jurisdictional mission, statutorily it can obviously not be qualified as a judge. Consequently, the only way to conceive of "companies' jurisprudence" would be to break the conceptual link between judge and jurisprudence. This would mean admitting that entities other than the judge can produce jurisprudence and that this source of law is distinguished only by its mode of conception and no longer by the identity of its designer. On this point, no truth or untruth seems to be able to be established since what is ultimately sought is a relevant way of reporting a reality. Consequently, the breaking of this link will appear justified – or not – with regard to the opportunity that exists to broadly conceive the notion of jurisprudence. Now, both a theoretical (A) and a practical (B) opportunity to overcome this organic obstacle in order to fully welcome the concept of "companies' jurisprudence" seems to be emerging.

(22) *Cf. supra*, note 7.

A. The theoretical opportunity to overcome the organic obstacle

14. Jurisprudential' production not emanating from judges. Going beyond an organic conception of jurisprudence seems justified by the need to better understand the various normative phenomena of which our legal system is both the theatre and the witness. Several contemporary phenomena indeed seem to functionally resemble jurisprudence without emanating from judges. In this respect, we should first mention the decisions produced by certain regulatory authorities. In the course of their various missions, some of them exercise jurisdictional functions (23) since they are called upon to settle a dispute by mobilising legal rules. This is the case, for example in France of the *Autorité de la Concurrence* (French Competition Authority) or the *Autorité des marchés financiers* (French Financial Markets Authority) when they adopt decisions or impose sanctions on economic operators. On this occasion, in the same way as a judge or the Facebook Oversight Board, these authorities apply general and pre-existing rules to answer concrete questions and may, in this context, mobilise an interpretation that enriches the content of a rule or even creates a new rule. It is therefore logical that the term "jurisprudence" is sometimes used to designate the normative production of these authorities when they adopt decisions, (24) even though they are statutorily administrative authorities and not Courts. Similarly, while it is accepted that arbitrators are private persons entrusted with the exercise of jurisdictional functions, the expression "arbitral jurisprudence" is frequently used to describe the body of decisions rendered by arbitral tribunals. (25) Although it may have been debated with regard to the characteristics of arbitration, (26) the use of this

(23) In the context of the application of Article 6 of the European Convention for the Protection of Human Rights and Fundamental Freedoms, the European Court of Human Rights assimilates the regulatory authorities when they pronounce sanctions to "Courts" pronouncing on "criminal matters." It thus distinguishes the status of jurisdiction from the exercise of jurisdictional functions and the guarantees they entail. On the interpretation of the concept of "criminal matters" within the meaning of Article 6 of the ECHR, see ECHR, 8 June 1976, *Engel and Others v. The Netherlands*, Appl.

(24) The *Autorité des marchés financiers* – AMF (French Financial Markets Authority) itself describes its decision-making practice as "jurisprudence", www.amf-france.org. See AMF publication, *2003-2019, Les principes directeurs de la jurisprudence de l'AMF.*

(25) D. Hascher, "Arbitrage du commerce international", *Rép. de droit international*, Paris, Dalloz, 2020, No. 132, quoting an ICC award of 1982 stating that "*les décisions des tribunaux arbitraux forment progressivement une jurisprudence dont il échet de tenir compte*" (which can be translated as: "the decisions of arbitral tribunals are progressively forming a body of case law which must be taken into account") (case No. 4131, *Recueil* 1974-1985, *op. cit.*, p 464).

(26) *Ibid.*, referring to the lack of hierarchy between arbitral tribunals (which does not seem to us to be a decisive obstacle to the constitution of jurisprudence). Similarly, the confidentiality and lack of publication of arbitral decisions are obstacles to the qualification of "jurisprudence" since they prevent the decision and the rule underlying it from being taken up by another Court and undermine their normative scope.

expression attests both to a potential normative capacity of these "private judges" when settling a dispute and to a possible application of the concept of jurisprudence to institutions other than Courts. Finally, private bodies are sometimes set up to guide and control the application of normative corpuses that are also of private origin. This is the case, for example, in France with the *Haut Comité de gouvernement d'entreprise* (French High Council for Corporate Governance), a body set up to monitor the application of the *AFEP-MEDEF code*, which was itself designed by professional associations of employers and intended for companies to implement governance principles. The role of this body is to ensure that the code is properly applied. (27) To this end, it issues opinions on the implementation by companies of the "comply or explain" principle with regard to the principles of governance prescribed by the *AFEP-MEDEF code*. Once again, this confrontation of abstract standards with specific cases may provide an opportunity to mobilise an interpretation (28) and therefore a technique for designing the standard that is similar to that of jurisprudence. Although these opinions are not systematically published, (29) which may cast doubt on the normative scope of the interpretations they contain, it is possible to detect in them a mechanism for devising norms similar to that of jurisprudence. Added to the example offered by the Facebook Oversight Board, the three configurations previously identified attest to a diversification of the entities responsible for applying and thus interpreting rules in the event of disputes.

15. Theoretical reception of these phenomena. In order to ensure the theoretical reception of these normative phenomena, a broadening of the concept of jurisprudence as traditionally understood by abandoning the organic criterion seems necessary. The application of such a criterion has the consequence of pushing all the phenomena described out of the category of jurisprudence. However, the admission of a concept of "company's jurisprudence" would make it possible to ensure a conceptual translation of the contemporary expansion of jurisprudential phenomena reflected in these different manifestations. However, this would in no way mean that the jurisprudence of judges would no longer be designated by the expression of jurisprudence. The admission of such a concept would

(27) See the presentation of its role on the website www.hcge.fr and Article 27.2 of the *AFEP-MEDEF code*.

(28) One of the tasks assigned to this committee is to interpret the *AFEP-MEDEF code* (*cf.* Article 27.2 of this code).

(29) They will only be used in the event of non compliance with the notice by the company concerned in the context of the committee's annual report. A certain timidity on the part of this committee, particularly with regard to the publication of these notices, has been highlighted, see N. Cuzacq, "Le mécanisme du *Name and Shame* ou la sanction médiatique comme mode de régulation des entreprises", *RTD com.*, 2017, p. 473.

only reflect the fact that the judge does not have a monopoly on the production of jurisprudential norms and that other actors, particularly private ones, can mobilise the method of creation specific to jurisprudence. The broadening of the concept of jurisprudence by admitting a possible contribution from companies appears to be consistent with the contemporary context of globalisation and the global retreat of the State institution in favour of other forces, particularly private ones, and which is reflected in particular by the increasingly active participation of non-jurisdictional actors in the implementation and therefore the interpretation of rules.

Although it is certainly theoretical, the possibility of admitting companies' jurisprudence is then not without practical consequences.

B. The practical opportunity to overcome the organic obstacle

16. Precondition for the determination of a rule of "companies' jurisprudence." Acknowledging that there is "companies' jurisprudence" is a necessary precondition for the possible framing of this jurisprudence. In other words, admitting that companies can develop norms of a jurisprudential nature makes it possible to highlight and identify a new facet of their normative power, which manifests itself in the very specific context in which they settle a dispute. However, like any power likely to influence the rights of individuals, it must be accompanied by a framework. There is therefore a real practical opportunity to identify the concept of "companies' jurisprudence": that of bringing out a requirement to determine the rules governing the development and scope of this jurisprudence with a view to guaranteeing the rights of the recipients of decisions adopted by companies.

17. Elements of the "companies' jurisprudence" rule. With regard to the model offered by the jurisprudence produced by judges, several elements of the framing of this "companies' jurisprudence" must be considered. The question of the dissemination of decisions rendered by a company must first be raised. Since the solutions adopted previously and the rules underlying them are intended to guide the company's future activity, the persons concerned must be able to access them. In order to ensure the proper reception of jurisprudence standards, but also to preserve the rights of those to whom they are addressed, the company should adopt rules and processes to ensure the proper dissemination of these decisions. In this respect, it is conceivable that if the decisions adopted are numerous, the company should, following the example of the highest public Courts, organise a system of prioritisation of decisions according to their normative scope. Another element of this jurisprudence system could also be the enactment of rules governing the reasons for decisions made by the company. Following the example of what is provided for in the Charter of the Facebook (30) Oversight Board, it is in the company's interest to regulate the process of giving reasons for decisions, as the quality of this reasoning will be a condition for the proper reception of the norm conceived and conveyed by the decision. Similarly, if it is accepted that these decisions may lead to the enactment of new standards, it would seem appropriate to provide for rules governing their application over time. The retroactive nature of the rules established in a particular case through interpretation, whether by a public or private judge, prompts us to clarify this point. Beyond that, admitting the normative power of companies when adopting certain decisions leads to the question of the status of the body in charge of settling these disputes: its composition, its competence, its independence, etc. Finally, and more centrally, the question of the identity of the body responsible for determining these elements of the rule emerges. Should it be left to the companies alone, in a purely self-regulatory logic, or, conversely, should it be subject to public control (31)? Should Facebook be left to manage the functioning of its Oversight Board alone or should the public authorities erect safeguards? If we conceive of this Board as "*a jurisdictional body of an international extra-state system,*" (32) this raises the question of the conciliation of this private legal order with State legal orders. (33) Should this reconciliation even exist? If so, how can it be implemented? These are all questions that can only emerge and whose importance can only be perceived once the reality of the normative power of companies when they adopt decisions that settle disputes has been brought to light, which is precisely what the concept of "companies' jurisprudence" allows.

(30) Oversight Board Charter, Procedure section, point 4 (decisions), www.oversightboard.com: "The final decision will include a decision on the content, together with a corresponding explanation in clear language of the board's reasons." It is also provided that in the event of a lack of consensus among the members of the Oversight Board "the reasons for divergence may be included in the decision of the panel to include all points of view and to give the floor to those who have expressed reservations or concerns."

(31) On that point, K. Langvart, "Regulating Online Content Moderation", *Georgetown Law Journal*, 2018, Vol. 106, No. 5, p. 1385.

(32) E. Farnoux, "La liberté d'expression et l'ordre public dans la *lex electronica*: sur la décision Trump vs Facebook du Conseil de surveillance de Facebook du 5 mai 2021", *op. cit.*, esp. p. 12.

(33) On this question and the relations of "relevance" S. Romano, *The legal Order*, London, Routledge, 2018.

The jurisdictionalisation of reputation by platforms

Luc-Marie Augagneur

Partner, Cornet Vincent Ségurel

"We can afford to lose money, even a lot of money.
But we can't afford to lose reputation, even a shred of reputation."
W. Buffett (1)

1. The very essence of compliance lies in delegating the regulation of certain risks to crucial operators which carry them, by setting (monumental (2)) goals rather than narrowly defined rules. This is particularly true for banks and insurance companies, which are exposed to risks of fraud, money laundering and terrorist financing through their services. This also applies in the industrial sector where companies have to deal with risks of corruption or infringements of fundamental rights by their suppliers or subcontractors. As for major platforms (search engines, marketplaces, intermediation platforms, app stores, social networks, etc.), they are part of a reputation economy (3) for which operators seek to obtain the greatest

(1) W. Buffett, *On Business: Principles from the Sage of Omaha*, Hoboken, J. Wiley & sons, 2010.

(2) M.-A. Frison-Roche (ed.), *Compliance Monumental Goals*, "Compliance & Regulation" Serie, Brussels, Journal of Regulation & Compliance (JoRC) and Bruylant, 2023.

(3) Far from being anecdotal, the place given to reputation in a society has often been significant. In ancient Rome, for example, it played a decisive role and already showed a capricious dimension. Reputation (*fama*) naturally had a more political than economic value, even if the Latinist J.-P. Néraudau observes that in Rome, in the course of time, "*la fama, régulatrice de la morale publique et privée, est devenue une commère versatile et vénale*" (free translation: "the fama, regulator of public and private morality, became a versatile and venal gossip.") Indeed, this author underlines that, etymologically, it is only a confused noise, a minimal degree of speech; that it often manifests itself in its representation by mixing the true and the false; and that it is translated in its practice as an unconscious and spontaneous impulse rather than as a rational evaluation (which would be the *existimatio*). It is moreover of unstable value, sometimes positive, sometimes negative, so that the term famosus will evolve from the meaning "*décrié*" ("decried") to "*fameux*" ("famous") between the Republic and the Empire (J.-P. Néraudau, "La fama dans la Rome antique", *Médiévales*, 1993, No. 24).

possible visibility through the best referencing, the best rating, the best opinions or the greatest number of likes/followers. As a result, one of the major risks they face, (4) and which they are therefore required to regulate, lies in the mechanisms of reputation manipulation. (5)

2. This manipulation can be carried out by professional users or by the platforms themselves. Users seek to improve their search engine ranking with SEO (*Search Engine Optimization*) techniques, which can be more or less artificial and questionable. In some cases, in order to harm other operators, some of them deliberately implement SEO techniques which are prohibited by search engines on a competitor's site (so-called *negative* SEO practices) to generate a bad reputation. Google has often been suspected of, (6) and even condemned for, (7) intervening in rankings to benefit its own services (so-called *self-preferencing*) or setting its algorithms in an opaque manner. In other cases, platforms impose downgrading penalties that may appear questionable, or even suspend or exclude user accounts or websites on more or less well-founded grounds of illegal content. Such assessment is often based on techniques linked to artificial reputation (infringing products or content, misleading advertisement, etc.).

3. In other cases, the manipulation of reputation on platforms is a matter of credibility of the users. It is the main issue concerning false reviews, positive (8) (in favour of the user) or negative (against a competitor), which are the main concerns on rating platforms (such as Tripadvisor), intermediation platforms (such as Uber) or marketplaces (such as Amazon). This false renown can also be the result of false clicks on buttons or of false subscribers, which are techniques implemented by click farms (9) or bots which simulate fictitious IP addresses. In some cases, the platforms themselves are suspected of being lenient about these manipulations, as

(4) Apart from the risks related to online hate, as well as the removal of content that may characterise or encourage the commission of various offences (terrorism, child pornography, fraud, counterfeiting, etc.).

(5) In the above-mentioned article, J.-P. Néraudau shows that, as early as ancient Rome, there was a fear of the manipulation of reputation by *homo novus* who wanted to gain a political position. So much so that Cato the Elder, fearing such manipulation, favoured the anonymity of victorious generals to avoid the exaltation of the leader and the orchestration of a complacent *fama*.

(6) *Autorité de la concurrence – ADLC* (French Competition Authority), opinion, 14 December 2010.

(7) European Commission, 27 June 2017, *Google Search (Shopping)*, AT.39740, confirmed by EU General Court, 10 November 2021, T-612/17.

(8) Journalist Oobah Butler used fake reviews to get his fictitious garden shed restaurant at the top of Tripadvisor's London restaurant rankings, even though he never served a meal there and the photographs showed dishes with shaving cream and coffee grounds.

(9) https://www.lesechos.fr/2017/06/les-fermes-a-clic-ces-usines-a-fabriquer-une-fausse-notoriete-sur-le-web-174325

not only do they earn revenues, proportional to the reputation of the cheaters, but their own credibility is at stake.

4. These reputation issues are not just a matter of coquetry, but of market regulation. In an economy that is increasingly based on online activity, even independently of sales through the monetisation of advertising traffic, and increasingly depersonalised in terms of relations with merchants, customer trust is essentially based on the quantitative dimension of the various rating and ranking mechanisms. The competition between operators to acquire the best reputation or the largest audience is therefore an essential factor in economic performance since it promises sales (10) (in proportion to the transformation rate) or advertising revenue. (11)

5. The main characteristics of the necessary reputation policing lie in the low unitary stakes of reputation offences (12) and in the massive nature of the relevant information. (13) The identification of an isolated false opinion has little economic consequence. Nicolas Colin and Henri Verdier have pointed out that the platform model is based on the economics of the multitude, (14) in which exchanges and interactions bring together a large number of users. There is also the viral nature of online reputation effects. The kinetic of information and its replication leads to such a fast dissemination that the speed of the corrective response to a reputational anomaly appears all the more necessary.

6. However, the justice system, in spite of possible complaints, is very ill-adapted to dealing with this type of disputes. It generally takes several weeks, or even months, to reach a decision, including in cases of emergency procedures. It relies on an individualised analysis of situations, a formalism and a contradictory analysis of circumstances, by counsels and magistrates, which involve resources that are disproportionate to

(10) Improved ranking on Amazon, as determined by the customer satisfaction score, can lead to an estimated 5 to 10 times increase in sales, *in* V. Coquaz and I. Halissat, *La nouvelle guerre des étoiles*, Paris, Kero, 2020.

(11) For content publishers, whose advertising space is often marketed using the resources of the same platforms, notably Google, which was recently condemned for abusing its dominant position by favouring its own interests in the auctioning of space *Autorité de la concurrence*, decision No. 21-D-11, 7 June 2021).

(12) Most of the practices mentioned (false positive reviews, false followers, false likes) in this study are likely to be qualified as misleading commercial practices within the meaning of Article L. 121-2 of the *Code de la consommation* (French Consumer Code). In other cases, they may consist of acts of unfair competition by competitors (denigration, false negative reviews, negative SEO), or even anti-competitive practices (self-preferencing of dominant platforms).

(13) In 2018, Google announced that it had sent website managers 180 million decisions regarding alleged manipulations of their site's ranking.

(14) N. Colin and H. Verdier, *L'âge de la multitude*, Malakoff, Armand Colin, 2012.

the stakes of false reputation. Finally, it is generally unable to assess the technical factors for identifying the origin and materiality of reputational manipulations.

7. In these circumstances, it appears that the platforms themselves exercise their own jurisdiction (Court-type activity) over reputation, by virtue of various obligations incumbent on them and at the cost of their credibility. They are led to seek out, identify and then sanction practices which distort competition on the merits of reputation. Given the massiveness of the information, these platforms use algorithmic means, in particular artificial intelligence, to automatically process not only the detection of manipulation, but also decisions to remove illegitimate content. This jurisdictionality appears particularly unique and almost contradictory to the essence of the function of judging, since it emanates from a machine-device that is placed under the responsibility of a stakeholder in the reputation market (the platform). The impossible equation of jurisdictionality without jurisdiction (I), calls for new forms of processual grammar (II).

I. THE ALGORITHMIC TREATMENT OF REPUTATION: JURISDICTIONALITY WITHOUT JURISDICTION AND WITHOUT LAW

8. An analysis of the way platforms detect and deal with reputation problems shows that they borrow characteristic features of court ruling, without having its legal attributes (A). However, beyond considerations linked to the instability of the notion of jurisdiction, the exercise of this similar jurisdictionality reveals a radical change in our legal concepts by giving normative power to data itself (B).

A. The simili-jurisdictional nature of platforms

9. The way in which platforms detect and remedy reputational manipulation is, overall, still rather uncertain and kept relatively secret, including from agencies whose mission is to improve the visibility and reputation of their clients. For example, regarding search engine ranking manipulation (which Google refers to as *webspamming*), we know that Google (which represents more than 90% of search queries) performs automated downgrading of sites that do not comply with its guidelines or which constitute "other deceptive practices" not designated by Google. (15) However, in the European Commission's proceedings, where Google favoured its own Google Shopping service by arbitrarily downgrading competing services, Google requested that the response to its downgrading algorithm be considered as protected by business confidentiality. Google is consequently explicitly claiming to rank results by non-transparent algorithmic means (16) and to arbitrate on bad SEO practices based on equally secret algorithms. (17) Each of these tools now incorporates artificial intelligence (18) for the automatic processing of natural language, which mathematically models content and analyses it by using machine learning.

10. Similarly, in its fight against fraudulent reviews, TripAdvisor claims to have an automated review analysis system based on "state-of-the-art analysis technology," (19) while refusing to disclose its exact parameters. (20) The company justifies this by the risk of users committing fraud when knowing these parameters, but also by the alignment of its interests with those of the users, arguing that "if people do not find the content reliable and useful, they will not come back to TripAdvisor." The lack of transparency is an argument of authority and serves itself as an authority to avoid any discussion on the reliability of this control. Faced with criticism about the authenticity of its reviews, TripAdvisor defends itself: "People [who criticise reliability] do not have access to technical data. We do." (21) As a result, for the two major platforms, Google and TripAdvisor, the algorithmic detection of false reputation is explicitly locked in black boxes.

11. However, when necessary, the processing of alleged manipulations by publishers is also subjected to a second level of human processing. By using TripAdvisor platform, if the automated system detects a suspicious review or if someone reports it, the review is sent to a moderation team

(15) European Commission, 27 June 2017, *Google Search (Shopping)*, para. 347-348.

(16) Google says: "To preserve the integrity of search results, it is important that we keep details about how search works out of the hands of dishonest individuals and spammers who try to manipulate our systems and promote misleading and low-quality content", https://www.google.com/intl/fr/search/howsearchworks/mission/creators/.

(17) Google states that it "invests in quality algorithms and conducts manual checks to prevent sites from improving their ranking in search results through manipulation or deceptive techniques."

(18) In particular the RankBrain algorithm, used since 2015.

(19) Tripadvisor 2019 review transparency report, https://www.tripadvisor.fr/TripAdvisorInsights/wp-content/uploads/2019/09/2147_PR_Content_Transparency_Report_11Aug19_fr_FR.pdf.

(20) Tripadvisor does reveal some parameters such as the location or characteristics of the device used to post the review or the frequency of reviews, but this limited information does not allow for sufficient predictability or a discussion of good application.

(21) *Ibid.*

which carries out an "in-depth analysis" and decides whether the publication criteria have been met. At Google, human intervention is more questionable and more processual. Google has admitted that human intervention in referencing exists independently of any user manipulation. (22) Through a subtle articulation between automatic and human means, a form of reputational jurisdiction is implemented by Google, leading to demotions or deletions of content pages in the referencing. In practice, publishers are notified of processing events by Google in the Search Console. The search engine offers them the possibility to "appeal removals once violations have been addressed" by submitting a "reconsideration request" to "human reviewers," which requires the applicant to explain the problem, describe the steps to resolve it and describe the result. (23) Google applies a processual form which borrows from proto-jurisdictionality. Nevertheless, it does not respect the principle of adversarial proceedings, since it expressly asks "not to send any other request before knowing the outcome of the appeal."

12. The way in which platforms intervene in reputational disputes has little in common with the role of a court in the sense of the Court of Justice of the European Union (CJEU). For the EU Court of Justice, the concept of a court or jurisdiction is subject to a series of criteria. It requires the considered authority to be established by law, to be permanent, to have subject matter competence, to act in accordance with an adversary procedure, to rule on the basis of applicable Law and to be independent. (24) But this definition is so strict that bodies which appear to fulfil the functions of courts are not considered to be courts. This is the case of several independent administrative authorities, particularly in the competition (25) field. Usually, these authorities are actual third parties in relation to the authority which submits a decision to them and their control is administrative by nature. The notion of jurisdiction appears all the more contingent as it is different from the notion of a court within the meaning of Article 6 of the European Convention for the Protection of Human Rights

(22) European Commission, 27 June 2017, *Google Search (Shopping)*, paras. 347-348.

(23) https://www.google.com/intl/en_us/search/howsearchworks/how-search-works/detecting-spam/.

(24) ECJ, 17 September 1997, *Dorsch Consult*, case C-54/96, pt 23.

(25) CJEU, 16 September 2020, *Anesco*, case C-462/19 (about the Spanish Competition authority); decision of the *Cour de cassation* (French Cout of cassation), *2ᵉ Chambre civile* (Second Civil Chamber), 30 September 2021, *FS-B+R* (about the French Competition Authority), No. 20-18.672.

and Fundamental Freedoms, which must be respected by competition authorities in terms of independence and impartiality.(26)

13. The legal diversity of bodies empowered to settle disputes seems to leave room for the conception of a meta-jurisdictional system in which platforms could exist. However, the characteristics are so different that the observer cannot fail to be confused. The jurisdictionality of these platforms is characterised by two major and relatively unexpected features: the absence of transparent rules along with the absence of actual rules resulting from the normative power of data, and cooperation between men and machines.

B. *Data is Law*, the normative power of data

14. By entrusting the identification and treatment of abuse to a "fraud model to identify electronic features undetectable to the human eye,"(27) TripAdvisor (like all other platforms or operators, particularly in the banking sector, for the detection of fraud) operates a regulation that is not based on a syllogism comparing a predefined rule (major or thesis) to a specific situation (minor or hypothesis) in order to deduce a solution. The algorithm classifies typical and atypical behaviour from which it infers abnormal behaviour with respect to centroids. Clusters that deviate from these centroids appear more or less suspicious, so that, through a probabilistic induction model, fraud is defined as a statistical deviance.

15. Considering the volume and the economic stakes of this regulation, one can only be troubled by the mutation from a dispute settlement system based on rules expressed as predicative statements to a probabilistic and inductive modelling. This approach negates the fundamental characteristics of the legal rule, including its abstract and general character, which makes it possible to ensure the predictability of the legal rule. On the contrary, this method is merely inferred from the data. One would be tempted to admit that *Data is Law*, in order to update Lawrence Lessig's famous saying (*Code is Law*(28)). However, this regulatory power of data,

(26) ECHR, 4 March 2014, *Grande Stevens and a. v. Italie*, Nos. 18640/10, 18647/10, 18663/10, 18668/10 and 18698/10, *D.*, 2015, 1506, obs. C. Mascala.

(27) Tripadvisor 2019 report on review transparency, *op. cit.*, p. 11, free translation of: "*modélisation de la fraude pour relever des constantes électroniques indétectables à l'œil humain.*"

(28) L. Lessig, "Code is Law, On Liberty in Cyberspace", *Harvard Magazine*, January-February 2000, https://www.harvardmagazine.com/2000/01/code-is-law-html. In this article, Lessig shows that freedoms in cyberspace are essentially determined by software code. For the first time, he highlights a new form of regulatory source from computer technology.

resulting from its algorithmic exploitation (often by artificial intelligence), raises decisive stakes. From the point of view of the rule itself, it raises the question of transparency and legal certainty, as well as the shift of control from probabilistic law to the search for statistical bias. From the point of view of the resulting Court-type decision making, it reveals a collective and teleological form.

16. The lack of predictability of the norm clashes with the fundamental requirement of legal certainty, which has acquired a higher place in the hierarchy of norms by having constitutional value. (29) Together with its corollaries, namely legitimate expectations (particularly in German and European Union Law) and the requirement that the law must be intelligible, legal certainty is a cardinal value of our legal system. Platforms' users whose reputation is determined, among other things, by algorithmic fraud detection mechanisms, find themselves in a similar situation as the tortured man in Kafka's *In the Penal Colony*. This man discovers the meaning of law and judgment only by the engraving of an abstruse text on his flesh. Kafka observes that "it is a torment to be governed by laws of which one is ignorant." Alain Supiot rightly sees this as a critique of the collapse of legality in the unleashing of industrial power. (30)

17. However, the statistical regulation of fraud seems to enjoy a fairly wide social acceptance. This phenomenon is undoubtedly linked to the perception, still often shared, that numbers do not lie. Nevertheless, it is now perfectly clear that the challenge of algorithmic regulation, particularly with regard to machine learning algorithms, lies in debiasing the source data and the algorithms themselves. These biases, whether voluntary or involuntary, are cognitive biases of designers of data models and algorithms, statistical biases of data collection and processing, or economic biases. (31) Their eradication, either by human means of correction or by algorithmic means, represents a challenge that is all the more considerable because it is based on new techniques and approaches to regulation.

(29) See for ex. M. de Salvia, "La sécurité juridique en droit constitutionnel français", *Cah. Cons. Const.*, December 2001, No. 11.

(30) A. Supiot, "Un artiste de la loi", *Le nouveau magazine littéraire*, February 2019, No. 14, *Kafka dossier*.

(31) P. Bertail, D. Bounie, S. Clémençon and P. Waelbroeck, *Algorithmes: biais, discrimination et équité*, Télécom ParisTech, February 2019, https://www.telecom-paris.fr/wp-content-EvDsK19/uploads/2019/02/Algorithmes-Biais-discrimination-equite.pdf.

Moreover, even if the artificial intelligences implemented within the framework of the platforms that are the subject of this study would not constitute high-risk AI, the draft European regulation currently under discussion subjects this second type of AI to strong requirements of bias prevention and rectification. (32)

18. In contrast to the usual individualised and singularised treatment of disputes, the algorithmic sanctioning of fraud proceeds from a computational analysis of the phenomena of the multitude. Rather than an individual assessment, this jurisdictionality bases its rationality on a law of large numbers that defines deviance in relation to centroid behaviour. The multitude, which is one of the fundamental characteristics of the digital economy of platforms, (33) thus appears both as a constraint on regulation and as a resource for its effectiveness.

19. Although the idea of collective jurisdiction is *prima facie* difficult to conceive, it is nevertheless found in archaic forms of justice (34) as well as in various modern forms. (35) Moreover, its justification lies not only in its methodology and technical constraints, but also in the very essence of compliance, namely its teleological character. As Marie-Anne Frison-Roche points out, the essence of Compliance Law is to "place the normativity of rules, decisions and reasoning in the goals pursued" (36) in order to satisfy its "useful effect." In this case, the effectiveness of the detection and treatment of false reputation requires that an approach based on massive data and systematic treatment be preferred to individual assessments, which would necessarily be ineffective.

20. The combination of the algorithmic phenomena of extremely limited adversary process and of the absence of pre-established rules and impartiality, creates a look-alike jurisdiction that appears both necessary

(32) The proposal for a regulation of the European Parliament and of the Council laying down harmonised rules on artificial intelligence (Artificial Intelligence Act), in its Article 10 provides that datasets must be "relevant, representative, free of errors and complete", that they must have "appropriate statistical properties" and that they must be subject to bias analysis and evolution throughout the data collection and processing chain.

(33) N. Colin and H. Verdier, *L'âge de la multitude, op. cit.*

(34) F. Ost, *Raconter la loi, aux sources de l'imaginaire juridique*, Paris, Odile Jacob, 2004. The author describes the way in which Aeschylus, in his trilogy of *The Oresteia*, shows the invention of justice through the transition from clan vindictiveness to individual responsibility under the function of a third party embodied by the figure of Athena.

(35) For example, group actions in civil matters or truth and reconciliation commissions in transitional and restorative justice.

(36) M.-A. Frison-Roche, "Dessiner les cercles du droit de la compliance", in *Études en la mémoire de Philippe Neau-Leduc. Le juriste dans la cité*, "Mélanges" Serie, Paris, LGDJ/Lextenso, 2018, pp. 483-496, free translation of: "*placer la normativité des règles, décisions et raisonnements, dans les buts poursuivis.*"

and atypical. But the risks and disadvantages which result from this represent a challenge for Compliance Law which is supposed to provide a framework.

II. THE OUTLINE OF AN ALTERNATIVE AND PARTICIPATORY JURISDICTION

21. Faced with confusing mechanisms that algorithms can have, French and European legislators are currently implementing a regulation for platform processes that we identify here as a form of jurisdictionality. While recognising the legitimacy of the platforms' function in this area, the legislators' approach oscillates between a traditional conception that consists in seeking to restore a transparent and contradictory framework (A) and a more innovative approach that consists in conferring a determining role upon third parties (B).

A. Limited and illusory transparency and adversarial system

22. To remedy the opacity of the platforms' algorithmic empire, regulations are gradually taking shape to impose both greater transparency and the possibility of a genuine adversary procedure based on sufficient human intervention.

23. Based on the belief that the algorithms used to classify and detect fraud are neutral, platforms have long been reluctant to reveal the underlying principles which govern them. However, several successive laws have forced them to be more transparent. In 2016, the French *law for a Digital Republic*(37) introduced provisions in the *Code de la consommation* (French Consumer Code)(38) that not only define the notion of online platform (by characterising them essentially by their content referencing function,(39) and their ability to influence reputation) but also subject

(37) French law No. 2016-1321 of 7 October 2016, *pour une République numérique* (for a Digital Republic).

(38) Current Articles L. 111-7 and following, later modified.

(39) Article L. 111-7, I: "*Est qualifiée d'opérateur de plateforme en ligne toute personne physique ou morale proposant, à titre professionnel, de manière rémunérée ou non, un service de communication au public en ligne reposant sur : 1° Le classement ou le référencement, au moyen d'algorithmes informatiques, de contenus, de biens ou de services proposés ou mis en ligne par des tiers ; 2° Ou la mise en relation de plusieurs parties en vue de la vente d'un bien, de la fourniture d'un service ou de l'échange ou du partage d'un contenu, d'un bien ou d'un service.*" (free translation: "Any natural or legal person offering, on a professional basis, whether paid or not, an online public communication service based on: 1° The classification or referencing, by means of

them to the requirement to disclose the criteria for ranking offers. (40) The so-called "Omnibus" Directive dated 27 November 2019 (41) extended this requirement to the whole European Union with regards to "the main parameters determining the ranking [...] and the relative importance of those parameters." (42) It is therefore odd that the chosen point of view for the construction of this transparency requirement is the one of consumer protection, the recipient of the information, rather than the one of the user companies whose reputation is at stake. It is only in parallel, in the context of the Platform to Business Regulation, (43) that the European legislator has provided for a relatively similar requirement (44) applicable to platforms for the purposes of informing businesses using their services in their general terms and conditions. (45) The legislator intends to remedy this asymmetry of information regarding the regulation of reputation resulting from referencing by making the rule explicit rather than leaving it to the discretion and arbitrariness of the platforms. However, this transparency is relatively incapacitated by the fact that the engines may only reveal the "main parameters," and furthermore these parameters may only represent "the most important" in determining, "individually or collectively," the listing. Article 5(6) also states that platforms cannot be required to disclose algorithms if knowledge of them would allow them to manipulate search results.

24. Similarly, it is Consumer Law that has introduced transparency in terms of monitoring online reviews on platforms. Here again, it was the *law for a Digital Republic* which compelled platforms to disclose the methods

computer algorithms, of content, goods or services offered or put online by third parties; 2° Or the bringing together of several parties with a view to the sale of a good, the provision of a service or the exchange or sharing of a content, good or service.")

(40) Article L. 111-7, II.

(41) Directive 2019/2161 of 27 November 2019 as regards the better enforcement and modernisation of Union consumer protection rules.

(42) Article 3 of Directive (EU) 2019/2161 creating a new misleading commercial practice by omission subject to the demonstration of an unfairness of the said practice, this demonstration being proof of a possible effect on the economic behavior of the consumer.

(43) Regulation (EU) 2019/1150 of 20 June 2019 on promoting fairness and transparency for business users of online intermediation services, whose incorporation into French Law led to the law *loi portant diverses dispositions d'adaptation au droit de l'Union européenne dans les domaines de l'économie, de la santé, du travail, des transports et de l'agriculture* – DDADUE (on various provisions for adaptation to European Union Law in the fields of the economy, health, work, transport and agriculture) sanctioning violations of the regulation as an unfair commercial practice between companies punishable by a fine of up to 5 % of turnover.

(44) Article 5 of Regulation 2019/1150.

(45) Article 7 of the Regulation also requires platforms to disclose any preferential treatment given to the platform itself regarding referencing, although this does not in itself prohibit discriminatory treatment; although the Digital Markets Act (DMA) Regulation provides for a ban on such self-preferencing in favour of gatekeepers, Article 6, d.

of publishing and processing reviews by describing the main means of moderation. The so-called "Omnibus" Directive is more challenging since, in addition to this information obligation, it makes the publication of consumer reviews conditional on the implementation of "reasonable and proportionate" measures to verify that these reviews originate from consumers. However, these transparency obligations remain largely insufficient to describe the complexity of algorithmic systems, leaving operators with a wide discretionary power.

25. It is also clear that the issue is not only one of transparency but also of an effective adversary procedure. Even before considering the process of challenging the algorithmic decision that has consequences for reputation, the first guarantee expected from the people affected lies in sufficient human intervention preceding any effect of the automated system. To date, in most cases, there is no prohibition against processing measures that are based exclusively on fully automated processing.(46) The European Regulation on a *Single Market For Digital Services*,(47) usually referred to as the *Digital Services Act* (DSA), provides details on human-machine interaction in the area of moderation of illegal content (including content affecting the reputation of users). As a result of the combination of Articles 14, 16 and 17 of the said regulation, the platforms will be able to detect and remove (or refuse to remove) illegal content (in particular regarding misleading advertisement resulting from false reviews, defamation, denigration) on the basis of a system based exclusively on algorithms. It is only starting from the appeal against the algorithmic decision, within the internal complaints system,(48) that human intervention becomes mandatory. It is therefore a real system of algorithmic jurisdiction over reputation, and more generally over illegal content,(49) by the platforms that the legislator is forced to approve if it wants to ensure efficient control over massive data.

(46) Article 22 of the General Data Protection Regulation prohibits taking decisions on the basis of such automated processing only in the case of personal data and for decisions having a legal effect or significantly affecting the data subject in a way similar to a legal effect.

(47) Regulation (EU) 2022/2065 of 19 October 2022 *on a Single Market For Digital Services*, entered into force on 17 February 2024.

(48) Article 20 of Regulation 2022/2065.

(49) This is particularly the case for hateful content, to the extent that the *Tribunal judiciaire de Paris* (Paris First Instance Civil Court) ordered Twitter, in a judgment of 6 July 2021, to make known, with a view to improving them, the algorithmic means of combating content that incites hatred and violence (*Tribunal judiciaire de Paris*, 6 July 2021, RG No. 20/53181).

26. However, the emergence of an adversary procedure will have to appear before human intervention. Article 17 of the DSA provides that the decision to remove illegal content must be reasoned and needs to contain the facts and circumstances on which the decision is based, as well as its legal basis and the reasoning for the violation of the rule. The regulation considers the conditions for a potential contradictory discussion of the automated decision, by ensuring that the language of the machine is accessible to human users through clear, easily understandable, precise and specific information. This accessibility is not only individualised, but also has a case-law scope, since Articles 15 and 24 will compel platforms to publish their reasoned decisions by specifically indicating the possible error rate of algorithmic means.

27. One might think that the procedure for challenging the algorithmic decision would have the purpose and effect of restoring the balance between platforms and users. But while the DSA requires human intervention (50) at the complaints handling stage in accordance with an easily accessible, expeditious and objective procedure, there is still no burden of proof at this stage and no guarantee of a minimum of impartiality by an independent panel. (51) In the Platform to Business Regulation, the complaint handling system appears even less processual under satisfactory conditions. Article 11 does not provide for any real adversary procedure, nor any normative reference, requirement to state reasons, evidence, guarantee of impartiality, or prohibition of exclusively algorithmic processing.

28. The regulations that have just been adopted give the platforms a high degree of freedom in the algorithmic treatment of reputation. The significant asymmetry of information, the limited adversary process, and, above all, anchor and authoritative effects of algorithmic processing, make it difficult to challenge decisions. Moreover, although transparency and adversary procedures are essential indicators of balanced jurisdiction in our normative reference system for resolving disputes, the legislator's apparent resignation in dealing with their ineffectiveness in individual situations, suggests that there is something else at play. In this case, it seems to us that it is the role entrusted to third parties in the apprehension of a collective regulation.

(50) Article 20 of Regulation 2022/2065 (this human intervention being at least partial since an exclusively algorithmic decision would be prohibited).

(51) Article 20(6) only requires that the decision be taken "under the supervision of appropriately qualified staff," without specifying the conditions of competence or independence.

B. A singular governance of jurisdictionality: the role of third parties

29. It would be illusory to think that users would be able to deal on their own with debates as complex and costly as the unravelling of data and algorithms, manipulations that platforms can exert to their advantage or inadequacies of control. As a matter of fact, the performance of review moderation by major platforms is only usefully challenged by operators with the appropriate technical resources. For example, Fakespot, which was recently removed from the Apple Store under pressure from Amazon,(52) uses its own artificial intelligence system to analyse the credibility of reviews. Similarly, in the *Google Shopping* case before the European Commission, the demonstration of the manipulation of referencing by Google was largely based on the analysis of the company Sistrix. The Commission's decision indicates that the weekly visibility index calculated by Sistrix showed a sharp drop in the ranking of price comparison sites in favour of Google Shopping when Google's new algorithm (Panda(53)) was launched. This vigilance requires not only financial resources and specific expertise, but also access to a significant volume of data(54) to exercise a countervailing power to the regulation of platforms.

30. The DSA is counting on these watchdogs to contribute to the effectiveness of the reporting of illegal content. The regulation creates a status of Trusted Flaggers,(55) which will be conferred by national coordinators of digital services, and which will require them to prove a particular expertise in detecting illegal content, the representation of collective interests and independence from relevant platforms. These whistleblowers will be given priority in examining their notifications and would, by their own status, have far greater credibility towards the platforms and courts.

31. This status of representation of collective interests is fully aligned with the phenomenon linked to the multitude of users and to a form of collective jurisdiction. Reputation appears almost as a common good justifying its own governance mechanisms. In this case, this status reflects the conception of a mutualised and participative regulation justifying a

(52) https://www.lefigaro.fr/secteur/high-tech/qu-est-ce-que-fakespot-cette-application-detectrice-de-faux-avis-qui-fache-amazon-20210723.

(53) European Commission, 27 June 2017, *Google Search (Shopping)*, *op. cit.*, para. 361.

(54) The Commission's decision on Google Shopping states that Sistrix uses a sample of one million keywords and analyses the first one hundred Google Search results for each.

(55) Regulation 2022/2065 of 19 October 2022, Article 22.

syndication of interests which, otherwise, would not be represented. The collective and participatory scope of this regulation is supported by the publication in a database of decisions taken by the platforms following complaints (56) compiled in an annual report. (57) Platforms would also be forced to detail, in another report, the purpose of their moderation algorithms as well as the related opportunity indicators. (58) All this information would obviously be extremely useful for Trusted Flaggers' missions…

32. However original it may seem in this system of jurisdictionality, the role of third parties in the judicial process is not as ground-breaking as one might think. Expert third parties can already be found in various procedural systems. This is the case, for example, of the *Amicus Curiae* called upon to give its opinion before a court. In addition, there are now roles for third-party watchdogs in the process of detecting offences. This is obviously the case of the whistleblower who plays an essential role in various areas of compliance. A little further away, the figure of the sycophant is another similar function. If his method of payment (59) had not led him astray and given him a despicable reputation, the sycophant initially appeared to be an essential sentinel in the functioning of Athenian democracy. (60) The Trusted Flaggers would thus combine the role of a vigilant third party with that of an expert third party, which to us seems to foreshadow the decisive and original role that they could play in this unique configuration of jurisdictionality.

33. The role of a third party appears geometrically unavoidable when platforms are simultaneously authors of decisions and interested parties. Another third party must therefore intervene as a possibility for a renewed form of jurisdictionality. This removal of part of the function of impartiality, like all the other characteristics of alternative jurisdictionality that we have described, translates into a new processual grammar.

*

* *

(56) Regulation 2022/2065 of 19 October 2022, Article 24, § 5.

(57) *Ibid.*, Article 15.

(58) *Ibid.*, Article 24.

(59) Collected from the fine imposed on the offender.

(60) N. Warembourg, "Le sycophante, un lanceur d'alerte? Remarques historiques sur la délation et le délateur dans l'Athènes démocratique", *in* M. Disant and D. Pollet-Panoussis (eds), *Les lanceurs d'alerte*, Paris, LGDJ, 2017, p. 53.

34. It is not so surprising that the upsurge of platforms into a process designed to resolve disputes has the effect of profoundly transforming the grammar and even the language of jurisdictionality. Marie-Anne Frison-Roche and Jérémy Heymann (61) have emphasised in this respect, with reference to Michel Foucault, how the prosecutor's and judge's functions exercising by a company under the injunction of compliance mechanisms, makes it both difficult and imperative to correlate words and things, while companies are working to bring the use of such powers under the jurisdictional vocabulary.

35. This earthquake in the language of Law and jurisdiction caused by compliance is, in the end, quite natural as soon as a party invites itself into the trial and is no longer external to it. Roland Barthes, for example, noted that Flaubert revolutionised the field of novel writing by allowing the subjectivity of the "writer" to emerge in the text through enunciation. (62) By no longer being "*extérieur à sa plume*" ("external to his pen"), the writer is no longer the "*simple procureur*" ("mere prosecutor") of a writing of something for an external cause. Barthes then demonstrates that this new writing is the expression of the verbal form of *mesotes*, that is, of the middle way described by Benveniste. The great linguist showed in a famous article (63) that between the active and passive voices of the sentence, each of which expresses a certain position of the subject in relation to the verb (diathesis), Latin and Greek admit a middle voice. In active diathesis, the subject performs the action. In passive diathesis, the action is performed by the subject. But in the middle voice, the subject no longer performs the action for another but for himself, affecting himself. The example Barthes takes in his text cannot fail to strike the compliance lawyer in this respect. He illustrates the active diathesis with the Greek expression *Nomous tithênai* (making laws for the city). The corresponding middle diathesis would then be *Nomous tithéstai* (making laws by including oneself in them). Now, it is precisely this inclusion of the subject in the process of the verb (thus of the action, of the norm) that expresses both the revolution in Flaubert's writing and the normative revolution that is compliance. For the very essence of compliance is the inclusion of the company not only in the production of norms but also, as this book

(61) M.-A. Frison-Roche, "The judge-judged. Articulating words and reality in the face of a conflict of interests", *this book*; J. Heymann, "The Legal Nature of the Facebook 'Supreme Court'", *this book*.

(62) R. Barthes, *La préparation du roman. Cours au Collège de France 1978-79 et 1979-80*, Class session of 8 December 1979, Paris, Seuil, 1979, p. 345.

(63) E. Benveniste, *Problèmes de linguistique générale*, Paris, Gallimard, t. I, 1966.

highlights, in a jurisdictional process in which it is led to become a prosecutor and judge of itself and of third parties.

36. The relationship between Law and language is so close that, in the rich book he has devoted to it,(64) Alain Sériaux sees language as an essential vector of performativity, which – he observes – is singularly true in *jurisdictio*, where Law is intimately linked to the way it is said.

37. But then, what would be this profound transformation of language conveyed by compliance? It is, of course, the one which is linked to the need to monitor a considerable volume of information, which constitutes so many risks in the pursuit of the monumental goals assigned to it. This language is the one of data and of artificial intelligence algorithms that give them meaning and scope. As we have seen, this way of "making data speak" in an inductive process gives rise to new normative forms that disrupt the characteristics of those we know. Artificial intelligence is clearly a different way of expressing ideas. This is so true that the experiment that led to two chatbots negotiating with each other led to the invention of a language of their own.(65)

38. We can thus understand the extent to which the jurisdiction of platforms, like the one of all companies that act as prosecutors and judges for themselves and others, borrows so little from the forms of jurisdiction that we know.

---

(64) A. Sériaux, *Le droit comme langage*, Paris, LexisNexis, 2020.

(65) E. Moreira, "Quand l'intelligence artificielle invente un langage incompréhensible par l'homme", *Les Échos* 24 June 2017, https://www.lesechos.fr/2017/06/quand-lintelligence-artificielle-invente-un-langage-incomprehensible-par-lhomme-174329.

The company judges itself: the Compliance function in the bank

ALAIN BRUNEAU

Chief Compliance Officer – Natixis

It is in the aftermath of the 1929 crisis that the first financial regulators appeared in the United States. Very quickly, these newly created regulators adopted the first laws and regulations concerning the sale and distribution of financial instruments, the insider information regime, among others, and in the wake of this, the compliance function was born.

It is first of all a function created by the regulator itself as a necessary tool of Regulatory Law, implementing compliance with the rules it sets out and which are specific to this industry. The compliance function was in a way an auxiliary of the regulator, within the banking institution, ensuring the proper understanding and application of the standards. Over time, and often as a result of new disorders or abuses, new rules were adopted and the compliance function developed and specialised. With the increasing complexity and stacking of standards, a need for anticipation has also emerged. By focusing more and more on the identification and the assessment of risks, compliance implements the required framework to respond to these risks even before a norm is adopted.

A preventive system has several advantages: i) it reduces the cost of compliance following the adoption of the norm; ii) it possibly avoids the sanction adopted in application of general principles, even in the absence of a norm. As such, the compliance function has, over time, shifted from the *ex post* to the *ex ante*, which is a characteristic of the newly created Compliance Law.

The consequences of the Libor manipulation scandal are an example of the movement from *ex post* to *ex ante* and of the development of Compliance Law. Indeed, from 2008 onwards, investigations by the American and then British regulators were opened concerning agreements and manipulations by certain traders of major banking institutions of the "Libor" index. The London InterBank Offered Rate, the main private index rate in developed economies, is used as the basis for calculating variable interest rates of most contracts. This index is present in transactions between banks, and it is also directly referenced in contracts with individuals, for mortgages or consumer loans. According to the UK Treasury, at the time of the events, financial contracts with a Libor reference represented approximately 300,000 billion dollars.

Without going into too much detail, the calculation of the Libor index was carried out as follows. A pre-determined panel of the largest banks indicated each day at what rate they received interbank funding. These contributions were averaged, and this average rate published daily was the Libor of the day.

There are several reasons for manipulating a bank's contribution, the first being to take advantage of a distorted rate by taking advance positions in the rates market. A second reason, which was relevant at the time, is linked to the emerging subprime crisis in the mid-2000s. During the crisis, it was important for banks to show that they had not lost the confidence of their peers and that the rate at which they were borrowing on the interbank market was stable despite the huge number of losses expected on the so-called subprime contracts. Hence the practice by some banks of contributing a lower rate than the actual rate at which other banks were lending to them, which was supposed to reflect the continued confidence of the industry, but which was nevertheless a manipulation of the index.

It should be noted at this stage of the analysis that, at the time of the events, there was no regulation governing contributions to the Libor index. The applicable rules were based on practice between the contributing banks and were hardly reflected in a contract. The European directive on market abuse,(1) which was adopted in 2003, only concerned financial instruments and its scope of application excluded foreign exchange and indices. Similarly, in the United States, the Securities and Exchange Act of 1934, which essentially applied to the dissemination of information by listed companies, did not apply to a situation of this type.

(1) Directive 2003/6/EC of 28 January 2003 on insider dealing and market manipulation.

In 2008, the US and UK central banks decided to investigate what was becoming a "case," following warning emails and phone calls, including from Barclays officials. However, the various forums of discussions between the banks' compliance departments were divided: in fact, there were no applicable regulations, therefore no possible breach according to some; others referred to the monumental goals of compliance and preferred to establish supervising principles to behaviours that undermine confidence in the economy for the benefit of a few. Thus, even before the decisions of the American and British supervisors to impose sanctions, the compliance functions adopted codes of conduct aimed at regulating these activities and reinforced the training of officers and staff directly responsible for contributions to Libor, but also to other indices such as Euribor. As of 2010, Barclays Bank separated the functions responsible for contributing to the indices from those proprietary trading interest rate products. Banks have also implemented monitoring programmes for these contributions and in some cases, where it was clear that staff had acted dishonestly, banks have preferred to dismiss these staff, (2) thus acting as judges of themselves before the regulator's judgment.

The first sanctions were adopted in 2012 and the chief executive of Barclays stepped down. Investigations were opened against multiple banks and fines totalled several billion euros against banks involved in the calculation of Libor and other interbank rates. It was only later that legislators adopted specific regulations applicable to index contributions. The second European directive on market abuse, the drafting of which began in 2011 and that was adopted in July 2014, only came into force two years later, on 3 July 2016. It included the manipulation of indices before a specific European regulation on indices (3) completed the reprehensive dimension of the Markets Abuses Regulation (MAR) by introducing a code of conduct.

This case shows that the normative process applicable to Banking and Financial Law is not different from the legislative process concerning other branches of Law. It is often in response to a problem that the legislator adopts a law to regulate a practice and prevent the problem from recurring. What seems to be different with Compliance Law is that before the

(2) Royal Bank of Scotland was the first bank to publicly admit to firing four traders in 2011 for manipulating interbank rates.

(3) The European Regulation (EU) 2016/1011 of 8 June 2016 on benchmarks. While the Regulation was adopted in June 2016, the European Commission's proposal for a draft Regulation dates from September 2013, immediately following the first sanctions adopted.

norm is adopted, the company that becomes aware of a risk can implement internal policies, monitor their effectiveness, and take any sanctions if necessary. Chronologically, we can see that we are indeed in the *ex ante* phase.

The movement from *ex post* to *ex ante* raises a twofold question: on the one hand, in the absence of a public norm that has already been enacted and must be respected, what rules can the company or its compliance department institute and on what basis? (I); on the other hand, in the absence of a body to monitor the correct application of these internally enacted rules, how can the company, in this case the bank, judge its own rules? (II) We will try to answer these two questions in the light of existing practice in financial institutions.

I. WHAT RULES CAN THE COMPANY ESTABLISH IN THE ABSENCE OF A PUBLIC NORM, AND ON WHAT BASIS?

The Libor crisis described in the introduction showed that the mechanisms of Compliance Law were already in place and made it possible, to a certain extent, to mitigate the consequences for a number of institutions which, prior to any legislation, adopted a code of conduct dealing with the subject of indices. It is interesting to analyse the catalyst for this shift from Regulatory Law to Compliance Law within banks. And the key is one word: reputational risk.

The consideration of reputational risk for a banking institution should not be overlooked. Unlike other industries, a bank's main asset is the public's deposits, and these are directly linked to the confidence of depositors. A bank's tainted reputation can have direct negative consequences even for the largest institutions: impact on the share price, questions or even examinations from supervisors, loss of business opportunities, adoption of remediation plans, and, in the ultimate cases, loss of liquidity and core capital. The cascading effects are even more important for a listed bank. For example, bad news affects the share price. A weakened share price requires more liquidity or borrowing from the interbank market. Prudential ratios are impacted. Deteriorating prudential ratios may lead the central bank to put in place safeguard and resolution mechanisms.

The triptych confidence-liquidity-maintenance of prudential ratios is thus posed, and many recent examples attest to the fact that the loss of confidence can lead to the disappearance of the institution. The failure of Lehman Brothers in 2008 was first of all a loss of confidence in its financial solidity, which led to a liquidity crisis and the inability of this bank to refinance itself with its peers, precipitating its fall.

Reputational risk can be linked to the balance sheet, but also to a lack of compliance or sometimes unethical actions. It is because there is an action that the public considers unethical that there is a challenge to the reputation of the person who committed it. Consequently, reputational risk is closely associated with a breach of ethics or a controversial application of rules. A significant breach of reputational risk may thus be subject to further scrutiny by regulators, who themselves are ultimately accountable to the political and public authorities and the electorate.

It is therefore to avoid the direct consequences of a reputational breach, as well as to avoid the sanction that could be imposed by a regulator, that the identification of issues likely to have an impact on reputation must take place as early as possible. The reputational risk is at least as important as the risk of a sanction, it being understood that the sanction itself generates a reputational risk.

Most banks have set up reputation risk committees covering both the products or services offered and the customers. These committees do not deal with credit or market risk, risks traditionally considered by the banker, but rather with the impact on the bank's reputation of its product offering and the quality of its customers. This enshrines a reality already in place in the financial industry since the application of strict know-your-customer rules: the company judges its partners in the name of safeguarding its reputation risk.

This is why Compliance Law requires the bank to adopt measures to judge third parties (A) and the consideration of reputational risk leads the bank to refuse to enter into transactions with certain third parties (B).

A. The regulations require the implementation of measures that call on the company to judge third parties

The collapse of Lehman Brothers was the largest in history and the symbol of the beginning of the most severe global economic crisis since the Great Depression. The bankruptcy of a medium-sized bank triggered a systemic crisis in the entire financial sector. In France, the role of the *Autorité de Contrôle Prudentiel et de Résolution – ACPR* (French Banking Supervisory Authority) is to ensure the development and implementation of both prevention measures and resolution mechanisms for banking crises. Among the preventive factors is, of course, the management of reputational risk.

In the recent legislative arsenal, we can mention the French so-called "Sapin 2" law, (4) which has notably mandated to set up tools for detecting breaches that could affect the reputation of an institution. In its transparency section, this law strengthens the protection of whistleblowers and sets out ethical rules for lobbyists. In the fight against corruption, the creation of a specialised agency, the *Agence française anticorruption – AFA* (French Anti-Corruption Agency - AFA), has called for the production of risk assessments of activities linked to corruption and enhanced due diligence on third parties (clients/suppliers). It should be noted that since 2016, these tools concern all companies in France and are not specific to banks.

It is interesting to look at one of the provisions of the French so-called "Sapin 2" law, more precisely to a requirement of the guidelines issued by the *AFA* concerning knowledge of the supplier. While banks in France are already subject to the provisions of the *Code monétaire et financier* (French Monetary and Financial Code) on the elements to be collected to attest a proper Know-Your-Customer (KYC), the *AFA*'s guidelines apply some of these principles to all companies in France with regard to knowing their suppliers. Beyond the elements to be collected to establish knowledge of the identity of a supplier, each company must assess the risk of corruption according to its own methodology and establish a classification of suppliers according to a risk grid. Since banks already have such a risk classification for their clients, it could be extended to suppliers, after adaptation if necessary. Thus, in application of this risk classification, for suppliers whose risk is assessed as being higher, specific contractual provisions will be introduced in the contract requiring the supplier to address to the compliance department, on a regular basis, various elements including annual reports, or to authorise the persons ensuring the duty of vigilance on the supplier to conduct specific audits at the supplier's premises. If the supplier refuses to accept this commitment or to comply with it, the contract is either not concluded or terminated. This illustrates that, starting with a regulatory provision aimed at fighting against corruption, if one accepts

(4) French law No. 2016-1691 of 9 December 2016 sur la transparence, la lutte contre la corruption et la modernisation de la vie économique (on transparency, fight against corruption and modernisation of economic life).

that the *AFA* guidelines can constitute a regulatory norm or at least constitute soft law with a general scope, the company can require the supplier to comply with its own definition of the elements to be implemented for an effective anti-corruption programme, or else see its service provision relationship terminated. This termination is done under the governing law applicable to the contract but it is still the result of the company judging third parties.

The whistleblower mechanism is more explicit in that it obliges the company to judge itself this time, and not to judge its partners. It obliges the company to make available to its employees or third parties a system for collecting and processing alerts on its operations while protecting the whistleblowers. These alerts may be anonymous or not. In both cases, they require the company to consider the facts within the specific framework of handling whistleblower reports and, after taking the necessary steps, to draw the consequences both on an organisational and personal level. Thus, as a result of a report, the company can dismiss an employee who is at fault, whereas without the report, the company might not have detected anything. Internal investigation mechanisms, often entrusted to the internal audit, the general inspection, or the legal or compliance departments, are like an investigation. The person in charge has all the means and access to all the information held within the company to establish the certainty of the facts. This amounts to having the company's procedures, their correct application, or the behaviour of an employee judged by the company itself. This judgement does not take place within the usual framework of permanent or periodic controls, which aim to reduce risks and ensure effective management of the company, but they are carried out within the framework of a system which must determine, *in fine*, who is responsible for the alleged facts and what personal consequences should be drawn from this responsibility, if any.

B. Consideration of reputational risk allows to refuse certain transactions

We have seen that it is possible, in application of the *AFA*'s recommendations, to terminate the relationship with a third party, taking into consideration both a corruption risk classification and the lack of remediation proposed by the third party that the company deems to present a high corruption risk. Returning more specifically to the banking business, it is also possible for a bank or a financial service provider to unilaterally terminate certain transactions with its client. Here again, consideration of reputational risk is an important element.

A recent court decision illustrates how a bank could legitimately, unilaterally terminate the service offer made to a customer. In the specific case, a person arrested for having severely assaulted a police officer on the sidelines of a demonstration in Paris wished to appeal to the public to raise funds to cover the costs of his defence. The former boxer, who is on trial in this case, used an online fundraising service, allowing those who wished to contribute to his cause to donate by paying online on a site hosted by a banking institution and specialised in fundraising. This fundraising service also allows contributors to write a note supporting the cause of the fundraising if they so wish. As the case was covered by the media, the funds collected quickly reached 145,000 euros and the messages posted by some contributors were of a hateful nature and clearly indicated support for the beating of a law enforcement representative.

Following the review carried out by the institution's compliance department, the latter took the unilateral decision to limit the amount of the pot and not to transfer the funds to the beneficiary (5) on the grounds that the fundraising was illicit. It is interesting to note that the case itself was not illegitimate. It is not prohibited to raise funds in order to defend oneself, to pay lawyers' fees in a lawsuit, including a criminal lawsuit. Similarly, the unilateral modification of the amount made available is not linked to a poor knowledge of the beneficiary or of the contributors (from a money laundering perspective). The contributors paid their contributions using bank cards issued by French banks, and the beneficiary presumably provided the necessary documents establishing his identity when opening his account. Issues related to financial security and terrorist financing seem to be excluded here. In addition to excessive media coverage that could damage the reputation of the institution that manages the fundraising, comments made by contributors calling for hatred or violence and supporting a cause that is contrary to public order are considered to limit the raising

(5) The account holder of the fund said that it "undertakes to ensure that the funds collected [...] will only be used to finance legal costs in accordance with our T&Cs and the legislation in force. Indeed, our TOS prohibit any incitement to hatred or violence. In view of the acts reproached to C. D. no other use of the prize fund will be accepted. The transfer of funds will only be carried out on presentation of proof of payment (estimate and lawyer's fees). The money will be transferred directly to the lawyer's dedicated account without any intermediary."

of funds. These comments are not made by the beneficiary and are added by third parties not involved in the contractual relationship between the beneficiary, the settlor, and the account holder. This is an illustration of the company becoming the judge of others, applying its own criteria, and determining what is lawful and what is not. Compliance Law has ruled *ex ante*, limiting the amounts that can be paid to the beneficiary, but the courts have gone even further.

Indeed, in application of Article 1162 of the *Code civil* (French Civil Code), the *Tribunal judiciaire de Paris* (Paris First Instance Civil Court), seized by the beneficiary who wished to recover the totality of the amounts perceived, cancelled the whole fundraising by a judgment of 6 January 2021, which ordered the restitution of the money to all contributors.(6) The judge mentioned that "the defence of public order, of general interest, takes precedence over specific interests and the contracts that express them, even with regard to the contractor who did not intend to undermine it."(7) This complete cancellation by the judge of the legal mechanism of the fundraising does not call into question the 'company's *ex ante* "judgement": it goes further, since where the bank had reacted by readjusting the contours of the funds available, the judge chose to exclude it. This underlines the fact that Compliance Law remains subject to ordinary Law, in this case to the French Civil Code.

The previous points demonstrate how Compliance Law, taking into account the monumental goals of compliance, recent laws calling for more transparency or the reputational risk, allows the bank to judge third parties, to terminate the contractual relationship with some or to limit access to products for others. In the bank, reputational risk management acts as an accelerator of the transition to *ex ante*. It is now necessary to examine how the banking company becomes a judge of itself.

---

(6) Judgment of the *Tribunal judiciaire de Paris* (Paris First Instance Civil Court) of 6 January 2021, between Mrs K.C., wife D. and the company SA Leetchi, No. 19/03587.

(7) *Ibid.*; free translation of: "*la défense de l'ordre public, d'intérêt général, prime les intérêts particuliers et les contrats qui les expriment et ce, même à l'égard du contractant qui n'entendait pas y porter atteinte.*"

II. THE INTERNAL SANCTION MECHANISM ESTABLISHED BY COMPLIANCE LAW IN THE BANKING INDUSTRY

The numerous regulations that apply to banks and the systemic risk attached to their activities imply a continuous surveillance system from regulators and central banks. This supervision takes the form of investigations that sometimes leads to the adoption of financial and disciplinary sanctions. Nonetheless, banks are also companies that remain subject to ordinary Law and thus liable to be sued in court.

We will examine the specificity of the mechanism of sanctions adopted *ex ante* by the compliance department (A) as well as the nature of those adopted by the regulator or the judge (B) to finally conclude that the company, judge of others and judge of itself, also seeks to protect itself from public sanction.

A. Internal sanctions or bans adopted by the compliance department

In order to protect themselves against reputational risk, banks have set up dedicated bodies or departments, or supplemented existing bodies or departments, with a reputational risk management component. An important financing project, such as the financing of a pipeline, is examined by the credit committee. This committee examines the solvency of the borrower, the guarantees provided and the viability of the economic project. This committee now also examines the impact on reputational risk and other aspects of compliance. Does the bank financing the transaction want to show that it is participating in the financing of a pipeline at a time when climate issues are becoming increasingly important? This is a separate issue from credit risk. The committees in charge of validating new products also include a compliance risk component. Does the product make it possible to modify the tax treatment of the subscriber? While tax specialists are better equipped to carry out this analysis, the regulations require ratification by the compliance function, which applies Compliance Law, initiates the contradictory debate by taking on the role of prosecutor. (8)

(8) Order of 3 November 2014, Article 35: "*Les entreprises assujetties prévoient des procedures spécifiques d'examen de la conformité notamment: - lorsqu'elles décident de réaliser des opérations relatives à des nouveaux produits* [...] *le responsable de la vérification, ou une personne dûment habilitée par ce dernier, donne un avis*

1. The compliance function is required by law to act as the company's prosecutor

There are the more explicit cases of conduct committees, in which the compliance department staff acts as a kind of prosecutor, in application of a Compliance Law intended by the legislation and set out in policies and procedures defined by the compliance department itself, policies which are also monitored by compliance. When compliance is impersonating the function of a "prosecutor," it does it in accordance with the procedural guarantees in adjusting his prosecuting behaviour towards individuals. Thus, the employee is given information about the grievance and is given time to develop his or her argument so that he or she can develop a point of view. This can lead to different people being responsible for the internal work of gathering information on the one hand and drawing conclusions on the other, especially if the seriousness of the facts justifies it, as the size of the institutions makes this arrangement easier in practice.

Non-compliance with the rules is dealt with in more or less the same way in banking institutions. "Conduct committees," involving management, human resources and the business lines, are set up to judge collegially those who do not comply with the rules. Within the committee, the compliance function acts as prosecutor and has the role of pointing out the breach and proposing a "sanction" for those who do not observe the internal rules defined by the company.

Some examples of what may fall under the assessment of a conduct committee are: general failure to comply with the bank's code of conduct or ethics and conflict of interest rules, failure to declare gifts or external mandates, failure to declare personal transactions or failure to attend mandatory training. These cases of non-compliance could be subject to a standard HR driven disciplinary procedure, which is often not appropriate for conduct cases, or be reviewed by a dedicated committee which decides on the "sanction."

This sanction mechanism is distinct from Labour Law. Contrary to the provisions of the *Code du travail* (French Labour Code), which governs disciplinary sanctions, the Conduct Committee may issue reminders (which do not have the status of a "warning" within the meaning of the French Labour Code) which are considered in the employee's annual appraisal.

écrit et systématique préalable à l'exécution de ces opération" (free translation: "Subject undertakings shall provide for specific compliance review procedures, in particular: - when they decide to carry out operations relating to new products [...] the compliance officer, or a person duly authorised by the compliance officer, shall give written and systematic advice prior to the execution of such operations.")

In the United States, there is both a stronger compliance culture and a less elaborate Labour Law than in Europe. This allows companies in this country to explicitly define the penalties payable by employees for failure to comply with the rules of compliance. (9) For example, we found that one financial institution, a subsidiary of a European banking group, imposes penalties of up to 10,000 dollars on those who do not comply with the rules on personal transactions. In addition, the disgorgement of the profit resulting from an unauthorised transaction is systematic in this country. Without going that far, Compliance Law in Europe increasingly provides for financial consequences for non-compliance. This is particularly the case for employees who are liable for the bank's balance sheet or liability, the material risk takers. The variable and discretionary remuneration of a risk taker can be reduced if a conduct committee confirms the breaches identified.

However, the disciplinary procedure provided for in the French Labour Code and the procedure resulting from a conduct committee may overlap. A conduct committee that concludes that an employee has committed a serious breach of duty and requires dismissal or another sanction provided for in the French Labour Code relies on the classic processes of Labour Law for the execution of the decision. Therefore, the human resources functions are also involved to conduct committees.

Finally, it should be noted that the structure of the conduct committees is not defined in a text and may vary from one establishment to another, particularly according to the size of the company. On the other hand, the same players are often present, and always the compliance department. In the largest banks, with numerous branches, there may be a mechanism for appeal to an umbrella committee, which is also responsible for ensuring consistency in the decisions taken by the local committees. This brings us closer to case-law.

2. The compliance function can act as the company's judge

In certain cases, the regulations provide that the compliance department must be able to judge the behaviour or appropriate honourability of an employee, including by calling this honourability into question if

(9) Penalties imposed by compliance for non-compliance are donated to associations or structures providing financial education to citizens.

breaches of Compliance Law are observed. This is notably the case provided for by the *Réglement général de l'Autorité des marchés financiers – AMF* (General Regulation of the French Financial Markets Authority) for the attribution of professional cards, which are necessary for certain employees to carry out their duties. Article 312-37 of these regulation state:

> "Before issuing one of the professional cards mentioned in Article 312-36, the compliance officer for investment services shall ensure that the applicant is honourable." (10)

The functions of trader and seller of financial instruments, clearer and compliance officer are, among others, subject to obtaining a professional licence, which is issued by the *AMF* directly (in the case of the compliance officer) or by the institution, under the supervision of the *AMF*. (11) In addition to assessing the competence and knowledge required to perform the function, the granting of a professional card is subject to an assessment of honourability. While the compliance department can check with the *AMF* on the person's background in case of doubt, (12) honourability is usually presumed and verified during the recruitment process, which also ensures that the competences and knowledge are acquired. All the assessment elements necessary for approval must be kept and transmitted to the market authority at its request. The compliance department thus makes a judgment – that of a person's good standing and honourability.

The impact of the consequence of a conduct committee on the granting of the professional card reinforces, if it were necessary, the power of judgment attributed to the compliance department. In this particular case, the General Regulation provides (Article 312-27):

> "When an investment service provider has been required to take disciplinary action against a person holding a professional licence because of a breach of professional obligations, it shall inform the AMF within one month." (13)

(10) Free translation of: "*Avant que ne soit délivré l'une des cartes professionnelles mentionnées à l'article 312-36, le responsable en charge de la conformité pour les services d'investissement s'assure que la personne candidate présente l'honorabilité requise.*"

(11) Article 312-20: "*Doivent être titulaires d'une carte professionnelle, délivrée par l'AMF ou le prestataire de services d'investissement en application des art. 312-29 et 312-36, les personnes concernées suivantes*" (free translation: "The following persons must hold a professional licence issued by the AMF or the investment services provider pursuant to Articles 312-29 and 312-36.")

(12) Article 312-37 of the AMF General Regulation.

(13) Free translation of: "*Lorsqu'un prestataire de services d'investissement a été conduit à prendre une mesure disciplinaire à l'égard d'une personne titulaire d'une carte professionnelle, à raison de manquement à ses obligations professionnelles, il en informe l'AMF dans le délai d'un mois.*"

This article requires at least two clarifications. The term "*mesure disciplinaire*" ("disciplinary measure") does not necessarily refer to the disciplinary sanction of the *Code du travail* (French Labour Code), but also includes any breach of conduct that would be observed by the institution or simply by compliance. As for the words "*manquement à ses obligations professionnelles*" ("breach of professional obligations"), the interpretation given by the supervisor is extensive. It is not only a question of compliance with legislative and regulatory standards, supplemented where necessary by market practices, but also covers all the compliance rules contained in the policies and procedures applicable within the company.

Notifying the *AMF* of a breach of these rules calls into question the employee's honourability and, by extension, his or her right to a professional card. Once again, this judgment rests with the compliance department, which must determine whether a breach of a compliance standard, formally recorded, allows the employee to retain all the attributes of honourability. Especially since Article 312-28 of the same General Regulation states:

> "The AMF keeps a register of professional cards. [...] The information contained in the register of professional cards shall be kept for ten years after the professional card is withdrawn." (14)

In other words, the holder of a professional card who fails to comply with an obligation under Compliance Law loses the benefit of the card. Without the professional card, the employee cannot continue to perform his duties and his employment contract has no object. Given that the *AMF* keeps a register of the allocation and withdrawal of professional cards, it becomes difficult for an employee whose card has been withdrawn to justify the reason for this withdrawal to another employer. In practice, the consequences of the compliance ruling are particularly important: the employee found guilty of non-compliance will not find a job in this sector of the industry. Especially since, with the entry into force of the European directive MiFID2, national registers of professional cards can be consulted by other national regulators, thus extending the ban in this respect to Europe.

The UK regulator, the Financial Conduct Authority (FCA), has a similar system for granting a professional licence, subject to a "fit and proper" opinion. (15)

(14) Free translation of: "*L'AMF tient un registre des cartes professionnelles.* [...]. *Les informations figurant sur le registre des cartes professionnelles sont conservées pendant dix ans après le retrait de la carte professionnelle.*"

(15) FCA Handbook, Section FIT 1.3 "The FCA would expect firms that are required to assess the fitness and propriety of staff being assessed under FIT to have regard to substantially the same factors as those outlined in FIT 2. In the FCA's view, the most important considerations will be the person's: (1) honesty, integrity and reputation; (2) competence and capability; and 3) financial soundness."

This Compliance Law mechanism, put in place by the regulator, confers a right to judge that is distinct from that of ordinary Law. The role of the prosecutor and the judge is sometimes performed by the same person, and the channels of appeal are narrow. This illustrates the *ex ante* enforcement applied by the bank, where the penalty it determines precedes the regulator's judgement, if any.

B. Sanctions by the regulator and the judge

Banks and financial institutions do not always come under the jurisdiction of the courts in the first instance, but rather under exceptional jurisdictions. There are so-called "sanction committees" judging in public or independent administrative authorities in France and abroad. These specialised jurisdictions have confirmed the emergence of the branch of Compliance Law. In addition to the specialised nature of the courts, Compliance Law applied to banks may change the nature of the sanction for breach of professional obligations. Indeed, the sanction can also be contractualised between the bank and its regulator, *via* a settlement, which was introduced in France in 2010 and whose scope was extended by the French law of 21 June 2016 on market abuse. (16) This contractualisation of the sanction constitutes the tangible link between the *ex ante* and the *ex post* and helps better apprehending the contradiction that constitutes for the company to be a "judge-judged."

The majority of sanctions adopted against financial institutions are now based on an agreement between the judge and the judged. Banks prefer to negotiate the terms, including financial terms, of the sanction with a specialised judge rather than leave it to the vagaries of civil procedures or even the shame of criminal proceedings.

We emphasized that the bank can often judge third parties and even judge itself, particularly through the powers conferred on the compliance function. The sanction power of the regulator, which regulates, controls and, if necessary, enforces decisions against the bank, illustrates that the paradox of the company judging itself is supported by another paradox: in this Compliance Law, the judge can end up being the judged.

(16) French law No. 2016-819 of 21 June 2016 *réformant le système de répression des abus de marché* (reforming the repression system of market abuse).

Despite its best efforts to respect and enforce *ex ante* the various professional obligations of the bank, the compliance department cannot prevent an *ex post* decision that would go beyond what it has determined.

To illustrate the contradiction of being the judge-judged, let us review a recent court decision. In a decision of 6 December 2018, which addresses the issue of honourability, the *AMF* Enforcement Committee found facts that "characterise a lack of honesty and loyalty on the part of Mr D., attributable both to him" (17) and to the bank that employed him. (18) The Committee then states that "Mr D. disregarded the obligation to respect the professional rules of *ED bank's internal rules*, as set out in Article 315-66 of the *AMF* General Regulation." (19)

Notwithstanding the internal sanction decisions taken by the bank against its employee, at the end of a conduct of business committee, the *AMF* considered that the facts were of a certain seriousness that justified the intervention of the Enforcement Committee. The Committee confirmed the ED bank's view of the loss of honourability of the employee holding a professional card and even tightened up the terms of the sanction by imposing a fine of 50,000 euros to the former employee. This confirmation and aggravation of the company's internal decision, insofar as it was "judging," was also accompanied by a sentence against the bank itself, for lack of control, (20) the judge thus becoming the judged in the same case.

In another area, the banks apply know-your-customer (KYC) processes that allow them to reject the entry into business relationships with potential clients with a considerable risk of money laundering. The banks exercise their right to judge third parties in the name of Compliance Law and to safeguard their reputation. The *Autorité de Contrôle Prudentiel et de Résolution – ACPR* (French Banking Supervisory Authority), acting as the bank regulator, periodically reviews the KYC process during examinations and may consider that the measures taken by the compliance department are not sufficient.

---

(17) Free translation of: "*caractériseraient un manque d'honnêteté et de loyauté de Monsieur D., imputable tant à ce dernier.*"

(18) AMF Enforcement Committee Decision No. 14 of 6 December 2018.

(19) Free translation of: "*à Monsieur D. d'avoir méconnu l'obligation de respecter les règles professionnelles issues des règles internes de la banque ED., posées par l'article 315-66 du règlement général de l'AMF.*"

(20) "If it failed to comply with its obligation, ED conducted an internal investigation and took sanctions against Mr D. and then fulfilled its obligation to inform the AMF without reservation."

Thus, in its 2 million euros sanction of 13 June 2019 against CEPAC, (21) the *ACPR*'s Sanctions Committee considered that the risk classification was not sufficiently developed to take into account "customers with a regular gambling profile in the region's casinos" (22) or that this classification did not take into account "the risk of financing terrorism via consumer loans." (23) These expectations of the regulator go beyond the control already carried out by the bank on its client. The regulator specifies *ex post* that the institution's *ex ante* system should be more intrusive or more judgmental.

In a more recent decision, (24) the *Cour d'appel de Paris* (Paris Court of Appeal) found *CEIDF* guilty of aggravated money laundering for the period between July 2012 and July 2014 in a case of fraud and Ponzi scheme considering that financial flows transited, among others, through bank accounts opened within the convicted institution. Without commenting on the merits of these two decisions, these decisions, whether adopted by the regulator or by the judge, illustrate that the treatment of Compliance Law issues by banks may not be sufficient. In the Court of Appeal's decision, it is particularly striking to note that the *ex ante* having been applied by the compliance department of the bank, i.e. that a suspicious transaction report had been transmitted to *TRACFIN* concerning the flows in question, the Court of Appeal considers that there is aggravated money laundering on the part of the institution even though, on the one hand, the Court, in the first instance, had completely exonerated the bank; on the other hand, the Court recalls in its decision that the *ACPR*, which had carried out an audit of the institution, had issued a positive report on the anti-money laundering process. The Court also noted that the institution had anticipated certain regulations by requesting documents that were not yet required at the time of the events "when nothing obliged it to do so." (25)

However, the court considered that "the bank failed in its obligation of reinforced vigilance as well as in its duty to report suspicious transactions, and that its attitude can be analysed as constituting the provision, with

(21) Decision of the *Commission des sanctions de l'Autorité de Contrôle Prudentiel et de Résolution* (Sanctions Committee of the French Banking Supervisory Authority) No. 2018-04 of 13 June 2019, *Caisse d'Épargne Provence Alpes Corse*.

(22) Free translation of: "*les clients ayant un profil de joueurs réguliers dans les casinos de la région.*"

(23) Free translation of: "*le risqué de financement du terrorisme* via *le credit à la consommation.*"

(24) Decision of the Paris Court of Appeal of 16 December 2021, pole 2, 13th chamber.

(25) Free translation of: "*alors que rien ne l'y obligeait encore.*"

full knowledge of the facts, of "assistance" to the defendants [...]." (26) This obligation of vigilance to detect money laundering operations is an obligation of means placed on the bank by the public authorities. By noting that this obligation of means was manifestly inoperative or too late, the Court ruled on the "judging" company, which is in its attributes, but the decision seems to transform this obligation of means into an obligation of result since its ineffectiveness turns into criminal misconduct *via* the qualification of "assistance" to money laundering, a term that will lead to criminal misconduct. This certainly permits the court to oblige the bank to compensate all the victims of the fraud, but using the criminal qualification to better repair civil damages is what the *Conseil constitutionnel* (French Constitutional Council) has ruled out about the so-called "Vigilance law" of 27 March 2017.

If the consequences of this decision are important and numerous for the organisation and the responsibility of banks and compliance officers, it is questionable on the criminal nature and the qualification of complicity that it retains. Indeed, the detection of a suspicious transaction is not an obligation of result, neither for the banks, nor for the police, nor for the judicial system. It is because banks are in a position to fight money laundering effectively that they are involved.

The Court first considered that "the bank did not handle this alarming information with the expected vigilance." (27) The Court may consider that the bank's duty of care was not fulfilled in this case. If an absence of vigilance in the fight against money laundering is raised, and this absence justifies the judge in retaining a failure of the bank to fulfil its obligations, this failure is necessarily of an administrative nature: the bank did not respect its professional obligations. However, the Court goes further and qualifies this "administrative" failure as a criminal offence:

> "It is therefore from that moment that the bank failed in its obligation of reinforced vigilance as well as in its duty to make a declaration of suspicion, and that its attitude can be analysed as constituting the provision, with full

(26) Free translation of: "*C'est donc à partir de ce moment que la banque a manqué à son obligation de vigilance renforcée ainsi qu'à son devoir de procéder à une déclaration de soupçon, et que son attitude peut s'analyser comme constituant l'apport, en connaissance de cause, d'un "concours" aux prévenus, assimilable à un soutien abusif*", decision of the *Cour d'appel de Paris* (Paris Court of Appeal) of 16 December 2021, *cited above*, p. 140.

(27) Free translation of: "*le traitement de ces informations alertantes n'a pas été approfondi avec la vigilance attendue.*"

knowledge of the facts, of a 'contribution' to the defendants, comparable to abusive support." (28)

In Criminal Law, the judge must demonstrate the element of intentionality against the person being judged. Either the intentionality of not doing something, or not complying with the rules, or the intentionality of contributing positively to violating the law. When it states "with knowledge of the facts," (29) the Court does not establish the intentional element. It is regrettable that the judgment does not seek this intentionality, whereas what distinguishes Criminal Law from Administrative Law is intention.

This decision of the Paris Court of Appeal thus interprets Compliance Law that would go beyond the consideration of good risk management to the realisation of the general interest, thanks to the shift to the *ex ante* described above. If it can be said that the Law thus puts companies in a position to act for the good of others, for example banks to detect and prevent the criminal behaviour of their clients, which gives them a kind of *ex ante* responsibility, this may eventually concern their civil liability. The monumental goals of compliance undoubtedly justify this. But shouldn't criminal liability remain rooted in proven malice, assuming at the very least proven actual negligence?

---

(28) Free translation of: "*C'est donc à partir de ce moment que la banque a manqué à son obligation de vigilance renforcée ainsi qu'à son devoir de procéder à une déclaration de soupçon, et que son attitude peut s'analyser comme constituant l'apport, en connaissance de cause, d'un 'concours' aux prévenus, assimilable à un soutien abusif.*"

(29) Free translation of: "*en connaissance de cause.*"

Compliance law in the construction industry and the contradictions, impossibilities and deadlocks that companies face

Jean-Marc Coulon

Head of Legal Affairs, Infrastructure Division, Bouygues Construction

The "building industry," which can be extended to the construction industry in its broadest sense, encompassing building, real estate, public works and civil engineering as well as road works, has the fundamental characteristic that it requires the physical projection of equipment, materials and human resources to the geographical location where the item, the product – in the industry, we refer to it as "the work" – is to be built in order to complete it.

This variable projection capacity of the participants in the construction industry explains why the latter comprises both superimposed layers and, to use a key concept of competition law, a multitude of relevant markets. A "global" market covering the whole world is the market for large and very large structures where only large and very large companies can compete. Below that are supranational regional markets covering a continent or part of a continent. The next most important level is, of course, the country-specific market. Lastly, there are the sub-national, regional and local levels. Each of these levels has its own microcosm and competition, logically made up of large and very large companies, medium-sized companies, small companies and even very small companies, depending on the situation.

For historical, political and cultural reasons, the development and structure of the construction market in each country are very different. The continental European model of the designer/builder has often been contrasted with the British model, where a distinction is made between the designer and the engineering companies, on the one hand, and the builder, on the other. This opposition of models has also significantly contributed to the structuring of the construction market.

To finish with the specificities of the construction industry, and this is much more systematic than in other industries where, clearly, partnerships also exist, it is also necessary to understand that the industry is a place *par excellence* for temporary associations between companies, in one form or another, that ensure the pooling of means so that participants complement others in order to meet the needs of a project.

In terms of its recent evolution, the construction industry, like many others, has not escaped, on the one hand, a generalised concentration phenomenon and, on the other hand, the emergence of a group of new Chinese participants, comprising very large companies taking advantage, first, of a vast and protected domestic market and then, in terms of exports, disrupting a situation that was previously dominated mainly by large continental European companies.

Lastly, and this circumstance is, of course, not neutral from the point of view of compliance, the construction industry, unlike others (banking, telecommunications, media, energy, etc.) and even though it is a heavyweight in the global, European (1) and national economy, is not a regulated industry.

*

* *

Inevitably, given this mixed picture, the penetration of compliance and, therefore, the incentives for companies in the construction industry to act with integrity are necessarily very variable.

This disparity is the result of several factors, both exogenous and endogenous.

(1) At the European level alone, the construction industry accounts for almost 10% of GDP, over 3 million companies and 13 million jobs.

Among the exogenous factors, those that are related to projects constituting the construction activity should be considered. This involves examining the influence that the companies in the construction industry, within the temporary associations referred to above, may have on compliance. Similarly, such influence may be exerted by capillary action from other sectors of activity in which compliance has a more long-standing, established and stabilised role, whether it's about clients, partners or suppliers, in particular those in, for example, the oil and gas, mining, energy and transport industries. Lastly, there is the influence of all kinds of lenders, equity investors, commercial and multilateral debt providers, credit and export insurance providers, in short, the financial industry that is very permeable with compliance.

It is also necessary to take into account the impact of compliance that results from seeking public investment for financing purposes. Companies in the construction industry are therefore subject not only to a regulator – in France, the *Autorité des Marchés Financiers* (French Financial Markets Authority), which itself issues compliance standards such as an *ad hoc* ethical alert system, a guide on governance and compliance, the second edition of which was published on 7 October 2020, etc – but also to pressure from their shareholder investors, the financial analysts, ...

Companies in the construction industry will be all the more sensitive to compliance if they are subject to the French law No. 2017-399 *relative au devoir de vigilance des sociétés mères et des entreprises donneuses d'ordre* (on the duty of vigilance of parent companies and ordering companies) of 27 March 2017 or the French law No. 2016-1691 *relative à la transparence, à la lutte contre la corruption et à la modernisation de la vie économique* (on transparency, fight against corruption and modernisation of economic life) of 9 December 2016, known as the "Sapin 2" law, which has brought about a real "compliance shock" in both the construction and other industries.

The *Agence française anticorruption – AFA* (French Anti-Corruption Agency – AFA), created by the French so-called "Sapin 2" law, after having noted in its report of 8 October 2020 the delay in the implementation of anti-corruption measures by small and medium-sized companies, has issued recommendations (2) specifically aimed at them, even though they are not legally obliged to implement a corruption prevention and detection system under the "Sapin 2" law. In late 2019, the French Anti-Corruption

(2) *Agence française anticorruption – AFA* (French Anti-Corruption Agency – AFA), *Anti-corruption guide for SMEs and Smaller Intermediate-sized enterprises*, 16 December 2021.

Agency began an audit of the construction industry that was completed in early 2021. The AFA has since published a practical guide to preventing the risk of corruption in the construction industry, in which it highlights the size difference between companies of this sector. Indeed, showing a wide disparity on their corruption prevention and detection mechanisms and, more generally, their maturity in terms of compliance.

In the absence of a regulator, the endogenous factors in the construction industry favouring compliance, while not non-existent, remain nonetheless modest.

Thus, various professional bodies in the construction industry have taken several initiatives in recent years to promote and raise awareness of compliance in the industry, including the *Ethibat* approach, which includes commitments in terms of ethics and compliance and was launched in 2015 by the regional branches of the *Fédération Nationale des Travaux Publics* (French National Federation of Public Works). On 11 January 2019, the *Fédération* published a new version of its standard-form of *société en participation*, the preferred corporate form in France for companies in the construction industry that wish to join forces, as referred to above, which contains statements and guarantees in terms of ethics and compliance. (3) Lastly, on 27 January 2021, it published its own ethical charter aimed at ensuring that its own activities in defending the construction profession are carried out "in compliance with the law and Competition Law rules." (4)

*

* *

In the relatively recent past, things were still quite simple.

One of the classic definitions of an enterprise, "the smallest combination of legal units that constitutes an organisational unit for the production of goods and services that enjoys a certain degree of decision-making

(3) *Fédération Nationale des Travaux Publics* (French National Federation of Public Works), *Société en participation. Exemples de statuts*, 12 October 2021, new Article 16: "*CONFORMITE. Ethique. Les associés déclarent et garantissent : qu'ils respectent les règles d'éthique et de conformité aux exigences et recommandations de leurs sociétés respectives, qu'ils ne participent pas, directement ou indirectement, à aucune forme d'ententes, qu'ils ne pratiquent pas, directement ou indirectement, une forme de corruption*" (free translation: "Compliance": "Ethics - The shareholders declare and guarantee that: they respect the ethical rules and comply with the requirements and recommendations of their respective companies, they do not directly or indirectly participate in any form of cartel, they do not directly or indirectly practice any form of corruption.")

(4) Free translation of: "*dans le respect de la légalité et des règles du droit de la concurrence.*"

autonomy, in particular for the allocation of its current resources," (5) taken from the 2008 French law *de modernisation de l'économie* (of modernisation of the economy) and adopted by *the Institut national de la statistique et des études économiques – INSEE* (French National Institute of Statistics and Economic Studies), exhaustively covered and described the role and economic and productive purpose assigned to enterprises.

However, over and above this traditional economic and productive purpose, companies have been, and continue to be, progressively tasked with avoiding or at least reducing the harmful impact that their activity generate in terms of compliance, employment, human rights and fundamental freedoms and, in the near future, the much more radical task of drastically transforming their modes of production in order to meet the constraints of the European taxonomy, in particular, and more generally, the challenge of environmental and climatic changes.

Focusing solely on compliance, this progressive movement applies in the prevention of ethical breaches by shifting the responsibility from the State to companies. Article 17 of the French so-called "Sapin 2" law, although far from exhaustively covering the contours of such movement, is an enlightening illustration.

It is a divestment of sovereign tasks that States no longer want or are no longer able to perform.

It is also an imperfect and incomplete divestment, in that certain guarantees are lacking, and the companies do not have the means to carry out the tasks thus delegated to them.

Lastly, it is a divestment but with sanctions.

As part of these sovereign tasks, the law delegates to companies the prerogative of issuing standards but also gives them the status of "auxiliaries of the justice system," assigning to them the tasks of public prosecutor and judge of both themselves and others.

Even if, as seen above, the construction industry is not at the forefront of compliance, many of its participants have acted as self-regulators by adopting, in more or less developed formats, standards, codes, charters, principles, compliance programmes, etc., thereby anticipating the

(5) Free translation of: "*la plus petite combinaison d'unités légales qui constitue une unité organisationnelle de production de biens et de services jouissant d'une certaine autonomie de décision, notamment pour l'affectation de ses ressources courantes.*"

obligations of the Article 17-II, para. 1, of the French so-called "Sapin 2" law (6) and thus fulfilling the role of "legislator."

The legally imposed (7) "internal whistleblowing system designed to enable the recording of alerts from employees on the existence of conduct or situations contrary to the company's code of conduct" is nothing other than an illustration of another role devolved to companies in the compliance area, namely that of "prosecutor."

Companies will become public prosecutors of (or against) themselves when, for example, alerted through their internal whistleblowing system, a third party, an independent administrative authority or a judge, or motivated by the leniency programme of the *Autorité de la Concurrence* (French Competition Authority) under the Article L. 464-2-IV of the *Code de commerce* (French Commercial Code), they initiate internal investigations.

Prosecuting others will be their role when implementing a whistleblowing system that is accessible to third parties or where companies file complaints with the police or prosecution authorities about the actions of third parties or of their own employees.

They also become "judges" of themselves when, for example, they negotiate the terms and conditions of their sanctions with a multilateral bank or take part in a *convention judiciaire d'intérêt public* (Judicial Public Interest Agreement) under Article 41-1-2 of the *Code de procedure pénale* (French Criminal Procedure Code), and "judges" of others when they apply other measures imposed by the French so-called "Sapin 2" law such as, under the corporate disciplinary regime, (8) when they apply more or less severe sanctions against their employees or exclude a stakeholder in application of the procedures for assessing third parties, (9) in application of that same law.

Such divestment of this threefold role is, however, imperfect, and incomplete.

(6) For example, the Bouygues Group adopted a Code of Ethics, the first version of which dates to 2006, that was subsequently completed by five thematic compliance programmes dealing, respectively, with anti-corruption, competition, conflicts of interest, financial information and stock market operations, embargoes and export restrictions.

(7) Article 17-II, para. 2, of the French law No. 2016-1691 of 9 December 2016 *relative à la transparence, à la lutte contre la corruption et à la modernisation de la vie économique* (on transparency, fight against corruption and modernisation of economic life).

(8) Article 17-II, para. 7, of the French law No. 2016-1691 of 9 December 2016, cited above.

(9) Article 17-II, para. 4, of the French law No. 2016-1691 of 9 December 2016, cited above.

The so-called legislation, in the field of corporate compliance, is not proper legislation.

Far from creating rights, duties, and obligations, enacting offences and defining sanctions, these codes, charters, principles, compliance programmes and compliance standards published by companies merely repeat or, at best, paraphrase the regulatory provisions.

Christophe Lapp highlights the vacuity of the exercise and the disempowerment of companies that it can entail. (10)

Their only virtue is to signify to stakeholders of the company, including their own employees, the company's appropriation of such regulatory provisions and, in so doing, to make them aware that if they breach them, they will not only be the subject of the sanction provided for in the regulations, but also of the company's disciplinary sanction. And this is precisely where another weakness arises.

The artificial nature of the company's role as "prosecutor," evoked above, becomes apparent where, for example, the company lodges a complaint with the Public Prosecutor – the State having a monopoly on initiating public action – who decides, on grounds that cannot be explained logically, not to prosecute the case and files it without further action in spite of the abundance and precision of the facts provided in support of the complaint.

We were talking about the sovereign tasks that States no longer want or are no longer able to perform…

The role of "judge" highlighted above appears equally illusory, for example when a *conseil de prud'hommes* (French First Instance Labour Court) did not hesitate to condemn a company for dismissal without real and serious cause after it had applied the disciplinary regime as required under the provisions of Article 17-II, para. 7, of the French so-called "Sapin 2" law while the employee's behaviour in question was clearly contrary to probity.

Having regard to the fundamental principles applying to proceedings, the fairness that must govern them, the adversarial principle, the provision of evidence, in short from the point of view of the provisions of Article 6 of the European Convention on Human Rights, it is preferable that companies do not become legislator, prosecutor or judge.

(10) Ch. Lapp, "Compliance in companies: the statutes of the process", *this book*.

Lastly, and this is one of the major innovations of the French so-called "Sapin 2" law, despite the paradoxical situation in which companies are placed, as described above, such divestment is accompanied by financial penalties and "name and shame" measures. (11)

In short, the company can be subject to sanctions for failure to define and apply a disciplinary regime allowing it to punish its employees in the event of a breach of the company's code of conduct but can also be just as much at fault when it implements that regime!

*

* *

As for its basic tasks, companies are in an inextricable situation, as they are required to legislate, prosecute, judge and sanction, under penalty of themselves being punished under compliance law, and yet they are simultaneously accountable for the quality of their preventive measures and incentives and the tools that are required to make them effective and the legitimacy and proportionality of their sanctions.

Companies are also confronted with contradictory requirements in relation to the provision of evidence. When they acts as "prosecutor" and "judge," they are subject to the fundamental legal principles of procedural law, a breach of which creates liability under ordinary paw, whereas they do not benefit from such principles when they are themselves assessed and judged and the burden of proof is reversed when they are required to prove the reliability of their corporate compliance system to the *Agence française anticorruption – AFA* (French Anti-Corruption Agency) or in court.

(11) Article 17-V of the French law No. 2016-1691 of 9 December 2016, cited above.

Compliance in Companies: The Statutes of the Process

Christophe Lapp

Partner

Advant Altana Paris

Companies have been assigned by a normative delegation the ambitious target, which the States are no longer able to achieve, of preventing the negative impact of their actions in areas as vast as human rights, fundamental freedoms, the environment and climate change, employment and professional relations – thus going beyond the fight against corruption and all other forms of extortion and breaches of probity that companies, as subjects of the law, cannot obviously disregard and for which they must be held accountable for their violation, both on a criminal and civil level.

The imperative is to avoid harm, which goes far beyond the prevention of offenses.

Of course, the Sates do not entrust all the companies with the realisation of this ambition. Essentially regulated companies are concerned, and those whose size or actions are likely to have an influence on social behaviour; however, the mechanisms designed and implemented by these companies will eventually irrigate the entire chain of their contractual relations, wherever they are located, even across borders.

To this effect, companies must put in place systems and measures aimed at eliminating the causes and means of the occurrence of a risk, and no longer merely to limit its realisation.

This is a challenging exercise. It proceeds from introspection, and foresight carried out at the end of the perspectives up to which the company will be able to focus and identify the risk factors thanks to its knowledge of the market in which it operates, its players, its practices and its possible biases.

The design of managerial systems and operational procedures will depend on the quality and depth of the exercise. Then comes the time for their implementation, their confrontation with reality and the measurement of their efficiency, which depends on their imperativeness.

Here, then, is the company invested with a delegation of regulation and sanctions against those who contravene it. In this respect, the company is indeed a prosecutor and a judge of itself by the application of its self-regulation.

However, this normative delegation proves to be imperfect, and can be perceived as being to the detriment of its beneficiary – the company – which is caught in the pincers of Compliance Law, whose jaws are those of prevention, which takes concrete form in all its processes (1), and those of the criminalisation of these same processes (2).

I. THE COMPANY'S PROCESSES: THE CONSTRAINED MAKING OF THE LEGAL RULE

Judging implies retaining a rule of law and applying it to claimant's allegations. What is the rule of law here that the company, that has become a judge, can apply? The one that it has conceived, defined and which is contained in its processes, i.e. its internal procedures, codified in its charter or its code of conduct – the term of " code" is not without incidence.

Many companies had not waited for the legislator or the regulator to put in place internal prevention procedures, whether in the form of a code of conduct or a charter of ethics, with the aim of defining rules of conduct to remove the means of committing an offence, in particular corruption, extortion or anti-competitive practices.

These initiatives were considered insufficient, and international pressure – in reality mainly from Common Law countries – led the French government to present, in March 2016, a bill on transparency, fight against corruption and modernisation of the economy which " aims to bring French legislation up to the best European and international standards and thus contribute to a positive image of France internationally."(1) Thus, "The bill provides for the creation of a service in charge of preventing and

(1) Free translation of: "*a pour ambition de porter la législation française aux meilleurs standards européens et internationaux et de contribuer ainsi à une image positive de la France au plan international.*"

assisting in the detection of corruption, as well as the obligation for large companies to put in place a corruption prevention system." (2)

This French law No. 2016-1691 of 9 December 2016 on transparency, fight against corruption and modernisation of the economy, (3) known as "Sapin 2" law, includes two fundamental innovations intended by its designers: to govern the company's internal procedures, and to bring Compliance Law into Criminal Law – whose induced effects on company behaviour must be assessed.

Besides, French law No. 2017-399 of 27 March 2017 on the (duty of vigilance of the parent companies and ordering companies (4)) compels certain companies to "establish and effectively implement a vigilance plan" (5) in order to prevent "serious attacks on human rights and fundamental freedoms, the health and safety of individuals, as well as the environment" (6) but it refers to the sole liability under Tort Law for breaches of these obligations, and not Criminal Law.

The legislator, in the context of these two laws, uses the same term "*mesures*" ("measures"), some of which are intended to prevent and detect, in France or abroad, the commission of acts of corruption or influence peddling, and the others of "*vigilance raisonnable*" ("due diligence"). The design of these "measures" is no longer left to the initiative of the company. The two laws list each step methodologically, in relatively similar terms, which include "*une cartographie des risques*" ("risk mapping"), "*des codes de conduite*" ("codes of conduct") and "*des procedures d'alerte*" ("alert procedures").

In addition to these preventive measures, there are also measures likely to ensure their effectiveness, such as evaluation procedures for stakeholders, contracting with the company, as well as control and sanction procedures of two types.

---

(2) Press release of the French *Conseil des ministres* of 30 March 2016, free translation of: "*Le projet de loi prévoit la création d'un service chargé de la prévention et de l'aide à la détection de la corruption ainsi que l'obligation, pour les grandes entreprises, de mettre en place un dispositif de prévention de la corruption.*"

(3) Free translation of: "*La loi n° 2016-1691 du 9 décembre 2016 relative à la transparence, à la lutte contre la corruption et la modernisation de la vie économique.*"

(4) Free translation of: "*La loi n° 2017-399 du 27 mars 2017 relative au devoir de vigilance des sociétés mères et des entreprises donneuses d'ordre.*"

(5) Free translation of: "*établi[r] et met[tre] en œuvre de manière effective un plan de vigilance.*"

(6) Free translation of: "*les atteintes graves envers les droits humains et les libertés fondamentales, la santé et la sécurité des personnes ainsi que l'environnement.*"

The first ones are those that the company is entitled to apply; this is how a "*régime disciplinaire*" ("disciplinary scheme") is provided for to enable "to sanction the company's employees in the event of violation of the company's code of conduct" (7) and of the ordinary Contract and Tort Law through the implementation of coercive measures contractually provided, or even the termination of commercial relations pursuant to the provisions of Article L 442-6, I, 5°, of the *Code de commerce* (French Commercial Code).

The second ones are those which apply to the company, and these sanctions are themselves of two types: the system of Tort Law, as we have just seen, to which the French law of 27 March 2017 refers, and the Criminal Law pursuant to the provisions of Article 17 of the French law of 9 December 2016.

Thus, whatever the sanction, its constituent elements are housed in the company's prevention measures, its risk mapping, its code of conduct or charter of ethics, its internal control systems.

The delegation of regulation to the company seems to be assured: the company defines the prevention and vigilance measures, to which it attaches a sanction in the event of non-compliance.

The repressive rule is contained in the statement of these measures, which constitute the company's processes.

But the conjunction of the French laws 2016-1691 of 9 December 2016 and 2017-399 of 27 March 2017 – to which are added various legal tools or instruments ranging from press releases, questionnaires and guides, to recommendations from the various regulatory authorities, have had the effect of locking the company into constrained processes whose obedient application assures the company of a presumption of compliance.

If the company indeed is at the heart of Compliance Law, because it is both a subject of Law and a globalised operator whose action extends beyond national borders, and because it determines the behaviour of numerous other economic operators or public authorities, the delegation for its benefit of a normative power should have been left under its sole responsibility, so that it can freely design and adopt the processes it deems necessary.

(7) Article 17, II, 7°, of the French law No. 2019-1691 of 9 December 2016, free translation of: "*de sanctionner les salariés de la société en cas de violation du code de conduite de la société.*"

However, the company is not immune from the judge, who is responsible for assessing the proportionality of the sanctions imposed by the company in execution of its preventive measures, as well as the insufficiency or inadequacy of its processes, which would not enable to avoid the occurrence of a risk of infringing any fundamental rights.

In this, the law of 27 March 2017 is consistent with the place of the company in Compliance Law, in consideration of its means and its influence on social behaviour.

By forcing it to implement the methodology designed by the legislator and meticulously specified by the regulator, the company is actually deprived of what founded the delegation, which was based on the company's knowledge of the market its players, and to its capacity to influence social behaviours.

The reality, beyond the administrative language of the evaluation reports of the implementation of the French laws of 9 December 2016 and 27 March 2017, is that the legislator and the regulator do not, in fact, trust the company; and by interfering in its processes, have taken back what was given to the company by the normative delegation, thus depriving it of its effects.

Professor Jean-Christophe Roda rightly describes the situation in the USA:

> "The classic model of 'deterrence' has never really been abandoned […] companies are […] forced to equip themselves with control mechanisms: the system then switches from 'voluntary compliance' to 'forced compliance.'" (8)

And makes the observation:

> "That one can no longer clearly distinguish between what concerns classic law or self-regulation." (9)

And that:

> "The boundaries between the functions of judge and regulator are blurring […]. Case law now imposes on corporate officers a real obligation to prevent

(8) Free translation of: "*Le modèle classique de* 'deterrence' *n'a jamais été vraiment abandonné* […] *les entreprises sont* […] *contraintes de se doter de mécanismes de contrôle: on bascule alors d'un système de* 'voluntary compliance' *à celui de* 'forced compliance.'"

(9) See J.-C. Roda, "La compliance en droit américain: le régulateur, l'entreprise et le juge", *in* N. Borga, J.-Cl. Marin et J.-Cr. Roda (eds), *Compliance: l'entreprise, le régulateur et le juge*, "Régulations & Compliance" Serie, Paris, Dalloz, 2018, pp. 235-248, paras. 5 and 24, free translation of: "*que l'on ne distingue plus clairement ce qui relève de la loi classique ou de l'auto-régulation.*"

> and monitor illegal behaviour within companies which, ultimately, can no longer be really distinguished from the compliance obligations drawn up by the regulatory authorities."(10)

If one can no longer distinguish, that obviously means a state of confusion.

Back to the topic of France, the normative disorder – to which the journal *Revue du Droit Public* has devoted an issue in 2006,(11) then a new one in 2016(12) – remains, if not getting worse.

Professor Yves Gaudemet noted that:

> "To the dispersion of sources and to the multiplication of institutions, with normative vocation, was added the disorder of the vocabulary."(13)

And evoked in his turn:

> "A chattering and descriptive regulation, unstable, characterised by the concern for detail, for immediacy, for the particular case, and at the same time a bias towards exhaustiveness; a regulation free of the legal qualifications and vocabulary, preferring that of a programmatic presentation, of communication, of incantation sometimes, of the pedagogy always, by persuasion or intimidation."(14)

What are the successive guidelines of the *Agence française anticorruption – AFA* (French Anti-Corruption Agency)(15) created by the French law of 9 December 2016, if not a programmatic presentation? Thus contributing to this normative disorder but whose immediate consequence is to get out of self-regulation.

---

(10) *Ibid.*, para. 24, free translation of "*Les frontières se brouillent entre la fonction de juge et celle de régulateur* [...]. *La jurisprudence fait ainsi aujourd'hui peser sur les dirigeants sociaux une véritable obligation de prévention et de surveillance des comportements illicites au sein des sociétés qui,* in fine, *ne se distinguent plus véritablement des obligations de compliance dessinées par les autorités de régulation.*"

(11) *"La régulation économique ou la dilution des normes"* ("The economic regulation or the dilution of norms"), *Revue du droit public*, No. 1-2017, p. 23.

(12) "*Le désordre normatif*" ("The normative disorder"), special issue of the *Revue du droit public*, 2006.

(13) Free translation of: "*À la dispersion des sources et à la multiplication des institutions, à vocation normative, s'est ajouté le désordre du vocabulaire.*"

(14) Free translation of: "*Une régulation bavarde et descriptive, instable, caractérisée par le souci du détail, de l'immédiateté, du cas particulier, et en même temps un parti d'exhaustivité; une régulation libre des qualifications et du vocabulaire du droit, lui préférant celui de l'exposé programmatique, de la communication, de l'incantation parfois, de la pédagogie toujours, par persuasion ou intimidation.*"

(15) *Agence française anticorruption – AFA* (French Anti-Corruption Agency – AFA), *The French Anti-Corruption Agency Guidelines*, 2021, https://www.agence-francaise-anticorruption.gouv.fr/files/files/French %20AC %20Agency %20Guidelines %20.pdf.

II. CORPORATE PROCESSES: CONFORMISM AND DISEMPOWERMENT

This disorder extends to the sanctions that the company can apply – or must apply, since it is granted the power of appreciation – when it discovers a contravention of its processes, committed by one of its employees or a party with whom it has a business relationship.

The party thus sanctioned obviously has recourse to a judge who will no longer be satisfied with a simple control of the respect of the procedural guarantees of the Repressive Law, of the fundamental freedoms including that of the right to privacy, and of the proportionality of the sanction to the breach; but who must above all, now question the legality of the penalty and, even more so, because of this descriptive regulation contained in the *AFA* guidelines, the legality of the " offence."

Jean-Marc Coulon is concerned. (16)

The company's process thus acquires the status of legality of the coercive and repressive measures required to ensure the effectiveness of Compliance Law.

This creates two dangers.

The first would be that of an evolution of Compliance Law into a mechanical Law which would be "processual" only in name since the company would respect a strict orthodoxy in order to avoid any subsequent liability. Such "Tick the Box" technique would thus constitute the proof of the company's vigilance and implementation of prevention measures and plans.

The *AFA* tries to protect itself from such danger in its latest guidelines of December 2020 (17) by specifying that:

> "8. These guidelines are not legally binding on the target organisations. The organisations mentioned in Paragraph 7 are free to adopt other methods, provided that their implementation enables compliance with the law."

---

(16) J.-M. Coulon, "Compliance Law in the construction industry and the contradictions, impossibilities and deadlocks that companies face", *this book*.

(17) *Agence française anticorruption – AFA* (French Anti-Corruption Agency – AFA), *The French Anti-Corruption Agency Guidelines*, 2020, paras. 8 to 11.

However, the *AFA* then establishes a presumption of conformity, and thus of legality, which renders this reminder of the normativity of its recommendations ineffective:

> "9. AFA refers to the guidelines when it performs its advice and monitoring tasks. It will only refer to these guidelines for audits commencing as from the sixth months following their entry into force.
>
> 10. These guidelines are binding on AFA in its auditing activities, meaning that the organisations mentioned in Paragraph 7 can invoke the guidelines if they have decided to comply with them.
>
> 11. This means that, an organisation mentioned in Paragraph 7 which states during an AFA audit, that it has followed these guidelines benefits from a prima facie presumption of compliance. This presumption may only be reversed if AFA demonstrates an ineffective, incorrect or incomplete application of the guidelines."

AFA also takes care of introducing its Guidelines as constituting "the French anti-corruption policy framework." (18) However, such "framework" appears to be a catalogue of procedural requirements and does not constitute a standard of conduct to which a regulator or a judge could refer to in order to ascertain whether the company has implemented vigilance and/or due diligence measures adapted to the risks inherent to its specific business.

As an example, the risk mapping, which stems from the introspection and foresight mentioned above, becomes:

> "124. The risk map is formalised, i.e. it takes the form of written and structured documentation with a detailed description of the methods used to produce the map, the measures taken to manage the risks and the roles and responsibilities of the different stakeholders."

And more: (19)

> "129. In this context, in order to identify, assess and manage corruption risks, it is recommended that the following steps be followed."

– and to describe these meticulous steps.

(18) *Agence française anticorruption – AFA* (French Anti-Corruption Agency – AFA), *Évolution du référentiel anticorruption: l'AFA publie ses nouvelles recommandations* (*The French anti-corruption policy framework: new AFA's guidelines published*), press release, 12 January 2021, free translation of: *"le référentiel anticorruption français."*

(19) *Agence française anticorruption – AFA* (French Anti-Corruption Agency – AFA), *The French Anti-Corruption Agency Guidelines*, 2020, para. 12, *op. cit.*

A reading of these guidelines makes it clear that these are programmatic measures which are imperatively prescribed and not, as previously stated, a standard of conduct.

Indeed, a company that thought it could evade this requirement would be exposed to a reversal of the burden of proof:

> "12. An organisation mentioned in paragraph 7 which decides not to implement all or part of the methods recommended in these guidelines cannot *a priori* be considered as not complying with the law. However, in the event the AFA challenges during an audit all or part of the measures taken by this organisation, it will be up to the latter to demonstrate that the choices it has made enable it to meet the requirements laid down by the law."

The company is clearly invited to "comply" with the AFA's prescriptions, rather than to design and implement its own self-regulation system.

The evidentiary aspect of compliance systems is not the subject of this article, and we shall not go any further here in the analysis pf the reversal of the burden of proof, except to say that it takes place "in the event that the AFA challenges," which leads to submit the company to the discretion of *AFA*, since its Guidelines are totally silent on the conditions under which the *AFA* would be legitimate to challenge the relevance of the company's measures.

There is no longer any confusion: the regulator does not trust the potential measures designed by the company on its own, even though the latter is deemed to have the best knowledge of the market, its players, constraints and risks. The company must comply with the *AFA*'s guidelines, which are of a binding nature, which leads to question the persistence of any normative delegation and of the company's accountability.

Indeed, regulators expect companies to adhere to the standards they have established under the various terms of recommendations, guidelines and charters, of which they are prolific. In order for the company to comply, there must be no deviation from the pre-established norm.

Even more concerning, the company is expected to convert to the standard issued by the regulator, which is said to have a higher value because of its expert status.

But Compliance Law is neither the Law of conformity, nor of conformism: it goes far beyond the general obligation on anyone to respect the law, and its ambition is far higher than to overcome the frustration of contravening a programmatic ritual.

The danger of conformism – which appears comforting both those who submit to it and those who establish it – has been clearly identified, in particular by the Office of the United Nations High Commissioner for Human Rights (OHCHR) in 2018. (20) As far as human rights are concerned, the statement deserves attention.

There was a warning against the risks of "overly detailed and proscriptive" obligations that could lead to "narrow, compliance-orientated" and "check-box process" behaviour. (21)

And more:

> "At the same time, States should be careful to guard against unintended consequences of legal interventions. Participants at the Geneva meeting discussed possible disadvantages of 'over-regulation'; for instance, the possibility that overly detailed and proscriptive legal regimes could discourage innovation and proactive behaviour by companies and encourage narrow, compliance-orientated, 'check-box' human rights due diligence processes On the other hand, too much flexibility may not provide sufficient levels of legal certainty for companies (especially if criminal sanctions are to be applied) and could make the regime difficult to enforce. This balance can be difficult to strike in practice, and States should give careful thought to the policy aims of legislation when reconciling these competing considerations." (22)

It is indeed the danger of conformism that is underlined here.

And the second danger is that of disempowerment in the performance of the duty to prevention.

Liability regimes, whether contractual or torts, undoubtedly have a dissuasive effect, even if the regulators consider this effect insufficient.

This dissuasive effect stems from the fact that the judge, in the liability litigation, confronts the incriminated behaviour of the company with a standard of behaviour that constitutes the normality of an ideal behaviour.

Yet it is an ideal that Compliance Law aims to achieve, in terms of prevention of corruption, extortion, breach of probity, and violations of human rights, fundamental freedoms, health, personal safety, and the environment, including global warming.

---

(20) OHCHR, "*Improving accountability and process to remedy for victims of business-related human rights abuse*" UN DOC.A/HRC/38/20/ADD.2, 1 June 2018.

(21) *Ibid.*, para. 17.

(22) *Ibid.*, paras. 17-18.

The stronger the procedural requirements, the more prescriptive and descriptive the regulations will be, and the more they are based on a catalogue of measures, vigilance plans and matrix systems, the less the company will be empowered with respect to its ability to achieve these essential objectives.

It could be argued that these standards taken into consideration by the judge, within the framework of a necessarily casuistic approach, would not offer a sufficient level of predictability and, consequently, of legal certainty.

This is the argument invoked by the defenders of a plethoric and often talkative regulation, as Pr. Yves Gaudemet wrote.

This is an error in reasoning. First of all, because it means answering a question of substantive Law, which is Tort Law, with processes.

Then, it is to divert Compliance Law. Or to reduce the judge's office to a dehumanised and disembodied control of legality. Yet Compliance Law is a practical Law, striving for a supra-national ambition. Orthodoxy should not replace the efficiency that is precisely sought.

The judge's office is obviously not excluded from Compliance Law – it is even the purpose of this book, devoted to the general question of the *Compliance Jurisdictionalisation,* (23) to recall this. The judge must take it over, beyond the control of legality, which does not take stock of the effectiveness of a measure. The Judge's office must remain that of full litigation, not *a posteriori* of the realisation of a damage, but during the execution of the company's processes, in order to assess their effectiveness with regard to the behavioural standard of the reasonably diligent company, taking into consideration the actual conditions in which it is.

Tort Law is a science of behaviour. It deters anti-social behaviours, especially since the concept of damage and the mechanisms of remedy have evolved.

Through a legal fiction, damage can now be inferred from the company's behaviour alone, and that is exactly the point.

(23) E.g. M.-A. Frison-Roche, "Reinforce the Judge and the Lawyer to impose Compliance Law as a characteristic of the Rule of Law", *this book*.

The preventive dimension of the sanction in Tort Law should not be neglected. It is often a matter of reputation and its viral propagation through social networks which enter in resonance, and for the company – concerned about its image – the incentive it constitutes is much more powerful and effective than conformism, which dispenses with the need to ask questions before it is too late. (24)

Compliance Law deserves more than the mere execution of recommendations, charters and guidelines abundantly issued by the regulators.

The "monumental goals" of Compliance Law require much more than that.

(24) See C. Sintez, *La sanction préventive en droit de la responsabilité civile – Contribution à la théorie de l'interprétation et de la mise en effet des normes* (*The preventive sanction in Tort Law – Contribution to the theory of interpretation and enforcement of norms*), "Nouvelle bibliothèque de thèses" Serie, Paris, Dalloz, 2011; M.-A. Frison-Roche, "La responsabilité *Ex Ante*" ("*Ex Ante* Responsibility"), Archives de philosophie du droit (APD), *La responsabilité*, t. 63, Paris, Dalloz, 2022, pp. 155-164.

The Legal Nature of the Facebook "Supreme Court"

Jeremy Heymann

Full Professor of Law (Jean Moulin Lyon 3 University)

1. "Making words and things coincide." Such is the general theme in which the present reflections are inserted, with a view to proposing a thematic apprehension of the company, instituted as prosecutor and judge of itself. "Words and things." One immediately thinks of Michel Foucault and his famous eponymous essay – an [a]rcheology of the human sciences, according to its subtitle (1) – in which the philosopher wonders about *épistémè*, that is to say the "conditions of discourse," which depend on a context, an era... (2)

So, what can we say, today, about this phenomenon of "jurisdictionalisation" of compliance? In what context is it taking place? What are the conditions that have made it possible? It does not seem insignificant that one could go so far as to speak of a "Supreme Court" for a body invited to hear appeals of decisions concerning content on digital social networks, managed by a private company. (3)

---

(1) M. Foucault, *Les mots et les choses. Une archéologie des sciences humaines* (1966), "Tel" Serie, Paris, Gallimard, 1990.

(2) Later, on the occasion of a debate with G. Preti (*"I problemi della cultura. Un dibattito Foucault-Petri"*, trans. A. Ghizzardi, *Il Bimestre*, September-December 1972, Nos. 22-23, pp. 1-4), Foucault specified that when he spoke of *épistémè*, he meant "*tous les rapports qui ont existé à une certaine époque entre les différents domaines de la science. [...] Ce sont tous ces phénomènes de rapport entre les sciences ou entre les différents discours dans les divers secteurs scientifiques qui constituent ce [qu'il] appelle épistémè d'une époque*" (M. Foucault, *Dits et écrits*, t. I [1954-1975], "Quarto" Serie, Paris, Gallimard, 2001, p. 1239). The objective being the determination of the common knowledge that makes possible practices, institutions, and theories.

(3) In the words of M. Zuckerberg himself, founder and CEO of Facebook (CNBC, 2 April 2018). See also K. Klonick's analysis, "How to Make Facebook's Supreme Court Work", *New York Times*, 17 November 2018.

In the words of Facebook's CEO, Mark Zuckerberg,(4) the initial idea was to envision a structure that would be similar to that of a "Supreme Court" – a body of qualified individuals, independent of the company, whose decisions could be appealed and who would have the power to make a final judgment "on what should be acceptable speech in a community that reflects the social norms and values of people all around the world."(5) A vast program, but with uncertain content...

2. "Words." While the analogy with the U.S. Supreme Court is obvious,(6) it seems impossible to make the two entities coincide perfectly, if only because the official name of this body created by the Delaware corporation Facebook eventually became the Oversight Board.(7)

Traditionally, the Board is understood – at least in the French language, in a second sense and by metonymy – as a "[g]roup of persons responsible for giving advice in certain public or private matters."(8) This seems to be the purpose of this "Oversight Board": according to the preamble of the Institutional Charter that created it, its purpose is to issue "policy advisory opinions on Meta's content policies."(9) However, its mission is also – and perhaps most importantly – to "protect free expression by making principled, independent decisions about important pieces of content."(10) In these words,(11) the Oversight Board is therefore an ambivalent body, assuming at the same time advisory and supervisory missions

(4) Founded on 4 February 2004, The Facebook, Inc. was quickly renamed Facebook, Inc., before being once more renamed "Meta" (Meta Platforms, Inc.) on 28 October 2021.

(5) The excerpt from which this quote is taken is as follows: "Over the long term, what I'd really like to get to is an independent appeal. So maybe folks at Facebook make the first decision based on the community standards that are outlined, and then people can get a second opinion. [...] You can imagine some sort of structure, almost like a Supreme Court, that is made up of independent folks who don't work for Facebook, who ultimately make the final judgment call on what should be acceptable speech in a community that reflects the social norms and values of people all around the world" (Mr. Zuckerberg, 2 April 2018, public statement, available on the Consumer News and Business Channel [CNBC] institutional website: www.cnbc.com).

(6) See below, at paras. 14-15.

(7) Although Facebook – now Meta Platforms – is headquartered in Menlo Park, California, it is formally incorporated in Delaware.

(8) According to the *Trésor de la langue française* (v° "Conseil", II, A°), a *Conseil* (Board) is defined as a "[g]*roupe de personnes chargées de donner des avis dans certaines affaires publiques ou privées.*"

(9) Oversight Board Charter (Feb. 2023), Introduction, para. 4.

(10) *Ibid.*

(11) In a third sense, the vernacular puts more emphasis on the decision-making authority of the board, defined as "a group of people constituted as the decision-making-body of an organization" (A. Stevenson and C. A. Indberg [eds], *New Oxford American English Dictionary*, 3rd ed., Oxford, OUP, 2010, v° "Board", 3). The legal language is more nuanced, indicating that the board is "a group of persons having managerial, supervisory, or advisory powers" (B. A. Garner [ed.], *Black's Law Dictionary*, 11th ed., St. Paul, Minn., Thomson Reuters, 2019, V° "Board", 1.).

with decision-making authority. A jurisdictional function seems to be *a priori* attributed to it.

3. "Things." Whatever name one chooses for the moment to designate this body created by the Facebook company, one must immediately recognise that words are powerless to decide, by the meaning one lends them – without even considering questions of translation (12) – the question of the legal nature of this so-called "Supreme Court." Do we not know of Courts which, although they have a jurisdictional function, can be seized for advice? (13) Do we not also know of Councils which, likewise, can be seized for advice? (14) And don't we know, with arbitration, a jurisdictional mode based on convention and of private origin?

Beyond words, the nature of Meta's Oversight Board therefore depends on "things": what it is, and what it is used for. However, the implications of such a characterisation can only be fully understood in the context in which the Board was created, and in the – new? – framework it has created.

4. Context. From a *micro* point of view, the challenges of setting up an Oversight Board are primarily assessed in terms of compliance: compliance of content published on social networks such as Facebook or Instagram with the standards issued by these companies; compliance of decisions – on moderation or assessment of this moderation – with the Law, whose substance and authority must also be assessed.

From a *macro* point of view, these same issues call into question everyone's conception of justice, starting with the 2.5 billion active users claimed by Meta Platforms, Inc. The context to be appreciated here is

---

(12) Every linguist is familiar with the famous paronomasia *traduttore-traditore*, which refers to the impossibility of achieving a perfect translation of an original work into a foreign language and is intended to underline the necessary – albeit debated – betrayal that translation would entail. On this concept, from a French perspective, see J. Du Bellay, *La Défense et Illustration de la Langue française* (1549), *in Les Regrets*, preceded by *Les Antiquités de Rome* and followed by *Défense et Illustration de la Langue française*, foreword by J. Borel, "nrf – Poésie" Serie, Paris, Gallimard, 1967, pp. 234-235. It should be added that every jurist specialised in the field of Comparative Law is also aware of the consequences of this paronomasia when comparing institutions of different legal orders. On these questions, see "La traduction juridique", *in Les Cahiers de Droit*, 1987, Vol. 28, No. 4, pp. 735 *et seq.*, with contributions by M. Beaupré, I. Kitamura, G.-R. de Groot, J. H. Herbots and R. Sacco. See also O. Moréteau, "Les frontières de la langue et du droit : vers une méthodologie de la traduction juridique", *RIDC*, 2009, 695.

(13) In France, referral to the *Cour de cassation* (French Court of cassation) for an opinion has been provided for since an Act of 15 May 1991 (Law No. 91-491 of 15 May 1991: *JORF*, 18 May 1991, p. 6790). See nowadays the relevant provisions of the *Code de l'organisation judiciaire – COJ* (French Judicial Organisation Code), Articles L. 441-1 to L. 441-4 and R. 441-1.

(14) In France, see e.g. *Code de justice administrative* (French Administrative Justice Code), Articles L. 113-1 and R. 113-1 to R. 113-4.

that of legal pluralism, in which the legality of a text and/or a decision no longer depends on a State or a group of States, but on the claim, by a private company, of a community of individuals that transcends borders and continents. (15) Thus, we can see that private powers are shaped in consideration of public powers, with a view to *ex ante* avoidance. The aim of this avoidance is to protect the private actor from state justice, while at the same time draping himself, in anticipation, in the virtue of respect for the Law. But what kind of Law are we talking about? Global Law? De-statized Law? Non-state Law elaborated/validated by a social community, but on what basis?

5. Plan. In order to better understand the Meta case, it is necessary to first identify it by studying its Oversight Board (I), before raising a certain number of questions (II).

I. IDENTIFICATION

6. Position of the problem. When contemplating the relations between public and private powers, it is traditionally considered that the settlement of conflicts and disputes between categorical interests falls to the state judge. Both the search for and the determination of the common good constitute the basis of his or her office, which is traditionally linked to a mission of public service. (16)

Facebook's creation of an Oversight Board is a further example of the search for a common good, by means of a body whose primary function would be to resolve a category-based conflict of interest(s), when the interests of users of the social networking platform in question collide with the

(15) Among the abundant legal literature, see the seminal work of G. Teubner, "'Global Bukowina': Legal Pluralism in the World Society", *in* G. Teubner (ed.), *Global Law without a State*, Aldershot/Brookfield USA/Singapore/Sydney, Dartmouth, 1997, pp. 3 *et seq*. See also the contributions by P. S. Berman, "Non-State Lawmaking through the Lens of Global Legal Pluralism" and R. Michaels, "What is Non-State Law? A Primer", in M. A. Helfand (ed.), *Negotiating State and Non-State Law. The Challenge of Global and Local Legal Pluralism*, Cambridge, Cambridge Univ. Press, 2015, pp. 15-40 and pp. 41-58 respectively; A. C. Cutler and Th. Dietz, *The Politics of Private Transnational Governance by Contract*, "Politics of Transnational Law" Serie, London/New York, Routledge, 2017; A. Peters, L. Koechlin, T. Förster and G. Fenner Zinkernagel (eds), *Non-State Actors as Standard Setters*, Cambridge, Cambridge Univ. Press, 2017; B. Shams, *Le conflit de lois et la production privée des droits fondamentaux: vers un renouveau théorique*, th. dactyl., IEP Paris, 2019. See also *Le pluralisme, Archives Phil. dr.*, 2005, t. 49, with contributions by D. Terré, "Le pluralisme et le droit", pp. 69 *et seq.*, and D. Boden, "Le pluralisme juridique en droit international privé", pp. 275 *et seq.*

(16) From a French perspective, see notably R. Chapus, "De l'office du juge: Contentieux administratif et nouvelle procédure civile", in *Études et documents du Conseil d'État*, 1977-1978, No. 29, pp. 11 *et seq.*, repr. in *L'administration et son juge*, "Doctrine juridique" Serie, Paris, PUF, 1999, p. 295.

interests of the company providing access to the service in question.(17) Is this office comparable to that performed by representatives of older institutions? Or is it something else?

7. Subdivision. To answer these questions, a brief overview of the main dispute resolution methods available – conceived as so many categories into which the Oversight Board's office could be classified – can be drawn up (A). The classification of the Oversight Board's office can then be proposed (B).

A. Available categories

8. Nomenclature. In addition to the state judicial framework for settling disputes that have degenerated into litigation, there are other methods of settlement available to the parties. Whether amicable or judicial, it should be emphasised from the outset that these methods of dispute resolution are centuries-old, and all share the common idea that conflict is consubstantial with a society and the personal interactions to which it gives rise. Without claiming to be exhaustive, and limiting ourselves to the main ones, we will list conciliation, mediation, amiable composition and arbitration as methods of dispute settlement other than legal proceedings.

9. Conciliation and mediation. While one could argue that mediation is a form of conciliation, it remains that these two methods share the common features of being amicable and peaceful methods of dispute resolution, through the choice of a third party, whose role is to act impartially and independently with the aim of helping the parties to settle their dispute themselves.(18)

(17) As a reminder, Facebook's Oversight Board is intended to "provide an accessible opportunity for people [who use Meta Platforms, Inc.'s services, including Facebook and Instagram (collectively referred to as "Meta")] to request its review and be heard" (Oversight Board Charter, Introduction). Two distinct social networking platforms are therefore concerned and grouped together under an emblematic common name.

(18) In France, Article 1530 of the *Code de procédure civile* (French Civil Procedure Code) defines these two methods as follows: "*La médiation et la conciliation conventionnelles régies par le présent titre s'entendent* [...] *de tout processus structuré, par lequel deux ou plusieurs parties tentent de parvenir à un accord, en dehors de toute procédure judiciaire en vue de la résolution amiable de leurs différends, avec l'aide d'un tiers choisi par elles qui accomplit sa mission avec impartialité, compétence et diligence*" (free translation: "conventional mediation and conciliation [...] are understood to mean any structured process by which two or more parties attempt to reach an agreement, outside of any legal proceedings, with a view to the amicable resolution of their disputes, with the help of a third party chosen by them who carries out his or her mission with impartiality, competence and diligence.")

Emphasising its independence and competence to deal with the claims submitted to it, (19) the Oversight Board seems to possess, *prima facie*, the qualities required of a mediator and/or conciliator. However, it is easy to see that the Oversight Board is not a third party truly chosen by the parties: whether it is "Facebook" or the user who is dissatisfied with the removal of content and/or a moderation decision taken against him or her, each of these parties is in fact offered, within the framework of an "appeal" procedure, only the Oversight Board as a third party likely to enable them to reach a settlement of their dispute. (20)

Furthermore, and more importantly, it is traditionally taught that the value of conciliation – like that of mediation – lies in the fact that the resolution of the dispute must come from the parties themselves, and not from the third party they have previously chosen. Considering the very terms of the "Oversight Board Charter," it is expressly stated that "[t]he board's resolution of each case will be binding," (21) which implies that the parties will have a decision *imposed* on them which they have not jointly reached.

Finally, it should be noted that the Board has "the discretion to choose which requests it will review and decide upon", (22) which seems hardly compatible with the diligence expected of a conciliator/mediator, and more generally with the spirit of a mediation or conciliation procedure, which should lead the parties to attempt to resolve their own dispute. These methods of dispute resolution, conceived as potential indicators of the Oversight Board's mission and function, therefore appear to have to be disqualified.

10. Amiable composition. Another form of dispute resolution available to the parties, amiable composition classically consists of submitting a dispute to a judge or arbitrator and giving him or her the power to settle it in equity, i.e. outside the legal rules that would otherwise apply. (23)

(19) See the "Principles" referred to on the Oversight Board's website, accessible via the following communication protocol: https://www.oversightboard.com. See also the Oversight Board bylaws, accessible via the same communication protocol.

(20) However, recourse to the Oversight Board by either party does not appear to be mandatory. Article 2 of the Oversight Board's Charter provides that "[p]eople using Meta's services and Meta itself *may* bring forward content for board review" (emphasis added). Section 1, subparagraph 1, of the same provision specifies that "[i]n instances where people disagree with the outcome of Meta's decision and have exhausted appeals, a request for review can be submitted to the board by either the original poster of the content or a person who previously submitted the content to Meta for review."

(21) Oversight Board Charter (February 2023), Article 4.

(22) *Ibid.*, Article 2, Sect. 1, para. 2.

(23) Under French Law, for example, this possibility is offered to the parties by Article 12, para. 4, and Article 1478 of the *Code de procédure civile* (French Civil Procedure Code), depending on whether the dispute is submitted to a judge or an arbitrator.

While it is true that the Oversight Board's role is to render its decisions outside the legal framework of a State, it does not appear to be vested with any power to rule in equity by the parties bringing the matter before it. Admittedly, the Oversight Board's charter expressly states that it "will not purport to enforce local law." (24) However, the Oversight Board does not claim to rule in equity either: its primary mission is to "review and decide on content in accordance with Meta's content policies and values," (25) while paying "particular attention to the impact of removing content in light of human rights norms protecting free expression." (26)

As a means of dispute settlement, amiable composition therefore appears to be equally disqualified to reveal the mission and function of Meta's Oversight Board.

11. Arbitration. The last available category in which the Oversight Board's mission and function could be classified as a dispute resolution method, arbitration, is intuitively related to the Oversight Board's office. As we know, the purpose of an arbitral tribunal is to settle disputes and put an end to them by means of an arbitral award, which is binding on the parties. (27)

However, it suffices here to note that unlike an arbitral tribunal, which must be set up to settle a specific dispute, the Oversight Board appears to be both unique and permanent. In addition, and above all, arbitration is a dispute settlement method based on agreement, which means that the members of the arbitral tribunal must be appointed by the parties, either by name or by means of some other appointment procedure. (28) However, the members of the Oversight Board are in no way chosen, let alone appointed, by the parties.

12. Transition. In view of the foregoing, the Oversight Board, while borrowing certain characteristics from several dispute resolution methods, cannot be classified in one of the main categories listed above. So how should it be classified?

(24) Oversight Board Charter (February 2023), Article 7, at the end.

(25) *Ibid.*, Article 2, *initio.*

(26) *Ibid.*, Article 2, Sect. 2, para. 3.

(27) The rates of spontaneous compliance with final arbitration awards are generally said to be good. Some authors venture an 80% rate. For a suggestion of an "empirical research to track and understand the ultimate fate of international commercial arbitration awards", see Q. Tannock, "Judging the Effectiveness of Arbitration trough the Assessment of Compliance with and Enforcement of International Arbitration Awards", *Arbitration International*, 2005, Vol. 21, No. 1, pp. 71-90.

(28) Under French Law, these two procedures are set out in the *Code de procédure civile* (French Civil Procedure Code), whether the arbitration is domestic (Article 1444) or international (Article 1508).

B. Qualification retained

13. Office and basis of the Oversight Board's decision-making process. According to the Oversight Board Charter, the main function of this body is to "review and decide on content in accordance with Meta's content policies and values." (29)

The request for review is submitted to the Board "by either the original poster of the content or a person who previously submitted the content to Meta for review. Separately, Meta can submit requests for review, including additional questions related to the treatment of content beyond whether the content should be fully allowed or removed completely." (30)

It should also be remembered that the Oversight Board "has the discretion to choose which requests it will review and decide upon". (31) To this end, "[i]n its selection, the board will seek to consider cases that have the greatest potential to guide future decisions and policies." (32)

Finally, regarding the basis of the decision-making process, the Oversight Board intends to rely not only on Meta's content policies and values, but also, "[f]or each decision, [on] any prior board decisions," (33) which "will have precedential value and should be viewed as highly persuasive when the facts, applicable policies, or other factors are substantially similar." (34)

In addition, the Board "will pay particular attention to the impact of removing content in light of human rights norms protecting free expression." (35)

14. Analogy with the US Supreme Court. Illustrating the process of jurisdictionalisation of compliance, the review of cases submitted – and upheld – by the Oversight Board is formally presented as a review of compliance with "Meta's content policies and values." Although this office is technically limited, an analogy with that of the Federal Supreme Court of the United States, as well as with the way it operates, seems appropriate with a view to qualifying said office. (36)

(29) Oversight Board Charter (February 2023), Article 2, *initio*.

(30) *Ibid.*, Article 2, Sect. 1, para. 1.

(31) *Ibid.*, Article 2, Sect. 1, para. 2.

(32) *Ibid.* The provision adds that "[i]n limited circumstances where the board's decision on a case could result in criminal liability or regulatory sanctions the case will be ineligible for board review."

(33) *Ibid.*, Article 2, Sect. 2, para. 2.

(34) *Ibid.*

(35) *Ibid.*, Article 2, Sect. 2, para. 3.

(36) It should be remembered that the Oversight Board was modelled on the U.S. Supreme Court (see above, notes 3 and 5).

After exhaustion of all prior avenues of appeal, the Oversight Board, like the Federal Supreme Court, decides on appeal.(37) Likewise, it has discretionary power to select the cases it intends to review, as does the US Federal Supreme Court.(38)

Although the Oversight Board Charter refers to the establishment by the Board of "its own set of procedures that its staff will use to select a pool of cases from which the board can choose,"(39) this set of procedures, which is not very explicit, does not seem to imply the issuance of any writ of certiorari. We are merely informed directly by the Oversight Board that it "only selects a small number of cases for review,"(40) and that it "prioritizes cases that are challenging, globally relevant and can inform future policy."(41)

15. Analogy with the US Supreme Court. Limitations. A comparison can therefore be made between the Oversight Board and the Federal Supreme Court of the United States, but the search for coincidence is hardly fruitful: *omnis comparatio claudicat*! Admittedly, the Charter refers to the future case-law of the Oversight Board, whose "prior decisions will have precedential value,"(42) as an authority that can serve as a basis for the decision-making process. This is a clear reference to the binding

(37) Under Article III, Sect. 2, para. 2, of the US Federal Constitution, "[i]n all Cases affecting Ambassadors, other public Ministers and Consuls, and those in which a State shall be Party, the supreme Court shall have original Jurisdiction. *In all the other Cases* before mentioned, *the supreme Court shall have appellate Jurisdiction, both as to Law and Fact*, with such Exceptions, and under such Regulations as the Congress shall make" (emphasis added).

As a reminder, paragraph 1 provides that "[t]he judicial Power shall extend to all Cases, in Law and Equity, arising under this Constitution, the Laws of the United States, and Treaties made, or which shall be made, under their Authority; – [...] to Controversies to which the United States shall be a Party; – to Controversies between two or more States; – [...] between Citizens of different States; – between Citizens of the same State claiming lands under grants of different States, and between a State, or the Citizens thereof, and foreign States, Citizens or Subjects."

(38) Under Section 1254 of Title 28 of the United States Code (28 U.S.C. para. 1254): "Cases in the courts of appeals may be reviewed by the Supreme Court by the following methods: (1) By writ of certiorari granted upon the petition of any party to any civil or criminal case, before or after rendition of judgment or decree [...]." This text derives from the original adoption of the Judiciary Act of 1925 [43 Stat. 936] – also known as the Certiorari Act or the "Judges' Bill," because of its original drafting/confection by Associate Justices W. R. Day, W. Van Devanter, J. C. McReynolds and G. Sutherland, at the request of Chief Justice William Howard Taft – by which the U.S. Congress intended to reduce the workload of Supreme Court justices and to extend the institution's discretionary power of case selection, by generalizing the practice of writs of certioriari (limited to certain matters only since the Judiciary Act of 1891, which also created the Federal Courts of Appeal). On the history of the "Judges' Bill", see in particular Merlo J. Pusey, "The Judges' Bill After Half a Century", Supreme Court Historical Society Yearbook, 1976, pp. 73-81.

(39) Oversight Board Charter (Feb. 2023), Article 2, Sect. 1, para. 3.

(40) This information is available on the Oversight Board's corporate website: www.oversightboard.com, in the "Appeals process" section.

(41) See previous footnote.

(42) See above notes 33 and 34.

precedent technique, and once again authorises a comparison between the judicial practice of the U.S. Supreme Court and that which the Oversight Board intends to implement. (43)

We can therefore expect that the Oversight Board will gradually develop distinctions between binding precedent and persuasive authority, and that sooner or later the Board will include the "distinguishing technique" in its "case-law," as can be seen in the case-law of the Federal Supreme Court and more generally in American judicial practice. (44)

However, while the Oversight Board's inspiration in defining its role and the decision-making process it intends to follow is clearly identified, there remains a fundamental difference between the "model" and its "replica": the latter is purely private in origin and does not derive its authority from any state constitution.

16. Jurisdictional nature. This fundamental difference raises the following question: does the private origin of the Oversight Board, and its overall composition, disqualify it as a jurisdictional body? In our view, the answer is negative. It seems to us that this Oversight Board, although of private and non-state origin, is nonetheless called upon to interpret the Law, i.e. to say what the Law is.

Admittedly, the basis for the Board's decisions is above all "Meta's content policies and values." (45) However, as we have seen, the Charter clearly states that the Oversight Board is required to pay "particular attention to the impact of removing content in light of human rights norms protecting free expression." (46) Although this legal frame of reference is rather flexible – not to say vague – it can nonetheless be seen as a form of obligation to "take into consideration" a binding legal framework, (47) which will nonetheless have the particularity of evolving according to the geographical context in which the case under review is located. An example is

(43) It should be noted that the Oversight Board Charter specifies that "any prior board decisions [...] should be viewed as *highly persuasive* when the facts, applicable policies, or other factors are substantially similar" (Oversight Board Charter, Article 2, Sect. 2, para. 2. Emphasis added).

(44) For a clear and simple presentation of these different techniques, see E. A. Farnsworth, *An Introduction to the Legal System of the United States*, 4th ed., New York, OUP, 2010, pp. 59 *et seq*.

(45) Oversight Board Charter (February 2023), Article 2, *initio*.

(46) *Ibid.*, Article 2, Sect. 2, para. 3.

(47) However, Article 7 of the Oversight Board Charter contains a reservation. Relating to "Compliance with Law", this provision states that "[t]he board will not purport to enforce local law."

provided by the decision concerning the account of the former President of the United States of America. (48)

Under the heading of Facebook's "values," the Oversight Board begins by recalling the company's commitment, as part of its corporate human rights policy, to respect rights in accordance with the United Nations Guiding Principles on Business and Human Rights (UNGPs). (49) The Board deduces from this the obligation for Facebook "to respect international human rights standards wherever it operates." (50) These standards are essentially identified by the Oversight Board as the stipulations contained in the International Covenant on Civil and Political Rights (hereinafter "ICCPR"), (51) as interpreted in General Comment 34 of the Human Rights Committee. (52)

However, the geographical framework does appear in the decision when the Board refers to the First Amendment to the Federal Constitution of the United States of 17 September 1787. Although the Oversight Board refuses to apply it – on the grounds that "the First Amendment of the U.S. Constitution [...] does not govern the conduct of private companies" (53) – it nevertheless intends to note that "in many relevant respects the principles of freedom of expression reflected in the First Amendment are similar or analogous to the principles of freedom of expression in ICCPR Article 19." (54) Consequently, after stating that any restrictions on freedom of expression must, under International Law, meet three requirements (clarity and accessibility of the rules; legitimate aim of the rules; necessity and proportionality of the rules to the risk of harm), the Oversight Board feels the need to specify that "First Amendment principles under U.S. law insist that restrictions on freedom of speech imposed through state action may not be vague, must be for important governmental reasons and must

(48) Case decision 2021-001-FB-FBR of 5 May 2021, available on the Oversight Board's corporate website: www.oversightboard.com, in the "Decisions" section. The decision explicitly locates the case in the "United States/Canada" region, but only the United States of America is identified as "affected country."

(49) Drafted to implement United Nations "Protect, Respect and Remedy's Framework", these Guiding Principles on Business and Human Rights were developed by the Special Representative of the Secretary-General on the issue of human rights and transnational corporations and other business enterprises. The Special Representative annexed the Guiding Principles to his final report to the Human Rights Council (A/HRC/17/31), which endorsed them in its resolution 17/4 of 16 June 2011. They were subsequently published (HR/PUB/11/4).

(50) Case decision 2021-001-FB-FBR of 5 May 2021, Section 4.III.

(51) Open for signature in New York on 16 December 1966, the Covenant entered into force on 23 March 1976, in accordance with Article 49. On 1 July 2023, 173 States ratified it.

(52) See Section 4.III of Case decision 2021-001-FB-FBR of 5 May 2021, for detailed references.

(53) Case decision 2021-001-FB-FBR of 5 May 2021, Sect. 8.3, para. 3.

(54) *Ibid.*

be narrowly tailored to the risk of harm."(55) Are we to understand that Facebook – now Meta – is comparable to a state? At the very least, in the Oversight Board's analysis, is it on an equal footing with States when it comes to protecting human rights?

Be that as it may, this decision clearly illustrates that the Oversight Board does indeed exercise, within a restricted framework, a jurisdictional mission: to state the Law, in the light of fundamental – and supposedly universal – principles for the protection of human rights, including freedom of expression. The Oversight Board's functions are therefore akin to those of a judge, albeit very limited.

17. Operational-level grievance mechanisms and dispute resolution body. Ultimately, the legal status of the Oversight Board appears to be twofold.

According to the Guiding Principles on Business and Human Rights, (56) this would be a non-state-based "grievance mechanism," which would more specifically take the form of a grievance mechanism "at the operational level."(57) Designed to be "accessible directly to individuals and communities who may be adversely impacted by a business enterprise," this type of mechanism does "not require that those bringing a complaint first access other means of recourse,"(58) and its aim would be that those bringing a complaint "can engage the business enterprise directly in assessing the issues and seeking remediation of any harm."(59) This seems to be the hallmark of the Oversight Board.

That said, it is fair to say that this first qualification, which is more descriptive than definitive, lacks precision. We therefore prefer the term "dispute resolution body," which seems the most appropriate to define the Oversight Board. As an independent body – albeit one originally set up by a private-sector company – the Oversight Board's role is certainly, and above all, to monitor compliance. (60) It is also true that the Oversight Board can be considered an institutional ombudsman since its mission is also similar to that of a defender of the rights of users of social networking platforms such as Facebook and Instagram. However, the Oversight Board is best qualified as a dispute resolution body, since its jurisdictional

(55) Case decision 2021-001-FB-FBR of 5 May 2021, Sect. 8.3, para. 6.
(56) See above note 49.
(57) Guiding Principles on Business and Human Rights (UNGPs): HR/PUB/11/4, 2011, p. 31, Principle 29.
(58) *Ibid.*
(59) *Ibid.*
(60) See above No. 4.

mission necessarily includes the other two, and ultimately takes precedence over them.

18. Transition. Identified as a dispute resolution body, the Oversight Board appears to have a preventive function. From a strictly *ex ante* perspective, the first consequence of the Oversight Board's jurisdictional role is that it will rule ahead of a – state – judicial decision... which may have the corollary of preventing active users of the Facebook and Instagram social networks from taking their cases to state courts. Should we fear competition between the Oversight Board and state courts? Could a decision taken by the Oversight Board become *res judicata*? In other words, the creation of this Oversight Board raises several questions, which, in view of this body's still recent practice, we will consider as open issues.

II. QUESTIONS

19. Subdivision. The questions raised by the creation and establishment of the Oversight Board are logically numerous, given the extent to which the exercise by this body of its mission(s) somewhat upsets what might be described as the established order. Can we entrust a private body with the task of protecting the fundamental rights of over two billion people? Are we witnessing a privatisation of the protection of human rights, and in particular freedom of expression? (61) These questions suffice to demonstrate that the issues raised essentially concern the legitimacy of the Oversight Board (A) and its authority (B).

A. Legitimacy

20. *A priori* approval. The legitimacy of the Oversight Board, as a private body for the preventive resolution of disputes, is a key question for any observer of the system that has been set up.

Let's be clear from the outset: there is nothing shocking about entrusting a private person, and a qualified one at that, with jurisdictional powers. Are we thinking of calling into question arbitration, whether institutional or *ad hoc*? The development of arbitration as a means of resolving disputes,

(61) In the same vein, see V. Ndior, "Le Conseil de surveillance de Facebook et la protection des libertés", *RDLF*, 2022, chron. No. 23, III.

and the competition between the world's major arbitration centres, clearly argue in favour of a negative response.

Nor is it shocking that an international non-governmental organisation should be at the origin of a jurisdictional means of settling disputes in a specific field or area. Wasn't the Court of Arbitration for Sport (CAS) intended, and then set up, to constitute a jurisdiction specific to sport, and sporting activities in particular? (62)

In a pluralist context, it is not questionable that private bodies can take on a jurisdictional mission, what's more on the basis of standards developed at international level by organisations such as the UN. It is worth recalling here that Facebook – now Meta – clearly intends to comply with the guidelines drawn up by the Office of the United Nations High Commissioner for Human Rights.

21. Discretionary case selection. Risks. Even though the creation of a non-judicial grievance mechanism is *a priori* endorsed, the fact remains that the exercise of *jurisdictio* by the Oversight Board raises questions: is it indeed the role of such a body to set itself up, *volens nolens*, as a reference jurisdiction on the exercise and safeguarding of the human rights of social network users? Above all, the practice of discretionary selection of cases for analysis by the Oversight Board is questionable. In a document available on its institutional website, the said Board explains its "overarching criteria for case selection": these are cases "that raise important issues for precedential impact." (63)

While these criteria are intended to be reviewed annually by the Oversight Board, the fact remains that the cases selected for review "will be significant for public discourse, affect a substantial number of people, and ensure geographic and linguistic diversity. They will seek to reflect the concerns of the people and communities who use and are affected by Facebook and Instagram around the world." (64) Shifting the conception of the appeal system more towards *ius constitutionis* (i.e. uniform interpretation/application of principles from a general interest perspective) than *ius litigatoris* (i.e. deciding a dispute in a given case), this stance by the Oversight Board is not without its critics, however, as it is hard to see,

(62) On CAS, see notably J.-P. Karaquillo, "Droit international du sport", *RCADI*, 2004, Vol. 309, pp. 107 *et seq*. The author presents the organization of the CAS as "a guarantee of independence and accepted authority" (free translation: "*un gage d'indépendance et d'autorité acceptée*", *eod. loc.*).

(63) Overarching Criteria for Case Selection (2023), p. 2.

(64) *Ibid.*

a priori, what objectively constitutes "important issues for precedential impact" justifying the review of a case by the said Board. (65) Is there not a risk, then, of questions being dismissed as being of little importance, or even inappropriate from the point of view of the policy defended by Meta? This is to rephrase a classic question about the legitimacy of a body with a jurisdictional mission to hear certain cases, on the grounds that said body would be both judge and party – due to the origin of its creation and/or its representation (66) –, which leads us to approach now the issues in terms of authority.

B. Authority

22. *Res judicata* and *imperium merum*? What is the authority of an Oversight Board decision? Under Article 4 of the Charter, the "board's resolution of each case will be binding and Meta will implement it promptly, unless implementation of a resolution could violate the law [of the affected country]." Each decision is therefore binding and enforceable *per se*.

But what happens if enforcement is refused, or only partially enforced? In such cases, can the authority of the decision be imposed other than by recourse to state coercion? Where is the Oversight Board's *imperium merum*? It has none. And supposing a decision is not implemented spontaneously, will a state judge see it as a jurisdictional act likely to be granted exequatur? This is a relatively old question in the field of arbitration… Furthermore, if a decision is challenged on the merits before a state court, will it be considered as fact or Law? Will the state judge feel bound by any *res judicata*? Given the current state of available sources, we can only speculate.

What are we to make of the normative content of these decisions, which have taken international human rights standards into consideration? Are they the first signs of the emergence of a Global Law? Are more than 2.5 billion users, and the diversity of the members of the Oversight Board, enough to justify the emergence of such a right? For which authority?

(65) In a former version, the Board mentioned cases that "will be of critical importance to public discourse."

(66) For an illustration, concerning the US Supreme Court, see J. C. Calhoun's criticisms, in R. Meriwether, W.E. Hemphill and C. N. Wilson (eds), *The Papers of John C. Calhoun*, 28 vols, Columbia, Univ. of South Carolina Press, 1959-2003, esp. vol. XI (1829-1832); R.M. Lence (ed.), *Union and Liberty. The Political Philosophy of John C. Calhoun*, Indianapolis, Liberty Fund, 1992, esp. pp. 229-230, and at pp. 406 *et seq.*

These are all questions that remain unanswered for the time being, but which the advent of a Compliance Law must consider and already incorporate into the reasoning behind the relationship that will inevitably be maintained between state legal systems and the Oversight Board (or, more generally, any equivalent body set up by other companies).

*

* *

23. Conclusion. At the end of this study, the proposed analysis of the Oversight Board reminds us of a traditional nursery rhyme:

Something old
Something new
Something borrowed
Something blue… (67)

While the nursery rhyme is primarily about what a bride needs to have a happy and fruitful marriage, the "words" and "things" mentioned in the nursery rhyme seem to characterise what the Oversight Board is all about: something that is both new and old, something borrowed (from other models) and… something blue: after all, isn't that the colour of the Facebook logo, as well as that of the Meta logo?

Time will tell whether the marriage of jurisdiction and compliance will be a happy one for the Oversight Board, but both its existence and practice already reveal the vivacity of contemporary legal pluralism.

(67) "*… and a* [*silver*] *sixpence in her shoe.*" These are the opening lines of a nursery rhyme that is extremely popular in the English-speaking world. On the origin of this folklore, see W. Crooke, "*The Wooing of Penelope*", *Folk-Lore*, 1898, Vol. IX, No. II, pp. 97-135, esp. p. 128.

Internal investigations within companies

DAPHNÉ LATOUR

Attorney at Law

Member of the Paris Bar

DL Avocats Law Firm

Internal investigation, which can be defined as an investigation requested by a company's management or an *ad hoc* committee to collect data on potential illegal facts committed within the company with a view to legally qualify them, to decide whether a disciplinary or a judicial proceedings should be opened to end such acts, and to sanction and avoid such acts happening again, is a common legal practice which is growing quickly in France especially since the enactment of the French so-called "Sapin 2" law. (1)

Indeed, this law created French Deferred prosecution agreements, known as *Convention judiciaire d'intérêt public – CJIP* (Judicial Public Interest Agreement). And, even if executing an internal investigation is not *per se* a legal condition for a company to benefit from a *CJIP* proposed by the prosecutor – among the few *CJIP* already signed so far, only one was preceded by an internal investigation – the *Parquet national financier – PNF* (French National Financial Prosecutor's Office) expressly mentioned in the common guidelines co-written with the *Agence française anticorruption – AFA* (French Anti-Corruption Agency – AFA), published in 2019, that companies need to actively participate in the determination of the truth.

(1) French law No. 2016-1691 of 9 December 2016 *relative à la transparence, à la lutte contre la corruption et à la modernisation de la vie économique* (on transparency, fight against corruption and modernisation of economic life).

However, despite the growing attraction for internal investigation and the fact that it may generate criminal, reputational, financial, organisational and strategical risks, the French legislator has thus far not established any rules constraining such practice. This gap has moreover been pointed out by Mr. Gauvain and Mr. Marleix in the Information report on the assessment of the impact of law No. 2016-1691 of 9 December 2016 on transparency, the fight against corruption and the modernization of economic life, known as "Sapin 2 law" (2) They suggested to more legally frame internal investigation and grant individuals submitted to such investigation more rights and guarantees.

Thus, as of the end of 2023, no legal specific and unified rules apply under French Law to regulate internal investigation, companies and their counsel tend to circumvent it and to, instead, apply dedicated Common Law principles, fundamental rights of the European Convention for the Protection of Human Rights and Fundamental Freedoms, French Criminal Law and procedural rules, as well as Labour Law and its sometime contradictory precedent regarding defence of employee's rights.

Such legal insecurity, coming from both uncertainty and unpredictability of the rules, is even more stressful for companies that, at the same time, they are increasingly asked to be more responsible *vis-à-vis* their employees acts and to regulate themselves if no legal regulations apply.

Private companies are now asked to both perform state duties and have moral, or at least ethical, behaviour. They and their managers are required to be omniscient and able to prevent misdemeanours, acts which are facilitated by the modernisation of technological tools and encouraged by growing worldwide poverty. And, in case of failure, companies should, at least, be able to detect and prevent them, by implementing adequate procedures that an internal investigation would have precisely helped to design.

How, under such circumstances, to effectively investigate oneself? All while bearing in mind that such efficiency will differ depending on whether it is viewed from the judicial authorities or companies' point of view. What rules should a company be compliant with, regardless of whether a preliminary investigation or a judicial investigation has already

(2) Free translation of *Rapport d'information sur l'évaluation de l'impact de la loi n° 2016-1691 du 9 décembre 2016 relative à la transparence, à la lutte contre la corruption et à la modernisation de la vie économique, dite "loi Sapin 2"*, presented by MM. Raphaël Gauvain and Olivier Marleix, Reporters of the Law Commission, Deputies, 7 July 2021.

been opened, or a *CJIP* is about to be negotiated or if the investigation is just to deal with an alert? Which of the company's or employees' rights and principles – which may be opposing – should prevail?

This article's objective is to disentangle what a company can do from what it should do, while acting as both prosecutor and party. To do so, we will (I) examine circumstances under which and reasons for which a company would like to open an internal investigation, (II) examine situations where investigations are legally required as opposed to cases where it is just recommended and (III) analyse all relevant risks and the way to prevent them.

I. WHEN AND FOR WHAT MAIN REASONS MAY A COMPANY HAVE TO OPEN AN INTERNAL INVESTIGATION?

An internal investigation, as a risk management tool, may be opened by a company, at its managers or an *ad hoc* committee's demand, in the event of a breach of law or internal rule. In particular, it may occur after one of the five following events occurs. (3)

The first event is an alert (4) coming from an employee or an external stakeholder, who may or may not have used a dedicated internal whistleblowing system (consisting of either a digital platform, an email address or simply a hotline, depending on the resources of the company in question.) (5)

The second event is the company's own spontaneous discovery, resulting from an internal control or an internal audit (global or targeted).

The third event is discovery coming from an external stakeholder, such as an auditor or a bank, while executing a control or an audit.

(3) A company may decide to initiate an internal investigation into facts potentially constituting a criminal offense, such as insider trading, even if the day the facts are discovered they are legally time-barred if the company anticipates that disclosure to the public, without it having full knowledge of the facts, and therefore without having been able to prepare its defense communication, would be likely to cause serious reputational damage, or if it can still act on a contractual basis against the author of the facts (for example, if the author is a current employee).

(4) The "Sapin 2" law requires that any alert which fulfills certain legal conditions relating to the author of the alert and its content must be processed. In-depth processing requires the conduct of an internal investigation. This regulation also applies to anonymous alerts.

(5) The regulator will not consider that a simple email address to be inadequate as a professional whistleblowing system for a VSE or SME.

The fourth event is the discovery by a regulatory authority, or more generally an independent administrative authority (such as the *Agence française anticorruption – AFA* [French Anti-Corruption Agency], the *Autorité des marchés financiers – AMF* [French Financial Markets Authority], the *Autorité de la concurrence – ADLC* [French Competition Authority], the *Direction générale de la concurrence, de la consommation et de la répression des fraudes – DGCCRF* [French Directorate General for Competition Policy, Consumer Affairs and Fraud Control]), while executing a control or an investigation.

The fifth event is the discovery by a police officer, prosecutor or an investigating judge during a preliminary investigation or a judicial investigation.

When a company decides to open an internal investigation in the context of one of the above situations, knowing that it will be expensive and potentially disruptive, it will have several objectives. First, it seeks to end the wrongdoing or misdemeanour because it is required to do so and to avoid such information becoming public. Secondly, it aims to avoid, thanks to adequate procedures' implementation, such wrongdoing occurring again or, at least, mitigating future harm.

The internal investigation aims afterwards at gathering the facts as soon as possible and before the situation becomes aggravated,(6) which it can do thanks to a detailed and deep data analysis. Such data is collected from employees' email inboxes and computers,(7) notably thanks to the data mining algorithms applied by audit firms mandated by the company or its lawyers.

Once the facts have been established, the company will determine their legal characterisation, to determine whether a breach of the law has been committed, and if so, its exact nature and extent, and the roles and responsibilities of relevant individuals, which will allow it to assess the risks and potential judicial consequences for all actors including the legal entity.

(6) In other words, they have become so important that mitigation of their negative impact would no longer be possible or would be of little effect. This is especially true as the more reprehensible facts are, the more important they will become within a company and the more they will tend to spread outside the company. The risk to the company's image is now more fundamental than ever and in the age of social networks, the slightest misstep or scandal, and the slightest revelation can very quickly become viral and ruin, in just a few hours, a reputation or brand image and therefore part of the market capitalisation of a company, especially if it carries out B to C business.

(7) The role of *Directeur des Systèmes d'Information – DSI* (Information Systems Directors) has become essential in internal investigations because they manage and control access to the data which is the raw material for investigations.

The company will then, depending on the investigation report's conclusions and recommendations, open a disciplinary proceeding against employees who committed wrongdoing, if one or several misconducts have been evidenced. A judicial proceeding may be envisioned to sanction them and to send a zero-tolerance message regarding illegal and unethical conduct. (8)

Finally, in the event that legal proceedings have already been opened against it, as a legal person, or some of its employees, a company may wish to provide, in particular through such a report, support to physical persons who may have more limited resources. It may choose to do so both to emphasise the message of full cooperation, and, thus, to increase or restore its credibility and its image despite past wrongdoing, but also to possibly be able to benefit from a *CJIP*, allowing the company to have a reduced sentence.

It is important to note that there is still some uncertainty as to whether an investigation report, even one drafted by a lawyer, can benefit from the protection afforded by lawyer-client privilege. As a result, and insofar as the report may be made public or communicated to any authorities, particularly judicial ones, it is recommended, in all cases, that the investigation report should not contain any information likely to incriminate the company that commissioned it or one or more of its employees. Thus, if the report is drawn up by a lawyer, the latter must take care not to mention in it any sensitive information that he wishes to remain confidential. They should either refrain from including such information in a written document, or ensure that it is included in a document in which there is no doubt that the protection of their lawyer-client privilege will be respected (such as, for example, direct correspondence with their client in which they detail their defence strategy in the event of litigation).II. When are internal investigations legally mandatory as opposed to just recommended best practice?

(8) The internal investigation is a "weapon" to be wielded with precision and know-how. On the one hand, it must be carried out in a very discreet and confidential manner because the law requires that to the extent possible – because it is not always possible – the identity of the whistleblower, the alleged wrongdoer and the facts disclosed remain confidential, and hence can only be processed by a small circle of authorised and trained investigators. On the other hand, internal investigations can serve as an example to employees that a company is uncompromising and carries out in-depth investigations whenever necessary. This communication could internally discourage potential future offenders and to externally assert the company's ethical righteousness. Hence, the company may communicate the existence of an investigation, even if this is not necessarily to its advantage (in practice, the new leaders will communicate on it only to show that they have been able to wipe out the past), but it must obviously not communicate the content of the investigation itself. This is also to prevent defamation if in the end no judicial decision has definitively settled the "truth."

An internal investigation is (A) mandatory under certain circumstances according to the terms of the "Sapin 2" law though (B) a company may also decide to opt to conduct one even when not obligatory.

A. Mandatory internal investigations

Since the entry into force of the "Sapin 2" law, any French company with more than fifty employees (9) has the obligation to implement a professional alert system allowing the collection and processing of alerts submitted by internal and/or external employees. Failure to do so is sanctionable in accordance with Article 17. Thus, even if the maximum administrative (10) fine incurred for failure to comply with the obligations laid forth in Article 17 covers the eight pillars of a compliance program, the *AFA* could quite decide, while executing a control, to impose such a fine on a company if it determines that the company received numerous alerts but knowingly decided to ignore them and failed to process them, even if it validly satisfied the other seven pillars. Allowing the effective reporting of alerts (11) and dealing with said alerts, therefore, constitute two legal obligations for these companies.

The treatment of alerts involves carrying out internal investigations on the alleged wrongdoing that has been reported. Therefore, each time a company receives a valid alert – meaning meeting all legal criteria –, whether it is anonymous or issued by an identified person, it has the legal obligation to launch a thorough internal investigation, in order to assess the nature and extent of the facts and establish an appropriate sanction and action plan. The exception is cases where the alert is poorly or insufficiently founded or *prima facie* inadmissible.

Except in cases where the company considers that there is an interest therein, in particular if it wishes to benefit from a *CJIP*, a company is not, in principle, obliged to disclose wrongdoing of which it is aware. Therefore, it is not subject to an obligation similar to that of Article 40 paragraph 2 of the *Code de procédure pénale* (French Criminal Procedure Code) for public

(9) French law No. 2016-1691 of 9 December 2016, Article 8, III.

(10) Fine of EUR 200,000 for physical persons and EUR 1,000,000 for legal persons, and display and publication of the sentence as a secondary penalty.

(11) French law No. 2016-1691 of 9 December 2016, Article 13, free translation: "the offense of obstructing the transmission of a report is subject to a fine of EUR 15,000 and one year's imprisonment for physical persons and a fine of EUR 75,000 for legal persons."

officials, except in two cases: when constituent elements of (i) Article 434-1 of the *Code pénal* (French Criminal Code), providing that "*Le fait, pour quiconque ayant connaissance d'un crime dont il est encore possible de prévenir ou de limiter les effets, ou dont les auteurs sont susceptibles de commettre de nouveaux crimes qui pourraient être empêchés, de ne pas en informer les autorités judiciaires ou administratives est puni de trois ans d'emprisonnement et de 45 000 euros d'amende*" (12) and/or of (ii) Article 223-6 (13) of the French Criminal Code, are characterized.

B. Recommended internal investigations

First of all, except in the limited case of the application of Article 434-1, paragraph 1, of the aforementioned French Criminal Code, it is important to remember that a company, through its manager, does not have the general obligation to disclose to the prosecutorial authorities the offenses committed by its employees, of which it would have been aware. Therefore, it is not obliged to initiate an in-depth internal investigation into criminal acts or breaches of which it would have been aware in order to make and send a comprehensive report to the prosecutorial authorities.

However, a company that has committed, through one or more of its employees, an offense against probity (corruption, influence peddling, tax evasion), money laundering and/or an offense provided for in the *Code de l'environnement* (French Environmental Code) or a related offense (14) may wish to benefit from a *CJIP* as an alternative to prosecution. And, this new

(12) Free translation: "The fact, for anyone having knowledge of a crime of which it is still possible to prevent or limit the effects, or of which the perpetrators are likely to commit new crimes that could be prevented, failing to inform the judicial or administrative authorities is punished by three years imprisonment and a fine of EUR 45,000."

(13) Free translation of the Article 223-6 of the *Code pénal* (French Criminal Code): "Anyone who can prevent by his immediate action, without risk to him or to third parties, either a crime or an offense against the bodily integrity of the person voluntarily abstains from doing so is punished by five years' imprisonment and EUR 75,000 fine. Will be punished with the same penalties whoever voluntarily refrains from bringing to a person in danger the assistance which, without risk for him or for the thirds, he could lend him either by his personal action, or by provoking a help. The penalties are increased to seven years' imprisonment and a fine of EUR 100,000 when the crime or offense against the bodily integrity of the person mentioned in the first paragraph is committed on a minor of fifteen years or when the person in danger mentioned in the second paragraph is a minor of fifteen years."

(14) Article 41-1-3 of the *Code de procedure pénale* (French Criminal Procedure Code), inserted by the French law No. 2020-1672 of 24 December 2020 *relative au Parquet européen, à la justice environnementale et à la justice pénale spécialisée* (relating to the European Public Prosecutor's Office, environmental justice and specialised criminal justice).

legal instrument necessarily imposes a specific regime with its own conditions, among which the internal investigation, as a factor of cooperation, is highly appreciated.

In American Law, a company that negotiates a Deferred Prosecution Agreement (DPA) with the American Department of Justice (DOJ) in order to avoid legal proceedings for violation of the provisions of the Foreign Corrupt Practices Act (FCPA) can, depending on the degree of its voluntary disclosure with regard to the facts and of its level of cooperation during the investigation, benefit from a reduced penalty ranging from 25 to 50% of the total fine incurred.(15) Under French Law, if a company wishes to negotiate a *CJIP* with the public prosecutor's office, it has an interest in opening an internal investigation into the incriminated facts, both to be able to benefit from such a transaction, and to see the amount of its fine reduced – even if French Law does not offer a systematic grid as is provided in US Law.

Indeed, it is set out in the *Guidelines on the Implementation of the convention judiciaire d'intérêt public (Judicial Public Interest Agreement)*, jointly established by the *AFA* and the *PNF*, on 26 June 2019(16), that, on the one hand, executing an internal investigation is a prerequisite for the public prosecutor's proposal of a *CJIP,* to a company which is otherwise legally eligible for it and,(17) on the other hand, that the realisation of such investigation will be taken into consideration as mitigating factor when determining the amount of the public interest(18) fine.

---

(15) FCPA, July 2020: "FCPA – A Resource Guide to the U.S. Foreign Corrupt Practices Act – Second Edition", https://www.justice.gov/criminal-fraud/file/1292051/download.

(16) It is important to note that the PNF issued updated and more detailed guidelines on the CJIP, on 16 January 2023, entitled *"Lignes directrices sur la mise en oeuvre de la convention judiciaire d'intérêt public"*.

(17) *PNF & AFA, Guidelines on the Implementation of the convention judiciaire d'intérêt public (Judicial Public Interest Agreement)*: "This also applies when the legal person has previously been granted a CJIP or a resolution agreement entered into with a foreign authority for offenses against probity" (AFA's translation). In addition to the legal conditions, factual criteria are assessed by the public prosecutor when examining the advisability of resorting to a *CJIP* and among these are the "degree of cooperation with the judicial authorities" (AFA's translation). Finally, "The cooperation of the legal person in the criminal investigation is a prerequisite for entering into a CJIP" (AFA's translation).

(18) *Ibid.*: "[The quality of the cooperation of the legal person] will also be taken into account when determining the amount of the public interest fine" (AFA's translation) by applying a reduction coefficient, and that will be taken into account as reducing factors the amount of the fine the criterion "excellent cooperation and complete and effective internal investigation" (AFA's translation).

More precisely, these Guidelines, explain the importance of the following when a company seeks to benefit from a *CJIP*:

- voluntary disclosure/self-reporting by the company to the prosecutorial authorities of the offenses within a reasonable time;
- the "degree of cooperation with the judicial authorities" which will influence (a) the willingness of the prosecution to propose a *CJIP* and (b) the amount of the proposed fine;
- in the event of parallel investigations conducted by a judicial authority and the company, "regular exchanges between the prosecution and the legal person's counsel/lawyers," in order to "ensure good coordination" between the two teams of investigators, to achieve an optimal common result. In practice, the public prosecutor's office, which may have less resources than the company, and which is not on site, may wish to be informed in real time of the company's progress; and
- transmission by the company to the public prosecutor's office of the report of its internal investigation "within a timeframe compatible with the requirements of the judicial investigation." The Guidelines do not provide further details, which suggests that it is imperative that the company acts in good faith and delivers its conclusions to the prosecutorial authorities (or to the investigating judge if a judicial investigation has been opened) as soon as possible, and, at all least, before the conclusion of the public prosecutor's office's investigation. This is particularly true as the internal investigation period is typically shorter than that of the judicial investigation.

Thus, even if the "Sapin 2" law does not require it – and among the *CJIPs* signed to date, it appears that some companies did not conduct internal investigation beforehand, in particular when a judicial investigation had already been carried out (19) – it is strongly recommended that a company wishing to benefit from a *CJIP* carries out an in-depth internal investigation. The company should report regularly and progressively to the "prosecuting" public prosecutor's office in order to show its full cooperation in the establishment of the truth with regard to the judicial authority.

(19) *Tribunal de grande instance – TGI* (French First Instance Civil Court) of Nanterre, *CJIP*, 4 May 2018, *SAS Poujaud*.

Also, regardless of the image the company may wish to convey either to the public, if the completion of the internal investigation is made public, for reasons of crisis management communication, or to the public prosecutor's office, to be able to access a *CJIP* and benefit from a reduced quantum of sentence, there remains an obvious interest for companies to carry out such an investigation each time it wishes to negotiate a *CJIP* or each time it is the subject of a legal procedure. Indeed, it is important for companies to be perfectly aware of the relevant facts that can be attributed to it, and therefore of the risks, and in particular criminal ones, to which it is exposed. This will provide the company with leverage for eventual negotiation with the authorities.

Thus, companies are increasingly confronted with situations during which an internal investigation is necessary (whether in terms of infringements of Labour Law, Financial Law or Competition Law) and in which there is a risk of sanction if the investigation is not carried out. Moreover, companies face risks in the deployment of internal investigations. Therefore, they must understand them and their procedures to determine what they can and should carry out during internal investigations, in order to limit them and/or lessen their detrimental effects.

II. WHAT ARE THE RISKS INCURRED BY A COMPANY CARRYING OUT AN INTERNAL INVESTIGATION AND HOW CAN IT PROTECT ITSELF AGAINST THEM?

In addition to the risk of administrative sanctions imposed by the *AFA*, notably for failure to properly process their alerts by carrying out internal investigations, companies face ancillary risks when they decide to carry out internal investigations, including: impact on activity, demotivation of employees and the risk of sensitive confidential information, relating to industrial know-how, being apprehended, if an investigation is carried out by a foreign authority at the same time (which is beyond the scope of this article). On top of this, a company may incur two main categories of risks: (A) those inherent to its dual status of "self-prosecutor" and party and (B) those linked to non-compliance with the applicable Law and, in particular, with the rights of the parties involved in the investigation, such as employees. Companies must therefore do a risk-benefit balance before launching internal investigations, when they are not legally obliged to do so.

A. Specific risks inherent to the status of "self-prosecutor" and "party," both shouldered by the company during an internal investigation

The company faces (1) a risk of destruction or alteration of evidence, as well as (2) potential conflicts of interest.

1. The risk of destruction or alteration of evidence

First, as soon as a company decides to open an internal investigation, there is a significant risk that its managers or employees, contrary to the company's own interests, seek to destroy evidence (such as emails, audio, video recordings, documents such as contracts, etc.) to exonerate themselves or under the belief that they are acting in the interest of their company. Such an act may even be a thoughtless reflex. Nevertheless, this destruction or alteration will have heavy and counterproductive consequences for the company. For example, because the metadata associated with these elements are themselves recorded in clouds or equivalent storage spaces, to which these "destroyers" have no access, not only is it unlikely that the individuals will succeed in completely eliminating the elements that they considered harmful, but they would have more certainly drawn the attention of the company, the police or judicial investigators to the matter they sought to conceal, thereby aggravating their case, whether or not they had something to be ashamed of. And, at the same time, they will harm the company's case, as it will be suspected of having ordered this destruction.

The destruction or removal of evidence constitutes an offense (20) punishable by three years imprisonment and a fine of 45,000 euros. The company must therefore not destroy evidence and ensure that its employees do not destroy it, by informing them in advance of the potential incurred sanctions.

(20) Free translation of the Article 434-4 of the *Code pénal* (French Criminal Code): "Is punished by three years' imprisonment and a fine of EUR 45,000 the fact, with a view to obstructing the manifestation of the truth: 1) To modify the inventory of a crime or of an offense either by the alteration, falsification or erasure of traces or clues, or by bringing, moving or deleting any objects; 2) To destroy, remove, conceal or alter a public or private document or object likely to facilitate the discovery of a crime or of an offense, the search for evidence or the conviction of the guilty. […]"

2. The risk of a conflict of interest

Several levels of conflicts of interest (21) can arise when conducting an internal investigation.

First, the company, as a legal person, may have an interest in concluding a *CJIP,* if it turns out that some of its employees have committed one or more of the offenses allowing it to be eligible for the use of such a tool, in particular in order to (i) benefit from a reduced sentence, (ii) preserve its brand image with the public, by showing its willingness to cooperate with the justice system and to work towards establishing the truth and (iii) be allowed to continue to apply for public tenders.

However, at the same time, as the *CJIP* leads to an internal investigation, and, therefore, the characterisation of offenses attributable to natural persons, the directors of the company negotiating it, who cannot benefit from such a tool in their personal capacity, (22) often do not have any interest in carrying out the review. If they are decision-makers (for example, the Managing Director or an operational Director who is a member of the Management Board), they may be tempted either to prevent the effectuation of an internal investigation upstream, or to orient its conduction and, if necessary, its results downstream. Likewise, they could have an indirect personal interest in protecting an employee who committed the offenses.

To avoid the occurrence of such conflicts of interest, it is recommended to establish an investigation procedure early on, providing the structure to be put in place when an alert, or facts potentially constituting offenses, is brought to the attention of management and requires an internal investigation. This procedure should appear in the Internal Regulations. Ideally, such an investigation procedure should include a provision according to which the decision to open an investigation and the monitoring of its progress has to rest with a fully independent *ad hoc* committee. The procedure

---

(21) G. Cornu (ed.), *Vocabulaire juridique de l'Association Henri Capitant*, 13th ed., Paris, PUF: "[*Le conflit d'intérêts est*] *une situation dans laquelle la mission professionnelle ou institutionnelle confiée à une personne entre en conflit avec son intérêt propre de sorte que l'indépendance, l'impartialité et l'objectivité de son jugement en sont altérées.*", free translation: "[the conflict of interest is] a situation in which the professional or institutional mission of a person comes into conflict with his personal interest so that the independence, impartiality and objectivity of his judgment are altered."

(22) The Gauvain and Marleix Report of 7 July 2021 on the application of the French so-called "Sapin 2" law and the "Sapin 3" bill, tabled in the *Assemblée Nationale* (French National Assembly) on 19 October 2021. The report proposed to create in this regard a *Comparution sur Reconnaissance Préalable de Culpabilité – CRPC* (guilty plea procedure) specific for the managers of a company negotiating a *CJIP*, as this tool is not open to them. Due to the lack of guarantees available to them, they will inevitably be legitimately reluctant to negotiate a *CJIP* for their company as this could potentially incriminate them by the same time.

should also state that, on an *ad hoc* basis, each person involved in the conduct of the investigation likely to be in a conflict of interest shall be excluded from it. Conflicts are solved by their disclosure. Therefore, total transparency and the appropriate continuous segregation of each person's tasks is necessary.

B. Risks, particularly criminal, incurred by the company for violation of its employees' rights

The progress of the internal investigation must meet a pre-established plan. The investigation will consist of defining a spatio-temporal research perimeter, identifying the roles of relevant actors, collecting, analysing and storing data potentially constituting evidence (emails, video or audio recordings, meeting reports, etc.). The investigation must also consider testimonies collected during hearings/interviews with employees or third parties, to facilitate the legal characterisation of the facts into a precise report, in order to provide the company with an analysis of the risks that these infringements cause and with recommendations on the disciplinary, organisational and/or legal sanctions to be pronounced.

But the internal investigation itself, as a tool in the service of the employer's managerial power, is susceptible to abuse or "mishandling" in good faith, which can pose risks to the company. Indeed, the company risks infringing the most fundamental (1) substantive and (2) procedural principles.

1. The risk of violating the substantive rights of the employee

First, it is worth mentioning the employee's right to privacy. Each individual's right to the respect for his/her private life (23) has long been recognised within the company for all employees. (24) Thus, even if the content of the devices (25) made available to the employee is presumed to be professional and, therefore, the company is, in principle, free to take knowledge of it, without needing the employee's presence nor the employee's prior notice, there are exceptions to this principle.

(23) European Convention for the Protection of Human Rights and Fundamental Freedoms, Article 6; *Code civil* (French Civil Code), Article 8.

(24) Decision of the *Cour de cassation* (French Court of cassation), *Chambre sociale* (Labour Chamber), 2 October 2001, No. 99-42.942, *Nikon*.

(25) Computer, cell phone or even business instant messaging.

The company cannot freely consult: (i) what has been identified by the employee as "staff," unless the employee was aware of the existence and content of the applicable IT charter, and knowingly violated its principles, (ii) the content of an employee's email apparently pertaining to his/her private life, even if the subject of the email had not been expressly labelled "personal," (26) or (iii) any email sent from, or received on, by an employee on his/her personal messaging platform, even if received during working hours, on a professional computer and at the place of work.

Likewise, the use of video surveillance is strictly regulated by Law. It is authorised to control the activity of the employee on the condition that the *Comité social et économique – CSE* (Social and Economic Committee) of the company, as well as the supervised employees, have been informed beforehand, and then in order to ensure the safety of the supervised employees and, thus, even without having them been previously informed. On the other hand, a surveillance process installed without the knowledge of the supervised employee or in an intimate place, and for a reason other than its security, such as to control its activity (even an activity authorised to be so), is prohibited. Note, also, that not all the employee's activities can be controlled.

The second substantive right of an employee interfering with the conduct of an internal investigation is his/her right to private property. (27) Indeed, the employee has the right to the respect of his/her private property, (28) even if within the company this right may clash with the equivalent right of the employer to his/her own private property. Thus, for example, the employer does not have the right to consult files classified as "personal" on an employee's professional computer, though it is the property of the employer. The courts have nonetheless circumscribed this right for the employee, who is not allowed to abuse it by qualifying all of their files or their entire hard drive as "personal". If he/she does so, each

(26) In practice, it is not always easy to know in advance whether the content of a professional email will contain information of a personal nature, so it is possible that the employer has wrongly gained knowledge of information to which he/she did not have the right. The outcome is then that the employer will not be able to oppose this information to the employee as proof of grounds for sanction, because this would be inadmissible before a tribunal or court.

(27) *Déclaration des droits de l'Homme et du citoyen* (French Declaration of Human and Civic Rights), 26 August 1789, Article 17; *Code civil* (French Civil Code), Article 544.

(28) For example: the employer has the right to consult the content of a personal USB key owned by an employee as soon as it is connected to his/her professional computer, and to consult the copy saved onto professional computers if the USB is no longer physically connected. See decision of the *Cour de cassation* (French Court of cassation), *Chambre* sociale (Labour Chamber), 12 February 2013, No. 11-28.649.

of the files contained on the hard drive, considered separately, will not be barred from consultation by the employer. (29)

Faced with the obligation to respect these employee's fundamental rights, the company must be very careful in the conduct of its internal investigations, if it does not itself want to be the subject of legal proceedings (bearing in mind that the threat to private life constitutes an offense punishable by a penalty of one year imprisonment and a fine of 45,000 euros (30)) and if it wants the fruit of the investigation to be admissible as evidence. To do this, investigators must be trained and competent.

2. The risk of violating the employee's procedural rights

The right to the respect of the principles of proportionality and evidence fairness

The employee is first of all protected by the principle of proportionality, which governs the entire internal investigation, and the principle of evidence fairness.

In principle, the internal investigator's specific task is to collect evidence that may either support or disprove alleged misconduct and must, during the collection, respect the principles of proportionality and loyalty.

Indeed, for evidence to be admissible before a tribunal or a court, it must have been obtained legally. Thus, the use of coercion and blackmail, for example, are prohibited, unless the right to the evidence outweighs the infringement of the right violated (in this case the right to privacy), (31) and if not, the evidence must have, at the very least, been obtained fairly and not as the result of a ruse which had the aim of inciting the commission of the offense pursued. It should be noted that the principle of evidence fairness stems from the right to a fair trial (32) and the right to

(29) ECHR, 22 February 2018, *Libert v. France*, No. 588/13.

(30) Free translation of Article 226-1 of the *Code pénal* (French Criminal Code): "Is punished by one year's imprisonment and a fine of EUR 45,000, the fact, by means of any process, to willfully violate the privacy of others: (1) by capturing, recording or transmitting, without the consent of their author, words spoken in a private or confidential capacity; (2) by fixing, recording or transmitting, without the consent of the latter, the image of a person in a private place. [...]."

(31) Decision of the *Cour de cassation* (French Court of cassation), *Chambre sociale* (Labour Chamber), 25 November 2020, No. 17-19.523, free translation: "the judge having to assess whether the use of this evidence has undermined the fairness of the proceedings as a whole, by weighing the right to respect the personal life of the employee and the right to proof, which can justify the production of elements detrimental to the personal life of an employee on the condition that this production would be essential for the exercise of this right and that the infringement would be strictly proportionate to the aim pursued."

(32) European Convention for the Protection of Human Rights and Fundamental Freedoms, Article 6.

the respect of defence rights, which, in criminal matters, requires that the evidence be the subject of an adversarial discussion. (33)

An employee's rights of defence

Moreover, even if no text has expressly provided for it, companies must respect their employees' defence rights during internal investigations and in its conduct of employee's interviews.

Thus, the company must respect the right of its employees to remain silent during the interview/hearing in which they have consented to participate. Employees are free to refuse to participate, but the fact that an employee refuses to attend an invitation to an interview as part of an internal investigation may be considered by his/her employer as a violation of his duty of loyalty, from which the employer will be able to draw all the consequences, including dismissal for fault. (34) The employee also has the right to answer only certain questions of his/her choice, *a fortiori* if it appears that he/she can potentially be implicated in the facts. He/she has the right to leave the interview at any time and under any circumstances so as not to incriminate himself or herself. (35) The employee has, equally, the right to be assisted by his/her own lawyer before and at any time during the interview, but only if it appears that he/she could be implicated (36). Note that his/her lawyer is different from the lawyer of the company who will also have previously notified the employee of his/her right to have recourse to his/her own lawyer and the fact that, because the corporate attorney is not the employee's lawyer, professional secrecy will not apply to what this employee could confide to him during the interview, which

(33) *Code de procédure pénale* (French Criminal Procedure Code), Article 427, Alinea 2, free translation: "The judge can base his decision only on evidence which are brought to him during the debates and contradictorily discussed before him."

(34) Decision of the *Cour de cassation* (French Court of cassation), *Chambre sociale* (Labour Chamber), 22 March 2016, No. 15-10.503.

(35) This right remains fundamental even if it is now indirectly undermined by the fact that self-reporting is rewarded with a reduced sentence.

(36) *Barreau de Paris* (Paris Bar), "*Vademecum de l'avocat chargé d'une enquête interne*" ("Vademecum of the Lawyer responsible for an internal investigation"), *in Règlement intérieur du Barreau de Paris* (*Internal Regulations of the Paris Bar*), Annex XVI, Article 8, free translation: "[The investigating lawyer] will indicate to the interviewed person that he can be assisted or advised by a lawyer whenever it appears, before or during her hearing, that he may be accused of an act following the internal investigation." The employee's right to the assistance of his/her own lawyer would then be subject to the fact that a breach could be attributed to him/her, which is questionable. In the author's opinion, this right should be unconditional even if some believe that there is no reason that an employee has more rights during an internal investigation hearing than during a pre-termination interview.

can then be included into its report sent to the company.(37) However, in practice, employees rarely exercise their right to legal assistance during their interviews. Finally, the different parties can contractually agree on the rights of the employee questioned with regard to the verbatim of the minutes of the interviews. In practice, the employee is increasingly often authorised to read the minutes, rectify the points he/she considers that his words were misinterpreted and refuse to sign them, *a fortiori* if his/her requests for rectification have not been granted.

The employee's right to the respect of fundamental rights and guarantees relating to the collection and processing of personal data

First, to use a tool for collecting personal data relating to its employees, either inside or outside an internal investigation, a company must beforehand have individually informed the employees concerned, as well as the *Comité social et économique – CSE* (Social and Economic Committee), made a declaration to the *Commission nationale de l'informatique et des libértés – CNIL* (French Data Protection Authority), and mentioned the possibility of internal investigations in its Internal Regulations. The Internal Regulations should ideally mention the ability of the company to conduct an internal investigation under certain conditions and refer, if necessary, to the procedure regulating internal investigations, if there is one.

Personal data, which is sensitive and abundant in the context of an internal investigation, must therefore be collected for a specific goal which is legally permissible, predetermined, declared and proportionate to the purpose pursued. The data must then be handled and stored temporarily with precaution and respect to the so-called French law *"Informatique et Libertés"* (the French Data Protection Act) and of the European regulation on the protection of natural persons with regard to the processing of personal data and on the free movement of such data, known as the GDPR. The penalty for breach is 5 years imprisonment and a fine of 300,000 euros for natural persons,(38) and five times that for legal persons.

---

(37) *Barreau de Paris* (Paris Bar), *"Vademecum de l'avocat chargé d'une enquête interne"* ("Vademecum of the Lawyer responsible for an internal investigation"), *in Règlement intérieur du Barreau de Paris* (*Internal Regulations of the Paris Bar*), Annex XVI, Article 7.

(38) Free translation of the Article 226-21 of the *Code pénal* (French Criminal Code): "The fact, by any person holding personal data during their recording, classification, transmission or any other form of processing, of diverting this information from its purpose as defined by the legislative provision, the regulatory act or the decision of the *Commission nationale de l'informatique et des libértés – CNIL* (French data protection authority) authorising the automated processing, or by the declarations prior to the implementation of this processing, is punished by five years of imprisonment and a fine of EUR 300,000."

The company must also manage the risk of a violation of the confidentiality obligation that must surround the identity of the whistleblower, the facts disclosed and the identity of the alleged wrongdoer.

Companies must indeed be very vigilant each time they deal with alerts, because Article 9 of the "Sapin 2" law requires them, as well as any person aware of the information, to ensure that the identity of the whistleblower, the content of the facts disclosed, as well as the identity of the alleged wrongdoer remain confidential. A breach can result in a prison sentence of two years and a fine of 30,000 euros for natural persons, and a penalty of 150,000 euros for legal persons.

However, in practice, this obligation may be very difficult to respect, because an investigator may inadvertently name the whistleblower during the interview of the alleged wrongdoer, and because indirect elements of identification of the whistleblower or the accused person may be mentioned, for example during the interview of a potential witness, allowing the interviewee to identify one or the other. The most sensitive issues arise in harassment matters, where it is almost impossible not to reveal to the accused person the identity of his/her potential victim, since this person has a procedural right to know who is accusing him/her and for what facts, in order to be able to defend him/herself while respecting the rights of adversarial debate.

To prevent the occurrence of one or more of these risks, it is firstly essential that the internal investigators of the company draw up an investigation plan for each investigation, in accordance with the established investigation procedure. Such plan should, at a minimum, define the roles and responsibilities of each actor, the different stages of the process and the method of implementation, as well as the rights, obligations and remedies of the parties involved in the investigation and the objectives of the investigation in terms of operational working documents to be produced (investigation report, action plans, etc.).

Secondly, investigators should be trained in investigative techniques, and in particular interview techniques. Since these interviews may create major psycho-social risks, it is necessary to anticipate them when conducting an interview. It is also essential that the investigators know the applicable legal rules and internal proceedings, in particular the rules relating to the various professional secrets potentially at stake.

Thirdly, those who carry out internal investigations must be limited in number, in order to avoid, as much as possible, "leaks" of confidential information, (39) which could either cause the loss of confidential information or damage the reputation of the company. Investigators should respect the presumption of innocence from which everyone must be able to benefit until proven guilty, and have the essential qualities of discretion, diplomacy, independence, objectivity, fairness, humanity and circumspection.

(39) An investigation can have a financial dimension including exchanges of key internal financial data, the exchange of customer lists (also including personal data) or the exchange of elements relating to manufacturing and business secrets (patents, strategic plans, etc.). All this information must be handled with great care and discretion.

Shaping the Company through Negotiated Criminal Justice Agreements. French Perspective

Alexis Bavitot

Senior Lecturer in private law and criminal sciences
Deputy Director of the Institute of Judicial Studies

Jean Moulin Lyon 3 University

The prospect of a criminal trial is a hazard, an uncertainty, with potentially dramatic consequences in terms of bad publicity, and the effects attached to a conviction, in particular the entry in the judicial record which, for a company, can block access to public contracts. This is why the U.S. Department of Justice (DOJ) has considerably increased the use of agreements, particularly in the area of bribery of foreign public officials (on the basis of the Foreign Corrupt Practices Act – FCPA, the U.S. anti-bribery law).

Two of these agreements are particularly used. Firstly, the deferred prosecution agreement (1) (DPA), which is defined as the fact that the DOJ initiates public action while concomitantly suspending it with regard to the commitments made by the company, under the control of a judge. (2) Secondly, the non-prosecution agreement (NPA), which has similar effects, except that unlike the DPA, it consists of a settlement prior to any prosecution being

(1) F. Buthiau, "Le *deferred prosecution agreement* américain, une forme inédite de justice négociée", *JCP G*, 2013, p. 359.

(2) L. Giudice, "Regulation corruption: analyzing uncertainty in current Foreign Corrupt Practices Act enforcement", *Boston University Law Review*, 2011, p. 91.

initiated.(3) By acknowledging certain facts that led to the prosecution, the company agrees to cooperate with the prosecuting authority and to respect "obligations" such as the payment of a substantial fine and the implementation of a compliance program within the company to control and prevent the repetition of new offences in the future.(4)

Alongside this now common American practice, Criminal Law is in a state of wilderness on an international scale. The United States, like many other states, adopts a broad conception of territoriality, considering the impact of conduct on its economic market, which in a globalised economy amounts to a true ubiquity of the right to punish.(5) In the absence of conflict of law and conflict of jurisdiction at the international level in criminal matters, the applicable rule of jurisdiction is that of the quickest,(6) of the "price of the race."(7) Only the *ne bis in idem* principle can serve as an ultimate bulwark.

The United States has thus been free to develop a real judicial imperialism.(8) While abandoning its role as the world's policeman, the world's leading power has taken on the role of world prosecutor. The other legislators have noted that their large companies were subject to these agreements of the American justice.(9) Resounding cases, such as those affecting BNP Paribas or Alstom, served as scarecrows for companies.(10)

By legal mimicry, similar procedures have been developed, and other states have wished to develop their own imperialism: in Australia, Singapore, or in Europe (in Switzerland, Germany,(11) the Netherlands or the United Kingdom where the DPA was introduced in 2014 for offences

---

(3) L. Giudice, "Regulation corruption: analyzing uncertainty in current Foreign Corrupt Practices Act enforcement", *op. cit.*

(4) T. Amico, "La convention judiciaire d'intérêt public ou la compliance comme moyen de lutte contre la récidive", *in* N. Borga, J.-Cl. Marin and J.-Chr. Roda (eds), *Compliance: l'entreprise, le régulateur et le juge*, Paris, Dalloz, 2018, p. 79.

(5) A. Garapon and P. Servan-Schreiber, *Deals de justice, le marché américain de l'obéissance mondialisée*, Paris, PUF, 2013.

(6) A. Mignon Colombet, "La défense des entreprises à l'heure du droit global", *AJ pénal*, 2015, p. 347.

(7) V. Malabat, "La répartition *a priori* du contentieux", *in* V. Malabat (ed.), *Juge national, européen, international et droit pénal*, "Actes et études" Serie, Paris, Cujas, 2012, p. 88.

(8) F. Ganivet, "Entre enjeux de puissance et réinvention de la souveraineté, les autres visages du droit à l'heure de la lutte internationale contre la corruption", *Revue internationale de la compliance et de l'éthique des affaires*, 2018, No. 4, study No. 134.

(9) M. Audit, "Les lois extraterritoriales américaines comme facteur d'accélération de la compliance", *in* N. Borga, J.-Cl. Marin and J.-Chr. Roda (eds), *Compliance: l'entreprise, le régulateur et le juge*, *op. cit.*, p. 45.

(10) D. Rebut, "La CJIP au service du budget de l'État", *JCP*, 2017, No. 49, doctr. 1297.

(11) J. Lelieur, "Les instruments allemands de répression de la grande délinquance d'affaires: justice consensuelle et enquêtes internes", *in* K. Martin-Chenut and R. de Quenaudon (eds), *La RSE saisie par le droit*, Paris, Pedone, 2015, p. 571.

prosecuted on the basis of the UK Bribery Act adopted in 2010).(12) Everywhere, the principle is the same: an agreement is concluded with the company with contents quite similar to those concluded with the DOJ.

France already had special procedures. This is the case with the procedure of *composition pénale*, which is an alternative procedure to prosecution consisting, for the *procureur de la République* (French Public Prosecutor), in proposing one or more penal "measures" to the person who has committed an offence, before any prosecution is initiated. The *composition pénale* is therefore an alternative to prosecution by the public prosecutor. France also already applies the *Comparution sur reconnaissance de culpabilité – CRPC* (guilty plea procedure), which is not an alternative to prosecution, since the prosecution has already been initiated when this procedure is applied, but a form of simplified trial through the participation of the perpetrator who admits his guilt.(13) Nevertheless, this *CRPC* uses all the words that make people angry in the benevolent world of compliance(14): it implies a prior acknowledgement of guilt, has the effects of a judgment of conviction and is subject to registration in the criminal record.

The French legislator therefore succumbed to global mimicry by creating the *Convention judiciaire d'intérêt public – CJIP* (Judicial Public Interest Agreement) through Article 22 of the French so-called "Sapin 2" law of 9 December 2016, which introduced Article 41-1-2 of the *Code de procedure pénale* (French Criminal Procedure Code).(15) Applicable in matters of offenses primarily affecting probity, the *CJIP* was extended to tax fraud offenses by a French 2018 law.(16) Even more recently, the French law of 24 December 2020 on the European Public Prosecutor's Office, environmental justice and specialised criminal justice(17) created a new Article 41-1-3 in the French Criminal Procedure Code establishing, in terms

---

(12) E. Jouannet and H. Ruiz Fabri (eds), *Impérialisme et droit international en Europe et aux États-Unis*, "Unité mixte de recherche de droit comparé de Paris" Serie, Paris, Société de législation comparée, 2007.

(13) F. Molins, "Plaidoyer pour le plaider coupable : des vertus d'une peine négociée", *AJ pénal*, 2003, p. 61.

(14) E. Breen, "La compliance, une privatisation de la régulation?", *RSC*, 2019, Vol. 2, No. 2, p. 327.

(15) French law No. 2016-1691 of 9 December 2016 *relative à la transparence, à la lutte contre la corruption et à la modernisation de la vie économique* (on transparency, fight against corruption and modernisation of economic life).

(16) French law No. 2018-898 of 23 October 2018, *relative à la lutte contre la fraude* (on the fight against fraud).

(17) French law No. 2020-1672 of 24 December 2020 *relative au Parquet européen, à la justice environnementale et à la justice pénale spécialisée* (on the European Public Prosecutor's Office, environmental justice and specialised criminal justice).

similar to those of the previous article, a *CJIP* applicable to environmental matters.(18) In five years of application, there are now 13 *CJIP*-probity to which must be added since the few *CJIP*-tax fraud from 2018.

The *CJIP* uses original language for a criminal lawyer.(19) It does not refer to a perpetrator but to a "*mis en cause*" ("respondent").(20) It does not refer to penalties but to "obligations." It does not refer to offences but to "*manquements*" ("breaches"). A failure has a more moral connotation than the violation of a legal rule. It is a breach of duty rather than a breach of a criminal law. The *CJIP* newspeak is therefore more courteous, more pleasant to the litigant. Of course, the *CJIP* must be validated by an order of a judge. But this order does not entail a conviction, has neither the nature nor the effects of a judgment of conviction and is not registered in the judicial record.

The motivation of the legislator is essentially economic. The purpose of the *CJIP* (although terribly effective and costly for companies) is paradoxically to protect them, in particular from exclusion from public procurement procedures. In the world of natural persons, the offence is often also an immoral act, or at least an act contrary to morality, i.e. to the common practice. When applied to the liberal, global business economy, the penalty is primarily perceived as an unfair competitive disadvantage. It was therefore necessary to mark the difference with the *CRPC*, not to let the company suffer the accusatory wrath of a prosecutor or the inquisitorial wrath of a judge. The two French *CJIP-probity Systra SA*(21) and *CJIP – Sociétés Bolloré et financière de l'Odet SE*(22) are also very careful to point out that these agreements do not entail any declaration of guilt.

The legislator limits the scope of the *CJIP* to legal persons,(23) a point that is debated because the possible indictment before a criminal judge of the natural person acting on behalf of the legal entity must lead to the greatest prudence. If this *CJIP* concerns offenses listed exhaustively by the

(18) J.-B. Perrier, "La Convention judiciaire pour les infractions environnementales : vers une compliance environnementale", Paris, Dalloz, 2020, p. 396.

(19) J.-Y. Marechal, "Propos hétérodoxes sur la Convention judiciaire d'intérêt public", *Dr. pénal*, 2020, No. 6, p. 11.

(20) Free translation of M. Segonds, "La convention judiciaire d'intérêt public arbitrerait-elle une chimère?", *Dr. pénal*, 2018, No. 5, p. 38.

(21) *Convention judiciaire d'intérêt public – CJIP* (Judicial Public Interest Agreement), *Systra SA – PNF*, 12 July 2021, § 29.

(22) *Convention judiciaire d'intérêt public – CJIP* (Judicial Public Interest Agreement), *Sociétés Bolloré et financière de l'Odet SE – PNF*, 9 February 2021, § 39.

(23) M Galli, "Une justice pénale propre aux personnes morales. Réflexions sur la convention judicaire d'intérêt public", *RSC*, 2018, p. 359.

law (there are many forms of corruption, active or passive, in the national or international context, incriminated in a general or special way as in the judicial field or in sports), it should be noted that the active aspect of corruption is more targeted. In the world of the *CJIP*, the company is targeted as a corruptor, and in particular the private company more than the public one.

What is the nature of the *CJIP*? We know above all what it is not: it is not a judgment of conviction. The originality comes from the fact that it makes it possible to avoid either the prosecutor or the judge. (24) Indeed, the *CJIP* is possible at the investigation stage. In this case, it is an alternative to prosecution (it is implemented prior to the public action, before the decision of the prosecutor to prosecute). But it is also possible at the investigation stage, i.e. after the prosecutor's decision to prosecute. In this case, the *CJIP* is no longer an alternative to prosecution but an alternative to referral for trial, after the public prosecution. It is therefore an agreement that makes it possible either to avoid prosecution or to avoid a trial. The *CJIP* can thus be perceived as an *ex gratia* measure, i.e. a preferential measure for a company, which may benefit from it only once, at the discretion of the prosecutor, and derogating from the mechanisms of general Criminal Law (which bases responsibility on guilt) and of criminal procedure (oriented towards the search for judicial truth). (25)

These agreements with the prosecuting authority are part of what is known as negotiated justice, or the contractualisation of Criminal Law. (26) Negotiated justice is "the situation in which the criminal conflict is the object of a trade in the etymological sense of the term *negotio*, that is to say, of a debate between the parties in order to reach an agreement." (27) A negotiation involves at least two components. Firstly, it requires a dialogue, a place and time to argue in a contradictory manner. (28) Secondly, it

(24) N. Catelan, "De quoi la CJIP est-elle réellement le nom?", *in* Dossier *Les poursuites en droit pénal économique*, *Gaz. pal.*, 2021, No. 11, p. 69.

(25) See more generally M. Herzog-Evans, "Définir la désistance et en comprendre l'utilité pour la France", *AJ pénal*, 2010, p. 366.

(26) S. Brihi and A. Bousquet, "Les nouveaux enjeux de la privatisation du procès pénal", *La revue des juristes de Sciences Po*, 2021, No. 20, p. 1; E. Verges, "La procédure pénale hybride, à propos de la convention judiciaire d'intérêt public issue de la loi n° 2016-1691 du 9 décembre 2016 relative à la transparence, à la lutte contre la corruption et à la modernisation de la vie économique", *RSC*, 2017, p. 579; see already in this sense: M. Delmas-Marty, *Procédures pénales d'Europe*, Paris, PUF, 1995, p. 553.

(27) S.-M. Cabon, *La négociation en matière pénale*, "Bibliothèque de droit privé" Serie, Paris, LGDJ, 2016, t. 64, free translation of "*la situation dans laquelle le conflit pénal fait l'objet d'un commerce au sens étymologique du terme negotio, c'est-à-dire d'un débat entre les parties pour aboutir à un accord.*"

(28) P. Milburn, "De la négociation dans la justice imposée", *Négociations*, 2004/1, No. 1, p. 27.

requires a conciliation of different interests. The one who accepts to lose something (for the company to lose money by the fine) wants in exchange to gain something (the absence or the end of the proceedings). In this respect, the extension of the *CJIP* to the environment requires that Environmental Criminal Law be more visible. If prosecutions in this area remain too rare and penalties too lenient, it is not certain that companies have any interest in negotiating. (29)

This negotiated justice is decried by some as the mark of a dual speed justice system. These agreements are said to be reserved for the powerful, while people in *comparutions immédiates* (immediate appearances), most often young men in precarious situations, do not have the privilege of negotiating with the prosecutor (in France). This debate, as important as it is, is less topical today, and pragmatism now invites most commentators to accept negotiated justice agreements for at least two reasons. Firstly, because the success is exceptional for public finances. The *Parquet national financier – PNF* (French National Financial Prosecutor's Office), like the DOJ, brings in several billion euros, and the fines range from 420,000 to more than two billion euros, depending on the *CJIP*. France is holding its own against the DOJ in the fight against breaches of probity, which has not been the case for a long time. Secondly, because whatever one thinks of this justice of the powerful, France has embarked on this path, following in the footsteps of many other countries, and it would be difficult for the State to turn back. Without directly removing the criminal justice system, negotiated justice nevertheless promotes the idea that, before punishing, other mechanisms must be inserted, such as preventive compliance mechanisms, discussions between the company and the authority. The trial is not the only place to appease the altered social relationship. Even the sentence is no longer vertical and authoritarian but must be the result of a compromise. (30) It is now necessary to consult upstream, to improve the acceptability of laws, even criminal laws. (31) Through these agreements, the legislator offers the company the possibility of bypassing the trial and it would be very difficult today for the State to withdraw such an acquired right.

(29) E Russo, "CJIP : ajustements apportés par la loi du 24 décembre 2020 et autres sujets de réflexion pour l'avenir", *AJ pénal*, 2021, p. 68.

(30) F. Rouvillois, *L'efficacité des normes, réflexions sur l'émergence d'un nouvel impératif juridique, Fondation pour l'innovation politique*, "Étude" Serie, Paris, Fondation pour l'innovation politique, 2005.

(31) A Garapon, *Le gardien de nos promesses. Justice et Démocratie*, preface by Paul Ricœur, Paris, Odile Jacob, 1996, p. 213.

To negotiate in the best possible way, the company will shape itself. The revelation of the facts may have consequences "in terms of human resources, insofar as the individuals involved in the facts are likely to be heard, or even dismissed from the company."(32) This may also be an opportunity to resolve issues of personal data protection and confidentiality.(33) More precisely, the company will shape itself in the negotiation of the agreement. The company will shape the facts (I), shape its accusation (II) and shape the agreement that a judge will have to validate (III).

I. SHAPING THE FACTS

The company will seek to establish the scope of the facts that will be discussed during the negotiations. To do this, the company will investigate itself, like a prosecutor in a preliminary(34) investigation or an investigating judge in a judicial inquiry. Through this investigation, which is also requested by the public prosecutor in the *Guidelines on the implementation of the convention judiciaire d'intérêt public (Judicial Public Interest Agreement)* released by the *Parquet national financier – PNF* (French National Financial Prosecutor's Office) and the *Agence française anticorruption – AFA* (French Anti-Corruption Agency – AFA), the company will shed light on the facts at the origin of the accusation.(35) But on this occasion, it could also discover new facts that could be subject to criminal qualification. A "breach" can reveal an isolated fact of the company (the theory of rotten apples which most often leads to the mechanism of exclusion of the scapegoat so well described by Girard(36)) but also result from a more general policy of the company.

By investigating itself, the company will have to decide on the fate of the facts discovered. The investigator assesses, decides and separates. Should everything be revealed in the hope of being rewarded with a lenient penal measure? Shouldn't the company keep certain facts under wraps

(32) E. Daoud and H Partouche, "Étude comparative des CJIP : bilan et perspectives", *Dalloz actu.*, 27 April 2020.

(33) *Ibid.*

(34) C.-H. Boeringer and G. Courvoisier-Clément, "La convention judicaire d'intérêt public en enquête préliminaire. Des améliorations souhaitables pour un meilleur équilibre des droits des parties", *AJ pénal*, 2020, p. 455.

(35) S. Sfoggia and E. Daoud, "Le parquet national financier et l'Agence française anticorruption publient leurs lignes directrices", *AJ pénal*, 2019, p. 352.

(36) R. Girard, *La violence et le sacré*, Paris, Grasset, 1972; id., *Le bouc émissaire*, Paris, Grasset, 1982.

so as not to incriminate itself? In such a situation, could the company benefit from a new agreement later on if these facts were to be revealed?

With these negotiated justice agreements, the company has a particular interest in wanting to resolve all the difficulties, all the problems within the framework of a global negotiation. In particular because it is indeed quite possible that the legal entity does not benefit from two negotiated agreements. (37) There is no text that prohibits this, but according to the *AFA-PNF* guidelines, the fact of having a criminal record or having already benefited from an agreement negotiated abroad constitutes "in principle an obstacle" to a *convention judiciaire d'intérêt public – CJIP* (Judicial Public Interest Agreement). (38)

However, this disclosure of facts remains a risk if the agreement is not followed up. Article 41-1-2 III of the *Code de procedure pénale* (French Criminal Procedure Code) provides that if the agreement is not validated, or if the legal person exercises its right of withdrawal, (39) the public prosecutor may not refer to the statements made or the documents provided by the legal person during the procedure "*prévue au présent article*" ("provided for in this article") before the investigating or trial court. By referring to "*la procédure prévue au présent article*" ("the procedure provided for in this article"), the law refers to the proposal of a *CJIP*. This means that the facts revealed by the company prior to this proposal (and the authorities expect the revelations to be made as far in advance as possible) could be used in the course of any criminal proceedings subsequent to the failure of a *CJIP*.

The company therefore has an interest in the widest possible disclosure but also in the success of the *CJIP* procedure. By giving the company the power to investigate itself, while retaining the freedom to pursue absent or overdue disclosures, the public authorities have gained a substantial bargaining advantage. The company has much to lose in the refusal or failure of the agreement. The public authority thus places itself in a position to negotiate at the highest price. By letting the company investigate itself, the prosecutor gains an advantage.

(37) T. Amico, "La convention judiciaire d'intérêt public ou la compliance comme moyen de lutte contre la récidive", *in* N. Borga, J.-Cl. Marin and J.-Chr. Roda (eds), *Compliance : l'entreprise, le régulateur et le juge*, *op. cit.*, p. 79.

(38) S. Scemla, "Les lignes directrices du PNF et de l'AFA sur la mise en œuvre de la convention judicaire d'intérêt public en matière de corruption. La création de nouvelles conditions pour pouvoir bénéficier d'un accord?", *Rev. int. Compliance*, 2019, comm. 143.

(39) E. Daoud and H. Partouche, "Étude comparative des CJIP : bilan et perspectives", *op. cit.*

Moreover, by shaping the facts, the company will often have to deal with their extraterritoriality. The revelation of facts to the French authorities could indeed have consequences abroad. Moreover, these agreements often include coordination clauses between foreign prosecution authorities. For example, in the *Société Générale* case, an agreement was concluded between the DOJ and the *PNF* to consider these foreign proceedings. (40) This is a wish of the legislator, which has been fulfilled here and which is very important as we know that the extensive application of the territoriality principle is only weakly prevented by the *ne bis in idem* rule at the international level.

Thus, the company will shape the facts. In the world of criminal proceedings, the procedure is geared towards the search for judicial truth. A truth that we know to be subjective, imperfect, but we still find the idea of justice that founds the Law. The Law is not the just, but the Law is turned towards the requirement of justice and the criminal trial is the bearer of this promise. Unlike the agreement which seeks to avoid, in the most efficient way possible, a risk.

To avoid the penalty that has become a risk, the company will also be invited to shape its own accusation.

II. SHAPING THE PROSECUTION

In contrast to the criminal trial, where the right to remain silent and the right not to self-incriminate are fundamental values, the company will have to have an attitude close to self-accusation. (41) Previously, there was a difference depending on whether the agreement was made before or after public action was taken. The legal entity had to acknowledge the facts only at the stage of the investigation. This condition was removed by the French law of 24 December 2020. However, full cooperation in the investigation is still required, which seems to imply a *de facto* recognition of guilt, especially in our judicial culture where, unlike in the United States, responsibility and guilt are largely confused.

(40) *Convention judiciaire d'intérêt public – CJIP* (Judicial Public Interest Agreement), *Société générale – PNF*, 24 May 2018, paras. 41 to 45. The DOJ and the *Parquet national financier – PNF* (French National Financial Prosecutor's Office) have shared evidence and agreed to coordinate their investigations. There is also an agreement to share the fine.

(41) A. Kirry, A. Bish and A. Fleuriot, "Convention judicaire d'intérêt public : lignes directrices PNF/AFA, quel encouragement à l'auto-dénonciation?", *JCP E*, 2020, p. 1184.

By shaping its charge, the company will contribute to its ability to settle. According to the 2019 *AFA-PNF* guidelines, like what prevails for the DOJ in the U.S., spontaneous disclosure of the facts is not a necessary prerequisite for the agreement but is one of the main factors considered for such a proposal. (42) The *PNF* cites the example of Airbus, which contacted the British authorities very early on and thus benefited from a 50 % reduction in the amount of the penalty. The company must open its archives and files as soon as possible in order to hope to receive the largest possible criminal reward. (43)

However, late cooperation does not prevent agreement, as in the case of the *CJIP* company *SAS Egis Avia*, which only cooperated with the public prosecutor's office after a new manager had been appointed and had decided to cooperate. (44) In this case, the *PNF* accepted the *CJIP*, while considering the delay in the company's cooperation as an aggravating factor that justifies a high penalty.

The company thus shapes the prosecution. It is the prosecutor's auxiliary. If necessary, the wrath of Criminal Law will be there to remind the company of all the gains it can expect from this self-accusation. This is how the *Tribunal correctionnel de Paris* (Paris First Instance Criminal Court), by judgment of February 20, 2019, sentenced the Swiss bank UBS to a fine of 3.7 billion euros, in accordance with the prosecutor's demands, after refusing a *CJIP* whose proposed amount was less (more than one billion euros). The fine was reduced to 1.8 billion euros by the *cour d'appel de Paris* (Paris Court of Appeal), in a ruling dated December 13, 2021, but the signal remains strong against legal entities that might be tempted to resist shaping their own accusation. (45) The development of sliding scale fines (also called proportional fines) now allows the criminal judge to impose a higher sanction than would have been negotiated in an agreement. Once again, the cost-benefit calculation instituted by a utilitarian vision of punishment (46)

(42) *Parquet national financier – PNF* (French National Financial Prosecutor's Office) and *Agence française anticorruption – AFA* (French Anti-Corruption Agency – AFA), *Guidelines on the implementation of the convention judiciaire d'intérêt public (Judicial Public Interest Agreement)*, 2019, pp. 5 *et seq.*

(43) O. Claude and R. Saint George, "La CJIP Airbus : les nouveaux contours de la coopération dans le cadre de la justice pénale négociée", *AJ pénal*, 2020, p. 240.

(44) *Convention judiciaire d'intérêt public – CJIP* (Judicial Public Interest Agreement), *Egis Avia – PNF*, 28 November 2019.

(45) F.-X. Dulin, "Le rôle du parquet dans le choix de la sanction des infractions économiques et financières", *AJ pénal*, 2019, p. 15.

(46) A. Roux, "Les origines sociologiques: la perception des atteintes à la probité et son influence sur la législation anticorruption, De la conformité à la justice négociée", symposium of the *École nationale de la magistrature – ENM* (French National School for the Judiciary) and the *Agence française anticorruption – AFA* (French Anti-Corruption Agency – AFA), 17 May 2018, p. 8.

invites the company to participate in its own accusation.(47) It would be interesting to know the number of agreements proposed but refused by the companies, data which we do not have at this time.

It should also be noted that the company shapes the accusation for itself but also for others, in particular the manager. This is a major difference between French Law and the agreements signed with the US DOJ. Despite the conclusion of a *CJIP*, the legal representatives of the accused legal entity remain personally liable. Thus, by making all this information available to the prosecutor's office, the company is made an auxiliary prosecutor of itself but also a prosecutor of its representative. Thus, in the HBSC case, the former general manager of the bank benefited from a *Comparution sur reconnaissance de culpabilité – CRPC* (guilty plea procedure), almost a year after the conclusion of the *CJIP*. He was sentenced to a 12-month suspended prison term and a 500,000 euros fine.

The self-accusation of the company, instituted as prosecutor of itself, is thus heavy with stakes so that it can resort to an agreement. The content of the agreement itself will also depend on this shaping of the company's own accusation.

III. SHAPING THE AGREEMENT

Through a negotiated criminal justice agreement, the company will be able to shape the amount of the public interest fine to be paid and the contours of the compliance program.

The amount of the public interest fine paid by the company will obviously be the crucial point of the negotiation. In reality, it is more with the DOJ than with the *PNF* that the company will really be able to shape this amount. In the United States, the rules for determining the amount of the fine contain a scale that makes it possible to quantify the impact of a given behaviour on the amount of the fine that will be proposed. For example, if a company cooperates with the investigation, even if it does not self-report, the fine can be reduced by up to 25%.

(47) S.-M. Cabon, "Les procédures pénales accélérées ou négociées : une justice pénale rapide à quel prix?", *in* C. Claverie-Rousset (dir.), *Analyse économique du droit et matière pénale*, Paris, LexisNexis, 2018, p. 119.

In France, on the other hand, self-reporting offers no guarantee that a *convention judiciaire d'intérêt public – CJIP* (Judicial Public Interest Agreement) will be concluded, and there is no applicable scale of penalty reductions, but only factors that reduce or increase the penalty, intended to consider, in particular, the seriousness of the facts and the duration of the offense. The ceiling of the public interest fine is known, it is 30% of the average annual turnover calculated on the last three known annual turnovers at the date of the infringement.

It is then the contours of the compliance program that will also have to be shaped by the company. These agreements are in fact instruments for promoting compliance. According to Article 41-1-2, 2° of the *Code de procedure pénale* (French Criminal Procedure Code), the company may be subject to a compliance program for a maximum period of three years and under the supervision of the *Agence française anticorruption – AFA* (French Anti-Corruption Agency – AFA).

Although it appears in second place among the obligations that may be provided for in a *CJIP*, such a program is by no means secondary.(48) Firstly, because it must always be kept in mind that if the company does not comply with the obligations of the agreement, the public prosecutor's office regains its power to implement public action. It is finally an interesting process that is emerging: it is agreed under the threat of prosecution that the company will create voluntary normativity, failing which a penalty will be possible. This is a jurisdictionalisation of compliance, or "*hardisation*" ("hardening")(49) of compliance. Secondly, because such a program may present a real constraint, particularly financial.(50) The company will then have to shape this program, negotiate its duration, its cost and the control it will be subject to by the administrative authority.

In short, this shaping of the company will result in an agreement that will have to be validated by the order of a judge (the real one, a judicial judge who comes under the rule of Law, i.e. "a disinterested third party in

(48) P. Servan-Schreiber, "L'actualité des deals de justice", *in Les nouveaux défis de la compliance, RJSP*, 2019, No. 16.

(49) P. Deumier, "La responsabilité sociétale de l'entreprise et les droits fondamentaux", *D.*, 2013, p. 1564.

(50) See for ex. *Convention judiciaire d'intérêt public – CJIP* (Judicial Public Interest Agreement), *Bolloré – PNF*, 9 February 2021, para. 32: the cost of an AFA audit of the compliance system alone for a period of two years is estimated at EUR 4,000,000 (four million euros). The same compliance audit will cost Airbus EUR 8,500,000 (eight million five hundred thousand euros), see *Convention judiciaire d'intérêt public – CJIP* (Judicial Public Interest Agreement), *Airbus – PNF*, 29 January 2020.

the position of an impartial arbitrator above the parties"). (51) The president of the court must in fact proceed with the validation by "verifying the validity of the recourse to this negotiated procedure." (52) The aim is to ensure that the procedure is in the best interest of the public as opposed to the criminal route. (53) Thus, the control concerns the justification for recourse to the *CJIP*. (54) However, when we take a look at the agreements concluded up to now, we see that the orders are particularly short and very little reasoning is given. (55) The motivation of validation orders could be an essential point to develop in order to avoid feeding the idea that justice is by nature reserved for the powerful.

(51) C. Eisenmann, "La justice dans l'État", *in La justice*, Paris, PUF, 1961, p. 11, free translation of: "*un tiers désintéressé en position d'arbitre impartial au-dessus des parties.*"

(52) E. Scott and R. Best, "Le contrôle du juge sur la convention judiciaire d'intérêt public", *Revue internationale de la compliance et de l'éthique des affaires*, 2019, No. 3, study No. 93, free translation of: "*vérifiant le bien-fondé du recours à cette procédure.*"

(53) J.-H. Robert and M. Segonds, "Convention judicaire d'intérêt public. De l'art de l'ombre à l'art du clair-obscur", *Droit pénal*, 2018, No. 1, p. 38.

(54) S. Pellé, "L'effacement du juge en matière pénale: inexorable évolution ou véritable mutation de notre justice pénale?", Paris, Dalloz, 2020, p. 1476.

(55) By this weak control, France is closer to the United States than to the United Kingdom, see on this point T. Baudesson and C. Merveilleux du Vignaux, "Convention judiciaire d'intérêt public et deferred prosecution agreement: regards croisés (France, Royaume-Uni, États-Unis)", *Revue internationale de la compliance et de l'éthique des affaires*, 2021, No. 1.

Vigilance, being a judge and not judge

Samir Merabet

Full Professor of Law

University of the West Indies

Gradually, the idea is taking hold that there could be "supreme courts" instituted by companies (1) and, by extension, a jurisprudence of companies. (2) The prospect of a company taking the place of the judge, whether it be to apprehend its own activities or even those of third parties, customers or partners, is emerging. This is a worrying prospect, but is it not the legislator himself who is inviting companies to adopt such a position? Doesn't compliance, and especially vigilance, presuppose that the company occupies this role? Vigilance presents two diametrically opposed dangers. The company is caught between two fires. On one hand, there is a risk that it will perform its role at a minimum, so that the obligations imposed on it are ineffective, thereby risking its own liability. On the other hand, there is a danger that the company will exceed its role and replace the judge. The gradual extension of vigilance tends to confer a central role on the company and exposes third parties to the risk of arbitrariness in its implementation. How can one be a judge and not judge at the same time? The answer to this question cannot be uniform, as the duties of care are so diverse. In order to consider the reality of the risk in question, it is necessary to consider a nomenclature of duties of care (I), so as to identify the extent to which the company is invited to judge itself or others. If vigilance does indeed require the company to judge, the question of the possible proceduralisation of vigilance inevitably arises (II).

(1) J. Heymann, "The legal nature of Facebook 'Supreme court'", *this book*.

(2) C. Granier, "Reflections on the existence of companies' jurisprudence through Compliance matters", *this book*.

I. NOMENCLATURE OF DUE DILIGENCE

1. The diversity of duties of care. Behind the term *vigilance* are obligations of varying degrees of intensity. They do not all require the same degree of intervention by the company. How can they be distinguished? A first approach could be to consider a formal identification that leads to a distinction between *vigilance* in the strict sense, such as that imposed on parent companies by reason of the activity of their subsidiaries, and identified as such, and obligations that are similar to it, such as, for example, the duty of moderation of companies on social networks, which, although not called a duty of vigilance, is nonetheless close to it. The extension of compliance obligations leads to a blurring of the line between what exactly is vigilance and what is not. From the perspective that interests us, that of determining whether or not vigilance implies a judgement by the company, it is appropriate to adopt a more substantial approach, to consider the degree of control exercised by the company. Thus, two categories can be distinguished: negative *vigilance*, which implies the identification of a risk (A), and positive *vigilance*, which implies even more the neutralisation of the risk (B). At this stage, it is clear that the company will have to perform a different function, as *ex ante* intervention, at the heart of *vigilance*, may lead to *ex post* control, which is then similar to that exercised by the judge.

A. Negative *vigilance*: identifying a risk

2. The essence of due diligence: the identification of a risk. The primary function of due diligence is to ensure the preservation of "monumental goals" (3) by requiring the company to take a proactive approach to ensuring compliance with these higher goals. Vigilance plans designed for this purpose may include a wide variety of measures, but all share the same philosophy: to identify a risk and implement the necessary means

(3) M.-A. FRISON-ROCHE "Le droit de la compliance", *D.* 2016, p. 1871. See also M.-A. FRISON-ROCHE (ed.), *Compliance Monumental Goals*, coll. "Compliance & Regulation", Brussels, Journal of Regulation & Compliance (JoRC)/Bruylant, 2023. The first refers to the detection, prevention and management of risks so that events do not occur, while the second refers to mechanisms put in place to ensure that events do occur in the future, for example effective equality between human beings. On the power of these monumental goals over all compliance mechanisms, see M.-A. FRISON-ROCHE, "Legal Approach to Compliance Tools: Building by Law the Unity of Compliance Tools from the Definition of Compliance Law by its 'Monumental Goals'", *in* M.A. FRISON-ROCHE (ed.), *Compliance Tools*, coll. "Compliance & Regulation", Brussels, Journal of Regulation & Compliance (JoRC)/Bruylant, 2021, p. 35.

to prevent its occurrence. This can be called negative *vigilance*. This is typically the spirit of the French law of 27 March 2017,(4) which is about to be enshrined in European Union Law.(5)

3. This vigilance may first of all be internal to the company. In French Law, one of the manifestations of this duty of vigilance can be found in Article L. 225-102-4 of the *Code de commerce* (French Commercial Code), which requires the parent company to draw up a vigilance plan with a view to identifying the risks associated with the activities of its subsidiaries. How does such a duty of care manifest itself(6)? The due diligence plan must first of all allow for "a mapping of risks in order to identify, analyse and prioritise them."(7) The law also requires the company to consider "appropriate actions to mitigate risks or prevent serious harm."(8) Furthermore, the measures that must be implemented as part of this vigilance plan must only be "*raisonnables*" ("reasonable") according to the text. Thus understood, the duty of vigilance seems moderate. Admittedly, in large groups with numerous subsidiaries and countless subcontractors, this risk mapping work represents a particularly heavy task, from a human, material and financial point of view. On the other hand, the actions to be taken by the company are aimed solely at identifying and preventing risks, without the company having to take positive action itself after they have occurred. The accountability of the company sought by the duty of vigilance implies that it makes a judgment on its own activities by determining whether or not they are at risk, however, without being led to substitute itself for the judge or the public authorities.

4. Vigilance may then be directed towards third parties. This is the case, for example, with the obligations of vigilance instituted by Article 561-2 of the *Code monétaire et financier* (French Monetary and Financial Code), which subjects certain professionals to vigilance obligations. These obligations arise at the time of entry into a relationship,

(4) C. Hannoun, "Le devoir de vigilance des sociétés mères et entreprises donneuses d'ordre après la loi du 27 mars 2017", *Dr. Social* 2017, p. 806.

(5) Parl. EU, Resol. No. 2020/2129/INL, 10 March 2020, containing recommendations to the Commission on the duty of care and corporate responsibility, to which a proposal for a directive on the subject in question is annexed. On this resolution, see J. Camy, "La résolution du Parlement européen sur le devoir de vigilance", *JCP E* 2021. 1396; B. Lecourt, "Vers une directive sur le devoir de vigilance des sociétés", *Rev. Sociétés*, 2021, p. 335.

(6) B. Teyssié, "Le plan de vigilance. Trois années d'application", *D.* 2021, 1823.

(7) M.-C. Caillet, "Du devoir de vigilance aux plans de vigilance, quelle mise en œuvre?" *Dr. Social* 2017, 819, free translation of: "*une cartographie des risques destinée à leur identification, leur analyse et leur hiérarchisation.*"

(8) *Ibid.*, free translation of: "*des actions adaptées d'atténuation des risques ou de prévention des atteintes graves.*"

but also throughout the business relationship, through the duty to detect inconsistent transactions, accompanied by possible obligations to notify *TRACFIN* (France's Financial Intelligence Unit) in the event of persistent doubt. Here again, vigilance requires limited action by the company. To facilitate the implementation of these obligations, the *Agence française anticorruption – AFA* (French Anti-Corruption Agency – AFA) publishes guidelines to assist companies. (9) In addition to the traditional risk mapping, this time the company is invited to adopt more significant measures. Companies subject to Article 17 of the French law of 9 December 2016 known as "Sapin 2" (10) still need to consider more active measures. For example, Article 17, II, 7° of this law requires the implementation of a "disciplinary system allowing the company's employees to be sanctioned in the event of a breach of the company's code of conduct." (11) In this regard, the *AFA* recalls in its recommendations the necessary "gradation of sanctions." (12) This time, vigilance goes a step further. The company must adopt sanctions against persons who have behaved in a manner contrary to the measures intended to prevent the risk of corruption. The approach is still intended to be *ex ante,* but already assumes an assessment by the company of an employee's behaviour. The approach is classic and falls within the employer's disciplinary power. The fact remains that the duty of vigilance invites companies to take sanctions to ensure the objectives prescribed by the legislator.

Several observations can be made with regard to the two examples just considered. To begin with, it can be seen that the company is not called upon to act in a positive manner, but only to identify and prevent the risks. The approach is therefore perfectly in line with the *ex ante* logic on which Compliance Law is based. Consequently, the company's role is limited at this stage. It is not intended to replace the judge. Furthermore, the texts are relatively silent on the way in which the company must exercise this duty of *vigilance*. The legislator itself seems to concede this insofar as

(9) *Agence française anticorruption – AFA* (French Anti-Corruption Agency – AFA), *The French Anti-Corruption Agency Guidelines – Notice on the French Anti-Corruption Agency Guidelines to help Public and Private Sector Entities to Prevent and Detect Bribery, Influence Peddling, Extortion by Public Officials, Illegal Taking of Interest, Misappropriation of Public Funds and Favouritism*, 2021, https://www.agence-francaise-anticorruption.gouv.fr/files/files/French%20AC%20Agency%20Guidelines%20.pdf.

(10) French law No. 2016-1691 of 9 December 2016, *relative à la transparence, à la lutte contre la corruption et à la modernisation de la vie économique* (on transparency, fight against corruption and modernisation of economic life).

(11) *AFA* Guidelines, cited above, free translation of: "*régime disciplinaire permettant de sanctionner les salariés de la société en cas de violation du code de conduite de la société.*"

(12) *Ibid.*, p. 47, free translation of: "*gradation des sanctions.*"

Article L-225-102-4 of the *Code de commerce* (French Commercial Code), which was discussed earlier, states that "a decree in *Conseil d'État* (French Council of State) may supplement the due diligence measures provided for in this article. It may specify the procedures for drawing up and implementing the due diligence plan." (13) Since then, further details have not been provided. At this stage, we can see that the company's vigilance obligations are not intended to take the place of the judge. It could even play too passive a role to ensure that the objectives pursued by the legislator are effectively met. The risk is therefore not excessive vigilance, but on the contrary, the faulty failure of the company when it is invited to take responsibility for its own activity.

B. Positive *vigilance*: neutralising a risk

5. Beyond vigilance. Beyond the obligations of vigilance *stricto sensu*, are there no other duties of the same nature that do not bear their name? If *vigilance* consists of the company preserving monumental objectives, such as fighting corruption or preserving the environment, by implementing measures to neutralise practices likely to undermine them, then it is possible to identify many others beyond the perimeter of the examples envisaged so far. Doesn't the same logic apply to companies such as Facebook or Twitter, which are asked to ensure the proper conduct of electoral polls, or the treatment of the health crisis? When the French so-called Avia (14) law, partly censured by the *Conseil constitutionnel* (French Constitutional Council), (15) required social networks to fight against the spread of false news, was it not a question of vigilance that did not bear its name? When Twitter censored some tweets by former President Donald Trump (16) or Facebook deactivated his account, (17) was this not also a form of vigilance? When the company is called upon to intervene, no judge has previously ruled on the legality of the content. Unlike the negative vigilance previously envisaged, the approach is no longer merely preventive.

(13) Free translation of: "*un décret en Conseil d'État peut compléter les mesures de vigilance prévues au présent article. Il peut préciser les modalités d'élaboration et de mise en œuvre du plan de vigilance.*"

(14) French law No. 2020-766 of 24 June 2020, *visant à lutter contre les contenus haineux sur Internet* (to combat hateful content on the Internet).

(15) Decision of the *Conseil constitutionnel* (French Constitutional Council), 18 June 2020, DC No. 2020-801.

(16) T. Tasente, "Twitter Discourse Analysis of US President Donald Trump", *Technium Soc. Sci. J.*, 2020, Vol. 67, No. 2.

(17) T. Tasente, "Facebook Discourse Analysis of US President Donald Trump", *Technium Soc. Sci. J.*, 2020, Vol. 26, No. 5.

The company must make a decision *a posteriori*, in order to understand the behaviour of a user of its services. It is no longer just a matter of ensuring compliance with the general terms of use that bind the company and its customer. The company is now required to check itself that the activity of a customer or partner does not contravene the law. The company is thus called upon to play the role which until now has been the responsibility of the judge and, more generally, of the public authorities.

6. From *ex ante* to *ex post*. The idea underlying the approach in question here is the same as in the case of negative vigilance, with the difference that this time the company is not content to identify a risk, it will also act positively to neutralise it before any request from an authority. The logic is therefore quite distinct from that imposed by Article 6-1 of the French law *pour la confiance dans l'économie numérique* (for Confidence in the Digital Economy), which obliges hosts to delete any content of a terrorist or child pornographic nature after an injunction from the administrative authority. (18) Since this law came into effect, the legislative arsenal has been expanded, in particular with the European Regulation of 29 April 2021 *on addressing the dissemination of terrorist content online*, (19) which in Article 1 envisages "reasonable and proportionate duties of care to be applied by hosting service providers in order to address the dissemination to the public of terrorist content through their services and ensure, where necessary, the expeditious removal of or disabling of access to such content."

In part, the host's obligation to remove content is conditional on a prior injunction from an authority. (20) In addition, the host must also take "specific measures to protect its services against the dissemination to the public of terrorist content," (21) the text specifying that "the decision as to the choice of specific measures shall remain with the hosting service provider" while listing some examples of possible measures. In the same vein, the *Digital Services Act* increases the moderation obligations on companies. (22)

(18) E. Dreyer, *Droit de la communication*, Paris, LexisNexis, 2018, No. 668 and No. 1971 *et seq*.

(19) On this text: E. Dreyer, "« Commentaire du Règlement (UE) 2021/784 du 29 avril 2021 relatif à la lutte contre la diffusion des contenus à caractère terroriste en ligne", *RSC*, 2021, p. 627.

(20) Regulation (EU) 2021/784 of 29 April 2021 on addressing the dissemination of terrorist content online, Article 3.

(21) *Ibid.*, Article 5.

(22) P. Auriel, "La liberté d'expression et la modération des réseaux sociaux dans la proposition de Digital Services Act", *Revue de l'Union européenne*, 2021, p. 413; C. Marzo, "Vers un devoir de vigilance des plateformes numériques?", *Dr. Social*, 2021, p. 708.

7. The risk of prejudice. In the case in point, the company must, *ex ante,* implement the necessary content moderation tools to remove certain speech, whether it is an apology for terrorism, incitement to hatred or disinformation. It is therefore required to delete content or even a user's account, in the light of a moderation policy that it will have decided on itself and in the absence of any administrative or judicial injunction. Very often, this task is carried out by means of an algorithmic tool, as the volume of content to be moderated does not allow for human control. This positive vigilance is therefore most often an automated vigilance, delegated to computer systems. The dangers of such an approach are already apparent. It is therefore a form of judgement that is made not only by a company, but even more so without human intervention, which does not go without posing difficulties with regard to the legitimacy of the decisions that are taken.

To sum up: to ensure compliance with higher imperatives, the company develops a moderation policy and the tools to implement it and then decides to adopt a sanction itself. The company must therefore make a judgement on content and behaviour, which inevitably exposes users to the risk of arbitrariness. The company is once again caught in the crossfire: on the one hand the faulty failure to act, on the other the spectre of censorship. The criticism levelled at Facebook and Twitter by users, associations and politicians is numerous. The company's inaction is criticised as much as its action. This time, positive vigilance seems to imply a judgement by the company, which makes the question of its proceduralisation legitimate.

II. VIGILANCE CONTROL

The extension of duties of vigilance, whether or not they are identified as such, legitimately raises concerns. The aim of compliance is to make companies more responsible and, to this end, to invite them to take an active part in the construction of the Law, by helping to determine their own obligations in order to achieve the objectives set by the legislator. (23)

(23) In this sense, M.-A. Frison-Roche, "Compliance and Incentives: a Promising Tandem", *in* M.-A. Frison-Roche (ed.), *Compliance Tools, op. cit.*, p. 141.

Progressively, the company is no longer only invited to participate in the elaboration of the rule, but also to apply it itself. In these circumstances, as soon as a private operator is invited to exercise the role of a regulator, it is legitimate to question the appropriateness of framing its action by procedural rules (A). This is still the easiest thing to admit, the difficulty being more in determining the procedural rules to be adopted (B).

A. The value of monitoring

8. Procedure as a bulwark against arbitrariness. As vigilance expands, the risks multiply. Therefore, the implementation of procedural rules governing vigilance is necessary and in the interest of all stakeholders. Firstly, the procedure is in the individual interest of the company's customers or partners who may be victims of arbitrary action or discrimination when exercising the company's duty of vigilance. The clarification of the rules governing its implementation should eliminate this risk. When the company itself adopts a sanction against the user of one of its services, the risk is all the greater as the decision will often be given "as a last resort" in the sense that few users will be able to legally challenge the moderation decision against them. In many cases, the user will accept the deletion of his or her content or create a new account if it is deleted. Secondly, the procedural framework of vigilance serves the general interest. In the case of negative vigilance, there is a risk of ineffectiveness of Compliance Law. However, the objectives pursued are of such importance that it is crucial that they are effectively ensured. In the hypothesis of positive vigilance, beyond the mere effectiveness of the law, other risks may be feared. The fight against fake news or hate speech can lead in the opposite direction to excessive restrictions on access to information or freedom of expression. If not properly framed, such vigilance can be more dangerous than the evils it is intended to fight. Finally, establishing procedural rules can also serve the interests of the company itself. When the implementation of vigilance obligations is not clearly identified, the risks of liability are greater for the company. If it limits its intervention, it may be held liable. If it exceeds its role, it may be held liable! The approach is not without its faults either. Compliance already imposes significant obligations on companies, and laying down rules of procedure that are too formal could make their burdens even heavier. It is therefore necessary to identify the rules that are strictly necessary to avoid the risks that have so far been envisaged.

B. The scope of control

Now that the need for greater proceduralisation of vigilance has been established, it is necessary to determine the procedural rules that are to be applied. The intensity of the rules to be implemented depends on the intensity of the role played by the company, as the risks are not the same. Negative vigilance entails a risk of ineffectiveness of the compliance rules. Positive vigilance, on the other hand, entails the risk that the company will substitute itself for the judge and expose third parties to arbitrariness. Each of these risks calls for the implementation of different procedures.

9. Framing negative vigilance. The objective is to ensure that the company's risk control is respected. In many cases, however, the duty of vigilance imposed on the company is relatively vague, and it is up to the company itself to develop the procedures designed to achieve the stated objectives. While it is wise to leave it to the company to determine the best way to comply with the objective, the absence of any indication to this effect is not satisfactory. On the one hand, it is feared that the procedures implemented are merely cosmetic and do not really achieve the desired objective. On the other hand, the company risks being held liable if it does not validly comply with the stated objective. In any case, the implementation of vigilance would benefit from being more closely supervised to avoid these pitfalls.

In order to facilitate the implementation of this duty, and to avoid the pitfall of a lack of effectiveness as well as that of an excessive role for the judge, are there any instructions to guide the company in the implementation of its duty of vigilance? The law is often silent on the method to be followed to achieve the objective with which the company must comply. To be convinced of this, let us take the example of the fight against money laundering and terrorist financing. The professionals referred to in Article L. 561-2 of the *Code monétaire et financier* (French Monetary and Financial Code) are bound by a duty of vigilance under Article L. 561-4-1 of the same Code. According to this provision, companies "shall define and implement systems for identifying and assessing the money laundering and terrorist financing risks to which they are exposed and a policy adapted to these risks. In particular, they shall draw up a classification of the risks in question according to the nature of the products or services offered, the transaction conditions proposed, the distribution channels used, the characteristics of the customers, and the country or territory of origin or destination of the funds."(24) The task is immense and companies would benefit from more support in implementing this duty of care. If they fail to do so, companies may be exposed to heavy penalties. The banking sector is particularly revealing in this respect. The *Autorité de Contrôle Prudentiel et de Résolution – ACPR* (French Banking Supervisory Authority) has already imposed significant sanctions for failure to comply with the duty of care. For example, a bank was sanctioned for a risk classification that was deemed insufficient because it did not sufficiently take into account nationality or country of residence, even though 36% of the clients in business relationships were of foreign nationality.(25) In the same vein, a bank was fined EUR 8 million for the inadequacy of its computerised monitoring tool and a failure to comply with its duty of care.(26) To facilitate the implementation of these obligations, the *Conseil d'orientation de la lutte contre le blanchiment de capitaux et le financement du terrorisme – COLB* (French Advisory Council on Money Laundering and Terrorist Financing) makes a number of recommendations. In particular, the Council provides an analysis of the various risks that each regulated profession is likely to face, with the aim of "refining knowledge of the risks so that their vigilance can be exercised as effectively as possible."(27) Among the initiatives designed to facilitate the implementation of this duty of vigilance is the initiative of the *Commission nationale des sanctions – CNS* (French National Sanctions Commission). This independent administrative institution, which is responsible for sanctioning breaches committed in this area by real estate agents, domiciliation providers and gaming and betting operators, proposed in its 2018 annual activity report a methodology for setting up risk assessment and management systems for these companies.(28) It proposes several steps: identification of risks,

(24) Free translation of: "*définissent et mettent en place des dispositifs d'identification et d'évaluation des risques de blanchiment des capitaux et de financement du terrorisme auxquels elles sont exposées ainsi qu'une politique adaptée à ces risques. Elles élaborent en particulier une classification des risques en question en fonction de la nature des produits ou services offerts, des conditions de transaction proposées, des canaux de distribution utilisés, des caractéristiques des clients, ainsi que du pays ou du territoire d'origine ou de destination des fonds.*"

(25) Decision *Autorité de Contrôle Prudentiel et de Résolution – ACPR* (French Banking Supervisory Authority), 4 February 2020, No. 2019-04, *Banque et Dr.*, 2020, Vol. 85, No. 3-4, obs. Nicolet.

(26) Decision *Autorité de Contrôle Prudentiel et de Résolution – ACPR* (French Banking Supervisory Authority), 22 February 2018, No. 2017-08, *Gaz. Pal.*, 2018, 1663, obs. M. Roussille.

(27) *Conseil d'orientation de la lutte contre le blanchiment de capitaux et le financement du terrorisme – COLB* (French Advisory Council on Money Laundering and Terrorist Financing), Activity Report, September 2019, esp. p. 12, free translation of: "*à affiner la connaissance des risques pour que leur vigilance puisse s'exercer de façon la plus efficace possible.*"

(28) *Commission nationale des sanctions – CNS* (French National Sanctions Commission), *Rapport d'activité 2018* (*Activity Report 2018*), pp. 23 *et seq.*

classification of risks and definition of risk management measures. The intensity of the envisaged risks requires a reaction from the company, the most important of which is to refuse to contract. This type of initiative could serve as a model and be extended to other companies subject to the due diligence requirement of Article L. 561-4-1 of the French Monetary and Financial Code to provide companies with guides describing precisely how to comply with their due diligence obligations. In this way, it is ensured that the due diligence plan adopted is not just a façade and the company knows where it stands, thus avoiding the risk of being held liable. Such a method could easily be implemented, particularly through legal tools. The example of the proposals made by the French National Sanction Commission is a good model. The company retains some room for manoeuvre in the implementation of its duty of vigilance; it is only accompanied while retaining the freedom to adapt the measures that it considers most appropriate.

10. Proceduralising positive vigilance. The proceduralisation of positive vigilance requires a different method. The risk here is that the company replaces the judge when implementing its duties. As soon as companies can impose sanctions on their users, as soon as they set up a kind of supreme court, as soon as we come to envisage a kind of corporate jurisprudence, is it not also necessary to envisage a procedure to regulate the power of the company? If so, what rules should be imposed? Insofar as the role of the company is partly similar to that of a judge, one might think that it would be sufficient to duplicate the principles governing the trial. Nevertheless, the analogy between the State judge and the company necessarily has its limits. Is it possible to apply the main principles of General Procedural Law? Certain principles seem difficult to reconcile with the company, such as the independence of the judge or the publicity of debates, even if the initiative led by Facebook demonstrates that companies that give themselves the means to do so can come close to the standards of state justice.(29) While not all companies can implement such procedures, it is possible to envisage thresholds to modulate the intensity of the procedural requirements for each company. Other principles can be more easily applied: the right to a reasonable timeframe or the adversarial principle. If we take the example of the moderation of social networks, this presupposes that the user whose content is deleted or whose account is

(29) C. Granier, "Reflections on the existence of companies' jurisprudence through Compliance matters", *this book*; M.-A. Frison-Roche, "The Judge-Judged; articulating words and things in the face of the impossible conflict of interests", *this book*.

suspended is informed of the reasons for doing so and is able to express his or her views before the authority that has to take a decision against him or her. One could be led to envisage a real procedure of vigilance prescribed by the legislator.

11. The proceduralisation of vigilance: the risk of a headlong rush. The decentralisation of the creation of Law from the State to companies necessarily implies a proceduralisation of the latter. It remains to be seen whether this is a movement towards which we wish to move. The role entrusted to the company exposes it to dangers, so it is necessary to provide a framework. Nevertheless, the more we proceduralise and legitimise the intervention of the company, the more the public authorities could be tempted to rely more and more on the companies, which could lead to a form of renunciation of what constitutes one of the attributes of sovereignty. We are faced with an impasse: on the one hand, we cannot allow companies to exercise such a role without any supervision, but on the other hand, it is not desirable that such supervision should further justify the regulatory missions entrusted to companies. As it stands, however, vigilance would benefit from being more formalised. Eventually, alongside civil, criminal and administrative procedures, a vigilance procedure could emerge.

CHAPTER II
PROCEDURAL LAW IN COMPLIANCE LAW

Procedural Principles in Compliance Law

NICOLAS CAYROL*

Full Professor at the University of Tours (France)

1. The question of "procedural principles in Compliance Law" in France is a classic example of a legal issue which involves studying a set of rules (procedural principles) in a particular field (Compliance Law), and identifying, as physicists would say, the "distortions" suffered by these rules in this "field." Given the issue is specifically about the relationship between two terms, and not about each term in itself, a simple definition of "procedural principles" and "Compliance Law" is all we need.

With regard to procedural principles, an authoritative definition from a seminal treatise on General Procedural Law(1) informs us that these are based on the principle that everyone has a right of access to a trial by judge; that there must be guarantees as to this judge's independence and impartiality; that the procedure before the judge must be fair, open to the public and take place within a reasonable time limit; that the judgment must be explained in open court; and that this judgment puts an end to the action initiated and prohibits new ones (*ne bis in idem*).

As for Compliance Law, and with reference to specialists in this emerging field of Law, it can be defined as an emerging(2) branch of Law that has arisen as an extension of Regulatory Law but which goes beyond Regulatory Law.(3) Its purpose is to combat particularly serious risks to the security of society, known as "systemic" risks, covering the following areas in particular: protection of human rights, protection of the environment, digital

* nicolas.cayrol@univ-tours.fr.

(1) See S. GUINCHARD *e.a.*, *Droit processuel. Droit commun et droit comparé du procès équitable*, 11th ed., Paris, Dalloz, 2021.

(2) See M.-A. FRISON-ROCHE, "Le droit de la compliance", *D.*, 2016, p. 1871.

(3) See M.-A. FRISON-ROCHE, "Le droit de la compliance au-delà du droit de la régulation", *D.*, 2018, p. 1561.

security (protection of personal data), financial security, competition and the fight against money laundering, corruption and various forms of trafficking (in arms, works of art, etc.). (4)

A vast field indeed. How to avoid getting lost and, above all, where to find the procedural principles?

2. And yet, when looking at Compliance Law, it is easy enough to see the presence of procedural principles here and there, which have long been observed and documented in Regulatory Law. (5)

For example, if we look at the provisions of the *Code monétaire et financier – CMF* (French Monetary and Financial Code) on banking matters, it is clear that the sanction procedure is now ingrained with the principles of "fair trial" which is built on a formal distinction between the prosecuting authority and the decision-making authority. (6) Thus, in the internal organisation of the *Autorité de contrôle prudentiel et de résolution – ACPR* (French Banking Supervisory Authority), there is a "Sanctions Committee," (7) made up of people solely responsible for these decisions and liable to be recused if there is a serious reason to doubt their impartiality. (8) This committee may not take up cases on its own initiative and a case may only be referred to it following a formal transmission of the case by the supervisory authorities. (9) The proceedings before this committee are public (10) and adversarial (11) and its deliberations take place in secret, without the presence of the rapporteur and the supervisory (12) authorities. The decisions it makes must be explained (13) and are subject to "*un recours de pleine juridiction devant le Conseil d'État*" ("full appeal to the French Council of State)." (14) All these features can be linked to procedural principles, so there is indeed a place for procedural principles in Compliance Law.

---

(4) See the recent *Code de la Compliance*, 4th ed., Paris, Dalloz, 2023.

(5) See already C. Deliscostopoulos, *L'encadrement processuel des autorités de marché*, Paris, LGDJ, 2002, preface by S. Guinchard.

(6) This was not the case in the past, which the *Conseil d'État* (French Council of State) eventually recognised (CE, 8 November 2010, *D.*, 2011, p. 1643, obs. Synvet). See also decision of the *Conseil constitutionnel* (French Constitutional Council), 2 December 2011, *QPC*, *JCP E*, 2012, 578, note Paclot.

(7) *CMF*, Article L. 612-9 (two members of the *Conseil d'État* [French Council of State], one member of the *Cour de Cassation* [French Court of cassation] and three persons chosen for their competence).

(8) *CMF*, Article L. 612-38, para. 5.

(9) The *Conseil d'État* (French Council of State) had previously ruled the contrary, see CE, 20 October 2000, *D.*, 2001, p. 2665, note Louvaris.

(10) *CMF*, Article L. 621-15, IV*bis*.

(11) *CMF*, Article L. 612-38.

(12) *CMF*, Articles L. 612-11 and L. 621-15.

(13) *CMF*, Article L. 612-38, para. 6.

(14) *CMF*, Article L. 612-16.

The same remarks would apply to a study of the provisions of the same code on financial matters in relation to the *Autorité des marchés financiers* (French Financial Markets Authority), or the provisions of the *Code de commerce* (French Commercial Code) on competition in relation to the *Autorité de la concurrence* (French Competition Authority), or the provisions on data protection and the *Commission nationale de l'informatique et des libertés – CNIL* (French data protection Authority), and so on.

3. As for distortions, they are also quite visible and it is not difficult to find original solutions, specific to Compliance Law, that reflect a particular understanding of procedural principles, or even their disregard.

The most obvious first step is the existence of *ad hoc* institutions with the power to sanction, which has the effect of removing litigants from the jurisdiction of their ordinary judge. (15)

The legal nature of these institutions is ambiguous, fluctuating between a jurisdictional dimension and one which is more administrative. Without being entirely jurisdictional, they do have various characteristics of courts, and they raise the same questions as them.

Perhaps the best way to illustrate this ambiguity is to reproduce the analysis of the *Autorité de la concurrence – ADLC* (French Competition Authority) given by the *Cour de cassation* (French Court of cassation), the highest court in the French judiciary, in a ruling of 30 September 2021, concerning an appeal on whether the provisions of the *Code de procédure civile* (French Civil Procedure Code) relating to the recusal of judges were applicable to the members of this Competition Authority. In this comprehensive explanation of its decision, it is noticeable that the Court of cassation relies on the case law of the *Conseil constitutionnel* (French Constitutional Council), the Court of Justice of the European Union and the European Court of Human Rights to reject the qualification of jurisdiction while noting the guarantees of jurisdictional order enjoyed by litigants: (16)

> "9. [The Competition Authority, charged by law with ensuring free competition and controlling economic concentration, is an independent administrative authority, whose organisation is based on a strict separation of the functions of prosecution and investigation, entrusted to a department placed under the

(15) See G. Wiederkehr, *Les principaux traits du pouvoir juridictionnel en France*, *in* D. d'Ambra, *Le rééquilibrage du pouvoir juridictionnel*, Paris, Dalloz, 2013, p. 8; L. Cadiet, J. Normand and S. Amrani Mekki, *Théorie générale du procès*, "Thémis" Serie, Paris, PUF, 2010, No. 47. For the historical analysis of the notion of ordinary judge, see B. Alix, *Le développement et l'usage du concept de judex ordinarius (XIIe – XVe siècles)*, PhD Thesis, Paris II, 2020.

(16) Translated by the author.

authority of a general rapporteur, and the powers of sanction, which are the responsibility of the college of the Competition Authority. In addition to this organisation, these texts set out the composition of this college and organise procedures before the Authority which aim to guarantee the impartiality and independence of the Authority, as well as the respect of the rights of defence.

10. It follows from the case law of the Constitutional Council that the Competition Authority is non-judicial in nature, even when it is called upon to pronounce a sanction having the character of a punishment (Const. Counc., 12 October 2012, No. 2012-280 QPC).

11. [Its decisions] shall be notified to the parties involved and to the Minister in charge of the economy, who may, within one month, bring an action for annulment or reversal before the Paris Court of Appeal.

12. [It] is a party to the proceedings, in accordance with the case law of the Court of Justice of the European Union (CJEU, 7 Dec. 2010, Vebic, C-439/08). The Chairman of the Competition Authority may lodge an appeal in cassation against the judgment of the Paris Court of Appeal annulling or reversing a decision of the Authority.

13. [It] may impose administrative penalties in order to ensure the effective application of Articles 101 and 102 of the Treaty on the Functioning of the European Union (TFEU). The Commission may refer cases to the Commission pursuant to Article 11(6) of Regulation (EC) No 1/2003.

14. It follows from these texts of European Union law, as interpreted by the Court of Justice of the European Union, that the Competition Authority is not a court or tribunal capable of referring a question to it for a preliminary ruling under Article 267 TFEU (CJEU, 16 Sept. 2020, Anesco, C-462/19, concerning the *Comisión Nacional de los Mercados y la Competencia*, the Spanish competition authority).

15. Furthermore, according to the European Court of Human Rights (e.g. ECHR, 23 Oct. 1995, Schmautzer, Umlauft, Gradinger, Pramstaller, Palaoro and Pfarrmeier v. Austria, Series A n°. 328 A-C and 329 A-C and ECHR, 27 Sept. 2011, A. Menarini diagnostics S.R.L. v. Italy, n°. 43509/08), compliance with Article 6 of the Convention for the Protection of Human Rights and Fundamental Freedoms does not preclude a "penalty" in administrative proceedings being imposed first by an administrative authority, provided that the decision of said administrative authority, which does not itself fulfil the conditions of Article 6, para. 1, is subject to subsequent review by a judicial body having unlimited jurisdiction. It states that the characteristics of a court of full jurisdiction include the power to review in all respects, in fact and in law, the decision taken by the lower court. In particular, it must have jurisdiction to consider all questions of fact and law relevant to the dispute brought before it.

16. However, the action for annulment or reversal before the Paris Court of Appeal, provided for in Article L. 464-8 of the Commercial Code, must be regarded as an action of full jurisdiction within the meaning of Article 6(1),

cited above. In particular, it confers on this court the power to rule on any grievance alleging an infringement of the Competition Authority's impartiality, whether it concerns the investigation phase, placed under the direction of the general rapporteur pursuant to Articles L. 461-4 and R. 463-4 of the Commercial Code, or the decision-making phase, entrusted to the college of the Authority.

17. It follows from the foregoing that Articles 341 *et seq.* of the Code of Civil Procedure establishing, before the judicial Courts ruling in civil matters, a procedure for recusal or dismissal on grounds of legitimate suspicion, do not apply to the *Autorité de la concurrence*." (17)

Other original solutions could be mentioned, especially in relation to the collection of evidence, which is the subject of special provisions that are noticeable for their inquisitorial nature, (18) but also in relation to the principle of publicity (of the proceedings or the decision), or certain aspects of the rights of the defence (right to remain silent, not to incriminate oneself), etc.

4. Under these conditions, dealing with this subject feels like assessing these particularities (to what extent does Compliance Law give rise to either an adapted or a derogatory General Procedural Law?), and trying to understand them (are these particularities justified or are they simply the dregs of a Law that remains imperfect?).

In a similar vein, however, another approach is possible by simply considering the chronological dimension. A survey of the successive reforms or developments in case law over the last twenty years, clearly shows that the procedural provisions in Compliance Law have been significantly improved, so much so that it now seems possible to assess the progress of General Procedural Law principles in Compliance Law, illustrating the progress made and the progress still to be made…

But this is beside the point and our analysis takes a different approach to the subject. We consider that the problem at hand is not so much to determine how much room has been set aside for General Procedural Law in Compliance Law as to question the former's right to interfere in the latter.

(17) Decision of the *Cour de cassation* (French Court of cassation), *deuxième chambre civile* (Second Civil Chamber), 30 September 2021, No. 20-18.672, BR, *D. actu.*, 11 October 2021, obs. N. Hoffschir. See also, decision of the *Cour de cassation* (French Court of cassation), *deuxième chambre civile* (Second Civil Chamber), 30 September 2021, No. 20-18.302.

(18) See e.g. *Autorité de contrôle prudentiel et de resolution – ACPR* (French Banking Supervisory Authority), *CMF*, Article 621-24. It follows from this text that investigators are not required to reveal to the supervised person either the documents concerning him or her that he or she holds or how they obtained them. The law even provides that investigators are entitled to use an assumed name to access information on the Internet.

I. ON THE LEGITIMACY OF PROCEDURAL PRINCIPLES IN COMPLIANCE LAW

5. How legitimate is General Procedural Law? A basic French textbook for all General Procedural Law specialists is Cornu and Foyer's *Procédure civile* (Thémis). From its first edition onwards, this book has opened with the example of a trial within which is the paramount notion of "*litige*" ("dispute").(19) Motulsky begins in the same way: the first section of the first chapter of his *Droit processuel* is entitled *Le litige juridique* (The legal dispute), the analysis of which leads to the classification of litigation, distinguishing between administrative, civil and criminal litigation.(20) So yes, litigation (or dispute) is indeed at the heart of General Procedural Law.

Its legitimacy stems from this, from a deep knowledge of disputes of all kinds, a knowledge that leads to better judgements. General Procedural Law experts are familiar with civil disputes between a contractor and a client, between parents fighting for the custody of their children. They are highly qualified in Magistrate's or Criminal Court trials when it comes to judging swindlers, thieves or rapists and perfectly familiar with full administrative litigation as well as litigation concerning the abuse of power...

But what does General Procedural Law know about compliance litigation? Of course, within the vast field of compliance, there are fairly ordinary disputes that fall within the common scope of General Procedural Law without any particular difficulty. But there are also unprecedented "cases" – to use a neutral term – with huge stakes and potentially catastrophic consequences. What do these have in common with the usual cases of General Procedural Law? What does General Procedural Law know about procedures in Compliance Law that are concerned with saving society, the state or the planet?

6. In many respects, Compliance Law is synonymous with a fighting Law, a Law by which society protects itself against threats to its survival, or at least its security and freedom. But what threatens the survival of a society, its security and its freedom? A dispute? No. Not an ordinary dispute, at any rate. In fact, isn't what threatens society what we call war? Shouldn't we say outright: "Compliance Law is a Law of war"? Is Compliance Law not the Law by which society arms itself against those who most seriously endanger its stability, who are the most dangerous?

(19) G. Cornu and J. Foyer, *Procédure civile*, Paris, PUF, 1958, p. 31.
(20) H. Motulsky, *Droit processuel*, Paris, Montchrestien, 1973, mimeographed, p. 5.

The narrative that such questions lead to, as I imagine it, is as follows:

"It is said that the fall of Constantinople in 1453 was due to the fact that the authorities were too busy discussing the sex of angels instead of organising their defence against the attacker.

Is discussing the principles of General Procedural Law in Compliance Law in 2021 not the same as discussing the sex of angels when there is an urgent need to organise the fight against the systemic risks facing the world?

When collective security is threatened, is there not more urgent work to be done than to discuss the individual right to recourse? When the rights of future generations are compromised, should the present generation be given free access to the judge?

Of course, a trial must be fair and equitable. But what does this platitude mean when the trial is not one of a common offender but of organisations that control the fundamental interests of everyone? What does this platitude mean when thieves and bandits, intoxicated by having stolen too much from society, proceed to corrupt it for their own benefit? Where is the equality of arms?

How can we dare to oppose a right to remain silent to the duty to tell the truth – the whole truth – about the nature and extent of the risks we face? Has history taught us nothing? For example, that disasters are born of blindness, of failing to demand the truth – the whole truth?

When society is threatened, it must defend itself. When the Revolution was threatened, the Convention wondered what kind of trial should be held for Louis XVI. Saint Just replied that the king could not be tried under the Law, that it was not a trial to be held but a political act to be carried out, that Louis XVI was not an accused individual but an enemy and that there was only one law for him, that of the law of nations, that is to say the Law of war.

Against whom are the rules of compliance?

Against the strong, the giants, the powerful. It's a question of curbing the insatiable appetite of the conquerors of all kinds, of throwing the conquistadors of personal data into the sea, of tracking down the privateers' algorithmic vessels wherever they may be.

Against the lords of finance, whose apparent strength gives them the confidence to transform promises into wealth, and therefore to mint money! Money, that common good which does not belong to them because it belongs to everyone, but of which they are the masters; we would be at their mercy if we did not force their respect.

Against the plunderers and polluters of natural resources, and other riders of the Apocalypse of climate change.

What Law do they have? What trial would be worthy enough? What good is a judge if he or she is unable to grasp the issues at stake? Who knows whether his or her judgements, based on outdated or deficient understanding, will not precipitate us into the abyss?

Yes, society must defend itself! Where is the new Saint Just for our time?"

7. This rhetoric, full of images and dramatic metaphors, does not make for an analysis. But it has at least two merits.

The first is to point out that the issue of the relationship between General Procedural Law and Compliance Law is fundamentally different depending on whether one believes that the legitimacy of General Procedural Law is indisputable or not.

The second is to help characterise this issue, however it is presented. It would be wrong to reduce the relationship between General Procedural Law and Compliance Law to a trivial problem concerning the logical relationship between two Laws, problem of the kind that lawyers deal with when they discuss, for example, the relationship between Civil Law and Criminal Law. In reality, the principal difficulty of the relationship between General Procedural Law and Compliance Law is not one of legal logic, but rather one of politics, concerning the conception of the Rule of Law and the relationship between security and freedom.

And it should be added that this political issue is made even more serious in Compliance Law by a dual dilemma, both existential and psychological. It is existential, because we have to overcome the anguish caused by the disasters that Compliance Law presents us with and psychological, because we need courage to face these disasters. But what is courage?

Here again, it is not a purely academic discourse that comes to mind. Let me put it this way:

> "As a defender of the Rule of Law, I love the principles of the right to a fair trial and I love them passionately. But in the context of Compliance Law, given the seriousness of the risks, loving them passionately is not enough, because you can't count on passion any more than you can count on good weather. Even if I were really able to do so when the time comes, would it not be foolish of me to rush onto the barricades waving the banner of procedural principles? If the dreaded circumstances arise, these principles may well be swept away at the same time as I am stupidly mowed down by machine gun fire."

II. THE NATURE OF COMPLIANCE LITIGATION

8. A more in-depth study of compliance "litigation" is therefore necessary. On analysis, there would appear to be two distinctive features.

The first is gigantism, the disproportionate size of the players and the risks involved. In Compliance Law, we speak of institutions *"d'importance systémique*" ("of systemic importance"), or even "*d'importance systémique mondiale*" ("of global systemic importance"). (21) We also speak of "*opérateurs cruciaux*" ("crucial operators") (22) and this is a characteristic feature of this litigation which cannot be ignored. In General Procedural Law, we are well aware that not all cases brought before the courts involve parties of equal strength. We know that there are unbalanced trials, for which the principles of General Procedural Law require a rebalancing act, so as to ensure relative equality. But we do not know what to do when the trial involves giants, when we are confronted not just with the enormous, but with the *enormously large*. (23)

The second is a corollary. In Compliance Law, the damage incurred can be so great and so serious that litigation is not only what must be resolved, it is also what must be avoided as far as possible. Litigation is not only what must be dealt with, it is also what must be anticipated and, as far as possible, prevented. So, compliance litigation has a dual aspect: *ex post* litigation for repression and reparation, and *ex ante* litigation for prevention. At the very least, good compliance litigation is litigation that does not arise, litigation that has been avoided.

9. Hence the importance, in Compliance Law, of "incentives," a euphemism used to designate all prescriptions aimed at avoiding catastrophic litigation such as, "incentives" to "map" risks, to analyse them, to divide them up, to erect "Chinese walls," to lay down "hedge buffers."

All this is accompanied by the threat of sanctions, sanctions that are as frightening as possible so as to thwart any calculation, and moreover "sanctions that are all the higher because they are negotiable in exchange for what the public authorities want." (24) Hence a litigation based on incentives, a litigation of the *ex ante*, a litigation that can be resolved by judgement, settlement or a "*convention judiciaire d'intérêt public*" ("Judicial Public Interest Agreement"). (25)

It follows that compliance litigation is not one but twofold and this duality may shed light on our subject.

(21) See *Code monétaire et financier* (French Monetary and Financial Code), Article L. 612-1, II, 2°*bis*.

(22) M.-A. Frison-Roche, "*Proposition pour une notion: l'opérateur crucial*", *D.*, 2006, p. 1895.

(23) A personal opinion: the fault of Competition Law. This Law, which abhors excessive concentrations, has little or nothing against gigantism.

(24) M.-A. Frison-Roche, "Resolving the Contradiction between 'Sanction' and 'Incentive' under the Fire of Compliance Law", *in* M.-A. Frison-Roche (ed.), *Compliance Tools*, "Compliance & Regulation" Serie, Brussels, Journal of Regulation & Compliance (JoRC)/Bruylant, 2021, p. 105.

(25) *Code de procedure pénale* (French Criminal procedure Code), Article 41-1-2.

III. RESPONSIBILISATION TRIALS

10. If Compliance Law is indeed a fighting Law and if compliance litigation is sometimes repressive, and sometimes preventive, then the combination of these two propositions leads to a distinction between two kinds of "struggle": on the one hand, retaliation after an infringement suffered; on the other hand, anticipation and prevention before the damage occurs.

It follows that these two kinds of litigation result in two different types of proceedings.

The first type of lawsuit is quite familiar, despite the often staggering sums involved. These are lawsuits caused by damage to the interests of society, and the aim of the trial is to put an end to the violation and to repair the damage caused. In the sense of Article 6 of the European Convention for the Protection of Human Rights and Fundamental Freedoms, this is ordinary "Criminal Law," and the principles of General Procedural Law are fully applicable.

The second type of lawsuit is more confusing. It is caused by a lack of professional rigour or discipline, carelessness or negligence, a risky initiative that creates insecurity and may threaten the stability of the system. This kind of trial can be found in all compliance disciplines, but it is a very particular kind of trial.

What name can be given to them and what is the nature of these lawsuits, which fall under the heading of *ex ante* anticipation litigation? Is this not what we call a lawsuit of *intent*?(26)

11. A lawsuit of intent... the idea is quite intriguing. Over time, we have learned to be wary of lawsuits of intent. It was an advance in procedure and in Law when we learnt how to recognise trials of intent, to give them a name ("interlocutory"), and to be able to eliminate them.

Yet, these "crucial operators" of compliance that we fear so much, that we place under surveillance, which we urge to be prudent and predictable in their precise and sophisticated accounting, to use rigorous self-checking procedures, these operators to whom we bring this alternative type of lawsuits, do we not consider them *irresponsible*? Irresponsible, not of course in the legal sense, but irresponsible in the common sense, i.e. we believe that they are capable of causing a disaster.

(26) The French original has a pun here, unfortunately lost in translation. The idiom literally translated as *trial of intent* actually means *to accuse someone of something based on second guessing their intentions.*

Lastly, going beyond interlocutory provocation, the compliance dispute calls for a different language. Rather than talking about a trial of intent against operators treated as irresponsible, perhaps we should talk about a "responsibilisation trial." (27)

Is this why there are doubts about how useful it is to simply assert the traditional procedural principles in Compliance Law? For what exactly does equality of arms and the rights of defence mean with regard to a person whose liability is not in question for what he or she has done, but who we want to instruct, to persuade and to educate? The person who has accepted he or she must sign charters of good conduct, who is taught to collaborate and to promise, and who is taught that after having promised, it is important to keep his or her promise? In short, the person for whom this trial is intended to make him or her "aware," to make him or her responsible because he or she is not yet fully responsible?

This brings to mind the beginning of the second essay of Nietzsche's *Genealogy of Morals.* In this work, Nietzsche tells the story of man, this "forgetful animal" who, by dint of effort, has become "consistent," "predictable," "calculable," and has eventually engraved in his memory the value of promises. (28) "This is simply the long story of the origins of responsibility," (29) he writes. But before reaching this point, before enjoying the "proud knowledge of the extraordinary privilege of responsibility"... (30) What an effort, what a sacrifice, what trials and tribulations endured to get there!

Given the new systemic risks that Compliance Law deals with, it is as if we are reliving this situation, because society needs a new form of responsibility, and this one, like the old one, has to be learned.

In this respect, today's compliance trials are also trials for the future. And like those of the past, they have a *pedagogical* function, i.e. to make a strong and lasting impression on people's conscience and to help instil responsibility for the future into their minds. Can or should this pedagogical dimension have an impact on the way procedural principles are applied in Compliance Law? It is difficult to reply to this question. (31)

(27) See e.g. the language of M. Delmas-Marty, *Résister, responsabiliser, anticiper*, Paris, Seuil, 2013.

(28) F. Nietzsche, *Zur Genealogie der Moral*, 1887, *On the Genealogy of Morals*, translated by D. Smith, Oxford, OUP, 1999.

(29) *Ibid.*

(30) *Ibid.*

(31) When one does not know, one likes to reason by analogy. Here is one: on 9 April 2021, the *Conseil constitutionnel* (French Constitutional Council) censured Article 12 of the French ordinance of 2 February 1945 (criminal proceedings against a minor), which provided that "*le service de la protection judiciaire de la jeunesse*

12. So, with regard to the procedural principles of Compliance Law, we would say that they mostly raise questions.

In a fundamental text entitled "*De la légitimité de la justice*" ("On the Legitimacy of Justice"), Dean Georges Wiederkher studied the legitimacy of the bodies with the power to judge. (32) Starting from the idea that "no power is legitimate in itself," (33) he notes that the legitimacy of a particular power can only come from the function it allows to be exercised, and on condition that this function is indispensable and can only be accomplished through this power. (34) But, he adds, "if the necessity and specific nature of the function are sufficient to legitimise the power by which alone it can be performed, they do not automatically entail the legitimacy of the institution to which the power is entrusted, nor of the judges who exercise the function." (35) Various specific conditions are necessary to legitimise the institution and the judges in charge of this function, foremost among which is independence, understood as freedom and not as power.

This line of reasoning, which Dean Wiederkehr uses in relation to judicial institutions, should be adapted to the institutions of compliance. Is the function of these institutions indispensable? Yes, it certainly is, given that society's safety is at stake. Can it only be exercised through these institutions and, in particular, why is this not possible through the ordinary judicial institutions? Because, as we have seen, compliance litigation (if indeed it is litigation) is not ordinary litigation, but litigation concerning the prevention of major systemic risks for society, which requires a pedagogy of responsibility.

---

compétent établit [...] *un rapport écrit contenant tous renseignements utiles sur la situation du mineur ainsi qu'une proposition éducative*" ("the competent youth protection service shall draw up [...] a written report containing all useful information on the minor's situation as well as an educational proposal"), without the minor being informed of his or her "*droit de se taire*" ("right to remain silent"), as his or her words recorded in a report sent to the judge were likely to contribute to his or her incrimination (Decision No. 2021-894 QPC). This decision is perplexing. Is it a good idea to explain to a teenager that he or she has the right not to talk to an educator about what he or she is being prosecuted for? What do we want him to understand by this? What kind of man do we want to make of him?

(32) G. Wiederkehr, *De la légitimité de la justice. Mélanges Jacques Héron*, Paris, LGDJ, 2008, p. 485.

(33) Free translation of: "*aucun pouvoir n'est légitime en soi.*"

(34) G. Wiederkehr, *De la légitimité de la justice. Mélanges Jacques Héron, op. cit.*, p. 486.

(35) *Ibid.*, p. 489, free translation of: "*si la nécessité et la nature spécifique de la fonction suffisent à légitimer le pouvoir par qui seul elle peut être assurée, elles n'entraînent pas automatiquement la légitimité de l'institution à qui le pouvoir est confié, ni des juges qui exercent la fonction.*"

Would we then maintain that compliance institutions have all the qualities required to perform their indispensable function and that their independence is sufficiently guaranteed? Well, shall we say that independence is of prime concern and enshrined in their title of *independent* administrative authorities. Moreover, although this "independence is necessarily relative and the guarantees limited," (36) in what are essentially political matters of direct interest to society, procedural rules are there to remind those in charge of the price to pay. The problem here is to avoid both the "misdeeds of dependence" and the "excesses of independence," (37) when, through hubris, the excitement of confronting giants, or the frustration of not always having the means to fight, one confuses independence with power.

The lesson that the principles of General Procedural Law addresses to jurisdictional institutions is also a highly useful one for the institutions of compliance, to help them legitimise their power, and beyond that to legitimise justice, which is indivisible.

(36) G. Wiederkehr, *De la légitimité de la justice. Mélanges Jacques Héron, op. cit.*, p. 489, free translation of: "*indépendance est forcément relative et les garanties limitées.*"

(37) *Ibid.*, p. 491, free translation of: "*méfaits de la dépendance*" and "*excès de l'indépendance.*"

Compliance Law, a New Guiding Principle for the Trial?

François Ancel

Conseiller à la Cour de cassation
(Judge at the French Court of cassation)

There is a certain paradox to make compliance a guiding principle for the trial. Compliance was originally designed precisely to reduce legal risk and avoid sanctions that companies, especially in the banking and financial sector, (1) face when they fail to comply with the multiple regulations that concern them. It may be against nature to try to emerge from Compliance Law the noblest principle known in General Procedural Law, a principle registered in the first part of the *Code de procédure civile* (French Civil Procedure Code) alongside contradiction, the rights of defence and so on.

The tools of compliance are designed to do without the judge: codes, conduct charters, alert procedures, algorithms or audits are developed to better evaluate the risk considered and reflect on procedures to avoid it. The judge is no longer necessary since the company can justify that it is always in compliance with the commitments it has made to comply with the mass of regulations that concerns it. (2)

Law of anticipation (of "*ex ante*"), how Compliance Law could absorb the office of the judge, which falls under the "*ex post*," to the point of giving rise to a guiding principle?

---

(1) See M.-A. Frison-Roche, "Le Droit de la compliance", *Recueil Dalloz*, 2016, p. 1871: "*substantif utilisé pour exprimer la maxime probatoire anglo-saxonne 'comply or explain'*" (free translation: "noun used to express the Anglo-Saxon probative maxim 'comply or explain.'")

(2) These preventive measures are put in place voluntarily, but can also be imposed by law: see the French law of 9 December 2016, so-called "Sapin 2" which forces companies of a certain size to structure themselves to prevent interne and international corruption, failing which they are sanctioned; or the French law of 27 April 2017, known as "Vigilance law" which obliges a ordering company to ensure compliance with safety and human rights rules throughout the chain of companies that provide a service for it.

If Compliance Law first invested in Banking and Financial Law, the multiplication of obligations to which companies are subject, in all areas (Labour Law, Antitrust, Personal Data Protection Law, Environmental Law, etc.), has expanded its scope to other areas of Law. It can thus potentially cover all areas that contain a risk for the company. This extension of compliance to all branches of Law therefore allows us to question its impact on General Procedural Law.

A narrow gate to such consecration opens if one is willing to return to the very definition of compliance and the purpose of the trial (I) and if one accepts to look at practices that have developed in recent years (II).

I. THE DOOR OPEN TO GUIDING PRINCIPLES: THE PURPOSES OF COMPLIANCE, THE PURPOSE OF THE TRIAL

A. The purposes of compliance

The assertion that compliance would postulate the eviction of the judge is based on a mistaken conception of what Compliance Law is. Indeed, to affirm the possible eviction of the judge is to suppose that compliance has the sole purpose of ensuring compliance with regulations and that, thanks to a performing compliance programme, there will no longer be any violation of it.

It is forgetting that far beyond the objective of respecting a mass of regulations, Compliance Law is above all animated by the higher will to preserve States from systemic dangers such as corruption, money laundering, climate imbalance, hatred, misinformation… all goals that have been qualified by doctrine as "monumental goals" and which participate in the Rule of Law. (3)

This purpose alone justifies the intervention of the judge, since it is up to him to ensure the primacy of the Law by exercising control over the one who promulgates these rules, to ensure respect for the fundamental rights of individuals.

(3) See M.-A. Frison-Roche (dir.), *Compliance Monumental Goals*, "Compliance & Regulation" Serie, Brussels, Journal of Regulation & Compliance (JoRC)/Bruylant, 2023.

B. The purpose of the trial

The purpose of compliance thus revealed, entirely devoted to the pursuit of monumental goals, could find a new field of intervention in the trial, whose purpose also falls under a monumental goal: rendering justice while avoiding the procedural risks generated by the trial and the legal wrangling that obstructs the examination of the merits of the dispute.

If the right to a judge guarantees the realisation of all other rights (and has been qualified as the "first" fundamental right), the trial itself is the necessary and indispensable realisation of this right, a recourse being "truly effective only when it can be concretely practiced, but also in that it leads to a judgment, since it is this that gives meaning to the action."(4)

Through the necessary involvement of the parties, who are assigned the objective of participating in the work of justice, a principle of compliance could thus find a place in General Procedural Law to contribute to guaranteeing the right to a fair trial and, in particular, the right to a substantive review of the dispute by the Judge to bring a reparative solution to the dispute, and thus giving substance to the objective of the parties to bring the dispute to maturity so that it can be resolved. Such a purpose, coupled with its vocation to apply to all jurisdictions and in all areas, allows for a connection with the qualification of guiding principles which have the "essential objective of determining the respective roles of the parties and the judge in civil proceedings [...] and establishing certain fundamental guarantees [...]";(5) and whose rules are qualified as guiding principles, "although having the same positive value as other rules (all this value and only it) because of the influence that their generality of application (before all jurisdictions, in all areas), on the other hand their capacity, as maxims summarising the French conception of civil proceedings, to guide the interpreter in the application of the [French Civil Procedure Code]."(6)

Certain judicial practices can help give substance to its emergence.

---

(4) W. Baranès and M.-A. Frison-Roche, "Le souci d'effectivité du droit", *D.*, 1996, chron. p. 301, free translation of: *"véritablement effectif que lorsque non seulement il peut être concrètement pratiqué, mais encore en ce qu'il aboutit à un jugement, car c'est celui-ci qui donne sens à l'action."*

(5) G. Cornu (dir.), *Vocabulaire juridique de l'Association Henri Capitant*, Paris, PUF, 1987, p. 269, free translation of: *"objet essentiel de déterminer le rôle respectif des parties et du juge dans le procès civil [...] et d'établir certaines garanties fondamentales* [...]."

(6) *Ibid.*, free translation of: *"bien qu'ayant la même valeur positive que les autres règles (toute cette valeur, seule cette valeur) en raison du rayonnement que leur donnent d'une part leur généralité d'application (devant toutes juridictions, en toute matière), d'autre part leur aptitude, en tant que maximes résumant la conception française du procès civil, à guider l'interprète dans l'application du [Code de procédure civile]."*

II. PRACTICE OPEN TO THE EMERGENCE OF A PROCEDURAL COMPLIANCE PRINCIPLE

If one starts from the idea that Compliance Law prohibits those who are not in line with the discourse they hold when they have the ability to act on practices and thus on the future, certain instruments and principles that have emerged in civil procedure could allow for the emergence of a procedural compliance principle.

A. The practice of procedural protocols

The complexity of the procedure, particularly on appeal, which is the result of several successive layers of reforms of which application gives rise to divergent interpretations, encourages the parties involved in the trial to protect themselves against the risk of litigation.

This is not about avoiding litigation, but about setting up procedures to avoid as much as possible, once litigation has begun, procedural uncertainties and traps.

Undoubtedly, lawyers have already implemented these processes within their firms to reduce litigation risk, but they are not alone. Many jurisdictions have entered into conventions or procedural protocols with bar associations that mostly aim to facilitate the implementation of a procedural reform through recommendations and commitments made by each of the parties. (7)

It is known that the legal value of these protocols is limited. The *Cour de Cassation* (French Court of cassation) does not consider them to be subject to procedural sanctions in the event of non-compliance if such sanctions are not themselves provided for in the *Code de procédure civile* (French Civil Procedure Code). (8)

However, as the culture of compliance asserts itself, can this existing situation be maintained, which amounts to drawing no consequence from a procedural protocol? Compliance Law could contribute to change things

(7) This was the case on the occasion of the creation of the *Chambre commerciale intenationale de la cour d'appel de Paris* (International Commercial Chamber of the Paris Court of Appeal), with the procedural protocol signed on 7 February 2018.

(8) Decision of the *Cour de cassation* (French Court of cassation), *deuxième chambre civile* (Second Civil Chamber), 19 October 2017, No. 16-24.234.

here, especially since it is not intended to sanction the non-compliance with a procedure (or a program) as if the risk it was intended to prevent had actually occurred. Indeed, those who do not put in place alert procedures to combat corruption cannot see the contracts they have concluded declared tainted by corruption and thus cancelled. Their liability is different.

In civil proceedings, the same would apply. If a party fails to comply with the protocol between a bar association and a jurisdiction, this does not necessarily mean that its action will be contrary to a procedural rule sanctioned by the French Civil Procedure Code, but simply that it has not implemented it according to the process defined by the parties.

The question then arises as to what sanction this failure can generate. This task can be delicate because the range of sanctions in civil procedure is relatively limited (nullity of the act; inadmissibility of the claim or plea; forfeiture). Nevertheless, can the failure to comply with the protocol, when the parties have agreed to respect it, remain without consequences?

The integration of Compliance Law into the legal process could lead to a development and an authorisation to invent new forms of sanctions: why not consider the cost of the trial (French Civil Procedure Code, Article 700) or the access to legal recourse (limiting the right of appeal based on the deliberately adopted attitude in the first instance contrary to these commitments)?

Apart from the case of procedural protocols, there is in some of the emerging guiding principles a spirit that is not far from Compliance Law and that it would not disavow.

B. The principles of loyalty, coherence (estoppel), and efficiency: a variation of a procedural compliance principle?

All these principles contain the idea that it is necessary to sanction someone who is not in line with the discourse he holds, or whose procedural attitude is not in conformity with his commitment. In this respect, they are not far from Compliance Law.

Thus, the link between the principle of coherence or estoppel and the procedural compliance principle is quite naturally made by the importance they both place on respecting the commitment made and the possible sanctions in case of deviation from this commitment.

The same applies to the principle of loyalty. A decision of the *Cour de cassation* (French Court of cassation), based on the "principle of procedural loyalty governing the parties to an arbitration agreement," (9) is interesting in this regard, as it confirms that a party who undertakes to submit a dispute to arbitration cannot, without disregarding this principle of loyalty, subsequently work to obstruct any arbitral and judicial resolution of its dispute. A party to arbitration cannot therefore refrain from paying its share of the deposit, which has the effect of paralysing the arbitral proceedings, and then raise the exception of arbitration before the State judge, which has the effect of paralysing the ordinary proceedings. It is sufficient to replace here "principle of procedural loyalty" with "procedural compliance principle" and the solution would not be much different.

Finally, the principle of efficiency, particularly developed in Arbitration Law in order to give full effect to the arbitration agreement, (10) finds an echo in the procedural compliance principle, one of whose objectives is also to make the commitments made by the actors in the trial effective.

Thus identified and/or emerging, such principles could be perceived as variations of a more general procedural compliance principle. Only time will tell if it is destined to ultimately encompass them.

(9) Decision of the *Cour de cassation* (French Court of cassation), *première chambre civile* (First Civil Chamber), 9 February 2022, No. 21-11.253, free translation of: "*principe de loyauté procédurale régissant les parties à une convention d'arbitrage.*"

(10) See the substantive rule developed by the French Court of cassation in order to guarantee the effectiveness or validity of the international arbitration clause (decision of the *Cour de cassation* (French Court of cassation), *première chambre civile* (First Civil Chamber), 20 December 1993, No. 91-16.828, *Dalico*).

Privilege Lessons from the U.S.

Bryan Sillaman

Partner, Anti-Corruption
and Internal Investigations Practice Group, Paris Office

Hugues Hubbard & Reed LLP

Attorney at Paris, New York and Washington D.C. Bars

I. Thesis

The French legal profession is evolving, perhaps most significantly in the way that French lawyers are increasingly finding themselves interacting with regulators and prosecutors in the context of investigations involving corruption or corporate misconduct. France has already taken cues from its Anglo-Saxon counterparts, especially the U.S., over the last decade, by (i) adopting a mechanism allowing companies to resolve misconduct through a negotiated resolution (1) (the *Convention judiciaire d'intérêt public* – CJIP [Judicial Public Interest Agreement]); (ii) encouraging cooperation with the authorities, as a precondition to the possibility of entering into a CJIP; (iii) emphasising the importance of adopting and maintaining robust compliance programs; and (iv) conducting thorough investigations when an alleged misconduct has been reported.

As this evolution continues, France should heed additional lessons from the U.S. in particular, as it grapples with the role of legal privilege (*secret professionnel*) and its implication in the context of internal investigations, especially regarding cooperation with regulators and prosecutors.

(1) The French so-called "Sapin 2" law, promulgated on 9 December 2016, created a procedure allowing the public prosecutor to conclude a Judicial Public Interest Agreement with a legal person potentially involved in corporate misconduct. This alternative measure to prosecution is applicable to companies, associations, local authorities, etc. under investigation for acts of corruption, influence peddling, tax fraud, laundering of tax fraud and any related offense.

Requiring companies to waive legal privilege in order to be seen as cooperative in the context of a regulatory investigation or prosecution has been tried, unsuccessfully, in the U.S., and should be avoided in France as well. *A robust ecosystem of efficient and effective prosecution of corporate misconduct – built on a delicate balance of trust between the public authorities and French lawyers – must maintain as sacrosanct the essential principle of* secret professionnel.

II. THE U.S. EXPERIENCE

In the U.S., Department of Justice ("DOJ") policy and practices have been announced through a series of memoranda, typically issued by Deputy Attorneys General ("DAG"). Among other things, these Memoranda provide guidance to DOJ prosecutors as to how they approach their jobs and, more specifically, how they should engage with companies seeking credit for cooperation. The importance of these Memoranda became heightened in the wake of high-profile corporate misconduct / fraud events in the late 1990s and early 2000s, such as Enron and Worldcom.

In 2003, DAG Larry D. Thompson issued a Memorandum that, among other things, encouraged companies to waive legal privilege in order to avoid prosecution and gain credit for cooperating with the authorities. The outcry from the legal profession was immediate and vocal. This eventually resulted in a revisiting of this posture, through the issuance of a subsequent Memorandum by DAG Paul McNulty, which stated clearly that "[w]aiver of attorney-client and work product protections is not a prerequisite to a finding that a company has cooperated in the government's investigation". (2) That approach has been further reinforced and clarified to date, (3) such that prosecutors in practice now avoid asking companies to waive privilege and assess cooperation only on whether companies have provided full and complete underlying factual (*i.e.*, non-privileged) information.

The result is a delicate balance that depends on mutual trust and confidence between DOJ prosecutors, companies and their outside counsel – trust that must be continually demonstrated through proactive and innovative means of sharing information without necessarily waiving privilege.

(2) Memorandum of Paul J. McNulty, Principles of Federal Prosecution of Business Organizations, 5 July 2007.

(3) See, *e.g.*, Memorandum of Mark Filip, Principles of Federal Prosecution of Business Organizations, 28 August 2008.

III. FRANCE'S CURRENT PATH

France seems to be heading in the unfortunate direction set out in the Thompson Memorandum, which is to hinge cooperation credit and the possibility of a CJIP on a company's willingness to produce materials, even those covered by *secret professionnel*. First and foremost, the 2019 Guidelines on the Implementation of the CJIP, (4) co-written by the *Parquet national financier* – PNF (French National Financial Prosecutor's Office) and the *Agence française anticorruption* – AFA (French Anti-Corruption Agency) adopted a stand that encouraged companies to waive legal privilege, by reminding clients that they are not bound by the lawyers' professional secrecy, and that refusal from a company to forward documents could be assessed by prosecutors as bearing "an unfavorable effect on the level of cooperation of the company." (5)

In the revised January 2023 CJIP Guidelines issued by the PNF, (6) they refer to privilege more indirectly through the following concepts:

- by listing "good faith" conditions of cooperation necessary to be eligible to enter into a *CJIP*, including, but not limited to, the provision to the authorities of (i) a detailed internal investigation report and (ii) elements supporting the internal investigation's findings, such as minutes of personnel interviews; (7) and
- the unwritten principle of confidence between French attorneys and prosecutors (*foi du palais*) that should govern talks and negotiations in anticipation of a potential CJIP, which would nonetheless not prohibit the PNF – if such negotiations are not successful – to use disclosed information in case of a later prosecution. (8)

These January 2023 Guidelines were followed by the March 2023 Practical Guide on Internal Investigations issued by the *AFA* and the PNF, which stated that "under the current legislation and case-law, regardless of the status of the investigation team members, the document drafted following the internal investigation *is not protected by any legal privilege*." (9)

(4) *Parquet national financier* – PNF (French National Financial Prosecutor's Office) and *Agence française anticorruption* – AFA (French Anti-Corruption Agency), *Guidelines on the implementation of the Convention judiciaire d'intérêt public* (Judicial Public Interest Agreement), June 2019.

(5) *Ibid.*

(6) PNF, *Guidelines on the implementation of the judicial public interest agreement (CJIP)*, January 2023.

(7) *Ibid.*

(8) *Ibid.*

(9) AFA and PNF, *Internal Anti-Corruption Investigations. Practical Guide*, March 2023 (emphasis added).

This position was later criticised by the *Conseil de l'Ordre de Paris* (Paris Bar Council), which stated that the interview notes and the internal investigation report which would be established by an attorney and transferred to his/her client are fully protected by legal privilege. (10)

In that context, the extension of the legal privilege (*secret professionel*) to in-house lawyers (*juristes d'entreprise*) in France, who do not currently enjoy any such privilege surrounding their advice to in-house constituents, has been discussed at the French governmental level. An article of the *loi d'orientation et de programmation du ministère de la justice 2023-2027* (Ministry of Justice Orientation and Programming law for 2023-2027) that recognised a new category of legal privilege – under certain conditions – for *juristes d'entreprises* was approved by the French Parliament in October 2023. However, in a decision dated 16 November 2023, the *Conseil constitutionnel* (French Constitutional Council) struck out the provisions introduced on procedural grounds, ruling that such provisions did not have sufficient connection with the purpose of the Bill. (11) Although the *Conseil constitutionnel* does not directly address the situation regarding French legal privilege and its compliance with constitutional requirements, this decision still deals a further setback towards gaining confidentiality protections for in-house legal counsel.

While a new legislative initiative on the protection of in-house legal counsel should be introduced in the near future, observations from certain members of the French Parliament suggests that this new category of legal privilege would restrict powers of the French authorities. (12) Such an uncertain and sceptical view of legal privilege could severely impact the establishment of long-term trust and confidence between prosecutors, lawyers, and their clients. Companies must be able to feel that they can entrust lawyers (in-house and external alike) to conduct sensitive internal investigations on their behalf and advise them of their legal consequences,

(10) *Barreau de Paris* (Paris Bar Association), Résolution du Conseil de l'Ordre relative au "Guide pratique sur les enquêtes internes anticorruption" (Resolution of the Bar Council relating to the "Internal Anti-Corruption Investigations Practical Guide"), April 2023.

(11) Since Decision No. 85-198 DC of 13 December 1985, the French Constitutional Council requires a minimum level of connection between the stated purpose of a Bill throughout the parliamentary process, and the provisions of the law to be adopted. Since decision No. 2006-534 DC of 16 March 2006, the French Constitutional Council started censuring provisions constituting what are called "*cavaliers législatifs*" ("legislative riders") even if they were not contested by the authors of the referral.

(12) *Gouvernement français* (French Government), Observations du Gouvernement sur la loi d'orientation et de programmation du ministère de la justice 2023-2027 (Government observations on the Ministry of Justice Orientation and Programming law for 2023-2027), received at the *greffe du Conseil constitutionnel* (clerk's office of the Constitutional Council) on 1st November 2023, p. 30.

without fear that privileged reports or materials prepared by lawyers in these particular situations will be requested or demanded by the authorities in exchange for cooperation credit. (13)

To the extent that a company decides that it wishes to cooperate to resolve a corporate prosecution, it should be required and prepared to provide factual and non-privileged information, but must not be forced to reveal privileged communications with its lawyers. Doing so will have a chilling effect on a company's good-faith efforts to uncover the truth surrounding misconduct, and will ultimately work against prosecutors' interests if they lose the confidence of companies and their defence counsel – who can serve as a useful avenue through which they can work more efficiently by obtaining factual information regarding an investigation.

(13) As per January 2023 *PNF Guidelines on the implementation of the judicial public interest agreement (CJIP)* cited above, spontaneous communication of the internal investigation is an element that can demonstrate good faith of a company, to be considered when negotiating a CJIP.

Motivation and publicity of the decisions of the Restricted formation of the French Data Protection Authority (*Commission nationale de l'informatique et des libertés – CNIL*) in a Compliance Perspective

Alexandre Linden

Chair of the restricted formation of the *CNIL*,
Honorary Judge of the Court of Cassation

In the event of a breach of the rules on the protection of personal data, the *Commission nationale de l'informatique et des libertés – CNIL* (French Data Protection Authority)' s restricted formation has the power to pronounce measures such as a fine, an order to comply or a reprimand. It may or may not order their publication according to the terms it determines. An appeal, known as a "*recours de plein contentieux*" ("full remedy appeal"), may be lodged against its decisions before the *Conseil d'État* (French Council of State).

I. MOTIVATION

The obligation to give reasons for any decision adversely affecting a person is a democratic requirement. The quality of this motivation is therefore fundamental.

One of the difficulties in drafting *CNIL* decisions lies in the heterogeneity of their readers: persons directly concerned (individuals or representatives of the legal entity in question), jurists, publishers, commentators, Law professors, lawyers and other legal professionals, journalists, the general public, and, in the event of an appeal, the *Conseil d'État* (French Council of State).

In addition, for cross-border cases, which are subject to a European cooperation mechanism, the draft decisions, translated into English, are sent to other data protection authorities, which may raise objections. Some of these authorities belong to different legal traditions and maximum clarity is necessary to avoid any ambiguity.

The quality of the motivation mainly depends on the accuracy of the reasoning, the relevance of the application of the legal rule and the clarity of the expression.

It is essential that the reader of the decision understands without difficulty what led the *CNIL* to rule as it did. However, the Authority must not make basic simplifications, especially when dealing with technical issues. This requirement for clarity is all the more important since the *CNIL* has a pedagogical role to play in achieving compliance. Thus, for example, organisations carrying out processing operations similar to those targeted by a sanction decision must be able to understand the corrective measures to be taken in order to comply.

It is with this in mind that *CNIL* decisions have numbered paragraphs and are, as far as possible, short.

With regard to the length of decisions, the *CNIL* strives to strike a balance in order to avoid drafting lengthy decisions or on the contrary excessively concise decisions.

The development of the motivation may vary according to the type of legal issue at stake. Thus, if a delicate question arises, for which several solutions are conceivable, the motivation will be more developed. For example, the case law references will be more numerous. This part of the decision will be written with the idea that the French Council of State must be convinced of the correctness of the solution adopted.

In some other parts, the decision can target all data controllers. For example, even if it is not essential to justify the conviction for a breach of security rules, the decision will recall the recommendations of the *Agence nationale de la sécurité des systèmes d'information – ANSSI* (French National Cybersecurity Agency).

One might think that the quality of the decisions' motivation would reduce the number of appeals, but other elements may encourage the individual or legal entity in question to lodge an appeal: the amount of the fine, a question of principle, an impact on reputation.

But there is no doubt that the quality of the motivation is an important element for compliance.

II. PUBLICITY

A. The public or non-public nature of the Restricted formation's meetings

The principle is that the hearing is public. However, the *CNIL*'s rules of procedure provide that the chairman of the hearing may, at the request of the data controller in question or on his or her own initiative, restrict the public nature of the hearing in the interest of public order, or when the protection of secrets protected by Law so requires.

Between November 2020 and September 2021, out of twenty-two meetings of the Restricted formation, thirteen organisations requested that the hearing be held *in camera*, mainly on the grounds of infringement of business secrecy. Such request has been granted in only two cases.

Each meeting of the Restricted formation is announced on the *CNIL* website, but without an agenda or mention of the person or organisation concerned. This lack of publicity is intended to prevent the effects that the public designation of the respondents could have, particularly with regard to their reputation, even though no decision has been taken in their regard. This practice contributes, upstream of any decision, to the necessary balance between the requirements of public interest, of which publicity is a part, and the interests of the respondents. In reality, very few people – sometimes none – attend the hearings. Their public nature is thus to be put into perspective.

B. Publicity of sanction decisions

The publication of a sanction decision must be considered as an additional sanction and, as such, is necessarily subject to the principle of proportionality. Its legality is assessed, in particular with regard to the medium used and, where applicable, the length of time during which the publication is freely and continuously accessible. (1)

The French so-called *"loi Informatique et Libertés"* (French Data Protection law) does not specify the criteria to be taken into consideration on this point.

The balance between pedagogy, awareness and sanction is one of the elements that the *CNIL*'s Restricted formation takes into account when deciding whether or not to make public the measures it pronounces.

Most of the decisions of the Restricted formation are made public. The grounds taken into account for not publishing a decision include, among others, the size of the organisation, its market position, the consideration not to stigmatise a particular player, the lack of need to raise public awareness on an issue. In concrete terms, the reputational impact that the publication of a sanction would have on a small organisation or individual, its potentially disproportionate nature, or the fact that a player who has recently entered a market could be weakened by it, may justify the absence of publication.

Moreover, Article 20 of the French Data Protection law provides that the Chair of the *CNIL* may issue an order to comply and ask the Bureau – composed of the president and the two vice-presidents – to make it public. The criteria mentioned above are then taken into consideration. When an order to comply made public is followed by a decision to close the procedure, this decision is subject to the same publicity.

C. Arrangements for publication

The decisions of the Restricted formation ordering their publication are published on the *CNIL* website and the *Légifrance* website.

This publication is not necessarily complete. In fact, several data are omitted from the decisions before they are put online, such as data that may be covered by business secrecy (turnover, number of customers, etc.).

The decisions stipulate the duration of the publication – generally between one and two years – and specify that at the end of this period, the person or organisation concerned will no longer be identified by name.

(1) Judgment of the *Conseil d'État* (French Council of State), 28 September 2016, *Théâtre national de Bretagne*, No. 389448.

The Restricted formation may also order the publication, while anonymising the data controller.

It resorts to this method in particular when there is a pedagogical interest, such as raising the awareness of the actors of a sector with a view to ensure a better understanding of a legal obligation. This type of publication falls within the scope of the *CNIL*'s mission to inform and raise awareness.

For example, the *CNIL*'s Restricted formation has ordered the publication of anonymised decisions imposing fines on private medical practitioners for insufficiently protecting their patients' personal data and failing to notify a personal data breach to the *CNIL*.(2) Although the identity of the practitioners concerned has not been revealed, the publication of the decisions has undoubtedly had an impact regarding this profession and its obligations in terms of personal data security, notably because the specialised press reported them.

The *CNIL* publishes on its website press releases on the decisions adopted. They summarise the content of the decisions and have the advantage of being easy to read. They can be issued even if the decision has not been made public.

Their impact can be very important. For example, one of the most read pages on the *CNIL* website in 2021 (15,269 views as of 15 September) is a press release announcing fines of 150,000 and 75,000 euros against a data controller and its subcontractor for not having taken satisfactory measures to deal with credential stuffing attacks on the controller's website.(3)

The anonymisation of published sanction decisions, or even the simple fact of communicating on a decision, is therefore a tool at the discretion of the *CNIL*. Their purpose is not only educational, but also corrective in terms of compliance by organisations in a particular sector, or even by all organisations concerned by structural obligations in terms of personal data protection.

However, the *CNIL* is not in a position to control all the effects of a publication and a communication relating to sanction decisions.

(2) https://www.cnil.fr/fr/violations-de-donnees-de-sante-la-cnil-sanctionne-deux-medecins.

(3) https://www.cnil.fr/fr/credential-stuffing-la-cnil-sanctionne-un-responsable-de-traitement-et-son-sous-traitant.

Indeed, at the end of the time limit set by the decision, the *CNIL* does not have the power to prevent articles relating to sanctions from remaining online and identifying the persons concerned, despite the planned anonymisation. Moreover, even if there is no publication, the potential complainant(s) are informed of the meaning of the decision and sometimes relay the information.

In short, even as part of its repressive activity, the *CNIL* exercises its regulatory role by working for compliance, both through the motivation of its sanction decisions and through their publication and communication modalities.

The Difficulty for Compliance Enforcement Authorities to Comprehend the Rights of the Defence in Compliance Matters

Sophie Scemla

Admitted to both the Paris and the New York Bars,
Partner, Gide Loyrette Nouel

and

Diane Paillot de Montabert

Lawyer, Associate, Gide Loyrette Nouel

The French law No. 2016-1691 of 9 December 2016 *relative à la transparence, à la lutte contre la corruption et à la modernisation de la vie économique* (on transparency, fight against corruption and the modernisation of economic life), known as the "Sapin 2" law, has established a legal obligation for public and private sector companies falling within its scope (1) to deploy an anti-corruption program composed of eight measures, the implementation of which is highly restrictive.

(1) Under the terms of Article 17 of the French so-called "Sapin 2" law, which sets out the eight measures to be implemented, the private legal entities that fall within the scope of this article are "*sociétés employant au moins cinq cents salariés, ou appartenant à un groupe de sociétés dont la société mère a son siège social en France et dont l'effectif comprend au moins cinq cents salariés, et dont le chiffre d'affaires ou le chiffre d'affaires consolidé est supérieur à 100 millions d'euros*" (free translation: "companies employing at least five hundred employees, or belonging to a group of companies whose parent company has its registered office in France and whose workforce comprises at least five hundred employees, and whose turnover or consolidated turnover exceeds 100 million euros.")

These eight measures consist in the implementation of (i) a code of conduct, (ii) an internal whistleblowing mechanism, (iii) a risk mapping, (iv) procedures for assessing the situation of customers, first-tier suppliers and intermediaries, (v) accounting control procedures, (vi) a training program, (vii) a disciplinary system and (viii) an internal control and evaluation system for these measures.

The French so-called "Sapin 2" law also created the *Agence française anticorruption – AFA* (French Anti-Corruption Agency – AFA). The AFA has been assigned three main missions. The first one is to assist companies in preventing and detecting their corruption, influence peddling, misappropriation of public funds and favouritism risks. (2) The second one endows the AFA with a supervisory power which enables it, on its own initiative, to verify the quality and effectiveness of anti-corruption programmes implemented by entities subject to the provisions of the "Sapin 2" law. (3) Finally, the AFA's Sanctions Committee is responsible for sanctioning any breaches identified.

As part of its control mission, the AFA does not seem concerned with respect for procedural rules, which are not codified. It does not hesitate to infringe the rights of defence of the entities it controls, notably by not always respecting the adversarial principle or the right not to incriminate oneself.

In a report on the investigative powers of government agencies published in April 2021, (4) the *Conseil d'État* (French Council of State) noted that the powers given to government agencies had become stratified and multiplied. It deplored the absence of a common procedural base applicable to the various agencies, and thus proposed to improve the conduct and effectiveness of their controls by harmonising practices and simplifying their powers and responsibilities.

While the restructuring called for by the *Conseil d'État* is necessary, it seems important to remedy the numerous procedural shortcomings in compliance control and sanction procedures, which are detrimental to the rights of the defence.

(2) Sapin 2 law No. 2016-1691, 9 December 2016, Article 1.

(3) *Ibid.*, Article 3.

(4) *Conseil d'État* (French Council of State), study on "*Les pouvoirs d'enquête de l'administration*" ("The investigative powers of government agencies"), April 2021: https://www.conseil-etat.fr/publications-colloques/etudes/les-pouvoirs-d-enquete-de-l-administration.

While some of these shortcomings may be the consequence of the AFA's hybrid status (I), others are due to the absence of procedural rules (II), which does not permit to regulate the authority's actions, or to precisely guarantee the rights of the defence (III).

I. THE AFA'S HYBRID STATUS UNDERMINES THE RIGHTS OF THOSE SUBJECT TO THE "SAPIN 2" LAW

By way of introduction, it should be noted that the AFA is a "national service" reporting to the Minister of Justice and the Minister responsible for the budget. (5) Although the AFA has been assigned the task of carrying out binding controls on subject entities, it has not been granted the status of an independent administrative authority, as is the case for the *Autorité des marchés financiers – AMF* (French Financial Markets Authority) or the *Autorité de contrôle prudentiel et de resolution – ACPR* (French French Banking Supervisory Authority).

A. The scope of AFA's guidelines undermines the presumption of innocence

As the legislator has not given the AFA any regulatory powers, (6) it cannot present its guidelines (7) as a doctrine or standard that would be enforceable against those subject to the law. In this respect, the AFA stresses that its guidelines do not create any legal obligations, and that subject entities "are free to adopt other methods, provided that implementation of such methods results in compliance with the Act [i.e. *the Sapin 2 law*]." (8)

Paradoxically, the AFA considers that its guidelines constitute "*le référentiel anticorruption français*" ("the French anti-corruption policy framework") in the same way as the law and its implementing decrees, even though they do not have the same prescriptive power.

(5) "Sapin 2" law No. 2016-1691, 9 December 2016, Article 1.

(6) Under the terms of Article 3, 2°, of the "Sapin 2" law, the recommendations are designed as a tool to help entities subject to this law by providing them with details of the best practices to adopt in the fight against corruption.

(7) *Agence française anticorruption – AFA* (French Anti-Corruption Agency – AFA), *The French Anti-Corruption Agency Guidelines – Notice on the French Anti-Corruption Agency Guidelines to help Public and Private Sector Entities to Prevent and Detect Bribery, Influence Peddling, Extortion by Public Officials, Illegal Taking of Interest, Misappropriation of Public Funds and Favouritism*, 2021, https://www.agence-francaise-anticorruption.gouv.fr/files/files/French%20AC%20Agency%20Guidelines%20.pdf.

(8) *Ibid.*, para. 8.

Similarly, the AFA is attempting to establish a presumption of non-compliance against companies that have not followed its guidelines, by stating that they will have to "show that [the] choices [they have made] enable [them] to meet the requirements of the Act" (9) if the AFA was to contest the measures they implemented. This interpretation, which reverses the burden of proof, is open to criticism and runs counter to the presumption of innocence.

This situation is all the more prejudicial for companies as France's compliance arsenal in terms of breaches of probity is among the most restrictive in the world, as it punishes *per se* any failure to comply with the preventive obligations imposed by the French so-called "Sapin 2" law. Indeed, very few jurisdictions impose on companies to set up a compliance programme and to face sanctions in case of breach of these obligations. For example, while in the United States, the existence of an anti-corruption program enables companies to obtain a reduction of the *quantum* of the fine that may be imposed in the event of prosecution for corruption, (10) it is not mandatory to set up such an anti-corruption programme. Similarly, in the UK and Spain, the introduction of a compliance programme enables companies to obtain partial or total exemption from criminal liability, (11) but the absence of such a programme is not sanctioned.

B. AFA's conflicting missions undermine the effectiveness of its advisory role

Another difficulty, of a functional nature, concerns the antagonistic nature of the different missions that the legislator has entrusted to the AFA.

(9) *Ibid.*, para. 12.

(10) When a US attorney leads an investigation against a company, he or she determines whether the company has an effective compliance programme in place to decide whether to prosecute the company or negotiate a possible settlement, and to determine the appropriate sanction (*Justice Manual*, JM 9-28.300, A.5. and JM 9-28.800). The existence of an effective compliance and ethics programme allows 3 points to be deducted from the "culpability score" established by the court (*Sentencing Commission Guidelines Manual*, November 1st, 2018, Part C - Fines, paras. 8C2.4., 8C2.5.[f], and 8C2.6.).

(11) According to a January 2018 report by the *Direction générale du Trésor* (French Treasury Department), "*il existe un système de prévention et de détection de la corruption en Espagne, mais son application n'est pas obligatoire dans les entreprises et relève de leur propre volonté. De fait, ce système est plutôt utilisé afin de réduire la responsabilité pénale d'une entreprise au cas où l'un de ses employés venait à commettre un délit de corruption*" (free translation: "a system for preventing and detecting corruption exists in Spain, but its application is not mandatory in companies and is a matter of their own free will. In fact, this system is used to reduce a company's criminal liability in the event that one of its employees commits a bribery offence"); *UK Bribery Act* 2010, Article 7, (2): "it is a defence for C to prove that C had in place adequate procedures designed to prevent persons associated with C from undertaking such conduct."

The first part of the AFA's mission is to help subject entities to prevent risks of corruption. Under the aegis of its director, the authority is responsible for disseminating information on preventing infringement of probity, and for drawing up recommendations to help legal entities detect and prevent breaches of probity.

The second part of its mission is to ensure that reporting entities comply with the obligations arising from the French so-called "Sapin 2" law. Under the aegis of its director as well, the AFA is also responsible for monitoring the implementation of compliance programmes. In the event of non-compliance, the AFA's director may refer the matter to the Sanctions Committee, which may then sanction the entity in breach.

Thus, the AFA is supposed to be both an ally of the entities subject to the "Sapin 2" law, which it must advise, while at the same time being responsible for controlling and sanctioning them. This combination of completely opposite missions is likely to create a degree of mistrust among companies. As a result, the AFA cannot fully fulfil its primary mission of assisting those subject to the law, and companies do not beneficiate from the support they should receive under the terms of the law.

II. THE ABSENCE OF PROCEDURAL RULES UNDERMINES THE RIGHTS OF CONTROLLED ENTITIES

Unlike other areas, such as Stock Market Law, where the body of legislation has already been greatly expanded, notably under the influence of European Union Law, French Law on the AFA's powers of control and sanction is limited to the French so-called "Sapin 2" law, which is very incomplete, and to an implementing decree that does not contain procedural rules.

Case law on AFA controls is virtually non-existent. To date, the Sanctions Committee has handed down only three decisions, none of which have been appealed to the *Conseil d'État* (French Council of State), despite the manifestly questionable nature of certain positions taken by the Committee.

Only Article 4 of the "Sapin 2" law provides a semblance of a procedural framework for AFA controls. It states that AFA may carry out documentary or on-site inspections, and that its agents are bound by professional secrecy and must not be in a situation of conflict of interests.

The AFA has undertaken to supplement this scant normative framework by publishing a Charter of the rights and duties of parties involved in AFA controls (the "Charter").(12) While the Charter sets out numerous duties for companies, their rights are limited to being informed of the start of the control, its progress and its outcome.(13)

The AFA takes advantage of these gaps in the rules to take over powers that are not provided for by the law, and which are difficult for companies to challenge, given the imbalance in which they are when they are subject to controls of the authority.

III. THE RIGHTS OF THE DEFENCE ARE NOT SUFFICIENTLY PROTECTED IN THE CONTEXT OF THE AFA'S CONTROLS

The enactment of procedural rules governing the exercise of the authorities' supervisory missions is an essential guarantee for the companies being controlled.

The shortcomings of the regulatory framework in which the *Agence française anticorruption – AFA* (French Anti-Corruption Agency – AFA) operates undermine the rights of defence of controlled entities, firstly in terms of disclosure of documents during controls (A), but also at the various stages of the procedure (B).

A. The disclosure of documents is not sufficiently regulated

Unlimited right of communication. Article 4 of the French so-called "Sapin 2" law allows AFA agents to "obtain from the representatives of the controlled entity any professional document, whatever its medium, or any useful information."(14) In addition to the absence of any procedural framework setting out the procedures for handing over, retaining or returning documents, the generality of the terms used by the legislator is a source of uncertainty. Indeed, there are no restrictions on the type of documents that AFA agents may request.

(12) AFA, *Charte des droits et devoirs des parties prenantes aux controles prévus aux 3° de l'article 3 et au III de l'article 17 de la loi n°2016-1691 du 9 décembre 2016* (Charter of the rights and duties of the parties involved in the controls provided for in 3° of Article 3 and III of Article 17 of Law No. 2016-1691 of 9 December 2016), April 2019.

(13) *Ibid.*, IV, 3, i and ii.

(14) Free translation of: *"faire communiquer par les représentants de l'entité contrôlée tout document professionnel, quel qu'en soit le support, ou toute information utile."*

On the one hand, there is no time limit, as the AFA considers itself entitled to request the disclosure of documents or information prior to the date of entry into force of the "Sapin 2" law. (15)

On the other hand, there is no limit as to the purpose for which the information may be communicated, as the legislator has left the notion of "useful" information – which it has not defined – to the discretionary judgement of AFA's agents, without it being possible for controlled entities to oppose the communication of a document since they could be accused of obstruction.

It would seem to be appropriate for the legislator to intervene, to specify the limits of this duty of communication. Such a framework already exists in Stock Market Law and Competition Law. For example, the Controller of requests for connection data verifies the nature of the requests made by the *Autorité des marchés financiers – AMF* (French Financial Markets Authority) to telephone operators to obtain detailed invoices for telephone calls. (16)

An overly restrictive concept of professional secrecy. While the *Code monétaire et financier* (French Monetary and Financial Code) expressly states that lawyers' professional secrecy is enforceable against the AMF, (17) this protection is limited. For example, case law in stock market matters considers that exchanges between two correspondents in which a lawyer is merely a copy are not covered by professional secrecy. (18) Furthermore, the enforcement authorities consider that exchanges taking place directly between a company and its lawyer are no longer covered by professional secrecy if these correspondences are voluntarily handed over. In this respect, the authorities consider that unreservedly handing over the entire content of an e-mail inbox constitutes a waiver of the right to later invoke professional secrecy in respect of certain correspondence. (19)

This concept of the waiver of professional secrecy is extremely jeopardising as it could be interpreted as a general waiver of the protection of privilege by foreign authorities. This interpretation is open to criticism, as it seriously undermines the rights of the entities being controlled.

(15) AFA, 4 July 2019, *Sonepar*, decision No. 19-01, para. 9.

(16) Decision of the *Conseil constitutionnel* (French Constitutional Council), 21 July 2017, No. 2017-646/647 QPC, leading to the adoption of Article L. 621-10-2 of the *Code monétaire et financier* (French Monetary and Financial Code).

(17) Article L. 621-9-3, French Monetary and Financial Code.

(18) Decision of the *cour d'appel de Paris* (Paris Court of Appeal), 8 November 2017, No. 14/13384.

(19) Decision of the *Cour de cassation* (French Court of cassation), *chambre commerciale* (Commercial Chamber), 29 January 2013, No. 11-27.333.

In its Charter, the AFA makes a mockery of professional secrecy by asserting, without any nuance, that "audited entities may not invoke professional secrecy to refuse to fulfil any of these obligations," (20) in particular that of communicating any professional document requested, including those which would be covered by professional secrecy. (21) This assertion is seriously prejudicial to the rights of the defence and *contra legem*. It should not be enforced.

The offence of obstruction – a forced cooperation? Enforcement authorities assume that controlled entities must cooperate, in such a way that any obstruction on their part should be punished. Under the terms of the French so-called "Sapin 2" law, obstructing an investigation constitutes the offence of obstruction, so that failure to communicate elements or information requested by AFA investigators can be punished by a fine of 30,000 euros. (22)

For its part, the AMF has a considerable arsenal at its disposal to put pressure on any company that proves recalcitrant during a control. While there is also an offence of obstructing the AMF's missions, (23) the most effective lever remains the administrative breach of obstruction, (24) which allows heavy sanctions to be imposed directly by the AMF's Enforcement Committee. (25)

This arsenal available to the enforcement authorities is a veritable sword of Damocles for companies, which cannot resist requests to disclose numerous documents or information without running the risk of being accused of obstruction, thereby infringing two essential rights of

(20) Free translation of: "*les entités contrôlées ne peuvent se prévaloir du secret professionnel pour refuser d'accomplir l'une de ces obligations.*"

(21) AFA, Charter, IV. 4 "Duties of controlled entities."

(22) "Sapin 2" law No. 2016-1691, 9 December 2016, Art. 4.

(23) Article L. 642-3 French Monetary and Financial Code.

(24) Article L. 621-15, II, f), French Monetary and Financial Code: "*Toute personne qui, dans le cadre d'une enquête ou d'un contrôle effectués en application du I de l'article L. 621-9, sur demande des enquêteurs ou des contrôleurs et sous réserve de la préservation d'un secret légalement protégé et opposable à l'Autorité des marchés financiers, refuse de donner accès à un document, quel qu'en soit le support, et d'en fournir une copie, refuse de communiquer des informations ou de répondre à une convocation, ou refuse de donner accès à des locaux professionnels*" (free translation: "Any person who, as part of an investigation or control carried out pursuant to I of Article L. 621-9, at the request of investigators or controllers and subject to the preservation of a legally protected secret enforceable against the *Autorité des marchés financiers*, refuses to provide access to a document, regardless of the medium, and to provide a copy, refuses to communicate information or to respond to a summons, or refuses to provide access to business premises.")

(25) Doubts remain, however, as to the conformity of this breach with the Constitution, following the *Conseil constitutionnel* (French Constitutional Council)' s censure of a similar provision in Competition Law for failure to respect the principle of necessity and proportionality of penalties (Cons. const., 26 March 2021, No. 2021-892 QPC, para. 24).

defence: the right to remain silent and the right not to contribute to one's own incrimination.

The fact that these rules conflict with the right not to incriminate oneself has led the Court of Justice of the European Union to rule that the obligation to cooperate with the authorities should not result in a natural person being punished for refusing to provide answers that could reveal his criminal liability or liability for an offence punishable by administrative penalties of a criminal nature. (26)

B. The absence of a procedural framework during the investigation and before the AFA Sanctions Committee

Procedural shortcomings at the investigation stage. Hearings before the AMF are subject to meticulous procedural supervision. Persons questioned by investigators are given a fifteen-days' notice, and any statements they make before this deadline cannot be held against them unless they have expressly waived this period. (27) In addition, investigators are obliged to inform the interviewee that he or she has the right to remain silent and to be assisted by counsel. (28) They must also draw up minutes of the interview they have conducted. (29) All these guarantees are essential to ensure the effectiveness of the right to remain silent, as well as the respect of the adversarial principle.

On the contrary, there are no rules governing the conduct of interviews by the AFA's agents. Firstly, there is no time limit for convening the interview. In addition, the AFA's agents are not obliged to notify the interviewee of his or her right to remain silent or to be assisted by a lawyer when the interviewee is not the representative of the controlled entity. (30) Finally, the AFA's agents are not obliged to draw up minutes of hearings. The AFA's Sanctions Committee considers that the absence of minutes does not vitiate the procedure. (31) Respect for the adversarial principle, however, requires that the entity being controlled be given the opportunity to challenge the conclusions drawn from the interviews conducted during the control.

(26) CJEU, 2 February 2021, *DB v. Commissione Nazionale per le Società e la Borsa*, case C-481/19, para. 45.
(27) Article R. 621-34, French Monetary and Financial Code.
(28) *Ibid.*
(29) *Ibid.*
(30) AFA, Charter, II, 1, iii.
(31) AFA, 4 July 2019, *Sonepar*, decision No. 19-01, para. 12.

Procedural shortcomings in the sanction procedure. Article 6, paragraph 1, of the European Convention for the Protection of Human Rights and Fundamental Freedoms provides that the notification of grievances must be clear and precise. The AFA's Sanctions Committee reiterates the importance of this principle, insisting on "the obligation of precision in the statement of grievances," requiring that "the grievances referred to the Sanctions Committee [be] stated clearly enough to leave no doubt as to their content and scope," and that "failing this, the nullity of the procedure should be raised, where appropriate, *ex officio.*" (32) This is an essential requirement in sanction proceedings, as it enables the entity being audited to be fully aware of the allegations against it, and thus to mount a targeted and effective defence.

Although the AFA's Sanctions Committee seems to intent to guarantee the respect of the rights of the defence, it ultimately rejects the application of this rule. Indeed, it ruled that a "formulation of the statement of grievances that leaves room for a few imprecisions" is not grounds for invalidating the procedure, on the grounds that the company was "able to grasp the content and scope of the grievances and, consequently, to develop a useful and effective defence." (33)

This solution, in complete contradiction with the principles laid down by the Sanctions Committee itself, is highly questionable and contrary to the rights of the defence.

*

* *

It is regrettable that the rights of defence are not sufficiently taken into account by the enforcement authorities when it comes to compliance. As recommended by the *Conseil d'État* (French Council of State), procedural rules should be enacted to guarantee the rights of defence of controlled entities.

(32) AFA, 7 February 2020, *Imerys*, decision No. 19-02, para. 11, free translations of: *"l'obligation de précision dans l'énoncé des griefs"*, *"les griefs dont la Commission des sanctions est saisie [soient] énoncés de façon suffisamment claire pour ne laisser aucun doute sur leur contenu et leur portée"* and *"défaut il conviendrait de soulever, le cas échéant, d'office, la nullité de la procédure."*

(33) AFA, 7 February 2020, *Imerys*, decision No. 19-02, para. 12, free translations of: *"formulation de l'exposé des griefs laissant place à quelques imprécisions"* and *"pu appréhender le contenu et la portée des griefs et, par voie de conséquence, développer utilement une défense efficace."*

Adjusting General Procedural Law to Compliance Law by the Nature of Things*

Marie-Anne Frison-Roche

Agrégée des Facultés de droit

Professor of Regulatory Law and Compliance Law

Director of the *Journal of Regulation & Compliance (JoRC)*

Director of the *European School of Regulation and Compliance Law*

1. Thanks to Motulsky. Even if, as with any stroke of genius, one can find premises to the thing and precursors to the person, General Procedural Law (1) was an invention in Civil Law legal systems in a large part due to the Law professor Motulsky, of which we have an express trace through the notes taken from the course he gave about it at the French University of Nanterre where he was a professor, (2) laying down principles that can be found throughout his seminal work. (3)

2. General Procedural Law, beyond legal rules and Comparative Law. General Procedural Law goes far beyond the benefits of comparing different types of procedure. In his thesis, Motulsky asserted that Law must prevail, since it is on the basis of and in application of the laws that the

---

* This article is based on a bilingual working paper, along with additional developments, numerous technical references and hypertext links. It is accessible at the following address: https://mafr.fr/en/article/ajuster-par-la-nature-des-choses-le-droit-processu/.

(1) The expression "General Procedural Law" is used here to translate the concept forged by Professor Motulsky: *"droit processuel."* This notion designates the procedural principles inherent to every and any procedure, common to civil, criminal and administrative justice.

(2) H. Motulsky, *Droit processuel*, "Les cours du droit" Serie, Paris, Montchrestien, 1973.

(3) For example, H. Motulsky, "Le droit d'action et l'action en justice", *in* Archives de Philosophie du droit (APD), *Le droit subjectif en question*, Paris, Sirey, 1964, pp. 215-230; or "Le droit naturel dans la pratique jurisprudentielle : le respect des droits de la défense en procédure civile", in *Mélanges Roubier*, t. 2, Paris, Dalloz/Sirey, 1961, pp. 175 *et seq*.

judge gives concrete form to the prerogatives of individuals, by applying it to the particular cases submitted to him or her.(4) He also asserted that there is "Natural Law" in General Procedural Law, in particular in the legal mechanism of the action that allows a claim to be submitted to the judge, which is a subjective right, in the rights of defence that allow the person (even, or even especially, if he or she is guilty) to protect himself or herself against the forthcoming judgment,(5) and in the right to contradict the adversary.

3. The nature of things in General Procedural Law. The fact that in a State governed by the Rule of Law these elements are found in the various procedures put in place is an indication of their importance, but it is the nature of things that gives rise to these principles, without which there would be no more than a "process"(6) and not these pillars of General Procedural Law as the supreme courts maintain them. It is true that systems based on regulations and processes can be made to work effectively without concern for the Rule of Law, but Motulsky's point is that as soon as there is a Rule of Law concern, there can be no elimination of this "Natural Procedural Law," whatever the "procedure" or even the "process": it is always present, even in the silence of the texts.

4. The Judge reveals the general procedural substance of the law. The judge must reveal the invisible ink by which these general procedural principles are imposed. This does not mean adding to the legal rules, since Law necessarily tacitly contains the general procedural principles, unless there is an express and justified exception. Indeed, exceptions to the principles of General Procedural Law may exist, as all principles are subject to exceptions, but this can only be done explicitly. Thus, while General Procedural Law is broad, existing in the silence, not bearing an unjustified exception, such an exception can only be express and calls for a limited interpretation. All this is a given and can be found in the case law of the supreme, constitutional and ordinary courts, because it follows from the

(4) H. Motulsky, *Principes d'une réalisation méthodique du droit privé. La théorie des éléments générateurs des droits subjectifs*, preface by P. Roubier, Paris, Sirey, 1948, republished with a foreword by M.-A. Frison-Roche, coll. "Bibliothèque Dalloz", Paris, Dalloz, 1992, the foreword of M.-A. Frison-Roche, which summarises the substance of the book, is available in English at the following address: https://mafr.fr/en/article/avant-propos-a-la-reimpression-de-louvrage-dhenri-/.

(5) H. Motulsky, "Le droit naturel dans la pratique jurisprudentielle: le respect des droits de la défense en procédure civile", *op. cit.*

(6) See, for example, the "special procedure" established by Stalin, expressly ensuring that all principles of General Procedural Law were disregarded: Decision of the Political Bureau of the Soviet Communist Party, 5 March 1940.

very Nature of Things as long as we live in a Democratic Society and a State governed by the Rule of Law. (7)

5. Law tacitly derived from the concrete nature of things. General Procedural Law is therefore based on the nature of things. But it is a concrete conception of this nature that is needed, as Aristotle sets out. (8) An overly abstract conception, particularly as propagated in the texts of the eighteenth century, is less conducive to Compliance spirit. Compliance Law organises things in a new way which must be articulated with this Nature of Things expressed by the very classical Law. This is why the simple and iron principles of General Procedural Law find their way into places, notably companies, where they are not expected at first sight, in particular because there is no judge, the person around whom procedures are usually organised.

6. However, thanks to this nature of things, we can better define the link between General Procedural Law and Compliance Law in the company (I) and imagine the way in which the judge can take greater account of the particular dimension of the cases submitted to him or her when they involve Compliance Law (II).

I. THE NATURAL LINK BETWEEN GENERAL PROCEDURAL LAW AND COMPLIANCE LAW IN THE COMPANY

7. General Procedural Law is "naturally present" in the company when a person is at risk of being wronged by a decision. The principles of General Procedural Law, including the right to remain silent and, more broadly, the rights of the defence, and then the right to have the decision to which one has been subjected reviewed by a judge, are particularly important in companies. Case law has long recognised this, particularly in relation to the dismissal of company directors. The French case law has established and reiterated that a company director must be given the opportunity to put forward his or her arguments before suffering the

(7) For the body of positive Law in this area, see e.g. G. Lautenbach, *The Concept of the Rule of Law and the European Court of Human Rights*, Oxford, OUP, 2013; S. Guinchard, C. Chainais, C. Delicostopoulos, I. Delicostopoulos, M. Douchy-Oudot, F. Ferrand, X. Lagarde, V. Magnier, H. Ruiz-Fabri and L. Si, *Droit processuel. Droit commun et droit comparé du procès équitable*, 12th ed., Paris, Dalloz, 2023.

(8) Aristotle, *Nicomachean Ethics*, translated by T. Irwin, Hackett Publishing Company, 3rd ed., 2019. In this way, see generally M. Villey, *La formation de la pensée juridique moderne*, "Quadrige Manuels" Serie, Paris, PUF, 2013.

consequences of the Board's power to dismiss him or her, even though this power is *ad nutum.* (9)

It is remarkable that the judge ruled in this way because it is in the nature of things that in the event of such sanctions being applied, even if there is no intrinsic fault in the use of the Board's discretionary power to dismiss the company officer, the person concerned must have been given the opportunity to defend himself or herself. In this way, even those who are entirely at fault must be heard, and those who have full discretion to strike must listen to: this is the hallmark of the Rule of Law.

8. General Procedural Law is "naturally present" when, by order of Compliance Law, a company creates litigious situations within itself. Even if the regulations say nothing about it, it is therefore also up to the courts, particularly the Supreme Courts, to recognise this Nature of Things on which General Procedural Law is built: when compliance mechanisms oblige companies to strike, General Procedural Law must oblige, even in the silence of the texts, to arm those who may be struck, or even to stand up against systems which would too easily rule out these defences which are considered to be contrary to effectiveness. Thus, when a company is established by Compliance Law as being in a position to investigate itself, or a person for whom it is accountable – whether an employee, internal or external, or even a third party – General Procedural Law must apply to them. What applies in Corporate Law (10) to the benefit of corporate officers for a discretionary decision adopted to their detriment must apply *a fortiori* to any decision to sanction or settle a dispute organised by the company.

9. Maps of legal qualifications reshuffled by General Procedural Law in the implementation of compliance tools in the light of risk situations. General Procedural Law thus reshuffles the deck in terms of legal qualifications. It is all the easier for the judge to do this because it is his or her duty to give the situations submitted to him or her the right legal qualifications that they require. Thus, when a company takes action against one of its employees, including in the context of its disciplinary

(9) Decision of the *Cour de cassation* (French Court of cassation), *Chambre commerciale* (Commercial Chamber), 29 March 2011, No. 10-17.667; *Cour d'appel de Paris* (Paris Court of Appeal), 5 September 2016, case No. 15/07864. However, it is sufficient for the procedure to have enabled the interested party *"d'exprimer ses points de désaccord"* ("to express his points of disagreement") (Court of cassation, Commercial Chamber, 11 July 2012, No. 11-19.563, unpublished).

(10) Corporate Law itself has been profoundly modified by Compliance Law in that it mixes the latter with "governance." See A.-V. Le Fur, "Interest and 'raison d'être' of the Company: How Does It Fit Together with the Compliance Monumental Goals?", *in* M.-A. Frison-Roche (ed.), *Compliance Monumental Goals*, "Compliance & Regulation" Serie, Brussels, Journal of Regulation & Compliance (JoRC)/Bruylant, 2023, pp. 69-82.

powers, to detect, reveal or correct a breach, even if the procedure is not yet that of a sanction, because the internal investigation is potentially what leads to it, the procedural principles are tacitly present. First and foremost, therefore, the judge must give facts their proper name,(11) for example by saying that the *company* is a *court*, the *compliance officer* is an *investigator*, the company is a place of an interrogation, etc., as soon as it is *in fine* a sanction that looms for the person who, whether inside or outside the company, is a party to the situation.

10. General Procedural Law must also take into account the nature of Compliance Law, Law of *Ex Ante* Information. However, General Procedural Law must also take into account the "nature of things" constituted by Compliance Law, which consists of the *ex ante* creation of Information to detect and prevent situations and behaviours that are systemically relevant with regard to the Monumental Goals that define this branch of Law.(12) However, in order to prevent and detect systemically harmful situations and behaviours, such as corruption, the company or the supervisory administrative authority must gather and process Information *ex ante*. It would be denying the very existence of Compliance Law to block this collection of Information. *General Procedural Law cannot negate this and, in the nature of things, it must respect this principle of ex ante information gathering.*

11. The apparent opposition between General Procedural Law and Compliance Law. This seems to lead to an *a priori*, since General Procedural Law by its very nature leads to Information not being provided, whereas Compliance Law by its very nature leads to Information being provided. This opposing views also fuels the criticism often levelled at Compliance Law, notably by lawyers, as a kind of regulatory efficiency *process*, a concept that is particularly popular with totalitarian political regimes that have no concern for human rights, while, on the other hand, the authorities suspect companies of draping themselves in processual rhetoric in order to hide their misdeeds…

Both only serves to increase mistrust between States and companies, even though Compliance Law should be based on an alliance between the two. But this vision is inaccurate because it ignores the natural link between General Procedural Law and Compliance Law.

(11) M.-A. Frison-Roche, "The 'Judge-Judged'. Articulating Words and Things in the face of Conflicts of Interest", *this book*.

(12) This brings us back to the very definition of Compliance Law, another issue which is the subject of the book *Compliance Monumental Goals*, *op. cit.*

12. The natural link between General Procedural Law and Compliance Law in the company: when the transmission of information leads to a possible decision causing grievance. By order of the Law or out of a desire to serve a collective interest, the company will collect information from various people within it, just as it will itself provide Information to the body that will make good use of it to achieve a Monumental Goal, for example by transmitting information to the supervisory authority, the public prosecutor, an agency or a judge. This gives rise to an obligation to cooperate on the part of the person in possession of the information towards the person who will make good use of it, whether that person is an internal or external employee or a third party in relation to the company, (13) or whether it is the company itself in relation to one of the aforementioned external bodies.

But when the transmission of this information potentially leads to a decision that is prejudicial, in particular a sanction, then General Procedural Law, with the legitimate inefficiency inherent in the rights of the defence (distinct in this respect from the adversarial principle), of which the right to remain silent is an example, takes its place once again.

13. The distribution of principle between General Procedural Law and Compliance Law because of the risk incurred by the person involved in the situation within the company. Therefore, there is not one principle and one exception, but two principles. Firstly, the principle of Information, on which Compliance Law is based (the nature of which must be respected) and secondly the principle of Non-Information, on which General Procedural Law is based, when it takes the form of the rights of the defence (the nature of which must be respected).

14. It is not necessary to apply these two natures on a case-by-case basis with half-full glasses: they must both remain full and complete, but the classic Law must be applied in the following way. If there is no risk for the individual or the legal entity to be the subject of a decision adversely affecting them, they do not have to benefit from the ineffectiveness offered by General Procedural Law and must cooperate in the collection of information on which Compliance Law is based. But if the person, whether a natural person or a legal entity, is at risk of being harmed by a decision,

(13) On the major consequences of this for information, particularly because we are in an information economy and competition for information, see M.-A. Frison-Roche, "Assessment of Whistleblowing and Vigilance Obligation with regard to International Competitiveness", *in* M.-A. Frison-Roche (ed.), *Compliance Monumental Goals*, *op. cit.*, pp. 401-429.

then he or she must be able to benefit from the rights of the defence, in the full sense of the term, in particular the right to remain silent. This is exactly how the Court of Justice of the European Union reasoned in its landmark judgment of 2 February 2021, *DB v. Consob.* (14)

15. What is at stake: object and burden of proof when the two branches of Law do not converge. Neither of these two branches of Law is the exception to the other, and neither must give way its place to the other. When the two converge, for example when General Procedural Law itself produces Information, in particular through adversarial debate, there is no difficulty. A difficulty arises when General Procedural Law involves a mechanism for withholding Information (the right to remain silent), what in Compliance Law is known as a "disinformation" mechanism in that it constitutes a fact which must be fought.

The object of proof is therefore the demonstration of a situation in which the person in question is likely to be the subject of a decision adversely affecting him or her at a later date. Who must prove the existence of such a situation?

16. The issue: the object of proof and the burden of proving the existence of the potentiality of a decision causing grievance. The object of proof is clear: it is the existence of a possible decision in the future, even outside the company, even well after the investigation conducted by the company, then enabling the person facing this prospect to hinder the collection of information. What is less clear is who bears the burden of proving that the decision that could be taken would be prejudicial to the individual, thereby justifying that he or she should remain silent or lie from the investigation stage onwards.

Indeed, because of the presumption of innocence, it could be considered that it would be up to the person conducting the investigation, who must be qualified as a Prosecutor, or a Judge, (15) to demonstrate in all circumstances that the situation that is constituted, for example an interview, an interrogation, a request for Information, a questionnaire, etc., does not potentially lead to a decision causing grievance, in particular a sanction or a decision that makes him or her liable. Doing so, however, would transform the object of proof into a negative object (the non-potentiality of a

(14) CJEU, GC, 2 February 2021, *DB v. Consob*, case C-481/19.

(15) M.-A. Frison-Roche, "The 'Judge-Judged'. Articulating Words and Things in the face of Conflicts of Interest", *this book*.

decision giving rise to a grievance), which is not consistent with the general principles of the evidentiary system. (16)

However, in the same way, it would be excessive to require, in the *ex ante* environment in which Compliance Law is evolving, that the person questioned or the company itself immediately demonstrate that the *process* that the company is organising, that it is imposing on itself, or that it is being subjected to from the outside in the case of investigations organised by a supervisory authority, or that it is imposing on internal or external employees, already potentially contains a sanction. Because it is very difficult to prove the future, other than by adding to the dossier of one's own guilt.

17. The solution: dissociate the burden of plausibility – on the person alleging to be a "potential" defendant – and the burden of proof – on the "potential" attacker. Going back to the very structure of a trial and the division between the judge and the parties, as described by Motulsky, (17) the burden of proof rests on the person who is procedurally the plaintiff in the proceedings only because he or she is temporally the first to formulate an allegation, asserting the existence of facts to which he or she associates a claim: it is therefore the formulation of an allegation that triggers a burden of proof weighing on the person who has made the allegation.

Thus, the author of the allegation, according to which, in the information gathering process, there is potentially a decision causing grievance, is not the authority that is prosecuting or punishing (the company or the administrative authority), but it is the natural or legal person involved in the legal situation constituted by the search for information and the obligation placed on that person to respond. This person therefore "alleges" a fact: that in the situation, there is a possible decision adversely affecting him or her, in particular a subsequent incurrence of liability, damage to his or her reputation, a penalty, etc. Since he or she is alleging this, the administrative authority or the company has to take into account this fact. Since he or she is alleging this, since he or she has constructed this future fact, which is a potentiality (18), he or she must undergo the corresponding evidentiary burden.

(16) See *supra*.

(17) H. Motulsky, "Le rôle respectif du juge et des parties dans l'appréciation des faits", 1959, *in Écrits – Études et notes de procédure civile*, preface by G. Cornu and J. Foyer, Paris, Dalloz, 1973, pp. 38-59.

(18) On the notion of "potentiality" and "virtuality," by which Law can deal with a future event in the present, see generally M.-A. Frison-Roche, "L'immatériel à travers la virtualité", *in* Archives de Philosophie du Droit (APD), *Le droit et l'immatériel*, t. 43, Paris, Sirey, 1999, pp. 139-148.

But this cannot be a full and complete "burden of proof" because it would mean obliging the person to show either that he or she is guilty – since he or she would have to show the elements of guilt that are actually present in the situation, which is excluded by the right not to incriminate himself or herself – or that he or she would have to show his or her innocence in order to avoid the prospect of having to answer later for the acts in which he or she is involved, which runs directly counter to the aforementioned presumption of innocence.

All that is required, therefore, is a "burden of plausibility": the person involved in the evidentiary procedure initiated by the company or administrative authority must prepare a credible presentation showing that by providing information, whatever it may be, particularly in terms of the subject matter to which it relates, the virtuality of a decision giving rise to a grievance emerges. (19) It is only necessary to show this in a plausible way, not in a causal way.

18. The succession in time of the burden of plausibility, on the potential defendant, and the burden of proof, on the potential attacker. Once this burden of plausibility has been met, the burden is not only reversed, shifting to the shoulders of the other party, but changes in nature. Because this other person is not aggressive at the first time – a superior requesting Information, a compliance officer seeking clarification, an investigator from an administrative authority, etc., but later the bodies will be the attacker (the company or the regulatory body sanctioning), what has been "plausibly" demonstrated by the individual or legal entity at the *ex ante* stage of the investigation, a demonstration of plausibility which proves that the person is at risk from the time of the investigation, will mean that the person who puts that person in that position will either have to put up with silence, lies, etc., everything which in General Procedural Law does not converge with Compliance Law, or demonstrate that this demonstrated plausibility does not correspond to the truth.

It is then, in this second stage, because the person "concerned" will have first satisfied his or her burden of plausibility, that the "potential" attacker, who will have to make room for General Procedural Law even when it contradicts Compliance Law and blocks it, will generate for the company or the regulatory body a burden of proof with a different object of proof: to demonstrate that, in reality, the natural or legal person had

(19) On this notion of virtuality, which makes it possible to deal immediately with the risks of the future (in this case the risk of a penalty), M.-A. Frison-Roche, "L'immatériel à travers la virtualité", *op. cit.*

nothing to fear from the situation in which the request for Information was made and this is why this person must therefore fully cooperate. But for obtaining this "full cooperation," the company or the administrative body must prove that the person has nothing to fear, reversing the probability of sanction proven by this person in a first step. (20)

This is the kind of evidentiary system we should be aiming for once our legal system has reached greater maturity through the Jurisdictionalisation of Compliance. (21) This is the ambition of this book: to contribute to the maturity of Compliance Law in the Rule of Law systems, thanks to General Procedural Law, without diminishing Compliance Law principles and nature.

More generally, this implies that the courts themselves treat the cases brought before them in a specific way when they have a compliance dimension.

II. THE TRANSFORMATION OF THE ROLE OF THE JUDGE IN CASES INVOLVING COMPLIANCE LAW

19. The specific nature of cases involving Compliance issues. Because it is a question of making room for the nature of things that the Rule of Law entrusts to the care of the judge and the lawyer, General Procedural Law must also adjust to the extraordinary nature of Compliance Law when cases involving it are brought to the attention of the Judge. Indeed, Compliance Law is extraordinary in that it expresses the political claim to act now to ensure that the future is not catastrophic, in particular by detecting and preventing the occurrence of systemic risks, or even that it is better, in particular by building effective equality or genuine concern for others. (22) The fact that this is an *ex ante* branch of Law does not, in any way, precludes disputes, nor sanctions, as each branch of Law is open to compliance techniques – Contract Law, Tort Law, Public Law, Environmental Law, International Law, Arbitration Law, etc. – even

(20) For more developments on this system, M.-A. Frison-Roche, "The Judge, the Compliance Obligation and the Company. The Compliance Evidence System", *this book*.

(21) *Ibid.*

(22) M.-A. Frison-Roche, "Legal Approach to Compliance Tools: Building by Law the Unity of Compliance Tools from the Definition of Compliance Law by its 'Monumental Goals'", *in* M.-A. Frison-Roche (ed.), *Compliance Tools*, Brussels, Journal of Regulation & Compliance (JoRC)/Bruylant, 2021, pp. 35-46; *id.*, "Compliance Monumental Goals, Beating Heart of Compliance Law", *in* M.-A. Frison-Roche (ed.), *Compliance Monumental Goals*, *op. cit.*, pp. 33-58.

independently of the litigation specific to compliance obligations. How will the lawyer, who, in one capacity or another, represents an interest in such a case, bring that interest to bear? And how will the judge recognise and deal with such a case?

20. The case in which Compliance Law is involved: the notion of "Systemic Cases." Because it is the issue at stake that defines this new branch of Law, a disputed systemic issue, possibly disputed by several parties before the judge, the latter must take this into account in an essential way. Whether the dispute is civil, criminal or administrative, whether it is national, European, international, arbitral, etc., we always find the same general procedural perspective that is specific to these cases submitted to the judge: their systemic dimension. Therefore, I proposed a new procedural category of cases: the "Systemic Cases." (23)

21. The procedural consequences of Systemic Cases in which Compliance Law is involved. Compliance Law is by its very nature systemic, whether it involves detecting and preventing systemic failings or promoting and building virtuous systems. The disputes that may arise from its application are therefore of a "systemic nature." (24)

22. Consider that the Systems themselves are involved in the procedure, and even in the judicial decision. Because Compliance Law always involves a system, in that its Monumental Goal is to protect a system from dangers (Negative Monumental Goal) or to improve a system (Positive Monumental Goal), it must be considered that not only must the judge be mindful of the consequences that his or her particular decision may have on the systems, which is undoubtedly a consideration that must be taken into account in all jurisprudence, but it must be considered that the system itself is more strongly and radically involved in the case.

This is why the concept of "systemic case" has also been proposed, (25) which refers to disputes in which it is the interests of the systems that are directly at stake in the facts and claims brought before the court, either as a collateral effect of a claim made by one of the parties (particularly in

(23) M.-A. Frison-Roche, "The hypothesis of the category of systemic cases brought before the judge", 2021, https://mafr.fr/en/article/lhypothese-des-causes-systemiques/.

(24) On this new concept of "systemic cases," confronted with the judge's office, see the article cited above and the colloquium organised at the *Cour de cassation* (French Court of cassation), 5 July 2022, *L'office du juge et les causes systémiques*, coordinated by M.-A. Frison-Roche, with contributions from Ch. Soulard, First President of the Court of cassation, F. Raynaud, *Conseiller d'État* and F. Ancel, Judge at the Court of cassation.

(25) M.-A. Frison-Roche, "The hypothesis of the category of systemic cases brought before the judge", *op. cit.*

a liability action), or because the system itself (some of which have even sought to give it a legal personality, in particular the market system) may have "claims" and make allegations, in particular through the Regulatory Authorities. In such cases, it is essential for the Judge to make room for the systems involved by allowing, in one way or another, the arguments that directly concern their interests to be specifically expressed in the proceedings themselves, and then taken into account in the judgment. (26)

23. Consider that the future is itself the object of the decision, its knowledge being a central element of the procedure. Similarly, the system actually involved is not so much the past of the system, or even the present of the system, but the future of the system: the system whose disasters must be detected and prevented, the system whose improvements must be built. On the substance of things, this translates into an "*ex ante* responsibility" of the parties to the dispute and a new conception of the very notion of dispute, which takes on the same scope as the systems involved, (27) the judge having to understand and anticipate the future configuration that the systems involved must not have (if they are to avoid being struck by systemic disasters, which corresponds to the category of "Negative Monumental Goals") (28) or the future configuration they should have (if the aim is to build more virtuous systems, which corresponds to the category of "Positive Monumental Goals") (29). Litigation will therefore be longer and more technical.

The future of systems therefore lies in the systemic cases to which Compliance Law, by its very nature, gives rise, because knowledge of the future is a difficult thing and scientists are still the best placed to talk about it, which justifies a special place for them in all compliance litigation, since all systems have a very important technical and scientific dimension, whether in finance, banking, data, climate, digital technology, artificial intelligence, etc.

24. Open the adversarial debate to the various interests concerned by the future of the systems involved in the case. This does not mean that classical General Procedural Law should be erased, that Motulsky

(26) For more technical developments, see M.-A. Frison-Roche, "The hypothesis of the category of systemic cases brought before the judge", *op. cit.*

(27) On the growth of this scope, see N. Cayrol, "Procedural Principles in Compliance Law", *this book*.

(28) M.-A. Frison-Roche, "Compliance Monumental Goals, Beating Heart of Compliance Law", *in* M.-A. Frison-Roche (ed.), *Compliance Monumental Goals*, *op. cit.*, pp. 33-58.

(29) *Ibid.*

should be forgotten (30) and that the judge should only be the scribe of scientific scholars or copy what algorithms have produced: the Roman principle must be followed more than ever: *audi alteram partem*. (31)

Indeed, the systems have their own interests, most often defended by the Regulatory and Supervisory Authorities, interests which do not necessarily coincide with the interests of everyone or which do not coincide with the interests of everyone on the planet, because it is necessary to take into account the fact that Compliance Law has a less strict relationship with the territory than the more traditional branches of Law. (32) So those who speak for themselves must not impose their point of view, but their expert comments must take part in the adversarial debate organised by the judge. In this adversarial debate, both written and oral, the scholarly works used by the parties would benefit from being debated, and the courts should, as some great judges have done it, make a more frequent use of *amici curiae*. (33) The status that American Law gives to the expert is exemplary in this respect and would benefit from being taken up in France (34) in order to reflect the place that the system could have in the organisation by the Judge of the proceedings, which would thus give it its rightful place.

Subsequently, the judgment should, as it does with regard to the various interests involved, respond to the interests of the system implicated by the case, even if the parties to the dispute are narrower, for example two companies fighting, than the dispute itself, which, because it is a question of compliance, gives way to the system. This is also why the Public Prosecutor, even if it is only a matter of so-called "civil" litigation, should have its say, since we are dealing with a branch of Law that involves systems and the future of those systems, which does not fit into any of the three traditional procedures (civil, criminal, administrative).

(30) See *supra*, No. 13.

(31) J. M. Kelly, "Audi Alterant Partem", *The American Journal of Jurisprudence*, 1964, Vol. 9, No. 1, pp. 103-110.

(32) M.-A. Frison-Roche, "The Principle of Active Systemic Proximity: Corollary of the Renewal of the Principle of Sovereignty by Compliance Law", *in* M.-A. Frison-Roche (ed.), *Compliance Monumental Goals*, *op. cit.*, pp. 487-508.

(33) While this study was being drafted, the President of the *Tribunal judiciaire de Paris* (Paris First Instance Civil Court) ordered such an investigation in a case concerning duty of vigilance. See O. Dufour, "Total en Ouganda: le Tribunal de Paris fait appel à des *amici curiae* sur le devoir de vigilance", *Actu-Juridique*, 27 Oct. 2022. See also E. Hannezo, J.-C. Jaïs and C. Cavicchioli, "First decision by French courts on duty of vigilance law: dismissal of claims lodged by six NGOs against TotalEnergies", 1st March 2023, https://sustainablefutures.linklaters.com/post/102i8vw/first-decision-by-french-courts-on-duty-of-vigilance-law-dismissal-of-claims-lod.

(34) In this regard, O. Leclerc, *Le juge et l'expert. Contribution à l'étude des rapports entre le droit et la science*, preface by A. Lyon-Caen, "Bibliothèque de droit privé", Paris, LGDJ, 2005.

25. Designing an *Ex Ante* role for the Judge in line with Compliance Law. The Judge, thus enlightened by a debate in which the parties concerned, those involved in a particular dispute, the stakeholders because they are concerned, including in the future, and the system itself, whose voice is carried more particularly by the administrative authorities but also by the professional organisations, the judge must, as Motulsky wrote, (35) remain the master of the procedural organisation, including to bring these different parties to an agreement, which brings us back to the definition of Compliance Law as an alliance between the strengths of the various parties to achieve the goals set.

In the same way, the Judge must develop an *ex ante* office, consisting of drawing up judgements with the future of systems and the human beings who live in them as their object since, just as Compliance Law relies on the power of crucial operators so that, willingly or unwillingly, they make use of it for the good of systems and people, the considerable power of judges also has the future as its object.

(35) See *supra*, No. 2 *et seq*.

CHAPTER III
ARTICULATION BETWEEN COMPLIANCE LAW AND INTERNATIONAL ARBITRATION

Compliance and arbitration. An attempt at problematisation

Jean-Baptiste Racine

Professor at Paris-Panthéon-Assas University (Paris II)

Compliance exists and is implemented without necessarily being thought of as a discipline in itself. However, efforts must be made to generate knowledge because compliance introduces significant upheavals in the actions of companies by reconfiguring their role, as they are now associated with achieving goals that were originally foreign to them. This is the purpose of the present discussion on the theme of "Compliance and Arbitration." The arbitrator is a judge, in fact, the natural judge of international trade. Therefore, arbitration is naturally destined to intersect with compliance, which transforms the actions of companies in an international context.

However, the links between compliance and arbitration are not obvious. Our goal is not to provide firm and definitive answers, but rather to ask questions. We are only at the beginning of the reflection on this topic, which explains why there is currently few legal literature on the relationship between compliance and arbitration.(1) This does not mean that there are no connections. Simply put, these relationships may not have been fully explored yet or they are still evolving. The purpose is to reveal existing or potential connections between two worlds that have long operated separately: compliance, on the one hand, and arbitration, on the other. The central question is as follows: can the arbitrator be or become a judge of compliance, and if so, how?

---

(1) However, let us note the file directed by Ch. Dargham, J. Feigher, M. de Fontmichel and B. Siino, "Arbitrage et compliance: au cœur de la lutte contre la corruption en matière civile et commerciale", *Revue internationale de la compliance et de l'éthique des affaires* 2019, dossier 192. See also, G. Bertrou and D. Bayandin, "Arbitrage et conformité: dans quelles circonstances les tribunaux arbitraux peuvent et doivent-ils ordonner la divulgation par les parties de leurs bénéficiaires économiques effectifs?", *Rev. arb.*, 2021, 373.

To address the question, it is necessary first to define the terms of the subject. While arbitration no longer poses any problems of definition, compliance, on the other hand, is an open concept. Depending on what is encompassed by this term, a wide variety of measures may or may not fall within its scope. If we attempt a semantic analysis, "compliance," an English term, actually comes from the French word "*complaire,*" (2) which itself derives from the word "*plaire*" (to please). And in French, "*complaire*" has given rise to "*complaisance*"... (3) Nevertheless, it is not only about pleasing, but also about obeying. (4) When imposed by public authority, compliance carries a command within itself. There are several ways to approach this phenomenon. The first approach is procedural: compliance would be synonymous with a procedure or process and would lead to the internalisation within the company of compliance systems (in order to avoid the realisation of a risk). One author considers that the "method consists of a form of internalisation by the company of compliance systems, ultimately enabling it to assist states in achieving their goals." (5) Another author speaks of compliance as the "mandatory institution of an internal preventive procedure." (6) Compliance then affects the company in its structure and organisation, not just in its behaviour. The second conception refers to a teleological approach: compliance would be defined in relation to the goals pursued. From this perspective, the company becomes responsible for achieving goals assigned by states through a form of public/private co-regulation. These goals have been described as "monumental": fighting against corruption and money laundering, ensuring banking and financial stability, combating climate change, protecting human rights, etc. (7) In short, compliance would be the means to focus on the human being, the ultimate recipient of the legal system. (8) This is advocating for a "humanistic" approach to

(2) A. Gaudemet, "Qu'est-ce que la compliance?", *Commentaire*, 2019, 109.

(3) *Petit Robert*, v° "Complaisance".

(4) A. Gaudemet, "Qu'est-ce que la compliance?", *op. cit.*

(5) M.-E. Boursier, "Qu'est-ce que la compliance? Essai de définition", *D.*, 2020, 1419, free translation of: "*la méthode consiste en une forme d'internalisation par l'entreprise et dans l'entreprise de systèmes de conformité lui permettant in fine d'assister les États dans la réalisation de leurs buts.*"

(6) L. d'Avout, *L'entreprise et les conflits internationaux de lois*, Les livres de poche de l'Académie de droit international de La Haye, 2019, p. 757, free translation of: "*l'institution obligatoire d'une procédure interne à visée préventive.*"

(7) M.-A. Frison-Roche, "Du droit de la régulation au droit de la compliance", *in* M.-A. Frison-Roche (ed.), *Régulation, supervision, compliance*, Paris, Dalloz, 2017, p. 1; M.-A. Frison-Roche (ed.), *Compliance Monumental Goals*, "Compliance & Regulation" Serie, Brussels, Journal of Regulation & Compliance (JoRC)/Bruylant, 2023.

(8) M.-A. Frison-Roche, "La compliance", *in* J.-B. Racine (ed.), *Le droit économique au XXIe siècle. Notions et enjeux*, Paris, LGDJ, 2020, p. 97.

compliance. (9) In this view, it is conceivable to defend a positive vision of compliance, even though it is also criticised because it can be aggressive, violent, and unpredictable.

In any case, the definition of compliance can oscillate between what is and what should be, between compliance as it is practised and the ideal compliance, as it could and should be. There are several types of instruments: hard Law or soft Law (compliance can be imposed or simply desired, aligning with the concept of corporate social responsibility). (10) It can be subject to criminal sanctions (thus involving a form of preventive Criminal Law) or solely to civil sanctions (in addition to non-legal sanctions i.e. sanctions issued by the market). Despite the variability of instruments, the mode of intervention is always the same, namely *ex ante* intervention (an expression primarily used in economics, but also applicable to legal matters). This is how compliance mechanisms are primarily recognised (in addition to allowing for going beyond legal norms). (11) This is also where the transformation of Law is most radical, as historically, Law has generally intervened *ex post* (to punish past behaviour and/or repair damage incurred). *Ex ante* intervention lies in risk prevention: it is better to intervene upstream by involving economic actors to prevent the realisation of targeted risks, rather than intervening afterward once harm has been done and damage caused. This is often related to systemic risks. It is no coincidence that compliance originated in the banking and financial sector. It has now spread beyond that, considering risks of significant magnitude, systemic or global in nature. The protection of the environment is the most

(9) M.-A. Frison-Roche, "Subjective Rights, Primary and Natural Tools of Compliance Law", *in* M.-A. Frison-Roche (ed.), *Compliance Tools*, Brussels, Journal of Regulation & Compliance (JoRC)/Bruylant, 2021, p. 321. From the same author, see "Pour une conception humaniste du Droit des affaires et de son enseignement", *in Mélanges A. Couret*, Paris, Lefebvre-Dalloz, 2020, p. 985. See also, K. Magnier-Merran, "La compliance: nouvel ordre moral", in *Mélanges J.-P. et M. Storck*, Paris, Dalloz/Joly, 2021, p. 399.

(10) L. d'Avout, *L'entreprise et les conflits internationaux de lois*, *op. cit.*

(11) C. Kessedjian, "Le droit tendre (*soft law*) est-il apte à encadrer la responsabilité des entreprises pour leurs violations des droits de l'homme?", *in Mélanges E. Decaux*, Paris, Pedone, 2017, p. 1323, in particular p. 1336: "As for due diligence, it is both internal and external. Internally, it requires the company itself to implement verification processes on production processes, hence the proliferation of compliance departments. The very name 'compliance' indicates that it goes beyond mere legal compliance. The use of the English term in French is not just laziness or language quirk. It is meaningful. It allows for controlling entrepreneurial processes beyond the requirements of legal norms." (free translation of: "*Quant à la due diligence, elle est à la fois interne et externe. En interne, elle exige de l'entreprise elle-même la mise en place de processus de vérification sur les process de production, d'où la multiplication des départements compliance. Dont le nom même indique que l'on va au-delà de la seule conformité au droit. L'usage en français du terme anglais n'est pas une simple paresse ou coquetterie de langage. Il est signifiant. Il permet de contrôler les processus entrepreneuriaux au-delà des exigences de la norme juridique.*")

illuminating example in this regard, particularly in relation to the fight against climate change.

But what does arbitration have to do with it? The arbitrator is a judge who resolves disputes, usually of a contractual nature. Therefore, arbitration intervenes *ex post* to resolve a dispute that has arisen. So, what are the connections between the *ex ante* mechanism of compliance and the *ex post* mechanism of arbitration? If we present the reflection in these terms, the two would appear to be unrelated, as they do not operate at the same time, in the same legal timeframe. However, the distinction between *ex ante* and *ex post* needs to be nuanced. There is a *continuum* between the two. (12) *Ex ante* influences *ex post* and vice versa. This has been demonstrated in Regulation Law (13) and also applies to compliance. *Ex ante* can be normative or cognitive. (14) It is normative in that it establishes norms in advance (which will guide behaviour). It is cognitive in that it provides information that allows for proper functioning of *ex post* control.

In other words, it is within the dynamic of the *ex ante/ex post* relationship that the connections between compliance and arbitration can be addressed. Two illustrations can be provided, which do not exhaust the potential of the topic.

Firstly, an arbitrator, who by definition intervenes *ex post*, could use compliance resources, established *ex ante*, to assess the case before him or her. The most evocative example is drawn from anti-corruption. It is known that cases involving corruption often come to arbitration, as arbitration agreements are frequently included in contracts that conceal, enable, or accompany such practices (typically intermediary contracts). This is not new, as evidenced by the Lagergren award rendered in 1963. (15) The problem now also arises in investment arbitration. After a period of state complacency, (16) a vigorous reaction has emerged, thanks in particular to compliance tools. And after a period of timidity among some

(12) M.-A. Frison-Roche, "*Ex ante/ex post*", in *Dictionnaire bilingue du droit de la régulation et de la compliance*, https://mafr.fr/fr/glossaire-du-droit-de-la-regulation-et-de-la-compl/.

(13) M.-A. Frison-Roche, "Le couple *ex ante-ex post*, justification d'un droit propre et spécifique de la régulation", *in* M.-A. Frison-Roche (ed.), *Les engagements dans les systèmes de régulations*, "Droit et Économie de la Régulation" Serie, Paris, Presses de Sciences-Po/Dalloz, vol. 4, 2006, p. 33.

(14) M.-A. Frison-Roche, "Le couple *ex ante-ex post*, justification d'un droit propre et spécifique de la régulation", *op. cit.*, p. 48.

(15) J. G. Wetter, "Issues of Corruption before International Arbitral Tribunals: The Authentic Text and True Meaning of Judge Gunnar Lagergren's 1963 Award in ICC Case n° 1110", *Arb. Int'l.*, 1994, 277.

(16) Indeed, it is worth recalling that in the 1980s, Bruno Oppetit, with his well-known provocative intelligence, could describe corruption as an international trade usage. ("Le paradoxe de la corruption à l'épreuve du droit du commerce international", *JDI*, 1987, 5).

arbitrators, a keen awareness has arisen regarding the need not to give effect, within their jurisdiction, to such practices. (17) The question is how anti-corruption compliance (in France, stemming from the "Sapin 2" law) can potentially assist arbitrators in their task. Can compliance provide cognitive *ex ante* information that helps arbitrators establish corruption facts? Should non-compliance or insufficiently implemented procedures not be taken into account? Conversely, should adherence to compliance rules not be an indicator that arbitrators should consider to possibly infer the absence of corruption? What about anti-corruption clauses? (18) We believe that compliance rules can support arbitrators in their investigations regarding the materiality of corruption facts. Compliance potentially provides indicators (which relates to the practice of "red flags").

Secondly, an arbitrator can intervene *ex post* to exercise control over commitments made *ex ante*. This is the case in Merger and Competition Law. Since the early 1990s, the European Commission has been using arbitration for the *ex post* control of (so-called behavioural) commitments in the context of merger control and, more recently, antitrust control. (19) These commitments generally grant third parties access rights to assets or infrastructure (e.g., intellectual property rights). Arbitration is thus designed as the procedural means to control, in a civil context, compliance with these commitments, resulting in an "externalisation of the control of compliance with commitments." (20) This example illustrates that an arbitrator can be an *ex post* judge overseeing a control process that occurred *ex ante*. The connection with compliance becomes natural. Compliance also leads to the undertaking of commitments, particularly in the field of anti-corruption, followed by a monitoring process. While an arbitrator cannot act as a monitor, as he or she is responsible for resolving disputes

(17) E. Gaillard, "La corruption saisie par les arbitres du commerce international", *Rev. arb.*, 2017, 805. From the same author, see "The Emergence of Transnational Responses to Corruption in International Arbitration", *Arb. Int'l.*, 2019, 1. See also, S. Lemaire, "La preuve de la corruption", *Rev. arb.*, 2020, 185.

(18) J. R. Boles, "The Contract as Anti-Corruption Platform for the Global Corporate Sector", *U. of Pennsylvania J. of Bus. L.*, 2019, 807; N. Bonucci, "La place de la clause 'anticorruption' dans le contrat. Un instrument de compliance en plein essor", *Revue internationale de la compliance et de l'éthique des affaires*, 2020, dossier 235.

(19) L. Idot, "Une innovation surprenante: l'introduction de l'arbitrage dans le contrôle des concentrations", *Rev. arb.*, 2000, 591; G. Decocq, "Arbitrage et droit communautaire du contrôle des concentrations", *Rev. aff. eur.*, 2005, 16; L. Idot, "L'arbitrage et le contrôle des engagements en droit de la concurrence. Analyse du système", *in* P. Mayer (ed.), *Arbitrage et droit de l'Union européenne*, Paris, LexisNexis, 2012, p. 113; F. Emanuele, M. Molfa and P. D'Elia, "EU Merger Remedy Arbitration: Key Features and Strategic Issues in Light of the First Reported Arbitral Award", *RDAI*, 2013, 445.

(20) D. Théophile and G. Aubron, "L'arbitrage dans les engagements en matière de concurrence", *AJ Contrat*, 2014, 212, free translation of: "*externalisation du contrôle du respect des engagements*".

rather than ensuring compliance with measures, why not consider arbitration in this context, especially to resolve future disputes with third parties arising from the implementation of compliance programs? The *Cour de cassation* (French Court of Cassation) ruled on a contract termination justified by the counterparty's refusal to adhere to an anti-corruption policy implemented following a settlement agreement with U.S. authorities. (21) In that case, a French court was seized, but an arbitrator would also be an appropriate judge in this matter. To our knowledge, compliance authorities do not impose or recommend arbitration in this particular scenario, as competition authorities may do for the control of commitments. However, arbitration is certainly a suitable avenue, aligning with the logic of continuity between *ex ante* and *ex post*.

In any case, the arbitrator can serve as the judge of contractualised compliance. As long as there is a compliance clause in a contract (commitment to adhere to an anti-corruption program, commitment to respect human rights, etc.), (22) and the contract includes an arbitration clause, the arbitrator will be the natural and exclusive judge of compliance within the civil domain, i.e. within the scope of a contractual dispute.

(21) Decision of the *Cour de cassation* (French Court of Cassation), *chambre commerciale* (Commercial Chamber), 20 November 2019, No. 18-12.817; *Revue internationale de la compliance et de l'éthique des affaires*, 2020, Comm. 118, obs. C. Ascione Le Dréau and B. Grundler; *Gaz. Pal.*, 10 March 2020, 3, obs. J.-Chr. Roda; *D.*, 2020, 913, note J.-Chr. Roda: "The American legal group Biomet was subject to the rules of the United States Foreign Corrupt Practices Act (FCPA), which prohibits companies from engaging in acts of corruption involving foreign public officials. On 26 March 2012, Biomet entered into a deferred prosecution agreement (DPA) with the U.S. authorities to resolve investigations by the Department of Justice and the Securities and Exchange Commission. The agreement required Biomet to implement substantial cooperation from its employees, distributors, and commercial agents with healthcare professionals for a period of three years, extendable for an additional year. Based on the findings and assessments in this case, the court of appeal, without being obligated to delve into the detailed arguments of the parties, concluded that considering the rules established by the compliance program and the agreement reached, the breach of contractual obligations by the company EIC, which could potentially hold Biomet accountable, was sufficiently serious to justify the termination of the commercial relationship without prior notice. The court legally justified its decision." (free translation of: "*Le groupe de droit américain Biomet était soumis aux États-Unis aux règles, issues du 'United States Foreign Corrupt Practices Act,' interdisant aux sociétés visées de commettre des actes de corruption d'agents publics étrangers et* [...] *il avait, le 26 mars 2012, conclu avec les autorités américaines un accord dit de poursuites différées (APD), afin de mettre un terme aux enquêtes du Department of Justice and Securities and Exchange Commission, à la condition de mettre en place, pendant une durée de trois ans pouvant être prorogée d'un an, une coopération substantielle de ses employés, distributeurs et agents commerciaux avec les professionnels de santé ;* [...] *en l'état de ces constatations et appréciations, la cour d'appel qui, sans être tenue de suivre les parties dans le détail de leur argumentation, a estimé que, compte tenu des règles fixées par le programme de 'compliance' et de l'accord conclu, le manquement de la société EIC à ses obligations contractuelles, en ce qu'il était susceptible d'engager la propre responsabilité de la société Biomet, était suffisamment grave pour justifier la rupture de la relation commerciale sans préavis, a légalement justifié sa décision.*")

(22) See L. Hennebel and G. Lewkowicz, "La contractualisation des droits de l'homme. De la pratique à la théorie du pluralisme politique et juridique", *in* G. Lewkowicz and M. Xifaras (eds), *Repenser le contrat*, Paris, Dalloz, 2009, p. 221; M. Mekki, "Contrat et devoir de vigilance", *RLDA*, 2015, 86.

The difficulty lies in the fact that compliance is inherently cross-cutting. Compliance mechanisms are present in numerous areas such as Banking and Finance Law, Competition Law, Tax Law, Data Protection Law, Environmental Law, etc. While one can easily grasp the concept of a Compliance Law, compliance as a phenomenon is, in any case, pervasive throughout the legal system, "gradually permeating all branches of Law." (23) It is even described as an "expanding galaxy." (24) As a result, the arbitrator frequently encounters matters that involve the methods, tools, and principles of compliance.

Here are three examples:

– Arbitration has been facing challenges related to economic sanctions (such as embargoes) for several years. (25) This impact is not limited to the arbitrator's handling of the dispute but also extends to pre-arbitration operations (such as the payment of an advance on costs, constitution of the arbitral tribunal, etc.). The connection to compliance is evident, as texts that impose economic sanctions often include compliance measures, particularly in the United States (and compliance programs within companies also aim to prevent potential violations of economic sanctions). This type of compliance is often politically driven and can trigger extraterritorial effects. (26) It must necessarily be taken into account in the field of arbitration. (27) The importance of addressing this issue has led prominent institutions like the International Court of Arbitration of the ICC to adopt guidelines on ICC Compliance (May 10, 2016). These guidelines emphasise the implementation of compliance measures, "in order to ensure compliance with obligations imposed on ICC by relevant regulatory authorities." Beyond the role of the arbitration centre, the arbitrator also plays a crucial role in determining how to

(23) J. Mestre, "Compliance", *RLDC*, May 2020, p. 19, in particular p. 20 (free translation of: "*innerve progressivement toutes les branches du droit*").

(24) B. Parance, "Réactivité et adaptation au cœur des exigences de la compliance", *Gaz. Pal.*, 19 juin 2019, 46 (free translation of: "*galaxie en expansion*").

(25) J.-H. Moitry, "L'arbitre international et l'obligation de boycottage imposée par un État", *JDI*, 1991, 349; G. Bastid-Burdeau, "Les embargos multilatéraux et unilatéraux et leur incidence sur l'arbitrage commercial international", *Rev. arb.*, 2003, 754; M. Audit, "L'effet des sanctions économiques internationales sur l'arbitrage international", *in* E. Loquin and S. Manciaux (eds), *L'ordre public et l'arbitrage*, Paris, LexisNexis, 2013, p. 143; P. Mayer, "L'arbitre et les sanctions économiques", *in Mélanges L. Aynès*, Paris, LGDJ, 2019, p. 371.

(26) M. Audit, "L'arbitre international confronté à l'extraterritorialité des lois", *Rev. arb.*, 2015, 1001.

(27) J. El Ahdab and D. Mainguy, *Droit de l'arbitrage. Théorie et pratique*, Paris, LexisNexis, 2021, p. 947.

address economic sanctions in the course of the dispute resolution process. (28)

- Competition Law has intersected with arbitration since the late 1980s. The arbitrability of Competition Law disputes is now well established, and arbitrators regularly handle such cases. (29) At the same time, compliance has also become relevant in the field of Competition Law, albeit more prominently in the United States than in France. (30) The presence, absence, or adequacy of a compliance program aimed at preventing violations of competition rules can assist the arbitrator in assessing anticompetitive behaviour, similar to how such circumstances can aid in establishing acts of corruption. (31)
- The field of Environmental Law is also relevant. This multidisciplinary branch of Law (32) has found applications in arbitration, particularly in investment arbitration, where issues related to the environment are increasingly being addressed. However, even in "traditional" commercial arbitration, which involves contractual disputes, environmental matters are no longer foreign, especially in cases involving the sale of polluted sites. (33) Arbitration is also being recommended as a means to resolve disputes related to climate change, including interstate disputes, investor-state disputes, and private disputes between operators. (34) Therefore, arbitration has a role to play within the realm of climate justice and broader environmental issues. Simultaneously, a specific concept of environmental compliance is emerging, (35) as exemplified by laws like

(28) At the stage of setting aside proceedings, see for example, decision of the *Cour de cassation* (French Court of Cassation), *Première Chambre civile* (First Civil Chamber), 15 January 2020 (*Fincantieri*), No. 18-18.088, *Rev. crit. DIP*, 2020, 526, note L. d'Avout; *Rev. arb.*, 2020, 780, note L. Franc-Menget; Paris, 3 June 2020 (*Sofregaz*), No. RG 19/07261, *RDC*, 2020/4, 60, note M. Laazouzi; *Rev. arb.*, 2020, 1121, note J.-Y. Garaud, G. de Rancourt and C. Martini.

(29) L. Idot, "La place de l'arbitrage dans la résolution des litiges en droit de la concurrence", *D.*, 2007, 2681.

(30) J.-Chr. Roda, "Compliance et antitrust. Le discours de la méthode", *Revue internationale de la compliance et de l'éthique des affaires*, 2020, 109.

(31) See *supra*.

(32) G.-J. Martin, "L'environnement", *in* J.-B. Racine (ed.), *Le droit économique au XXI*e *siècle. Notions et enjeux*, *op. cit.*, p. 319.

(33) O. Boskovic, "L'arbitrage international en matière environnementale", *Energie-Environnement-Infrastructures*, April 2019, dossier 11; P. Thieffry, "L'arbitrage et le droit européen de l'environnement", *Rev. arb.*, 2019, 1069.

(34) ICC Commission Report, *Resolving Climate Change Related Disputes through Arbitration and ADR*, ICC, 2019. See, R. de Paor, "Climate Change and Arbitration: Annex Time before there won't be A Next Time", *J. Int'l. Dis. Settl.*, 2017, 179; P. Thieffry, "L'arbitrage au XXIe siècle face aux enjeux du changement climatique", *Rev. arb.*, 2022, 899.

(35) J.-N. Clément, "La compliance environnementale", *Revue des juristes de Sciences Po*, 2019, 127.

the French "duty of vigilance" law enacted on March 27, 2017. (36) This requires companies to contribute to environmental protection by integrating environmental considerations into their internal and external operations (within their sphere of influence). The introduction of a *convention judiciaire d'intérêt public* (Judicial Public Interest Agreement) for environmental matters through the French law of December 26, 2020, further emphasises the integration of compliance into this field (see Article 41-1-2 of the *Code de procédure pénale* (French Criminal Procedure Code). In short, when an arbitrator is entrusted with resolving a dispute related to Environmental Law, the question of its relationship with compliance arises naturally from this perspective.

Indeed, we can observe a renewal in arbitral practice in light of compliance. On the one hand, compliance is transforming the Law itself. It no longer relies solely on the binary legal/illegal or lawful/unlawful framework (as used, for example, by Luhmann to characterise the legal system). Compliance is reshaping the boundaries of legality, what is permitted and prohibited. (37) Because of its predominantly preventive nature, it leads to the *ex ante* management of identified risks. As noted by an author, "Compliance no longer solely relies on the vertical relationship between the company and the law but also on the establishment of a horizontal environment within the company that tends to reduce the risk of rule violations." (38) While classical Law operates vertically, compliance leads to the "horizontalisation" of obligations. This shift will undoubtedly have an impact on arbitration. For a long time, discussions have taken place regarding the relationship between arbitration and public policy, particularly the arbitrator's obligation to uphold public policy and the methods available to do so (39) (which logically leads the arbitrator to reason in terms of the binary lawful/unlawful, with the challenge in an international

(36) J. Rochfeld, *Justice pour le climat ! Les nouvelles formes de mobilisation citoyenne*, Paris, Odile Jacob, 2019, pp. 133 *et seq.*

(37) L.-M. Augagneur, "La compliance a-t-elle une valeur?", *JCP E*, 2017, 1522.

(38) A. Gaudemet, "Qu'est-ce que la compliance?", *op. cit.*, p. 110 (free translation of: "*La compliance ne table plus seulement sur le face-à-face vertical de l'entreprise et de la loi, mais également sur l'aménagement d'un milieu horizontal au sein même de l'entreprise qui puisse faire diminuer tendanciellement le risque d'infraction aux règles.*")

(39) See I. Fadlallah, "L'ordre public dans les sentences arbitrales", *RCADI*, 1994, V, 377; J.-B. Racine, *L'arbitrage commercial international et l'ordre public*, Paris, LGDJ, 1999; H. Arfazadeh, *Ordre public et arbitrage international à l'épreuve de la mondialisation*, Brussels/Paris/Zurich, Bruylant/LGDJ/Schulthess, 2005; G. A. Bermann and L. A. Mistelis (eds), *Mandatory Rules of Law in International Arbitration*, JurisNet, 2011; P. Mayer, "L'arbitre et l'ordre public", *in Mélanges E. Loquin*, Paris, LexisNexis, 2018, p. 231.

context of identifying the source of unlawfulness). (40) Among the means at the arbitrator's disposal, the concept of "*lois de police*" (mandatory laws) has naturally been invoked. (41) It is not insignificant that the doctrine reflecting on compliance has questioned whether the implemented compliance measures can be qualified as "*lois de police*", particularly in relation to the French law on the duty of vigilance. (42) Compliance, when its measures are qualified as "*lois de police*," can thus lead to a renewal of thinking and practices concerning the relationship between arbitration and "*lois de police.*" Beyond these mandatory laws, it is obvious to us that the objectives of compliance can contribute to a transnational public policy. (43) The goals of compliance align perfectly with what traditionally falls within the purview of such public policy: combating corruption, protecting the environment, respecting human rights, etc. The connection between the two is therefore natural. While the notion of transnational public policy is still debated and sometimes viewed with condescension, compliance provides a foundation for it to strengthen and gain legitimacy.

Under these circumstances, a 2012 ICC arbitral award can be subject to criticism in light of compliance considerations. (44) The dispute involved a consultant contract where the co-contracting party had implemented a code of ethics to combat money laundering and corruption risks. The co-contracting party invoked the content of this code of ethics to avoid payment of commissions that were normally due under the contract. The arbitral tribunal refused to consider the code of ethics on the grounds that there was no contractual reference to it. The arbitrators thus followed a purely contractual perspective on compliance. However, a reference to transnational public policy could have provided a solution regardless of the code of ethics not being explicitly incorporated into the contract. Furthermore, when considering compliance frameworks, particularly in anti-corruption matters, the adoption of codes of conduct is often a legal obligation imposed by

(40) Ph. Kahn and Ch. Kessedjian (eds), *L'illicite dans le commerce international*, Paris, Litec, 1996.

(41) Ch. Seraglini, *Lois de police et justice arbitrale internationale*, Paris, Dalloz, 2001; L. G. Radicati di Brozolo, "Arbitrage commercial international et lois de police", *RCADI*, 2005, t. 315, p. 265.

(42) O. Boskovic, "Brèves remarques sur le devoir de vigilance et le droit international privé", *D.*, 2016, 385; H. Muir Watt, "Devoir de vigilance et droit international privé. Le symbole et le procédé de la loi du 27 mars 2017", *Revue internationale de la compliance et de l'éthique des affaires*, 2017, No. 4, p. 48, in particular pp. 51 *et seq.*; E. Pataut, "Le devoir de vigilance – Aspects de droit international privé", *Dr. soc.*, 2017, 833.

(43) On which see in particular, P. Lalive, "Ordre public transnational (ou réellement international) et arbitrage international", *Rev. arb.*, 1986, 323; L. Chedly, *Arbitrage commercial international et ordre public transnational*, Tunis, 2002; C. Kessedjian, "Transnational Public Policy", in *ICCA Congress Series*, No. 13, Alphen aan der Rijn, Kluwer Law International, 2007, p. 857; P. Lalive, "L'ordre public transnational et l'arbitre international", in *Liber F. Pocar*, Milan, Giuffrè, 2009, p. 599.

(44) ICC award No. ICC-FA-2020-240, *JDI*, 2020, 1485, obs. H. Barbier and A. Fessas.

regulations. (45) In this regard, arbitrators' assessment will necessarily need to evolve in line with the tools used in compliance.

On the other hand, the intersection between compliance and arbitration sheds light on the transformation of the arbitrators' role. For a long time, arbitrators were seen and saw themselves as judges of the contract. A Swiss author once remarked that for arbitrators, the contract was a "sacred cow." (46) However, arbitration has gradually evolved due to two factors. Firstly, it has become, as commonly stated, the common means of resolving disputes in the field of international business (with 80 to 90% of international contracts containing an arbitration clause). It has thus become a "systemic" (and systematic) form of justice, in the sense that arbitration constitutes a sort of system of justice (as a network). (47) Secondly, as arbitration has expanded and the conditions for arbitrability have become more liberal, it has come into contact with an increasing number of public interests (such as in Competition Law). Moreover, the widespread use of investment arbitration, based solely on treaties, since the 1990s has brought arbitration into contact with the public interests represented by states. The combination of the systemic nature of arbitration and the presence of public interests means that arbitrators now have specific responsibilities. They are no longer just judges of contracts (or investments). They have, in a broader sense, become "regulators" in that they often have to reconcile private interests with public interests. (48) As Bruno Oppetit believed, "This task of defending collective interests assigned to the international arbitrator places the arbitrator's approach in an anti-individualistic reaction and a philosophy of the common good, which affirms the permanence of collective interests. It manifests, among other signs, the contemporary development of ethics, which often develops autonomously, on the margins of the Law." (49) It is not certain that

(45) H. Barbier and A. Fessas, obs. in *JDI*, 2020, *op. cit.*

(46) J. Werner, "Application of Competition Laws by Arbitrators", *J. Int'l. Arb.*, 1995, No. 1, p. 21, in particular p. 25.

(47) Regarding institutional arbitration in particular, an author argues that there exists an "*embryon de système de justice transnational*" ("incipient transnational justice system") (A. Mourre, "La Cour internationale d'arbitrage de la CCI, acteur de la régulation du commerce international", *Revue des juristes de Sciences Po*, February 2021, 1, in particular p. 3). See also, J.-B. Racine, "L'arbitrage comme système de justice internationale", in *Entre ciels et terres. Mélanges L. Ravillon*, Paris, Pedone, 2022, p. 311.

(48) L. Dossios et J.-B. Racine, "L'arbitre, juge des parties et/ou régulateur?", *RID éco.*, 2019, 105.

(49) B. Oppetit, *Théorie de l'arbitrage*, Paris, PUF, 1998, p. 127 (free translation of: "*Cette tâche de défense d'intérêts collectifs reconnue à l'arbitre international inscrit alors la démarche de ce dernier dans la réaction anti-individualiste et dans une philosophie du bien commun, qui affirme la permanence des intérêts collectifs ; elle manifeste, entre autres signes, l'essor contemporain de l'éthique qui se développe souvent aujourd'hui par des voies autonomes, en marge du droit.*")

the arbitration community as a whole has fully recognised the particular responsibilities that now rest upon it. It must do so if it wants the system to endure. In fact, the strong criticism directed towards investment arbitration can be seen as a signal. Arbitration is far from uncontroversial and is now in search of legitimacy.

What is the connection with compliance? In fact, compliance encompasses objectives and values that pertain, in a strong sense, to the public interest. It is a new mode of action by the state that delegates to companies the responsibility of safeguarding priority goals. It is therefore a delegation to the private sector of fragments of the general interest. The boundary between the public and private sectors becomes blurred, as does the line between the public interest and private interest. And states remain vigilant. Compliance is no longer a set of voluntary commitments or soft Law. It combines the most stringent and coercive methods, if necessary through Criminal Law. The world of arbitration cannot afford to be indifferent or insensitive to it. This is especially true since the goals pursued by compliance (the three most important being, *a priori*, the fight against corruption, environmental protection, and the preservation of human rights) are subject to strong social expectations that appear as true "*forces créatrices*" ("creative forces"). (50) There is social adherence to these goals, and arbitration can only reinforce its legitimacy by being a conduit, among others, for these objectives (from this perspective, the relationship between compliance and arbitration can be seen from the angle of convergence and not just confrontation).

Because precisely, compliance authorities are looking for channels of effectiveness. They could potentially find one through arbitration, provided that arbitrators have a systemic vision of their intervention. Each arbitrator is more than a transient judge; he or she is a link in a global chain. Compliance can thus lead, or even compel, the practice of arbitration to develop a systemic view of its intervention and assume a regulatory role, understood as a reconciliation between private and public interests (going beyond the sole framework of contracts or investments). This paves the way for a "compliant" arbitration.

However, this trend is subject to a limit and a nuance. The limit lies in the traditionally confidential nature of arbitration. Even though the status of confidentiality in international arbitration is uncertain, it is an

(50) I. Parachkévova-Racine, "La responsabilité sociale de l'entreprise", *in* D. Fenouillet (ed.), *Flexibles notions. La responsabilité civile*, Paris, Éditions Panthéon-Assas, 2020, p. 299.

advantage that is generally sought after by users. Compliance disputes, at least in the contractual realm, can thus escape public knowledge. An author has considered that "Decisions involving Contract Law and compliance are not so frequent, if only due to the play of arbitration clauses that make this dispute somewhat invisible." (51) How, then, can a confidential justice system serve as a channel for the effectiveness of compliance and a means to achieve its objectives? The answer is most likely the trend towards transparency in the field of arbitration, in general, and particularly in investment arbitration. Even though transparency may be criticised, it helps legitimise arbitration, especially when the public interest is at stake. The nuance lies in the fact that arbitration is fundamentally a private form of justice based on the parties' agreement. Arbitrators are not naturally mandated to take on the responsibility of safeguarding the public interest, unlike state judges for whom this task falls within their mission. (52) Under these conditions, one should not expect too much from arbitration, as it is not a panacea for all ills. However, such a view of arbitration should not lead us to deny reality. Arbitration has gradually become more "public" (as evidenced, in particular, by the movement towards transparency, which, in a literal sense, makes arbitration "public"). New duties and responsibilities rest on the arbitration community, which leads to arbitration becoming a mixed system, part private and part public. (53)

There is a strong convergence with the intervention methods of compliance in this regard, which leads to the privatisation of concerns for the general interest, delegating their management to the private sector. The evolution of arbitration towards taking into account public interests aligns with a fundamental movement that aims to reshape the role of the state and hold the private sector accountable. (54) Arbitration is thus a form of the private sector that is affected and should feel concerned (especially as a private sector of justice). It is possible to advance the idea

(51) J.-Chr. Roda, note under Com., 20 November 2019, *Gaz. Pal.*, 10 March 2020, p. 3 (free translation of: "*Les décisions mêlant droit des contrats d'affaires et compliance ne sont pas si fréquentes, ne serait-ce qu'en raison du jeu des clauses d'arbitrage qui invisibilisent un peu ce contentieux.*")

(52) An author (P. Thieffry, "L'arbitrage et le droit européen de l'environnement", *op. cit.*, p. 1106) expressed this idea by considering that "As a private judge, the arbitrator derives authority from the autonomy of the will, not from any mandate of the general interest. While she or he must ensure compliance with public policy, she or he is not tasked with replacing administrative authorities to advance the environmental cause" (free translation of: "*Juge privé, l'arbitre tire son autorité de l'autonomie de la volonté, pas d'un quelconque mandat d'intérêt général. S'il doit veiller au respect de l'ordre public directeur, il n'a pas pour mission de se substituer aux autorités administratives pour faire progresser la cause environnementale.*")

(53) B. Oppetit, *Théorie de l'arbitrage*, *op. cit.*

(54) I. Parachkévova-Racine, "L'entreprise", *in* J.-B. Racine (ed.), *Le droit économique au XXI*[e] *siècle. Notions et enjeux*, *op. cit.*, p. 275, in particular, pp. 295 *et seq.*

of "social responsibility" of arbitration, which refers to the assumption of public interest by the arbitration community (including all actors, especially the arbitrators themselves and arbitration centres), at least in certain targeted sectors. The main arbitration centres now pay attention to this aspect. In addition to the International Court of Arbitration of the ICC's 2016 guidelines on ICC compliance, it is worth noting that the London Court of International Arbitration (LCIA) added a dedicated article on compliance to its arbitration rules in 2020 (Art. 24A). (55) Moreover, there is now a kind of professionalisation of the arbitrator's role. (56) Arbitrators, who have recurring appointments, are forming an informal profession. The image of an arbitrator is no longer that of a solitary "freelancer" but rather that of an "infantryman" as part of a troop. This professionalisation necessarily leads to a keen awareness of the role, particularly the social role, that arbitrators are now called upon to fulfil.

It is also a matter of reputation for homes of arbitration (Paris, London, New York, Singapore, Hong Kong, Dubai, etc.). A home of arbitration can demonstrate its commitment to compliance rules to enhance its image. Compliance is often presented as a tool for competitiveness for companies. (57) Could we not say the same for homes of arbitration? Taking the example of Paris, declaring adherence to compliance tools and methods could be perceived as an advantage. This largely depends on all the actors involved: the arbitrators, arbitration centres, and also the judge in charge of reviewing the award. The reviewing judge plays a role because she or he will examine the final outcome of the arbitration, namely the award. If the judge is demanding and exercises control in light of international public policy, as is currently the case, especially regarding corruption and

---

(55) "24.9 Any dealings between a party and the LCIA will be subject to any requirements applicable to that party or the LCIA relating to bribery, corruption, terrorist financing, fraud, tax evasion, money laundering and/or economic or trade sanctions ('Prohibited Activity'), and the LCIA will deal with any party on the understanding that it is complying with all such requirements.

24.10 The LCIA may refuse to act on any instruction and/or accept or make any payment if the LCIA determines (in its sole discretion and without the need to state any reasons) that doing so may involve Prohibited Activity, or breach any law, regulation, or other legal duty which applies to it, or that doing so might otherwise expose the LCIA to enforcement action or censure from any regulator or law enforcement agency.

24.11 The parties agree to provide the LCIA with any information and/or documents reasonably requested by the LCIA for the purpose of compliance with laws relating to Prohibited Activity. The LCIA may take any action it considers appropriate to comply with any applicable obligations relating to Prohibited Activity, including disclosure of any information and documents to courts, law enforcement agencies or regulatory authorities."

(56) Y. Derains, "Le professionnalisme des arbitres internationaux", *Rev. arb.*, 2019, 659.

(57) Dossier thématique, "La compliance, facteur de protection et de compétitivité des entreprises françaises", *Revue des juristes de Sciences Po*, 2019.

money laundering, (58) Paris can establish itself as a "clean" and virtuous place for arbitration. Certainly, the reviewing judge will not assess the respect of compliance rules. In a judgment rendered in the Alstom case, the *cour d'appel de Paris* (Paris Court of Appeal) decided that "the review of the exequatur judge does not aim to verify whether contractual provisions – including compliance rules – have been correctly executed, but only to ensure that the recognition and enforcement of the award does not have the effect of enforcing a corrupt contract." (59) The solution is quite logical: the reviewing judge is not the judge of the contract but of the award. Only if the award itself, through the decision rendered, gives effect to a corrupt practice, will it be considered contrary to international public policy. (60) The arbitrator is thus on the front line because she or he is responsible for deciding the merits of the dispute. It is therefore up to the arbitrator to assess, if applicable, the respect or non-respect of compliance rules.

The consideration of compliance rules by arbitrators is also a way of sending a message to the compliance authorities themselves, who can rely on the support of arbitration in implementing compliance objectives (with a particular focus on the fight against corruption). In this regard, cooperation between the arbitrator and public authorities can take place. There has been talk of an "assisting arbitrator" ("*arbitre d'appui*"). (61) This form of judicial cooperation could result in exchanges of information between arbitrators and public authorities (such as judges or compliance authorities, for example the *Agence française anticorruption – AFA* (French Anti-Corruption Agency – AFA)), which may raise difficulties, especially regarding the typically confidential nature of arbitration. It is even possible that arbitrators may be compelled to cooperate by compliance authorities.

(58) J.-B. Racine, "Le contrôle de la conformité de la sentence à l'ordre public international: un état des lieux", *Rev. arb.*, 2022, 179.

(59) Decision of the *cour d'appel de Paris* (Paris Court of Appeal), 10 April 2018, *Rev. arb.*, 2018, 574, note E. Gaillard (free translation of: "*le contrôle du juge de l'exequatur n'a* [...] *pas pour objet de vérifier que des stipulations contractuelles – y compris les règles de conformité ("compliance") – ont été correctement exécutées, mais seulement de s'assurer que la reconnaissance et l'exécution de la sentence n'ont pas pour effet de donner force à un contrat de corruption.*")

(60) As E. Gaillard wrote (note under the decision of the *cour d'appel de Paris* (Paris Court of Appeal), 10 April 2018, *op. cit.*, p. 584), "While they have their utility, particularly when they provide for an automatic sanction for their violation, these [compliance] clauses pertain to the merits, and their application, whether right or wrong, by the arbitrators falls outside the control of the judge tasked with ensuring the conformity of the award with the requirements of public policy." (free translation of: "*Si elles ont leur utilité, notamment lorsqu'elles prévoient une sanction automatique à leur violation, ces clauses [de compliance] relèvent du fond et leur application, bonne ou mauvaise, par les arbitres, échappe au contrôle du juge chargé de s'assurer de la conformité de la sentence aux exigences de l'ordre public.*")

(61) K. Mehtiyeva, *La notion de coopération judiciaire*, préface by L. Cadiet, Paris, LGDJ, 2020, pp. 97 *et seq.*

This could open up a vast field, thus involving the arbitral community in the world of compliance.

If arbitrators were not to embrace the principles of compliance, the worst-case scenario would be an attitude of distrust or even hostility towards arbitration from compliance authorities. In the extreme, it would be conceivable for compliance authorities to seek commitments in compliance programs to no longer resort to arbitration. This would be a significant regression that must be avoided at all costs. That is why it is crucial for the entire arbitral community to be aware of the stakes involved in this matter.

Finally, it is obvious that arbitration is no longer able to escape, and will not be able to escape, the realm of compliance. How and to what extent remains to be seen in the future. There are, without a doubt, going to be repercussions. Compliance leads to a change in the world, and arbitration is naturally affected, just like everything else. It is essential to be aware of this and try to anticipate future developments. Because if arbitration does not align with compliance, compliance will inevitably make its way into arbitration.

What place is there for compliance in investment arbitration?

Eduardo Silva Romero

Partner at Dechert LLP

in collaboration with

Raphaelle Legru

Associate at Dechert LLP

The relationship between investment arbitration and compliance is a new topic. Compliance has only recently begun playing an increasingly important role in the realm of international business, particularly with the development of the globalised fight against corruption.

This relationship is nevertheless essential. Irrespective of the fact that the very existence of international arbitration is fragile and constantly under threat, the fact is that international arbitration still plays a crucial role in international business, which itself is constantly seeking to be more ethical.

On one side of this relationship, there is the concept of compliance, which provides a framework for international business law. As Professor Jean-Baptiste Racine observes, compliance can be understood as a process put in place by companies, and in particular multinational corporations, to regulate their activities to enable them "to assist states in achieving their goals," the ultimate goal being "to focus on the human being." (1) In short, ensuring compliance contributes directly to the public interest. (2)

---

(1) J.-B. Racine, "Compliance and arbitration. An attempt at problematisation", *this book*.

(2) Press release of Ethicorp.org and *Association Française des Juristes d'Entreprise – AFJE*, "Compliance & anticorruption: 3 ans après la promulgation de la Loi Sapin 2, la mise en œuvre par les entreprises en France n'est pas pleinement achevée", *Editions Législatives*, 31 January 2020, available at https://afje.org/medias/CAMPUS%20AFJE%202019/CP%20Etude%20ETHICORP%20AFJE.pdf.

More precisely, compliance entails that the international trade players conform to a set of rules, the content of which is essentially ethical, with the aim of fighting as much as possible against corruption, money laundering, environmental damage and other afflictions caused by what some refer to as the "prosperity of nations."

Incidentally, it could be said that the very existence of compliance arises from the States' failure in their fight for ethics in international business. Indeed, it is these very States, the respondents in investment arbitration proceedings, which would need the help of investment tribunals – the "natural if not the common judge of international trade" (3) – to restore lost ethics in international business.

On the other side of the relationship, there is investment Arbitration Law. Its recent evolution reveals clearly that it will only protect investors who respect the rules of compliance. In other words, only the "compliant investor" – that is, the ethical or "socially responsible" investor – would deserve to receive protection from investment arbitration tribunals.

Investment arbitration helps to monitor compliance, and thus assists States in their quest for business ethics, in three main ways.

Traditionally, investment arbitration has helped safeguard compliance through the monitoring of the legality of the investment (I).

More recently, investment arbitration has contributed to the development of compliance by ensuring that the investor is in possession of a "social license to operate," *i.e.* by ensuring that the investor has established good relations with the local communities of the investment project (II). (4)

The third way in which investment arbitration contributes to the development of compliance stems from criticism of the imbalance in investment treaties. This critique maintains that the system tends to protect international corporations wishing to invest, to the detriment of host States and, more specifically, of their right to exercise their sovereign power to regulate, including in social or environmental matters. (5) These criticisms have

(3) E. Gaillard, "L'ordre juridique arbitral: Réalité, utilité et spécificité", *McGill Law Journal*, 2010, p. 898 (free translation of: "*juge[s] naturel[s], sinon le[s] juge[s] de droit commun, du commerce international.*")

(4) K. Bergeron, M. Jébrak, S. Yates, C. Séguin, V. Lehmann, P. Le Meur, P. Angers, S, Durand and C. Gendron, "Mesurer l'acceptabilité sociale d'un projet minier: essai de modélisation du risque social en contexte québécois", *La Revue Electronique en Sciences de l'Environnement*, 2015, No. 3, p. 15.

(5) T. Gazzini, "Le TBI 2016 Maroc-Nigéria: Une importante contribution à la réforme des traités", *Investment Treaty News*, 26 September 2017, available at https://www.iisd.org/itn/fr/2017/09/26/the-2016-morocco-nigeria-bit-an-important-contribution-to-the-reform-of-investment-treaties-tarcisio-gazzini/.

led to the recent inclusion, in a new generation of bilateral investment treaties, of clauses relating to social rights, including the protection of the environment and public health, thereby establishing the central role that investment arbitration will be able to play in monitoring compliance (III).

I. THE TRADITIONAL APPROACH: MONITORING COMPLIANCE BY VERIFYING THE LEGALITY OF THE INVESTMENT

It is undisputed that the concept of "investment" is the gateway to the system of international protection offered to international investors. An investor can only benefit from the protection of a bilateral investment treaty – including the right to bring a claim against the host State before an international arbitral tribunal (whether that is ICSID, UNCITRAL or another forum) – if its investment meets certain requirements set out in the treaty and/or International Law. Among these requirements is the need for the investment to be legal, i.e. made and carried out in accordance with the national Law of the State hosting the investment.

In that regard, the convergence of global rules and instruments that regulate and condemn corrupt practices have led to the now common consideration that corruption is "an obstacle to jurisdiction in investment arbitration." (6) By refusing to even hear the claims of investors who have engaged in corrupt practices, investment arbitration is actively involved in the fight against corruption and, therefore, in protecting compliance.

The tribunals' review of the legality of the investment operates primarily in relation to the creation of the investment. If the investment is found not to have been lawfully created in accordance with the laws of the host State, tribunals may deny the investor, from the outset, the protection of the bilateral investment treaty, by declaring that it lacks jurisdiction or by declaring the claims inadmissible.

Two approaches are possible.

First, the treaty may contain an express requirement that the investment be made in accordance with the laws of the host State. In practice, the vast

(6) G. Martsekis, "La corruption comme obstacle à la juridiction dans l'arbitrage des traités d'investissement: une réforme stratégique", *ITA in Review*, 2019, Vol. 1, No. 2 (free translation of: "*un obstacle à la juridiction dans l'arbitrage d'investissement*").

majority of bilateral investment treaties contain such a requirement.(7) For instance, the France Model Bilateral Investment Treaty provides that "[i]t is understood that the [...] assets must be or have been invested in accordance with the laws of [the host state of the investment]."(8) In the words of the *Saba Fakes v. Turkey* tribunal, "[i]f this condition is not satisfied, the BIT does not apply."(9)

This inclusion in the treaties is not insignificant. The idea is to push States to report acts of corruption that may have taken place on their territory so as to expose them and, thus, remedy them. As has been stressed by commentators, these efforts should be encouraged as they can help to start a virtuous circle of self-reinforcing anti-corruption norms within the political sphere.(10)

Second, when the bilateral investment treaty does not expressly provide that the investment must be made in accordance with the laws of the host State, the tribunal, faced with a situation where the investment has been created illegally, may – and should – resort to general principles of International Law. The *Saur v. Argentina* tribunal noted that "the purpose of the investment arbitration system is to protect only lawful and *bona fide* investments" and that "it is incomprehensible that a State should offer the benefit of protection through investment arbitration if the investor, in order to obtain such protection, has acted contrary to the Law."(11) There would thus be a tacit condition of legality of the investment based on the general principle of good faith, a principle that would prevent a dispute arising out of an investment made in violation of the laws of the host State from being heard by an investment tribunal.

In *Hamester v. Ghana*, for instance, the tribunal declared that an investment cannot be protected – and the tribunal must decline jurisdiction – where the investment was "created in violation of national or international

(7) S. Schill, "Illegal Investments in Investment Treaty Arbitration", *Law and Practice of International Courts and Tribunals*, 2021, No. 11, p. 281.

(8) France model Bilateral Investment Treaty, Article 1 (free translation of: "*[i]l est entendu que les* [...] *avoirs doivent être ou avoir été investis conformément à la législation de* [*l'État hôte de l'investissement.*]")

(9) *Saba Fakes v. Republic of Turkey*, ICSID Case No. ARB/07/20, Award, 14 July 2010, para. 115.

(10) J. Yackee, "Investment Treaties and Investor Corruption: An Emerging Defense for Host States?", *IISD*, 19 October 2012, available at https://www.iisd.org/itn/fr/2012/10/19/investment-treaties-and-investor-corruption-an-emerging-defense-for-host-states/.

(11) *SAUR International v. Republic of Argentina*, ICSID Case No. ARB/04/4, Decision on Jurisdiction and Liability, 6 June 2012, para. 308 (free translation of: "*la finalité du système d'arbitrage d'investissement consiste à protéger uniquement les investissements licites et bona fide*" and "*est incompréhensible qu'un État offre le bénéfice de la protection par un arbitrage d'investissement si l'investisseur, pour obtenir cette protection, a agi à l'encontre du droit.*")

principles of good faith; by way of corruption, fraud, or deceitful conduct; or if its creation itself constitutes a misuse of the system of international investment protection under the ICSID Convention." (12)

It must be noted that it is almost unanimously recognised that only "serious" illegalities – *i.e.* an "illegal wrongdoing that is so egregious [...] as to be found to breach international public policy norms" – can lead a tribunal to decline its jurisdiction. (13) In practice, investments have generally been found to be illegal in cases involving acts of corruption. (14)

The relationship between investment arbitration and compliance is especially brought to the forefront in the context of corruption, as investment tribunals often use the so-called "red flags" method to identify potential "serious, concordant and specific" indicia of corruption. This "red flags" method is derived from US compliance practice. By applying this method, investment tribunals thus conduct genuine compliance investigations even if they do not expressly refer to the concept of compliance.

The famous *Metal-Tech v. Uzbekistan* case is a clear illustration of such an approach. To assess the legality of the intermediary contract at issue, the tribunal considered that it was "its duty to inquire about the reasons for [a] payment" made to a consultant in the amount of USD 4 million. To do so, the tribunal ordered the parties to produce briefs, exhibits and testimony, and to answer specific questions, before concluding that there was a *prima facie* case of bribery and, declining jurisdiction on that ground. (15)

(12) *Gustav F W Hamester GmbH & Co KG v. Republic of Ghana*, Award, 18 June 2010, para. 123.

(13) *Infracapital F1 S.à r.l. and Infracapital Solar B.V. v. Kingdom of Spain*, ICSID Case No. ARB/16/18, Decision on Jurisdiction, Liability and Directions on Quantum, 13 September 2021, para. 468.

(14) *Infinito Gold Ltd. v. Costa Rica*, ICSID Case No. ARB/14/5, Decision on Jurisdiction, 4 December 2017, para. 317 (in this case, the tribunal observed that since the legality requirement in the treaty affects the tribunal's jurisdiction, the tribunal must conduct its own investigation on the basis of the evidence of the case, particularly where there are allegations of corruption, which is a matter of international public policy); *Krederi Ltd. v. Ukraine*, ICSID Case No. ARB/14/17, Award, 2 July 2018, para. 384 (in this case, the tribunal observed that allegations of misconduct by an investor on the basis of bribery or similar conduct must be taken very seriously; this type of illegality must be considered contrary to international principles and, if proven, result in the loss of investment protection under the BIT); *Energoalians TOB v. Republic of Moldova*, UNCITRAL, Award, 23 October 2013, para. 261 (the tribunal found that under contemporary international law, only material and intentional violations of applicable laws by investors can serve as grounds for challenging jurisdiction; such violations include bribery, fraud, or other serious violations of domestic and international laws); *Álvarez y Marín Corporación S.A. and others v. Republic of Panama*, ICSID Case No. ARB/15/14, Award, 12 October 2018, para. 156 ("it is a severe and non-modifiable sanction, which should only be imposed if it is a proportionate response to an investor who has seriously violated the host state's legal system by investing") (free translation from Spanish).

(15) *Metal-Tech Ltd. v. Republic of Uzbekistan*, ICSID Case No. ARB/10/3, Award, 4 October 2013, paras. 194 *et seq.*

While arbitration has only recently started to ensure the observance of compliance rules as such, the refusal to arbitrate disputes arising out of commercial transactions tainted by corruption is not new. Judge Lagergren, for instance famously held that a dispute arising out of a corrupt contract was "*inarbitrable.*" In that case, even though neither party had contested his jurisdiction, he found that, by entering into such a contract, the parties had waived their right to have recourse to "the machinery of justice." (16) It is this same logic – based in part on the maxim *nemo auditur propriam turpitudinem allegans* – that is at least implicit in the reasoning of investment tribunals today. In the words of the *Inceysa v. El Salvador* tribunal, "the foreign investor cannot seek to benefit from an investment effectuated by means of one or more illegal acts and, consequently, enjoy the protection granted by the host State, such as access to international arbitration, to resolve disputes." (17)

The question arises as to whether the legality of the investment and, therefore, of compliance, is to be monitored when acts of corruption occur not at the time when the investment is made, but at the time of its performance. Some investment tribunals have taken the view that the legality clauses described above can only operate – and thus act as a barrier to the tribunal's jurisdiction – in cases where the illegality occurred at the stage of the creation of the investment. (18) Those tribunals have resorted to the "clean hands" doctrine – based on the common law concept of "equity" – according to which only those who have acted ethically deserve the protection of International Law. (19)

By way of illustration, in the *Al Warraq v. Indonesia* case, the State argued that the investor's claims were inadmissible on the grounds that the investor had been involved in money laundering and fraud during the performance of the investment. In short, the investor was requesting the tribunal's assistance with "unclean hands." The tribunal ruled in favour of the State and declared the claims inadmissible, noting, *inter alia*, that the investor's actions had "harmed the public interest." (20) The link between

(16) ICC Case No. 1110, 1963.

(17) *Inceysa Vallisoletana, SL v. El Salvador*, ICSID Case No. ARB/03/26, Award, 2 August 2006, para. 242.

(18) *Muszynianka Spólka z Ograniczona Odpowiedzialnoscia v. Slovak Republic*, PCA Case No. 2017-08, Award, 7 October 2020, paras. 300-301.

(19) C. Le Moullec, "The Clean Hands Doctrine: A Tool for Accountability of Investor Conduct and Inadmissibility of Investment Claims", *The International Journal of Arbitration, Mediation and Dispute Management*, 2018, Vol. 84, No. 1, p. 14 ("*The clean hands doctrine originates in common law jurisdiction where it evolved as part of the development of equity.*")

(20) *Hesham Talaat M. Al-Warraq v. Republic of Indonesia*, Final Award, 15 December 2014, para. 647.

the notion of "clean hands" and the public interest refers back, at least indirectly, to the notion of compliance, one of the main objectives of which is to "achieve the public interest goals set by the public authorities." (21)

This being said, the application of the "clean hands" doctrine is not unanimously accepted by investment tribunals. The majority of investment arbitrators, mostly positivists, do not feel comfortable declaring an investor's claims inadmissible on the basis of a general principle of International Law whose source and, therefore, existence is still controversial.

It seems to us that the increasing compliance requirements should nevertheless help to strengthen the "clean hands" doctrine and make its application more popular. In other terms, the generalisation of compliance practices could – should – help to establish the *opinio juris* that the aforementioned majority does not yet find in the acceptance of the "clean hands" doctrine.

II. A MORE RECENT APPROACH: MONITORING COMPLIANCE BY VERIFYING THE EXISTENCE OF A "SOCIAL LICENSE TO OPERATE"

Recently, investment tribunals have been involved in monitoring compliance by verifying that the investor has obtained a "social license to operate."

The term "social license to operate" refers to the perception by indigenous communities of the social legitimacy of a given investment project, often relating to mining. (22) It refers, in short, to the acceptance, by the parties concerned, of the operations that are being carried out. It forms part of the broader concept of corporate social responsibility, which in turn refers to a commitment by the company to meet the legal, ethical, and societal expectations of its stakeholders in order to ensure the sustainability and viability of its activities. (23) This concept entails, among other things, the protection of human rights, the protection of the environment,

(21) M-A. Frison-Roche (ed.), *Pour une Europe de la Compliance*, Paris, Dalloz, May 2019 (free translation of: "*concrétiser des buts d'intérêt général fixés par les autorités publiques.*")

(22) Report of SwissHoldings, "Responsabilité sociale des entreprises : le point de vue des entreprises", June 2015, available at https://www.economiesuisse.ch/sites/default/files/publications/Responsabilit%C3%A9%20sociale%20des%20entreprises%20-%20le%20point%20de%20vue%20des%20entreprises.pdf.

(23) A. Golli and D. Yahiaoui, "Responsabilité sociale des entreprises: analyse du modèle de Carroll (1991) et application au cas tunisien", *Management & Avenir*, 2009, Vol. 3, No. 23, p. 139.

public participation in the decision-making process, the right to access information, sustainable development, responsibility, and prior consultation with local communities regarding the exploitation of natural resources. (24) This concept has, recently, been invoked by States before arbitral tribunals against investor claims.

In *Copper Mesa v. Ecuador*, for instance, the tribunal expressly recognised the need for an investor to obtain a "social license to operate." In that case, the local communities had led a major campaign to resist the investor's mining operations in order to prevent massive deforestation, contamination of rivers and water sources, and threat to endangered species. The investor used intimidating tactics against these community members and, in particular, was responsible for the "reckless escalation of violence [...] recruiting and using armed men, firing guns and spraying mace at civilians." (25) The State argued before the arbitral tribunal that the investor's conduct constituted a serious violation of the legal principles governing corporate social responsibility, including the United Nations Global Compact and the OECD Guidelines. (26)

Although the arbitral tribunal ruled in favour of the State on this point, the facts of the case did not prevent it from concluding that the State had expropriated the investor and violated the standard of fair and equitable treatment contained in the applicable treaty, as a result of the State's withdrawal of two mining concessions owned by the investor. However, the lack of a "social license to operate," played a role in the genesis of the social conflict, led to a 30% reduction in the damages awarded to the investor, by virtue of the International Law concept of "contributory negligence." (27)

More recently, in the famous *Bear Creek Mining* case, a dispute arose due to the withdrawal by the Peruvian government of the investor's permits for the exploration and extraction of a silver mine, following social unrest and opposition from certain local communities which contested the environmental impact of the investment. The tribunal found that the company's efforts to obtain a "social license to operate," notably in accordance with the United Nations Declaration on the Rights of Indigenous Peoples, were insufficient.

(24) M.-M. Barnes, "The Social Licence to Operate: An Emerging Concept in the Practice of International Investment Tribunals", *Journal of International Dispute Settlement*, 2019, p. 344.

(25) *Copper Mesa Mining Corporation v. Ecuador*, PCA Case No. 2012-02, Award, 15 March 2016, para. 6.99.

(26) *Ibid.*

(27) *Ibid.*, paras. 6.99-6.102.

In this case, the tribunal found that the Peruvian authorities could not blame the investor since they had granted the permits with full knowledge of the facts. The tribunal found that the State itself had not sufficiently contributed to the protection of the rules of compliance and thus concluded that the investment had been expropriated. It is worth recalling that, while investment tribunals play a role in monitoring compliance and enforcing it *ex post*, ensuring compliance is primarily a matter for the State.

The tribunal nonetheless took into account the investor's lack of a "social license to operate" in valuing damages and deciding to award only the sunk costs incurred by the investor in establishing its investment. (28) More importantly, one of the co-arbitrators, Professor Sands, suggested in a dissenting opinion that damages should have been reduced even further considering that the foreign investor failed to obtain a social license to operate, thereby seeking to increase the international liability of foreign investors as regards certain social and human rights obligations. For Professor Sands, it was "obvious that the viability and success of a project such as this, located in the community of the Aymara peoples, a group of interconnected communities, was necessarily dependent on local support." (29)

One of the most recent examples to date of the significance of the "social license to operate" can be found in the *SAS v. Bolivia* case. In that case, indigenous communities challenged the investor's mining project, accusing the investor of polluting sacred spaces, of abusing its authority, of deceiving and threatening community members and condoning the rape of women, among other things. The government reached an agreement with the members of the local community, pursuant to which ownership of the mining concessions would revert to the State. The investor claimed damages for expropriation, but the State argued that such expropriation was justified by public and social utility. The tribunal found that, although the reversion of ownership was justifiable on the grounds of public utility and social benefit, the treaty nevertheless required the State to compensate the investor.

Although the investor's lack of a "social license to operate" has not, to date, resulted in the investor's claims being rejected, the concept is increasingly being considered by investment tribunals. A company which

(28) *Bear Creek Mining Corporation v. Republic of Peru*, UNCITRAL Case No. ARB/14/21, Award, 30 November 2017.

(29) *Ibid.*, Partial Dissenting Opinion of Professor Philippe Sands QC, 30 November 2017, para. 6.

chooses to invest today without having obtained a "social license to operate" may, at the very least, see its damages drastically reduced when the lack of this licence has led to social conflict.

It is worth highlighting that, while governments and investment tribunals now refer more directly to the notion of a "social license to operate," the importance given to the investment's social legitimacy is not entirely new. In *Glamis Gold v. United States*, for instance, in response to protests from local communities, the State enacted a law prohibiting the approval of any mining operation near a sacred Native American site unless the project provided for the pits to be backfilled and levelled, thereby preventing the investment from proceeding *in casu*. (30) In 2009, the tribunal rejected the investor's claim based on an alleged violation of the treaty's fair and equitable treatment standard, recognising the right of the host State to legislate in such circumstances.

It should be noted, however, that none of the cases mentioned in this article expressly refer to the notion of compliance as such (although the concepts of social responsibility are similar, if not directly inspired by it). It remains to be seen whether, with the growing interference of compliance in the legal language, the basis of arbitration awards dealing with this "social license to operate" will be less the traditional concepts mentioned, and more the notion of compliance itself. In any case, we believe that we will soon see a paradigm shift.

III. A NEW APPROACH: THE INCLUSION OF HUMAN RIGHTS AND ENVIRONMENTAL PROTECTIONS IN BILATERAL INVESTMENT TREATIES

Finally, there is a new trend whereby States are including social, environmental and human rights obligations incumbent on foreign investors into their bilateral investment treaties, thereby increasingly embedding compliance principles into legal instruments between States.

One illustration of this movement is the Netherlands Model Investment Agreement, published in March 2019, which, taking into account criticism from NGOs and host States, prioritises sustainable development objectives, and notably emphasises the social responsibility of international

(30) *Glamis Gold, Ltd. V. United States*, UNCITRAL, Award, 8 June 2009, para. 10.

companies. Under this treaty, the contracting parties "are committed to promote the development of international investment in such a way as to contribute to the objective of sustainable development" and "ensure that [their] investment laws and policies provide for and encourage high levels of environmental and labour protection and shall strive to continue to improve those laws and policies and their underlying levels of protection." (31)

The text of the Model Agreement also expressly provides that, when deciding on the amount of compensation awarded to investors, tribunals should "take into account non-compliance by the investor with its commitments under the UN Guiding Principles on Business and Human Rights, and the OECD Guidelines for Multinational Enterprises." (32)

Finally, the treaty confirms the right of States to regulate to "achieve legitimate policy objectives," such as public health, safety, public morals and the environment, and adds that the mere fact that a regulatory change adversely affects the investment or interferes with the investor's legitimate expectations does not constitute a violation of the treaty.

Three important consequences follow from this Netherlands Model Investment Treaty.

First, the text adopts the recent approach of investment tribunal awards to align violations of compliance rules by investors with the compensation awarded. Arbitral tribunals will thus have to reduce any damages due as a result of a treaty breach, applying a logic of shared or contributory fault on the part of the investor. This approach could therefore become more widespread in the future.

Second, the text enshrines the possibility that a violation of soft law principles, such as the United Nations Guidelines on Business and Human Rights and the OECD Guidelines for Multinational Enterprises, may give rise, indirectly, to a sanction through the reduction of any compensation.

Third, the objective is no longer only to protect and attract foreign investors; it is also to ensure that they respect the rights considered fundamental by the host State, which constitutes a turning point in relation to the spirit of the bilateral investment treaties of the end of the 20th century.

(31) Netherlands Model Investment Agreement, Articles 6(1) and 6(2).
(32) *Ibid.*, Article 23.

This search for a better balance between the rights of investors, on the one hand, and the rights of host States, on the other, is not an isolated effort undertaken by the Dutch government. The Canadian Model Investment Treaty, published in 2021, followed in the same vein. The European Union has similarly launched a process to modernise the Energy Charter Treaty to better meet the Union's climate objectives. Before that, for example, the treaty signed between Morocco and Nigeria in 2016 – described as "innovative" and "an important contribution to investment treaty reform"(33) – imposed obligations on foreign investors, including the requirement to comply with environmental screening and assessment processes, as well as a social impact assessment.

While these texts certainly mark a new trend in Investment Arbitration Law, whereby States tend to move away from the absolute protection of investors to devote more attention to respecting the environmental and social rights of host States, it is not the first time that States have shown an interest in such rights. A number of States have indeed been including in their treaties, for almost a decade, that a measure or regulation which has been adopted in a legitimate and non-discriminatory manner by the host State will not constitute a measure prohibited by the treaty, if the aim of that measure or regulation is to protect the environment, human health, consumer protection or another essential public interest. The majority of bilateral investment treaties signed by Latin American countries since 2004, for example, provide that the contracting parties recognise that it is not appropriate to encourage investments that require a relaxation of measures relating to health, safety or the environment.

Behind this idea of enshrining a principle of solidarity between international investors and host States in matters relating to environment, public health, safety, etc., is the underlying idea of compliance, which encourages international business relations while "*paying attention to the human being*" within these business relations.

*

* *

(33) T. Gazzini, "Le TBI 2016 Maroc-Nigéria: Une importante contribution à la réforme des traités d'investissement", *Investment Treaty News*, available at: https://www.iisd.org/itn/fr/2017/09/26/the-2016-morocco-nigeria-bit-an-important-contribution-to-the-reform-of-investment-treaties-tarcisio-gazzini/ (free translation of: "*innovant*" and "*une importante contribution à la réforme des traités d'investissement.*")

In conclusion, it is clear that investment arbitration plays a significant role in observing the rules of compliance by offering an *ex post* or *a posteriori* monitoring, by arbitral tribunals, of the legality of investments and of the investors' compliance with certain social requirements. Investment arbitration will participate more and more in the protection of compliance rules by deciding not to protect investors by applying the social, environmental and public health rules included in the new investment treaties, which are resolutely, from this point of view, more "solidarity-based" and, therefore, "humanistic."

The question nevertheless arises as to whether investment tribunals are aware of being the guardians of a compliance system or, rather, if they are simply acting as judges of the specific cases that have been entrusted to them. The question is still being debated. In short, while, for example, Gabrielle Kaufmann Köhler feels some responsibility towards ensuring, at the very least, a certain consistency in the decisions that are rendered in the community of international investors and host States, other leading figures in the field, such as Michael Reisman and Brigitte Stern, still conceive their role as that of a "contract judge." The evolution towards a new paradigm is, however, underway.

The arbitrator's position on compliance

Mathias Audit

Law Professor at the Sorbonne School of Law

(University of Paris 1 Panthéon-Sorbonne)

The issue of compliance has taken on considerable importance in contemporary law, and arbitration practice is no exception to this trend. It is undeniable that the compliance legal phenomenon, which initially came from across the Atlantic but which is now well established in European legal systems, has somewhat disrupted the mechanics of arbitration proceedings. It introduces a new dimension that cannot be ignored, but which does not fit easily into the traditional categories and usual practices of arbitration.

Indeed, the disruption is quite widespread and can occur at all stages of the arbitral process. But it is specifically from the arbitrator's perspective that the issue will be considered here. In other words, the question is how sole arbitrators, or arbitrators in a tribunal, are likely to consider compliance issues during arbitration proceedings.

This term has been used to designate "*the set of processes that ensure that the behaviour of the company, its managers and employees, complies with the laws, regulations, standards, professional practices and ethical requirements that apply to them.*"(1) It is thus a particular form of normative practice which consists in forcing companies to put in place internal processes aimed at preventing certain practices, primarily the commission of criminal offences such as money laundering, corruption or

(1) A. Gaudemet, *La compliance: un monde nouveau? Aspects d'une mutation du droit*, "Colloques" Serie, Paris, Éditions Panthéon-Assas, 2016, "Introduction", pp. 9-14, free translation of: "*l'ensemble des processus qui permettent d'assurer la conformité des comportements de l'entreprise, de ses dirigeants et de ses salariés, aux lois, règlements, normes, usages professionnels et exigences éthiques qui leur sont applicables.*"

influence peddling. It is therefore understood that compliance is a method of respecting standards, or "*a process*" (2) consisting in a company organising itself in the best possible way to prevent offences from arising within. Moreover, compliance actually implies a paradigm shift in the prevention of the commission of offences. It is an internalisation within the company of the mechanisms for preventing possible breaches of law. In Marie-Anne Frison-Roche's words, "*the subject becomes an agent of equality*" and the company acquires "*penal capacity.*" (3)

Yet these obligations to prevent, detect and punish infringements arising within the company may be invoked by a party to arbitration proceedings against its adversary. The arbitral tribunal must then adopt a position on this particular claim and it is the parameters for adopting this position that shall be examined here.

Among those parameters, the issue of proof is undeniably subject to the most heated debates. It is clear that in the area of corruption, *inter alia*, an original evidentiary system specific to arbitration is being gradually set up. This system, which involves using red flags, is currently attracting a great deal of attention. (4) However, it is not directly the implementation of this very specific evidentiary method that shall be considered here, but rather the questions that arise upstream in the logical sequence that should govern the arbitrators' reasoning.

In fact, before considering the issue of proof, it is necessary to determine beforehand the rule according to which the evidence must be produced. It is important to identify the applicable standard on the basis of which the conduct of the party concerned shall be assessed and, consequently, established on the basis of evidence. This is the starting point of the entire reasoning, which would lead to the arbitrators' decision on whether the parties failed to comply with their obligations in terms of compliance.

---

(2) E. Breene, "La compliance, une privatisation de la régulation ?", *RSC*, 2019, p. 327.

(3) M.-A. Frison-Roche, "Du droit de la régulation au droit de la compliance", *in* M.-A. Frison-Roche (ed.), *Régulation, Supervision, Compliance*, Paris, Dalloz, 2017, pp. 1-14, free translation of: "*l'assujetti devient agent de légalité*" and "*l'aptitude pénale.*"

(4) M. Audit, S. Bollée and P. Callé, *Droit du commerce international et des investissements étrangers*, "Domat Droit privé" Serie, Paris, LGDJ-Lextenso, 2019, No. 230. *See also*: decision of the *cour d'appel de Paris* (Paris Court of Appeal), 10 April 2018, No. 16/11182; *D.*, 2018, p. 1942, L. D'Avout and S. Bollée; *ibid.*, p. 2448, T. Clay; *RTD com.*, 2020, p. 283, E. Loquin; *Rev. arb.*, 2018. p. 574, E. Gaillard; *Cah. arb.*, 2018, p. 465, A. Pinna; *JDI*, 2019, p. 630, K. Mahtiyeva; *Gaz. Pal.*, 2019, p. 24, D. Bensaude; decision of the *cour d'appel de Paris* (Paris Court of Appeal), 28 May 2019, No. 16/11182, *Alstom*; *Rev. arb.*, 2019, p. 850, E. Gaillard; *JDI*, No. 2, April 2020, p. 10, E. Loquin; *Gaz. Pal.*, July 2019, p. 22, D. Bensaude; *D.*, 2019, p. 1956, S. Bollée.

Experience shows that there can be a certain amount of terminological and conceptual confusion from time to time in the debates that may take place within the course of arbitral proceedings. Such confusion is sometimes deliberately maintained by one of the parties when it is likely to serve its procedural strategy. Indeed, the notion of compliance is often equated with corruption, influence peddling, money laundering, embezzlement and sometimes even favouritism. However, all these concepts do not cover the same legal reality and assimilating them hastily could prove questionable.

Even if, generally speaking, Compliance Law is now increasingly conceptualised, including in French Law,(5) experience shows that, in arbitration, the distinction between this concept and other related notions, such as corruption or money laundering, is not always clear-cut, or at least not with complete clarity.

Needless to say, we do not dispute that there is a link between these criminally reprehensible behaviours and the compliance programs set up to prevent them. But this does not mean that they are perfectly comparable. For this reason, when a case that raises such questions is brought before an arbitral tribunal, the latter must first identify the compliance obligation (I). It can thereafter examine the consequences that should be attached to the breach of this obligation (II).

I. IDENTIFICATION OF A COMPLIANCE OBLIGATION

In the context of arbitration proceedings, the existence of a breach of a compliance obligation may be invoked against one of the parties. Such breach obviously does not exist *per se*; its recognition implies that a norm laid down an obligation in this respect, and it is this obligation that the arbitral tribunal must identify. To this end, it is important to note that there is an autonomy of the compliance obligation (A), the possible sources of which will then be considered (B).

(5) A. Gaudemet, see *supra*; M.-A. Frison-Roche, "Le droit de la compliance", *D.*, 2016, p. 1871; M.-A. Frison-Roche, "Du droit de la régulation au droit de la compliance", *in* M.-A. Frison Roche (ed.), *Régulation, Supervision, Compliance*, Paris, Dalloz, 2017, pp. 1-14; M.-A. Frison-Roche, "Compliance: avant, maintenant, après", *in* N. Borga, J.-Cl. Marin and J.-Chr. Roda (eds), *Compliance: l'entreprise, le régulateur et le juge*, Paris, Dalloz, 2018, pp. 23-36; M.-A. Frison-Roche, "Un Droit substantiel de la Compliance, appuyé sur la tradition européenne humaniste", *in* M.-A. Frison Roche (ed.), *Pour une Europe de la Compliance*, Paris, Dalloz, 2019; M.-A. Frison-Roche, "L'aventure de la compliance", *D.*, 2020, p. 1805.

A. Autonomy of the compliance obligation

It is established that questions of Criminal Law, and in particular that of corruption, are not new in arbitration practice, and one can mention here the widely known *Lagergren* award, named after the sole arbitrator who rendered it in 1963. (6) More generally, scholars have also been dealing with these issues for a long time. (7)

Nevertheless, it cannot be denied that the phenomenon has accelerated in the recent years. Furthermore, there has been a form of importation of Criminal Law concepts into Arbitration Law, such as corruption, money laundering or embezzlement. Moreover, this import has often generated a form of semantic and legal slippage. This implies that all these Criminal Law concepts have a strict definition within the branch of law from which they originate. More than other areas of law, Criminal Law relies on precisely defined concepts. The textual frameworks are not interchangeable, and this is probably a manifestation of the principle of strict construction of Criminal Law.

Yet this rigor of the concepts specific to Criminal Law has not always been maintained when they have been imported into arbitration practice. One example is the notion of corruption. In arbitration practice, corruption covers behaviours that include both passive and active corruption *stricto sensu* as well as influence peddling in terms of Criminal Law. In other words, the notion of "corruption" in arbitration does not cover exactly what is meant by the same term in Criminal Law. Another example is the distinction between corruption and the offence of favouritism.

However, this hypertrophy of the notion of corruption in arbitration has a clearly identified origin, which also gives it its justification. Arbitral tribunals are not competent to apply Criminal Law, *i.e.*, to recognise an offence and punish it. Consequently, the concepts that arbitral tribunals apply are not in fact those of Criminal Law; they are merely related to them. This has led to the inception of concepts specific to Arbitration Law, such as corruption, which relationship with Criminal Law is not nonexistent but remote.

---

(6) ICC Case No. 1110 (1963). Award entirely published in: J. Gillis Wetter, "Issues of Corruption before International Arbitration Tribunals: The Authentic Text and True Meaning of Judge Gunnar Lagergren's 1963 Award in ICC Case No. 1110", *Arb. Int.*, 1994, pp. 277-294.

(7) A. El Kosheri and Ph. Leboulanger, "L'arbitrage face à la corruption et aux trafics d'influence", *Rev. arb.*, 1984, p. 3; V. Heuzé, "La morale, l'arbitre et le juge", *Rev. arb.*, 1993, p. 179; P. Mayer, "La règle morale dans l'arbitrage international", *in Études offertes à P. Bellet*, Paris, Litec, 1991, p. 379.

This is confirmed by the fact that arbitral tribunals, like reviewing courts, rely on major international texts in order to qualify certain behaviours as corruption or money laundering, in particular the United Nations Convention against Corruption concluded in Merida in 2003 (also known as the Merida Convention), (8) or the Convention on Combating Bribery of Foreign Public Officials in International Business Transactions concluded under the aegis of the OECD in 1997 (also known as the OECD Anti-Bribery Convention). (9)

In a noteworthy decision of 2017, *Republic of Kyrgyzstan v. Belokon*, (10) the *cour d'appel de Paris* (Paris Court of Appeal) refused to grant exequatur to an arbitral award because of money laundering acts, as defined in Article 23 (1) of the Merida Convention. The Court noted that "*the fight against the laundering of money derived from criminal activities is the subject of an international consensus expressed in particular in the United Nations Convention against Corruption, signed in Merida on December 9, 2003*" (11) and that "*it is not the task of this Court to determine whether a party to the arbitration may be found guilty of the offence of money laundering under the Criminal Law provisions of a national legal system, but only to investigate whether the recognition or the enforcement of the award is of such nature as to hinder the objective of combating money laundering, as defined by the Merida Convention, by allowing a party to benefit from the proceeds of illicit activities of this nature.*" (12) In this case, the Paris Court of Appeal fetched the definition of money laundering that it implemented in the Merida Convention.

(8) United Nations Convention against Corruption (UNCAC), 2003.

(9) Convention on Combating Bribery of Foreign Public Officials in International Business Transactions, 17 December 1997.

(10) Decision of the *cour d'appel de Paris* (Paris Court of Appeal), 21 February 2017, No. 15/01650; *D.*, 2017, p. 2054, L. d'Avout and S. Bollée; *ibid.*, 2559, T. Clay; *Rev. arb.*, 2017, p. 915, M. Audit and S. Bollée; *RTD com.*, 2019, p. 42, E Loquin; *JCP*, 2017, Doctr., 1326, C. Seraglini; *Cah. arb.*, 2017, p. 668, B. Poulain; *Bull. ASA*, 2017, p. 551, L.-C. Delanoy.

(11) Free translation of: "*la lutte contre le blanchiment d'argent provenant d'activités délictueuses fait l'objet d'un consensus international exprimé notamment dans la Convention des Nations Unies contre la corruption faite à Mérida le 9 décembre 2003.*"

(12) Free translation of: "*il n'entre pas dans la mission de cette cour, saisie d'un recours en annulation d'une sentence internationale, de rechercher si une partie à l'arbitrage peut être déclarée coupable du délit de blanchiment en application des dispositions pénales d'un ordre juridique national, mais seulement de rechercher si la reconnaissance ou l'exécution de la sentence est de nature à entraver l'objectif de lutte contre le blanchiment en faisant bénéficier une partie du produit d'activité de cette nature, telles que définies par* [...] *la convention de Mérida.*"

Subsequently, in the famous *Alstom* judgment of 28 May 2019,(13) the same Court also defined corruption by reference to the Merida and OECD Conventions. It stated that "*the fight against corruption is an objective pursued, inter alia, by the OECD Convention on Combating Bribery of 17 December 1997, which entered into force on 15 February 1999, and by the United Nations Convention against Corruption executed at Merida on 9 December 2003, which entered into force on 14 December 2005.*"(14) The Court goes on to state that "*according to the consensus expressed by these texts, bribery of a foreign public official consists in offering to the latter, directly or indirectly, an undue advantage, for himself or for another person or entity, in order for him to perform, or refrain from performing, an act in the exercise of his official duties, with a view to obtaining or retaining a contract or other undue advantage in connection with international trade activities.*"(15) Here again, the qualification of the offences – the commission of which entails the violation of international public order – is based on international conventions.

However, it should be noted that reference to international instruments is not systematic. In a recent *Aboukhalil v. Senegal* decision dated 12 October 2021,(16) the Paris Court of Appeal refused to adopt the definition of illicit enrichment as defined in Article 20 of the Merida Convention, noting that "*the offence of illicit enrichment does not exist under French Law.*"(17) Having undertaken an *in concreto* examination, the Court ruled that "*the facts complained about could not be classified as any other criminal offence under French Law and in particular could not be assimilated*

(13) Decision of the *cour d'appel de Paris* (Paris Court of Appeal), 10 April 2018, No. 16/11182; *D.*, 2018, p. 1942, L. d'Avout and S. Bollée; *D.*, 2018, p. 2448, T. Clay; *RTD com.*, 2020, p. 283, E. Loquin; *Rev. arb.*, 2018, p. 574, E. Gaillard; *Cah. arb.*, 2018, p. 465, A. Pinna; *JDI*, 2019, p. 630, K. Mahtiyeva; *Gaz. Pal.*, 2019, p. 24, D. Bensaude; Decision of the *cour d'appel de Paris* (Paris Court of Appeal), 28 May 2019, No. 16/11182, *Alstom*; *Rev. arb.*, 2019, p. 850, E. Gaillard; *JDI*, No. 2, April 2020, p. 10, E. Loquin; *Gaz. Pal.*, July 2019, p. 22, D. Bensaude; *D.*, 2019, p. 1956, S. Bollée.

(14) Free translation of: "*la lutte contre la corruption est un objectif poursuivi, notamment, par la Convention de l'OCDE sur la lutte contre la corruption du 17 décembre 1997, entrée en vigueur le 15 février 1999, et par la Convention des Nations Unies contre la corruption faite à Merida* [sic] *le 9 décembre 2003, entrée en vigueur le 14 décembre 2005.*"

(15) Free translation of: "[s]*uivant le consensus exprimé par ces textes, la corruption d'agent public étranger consiste à offrir à celui-ci, directement ou indirectement, un avantage indu, pour lui-même ou pour une autre personne ou entité, afin qu'il accomplisse ou s'abstienne d'accomplir un acte dans l'exercice de ses fonctions officielles, en vue d'obtenir ou de conserver un marché ou un autre avantage indu en liaison avec des activités de commerce international.*"

(16) Decision of the *cour d'appel de Paris* (Paris Court of Appeal), 12 October 2021, No. 19/21625.

(17) Free translation of: "*l'infraction d'enrichissement illicite n'exist*[e] *pas en droit français.*"

to the offences of corruption, influence peddling, illegal taking of interest or misappropriation of funds, and even money laundering." (18)

Whether or not these Criminal Law concepts are adopted, they are in any event separate from the notion of compliance. Indeed, there is no equation between this notion and the criminally reprehensible behaviours that it aims to eradicate. In other words, the lack of compliance by a company involved in arbitration proceedings does not necessarily imply that corrupt or money laundering practices can be imputed to it. The mere fact that a company is not "compliant" does not mean that its employees, its managers or itself have committed any criminally reprehensible acts.

The scope of compliance is clearly separate from the commission of these acts. Compliance only implies the implementation of internal protocols within the company, aimed at preventing the commission of such acts. It can also be manifested in other areas, such as compliance by the same company with unilateral sanctions programs or embargoes imposed by a State.

Therefore, it is exclusively in the field of implementation of internal prevention mechanisms within the company that compliance is situated, *i.e.*, on a different level from the commission – if any – of the criminal offences that compliance is precisely intended to prevent. Hence, in order for an arbitral tribunal to recognise a breach of a compliance obligation, *i.e.*, a breach of an obligation to comply, the source of such obligation must have been identified beforehand.

B. Source of the compliance obligation

It is a truism to say that, where there is a breach of compliance, there must be a pre-existing compliance obligation on the part of the party concerned. In other words, there is no such thing as an immanent compliance obligation; it is necessarily imposed by a norm. In this respect, there are several possible sources of this obligation.

The first is undoubtedly contractual. It is indeed possible that the contractual agreement between the parties to the dispute imposes a compliance obligation on one of them. For example, an intermediary agreement

(18) Free translation of: *"les faits reprochés ne pouvaient pas recevoir une autre qualification pénale en droit français et notamment ne pouvaient être assimilés aux délits de corruption, de trafic d'influence, de prise illégale d'intérêts ou détournements de fonds, et même de blanchiment."*

may provide – and this is now common – that the intermediary will not only refrain from any corrupt or other such practices within the framework of its mission, but will also ensure, by setting up internal control and audit processes, that the entire chain of execution and decision making within its company tends towards avoiding such practices.

In addition to the contract, the law can also impose a compliance obligation. Some national laws impose a legal obligation upon companies of a certain size to implement a compliance program. This is particularly the case of the UK Bribery Act, (19) which establishes an offence of failure of commercial organisations to prevent bribery. (20) The company will be liable if it benefits from bribery committed by a person "*associated*" with it. (21) In other words, not only does the statute incriminate bribery, it also – and autonomously – incriminates the failure of a company to implement a compliance program aimed at preventing corrupt practices by its representatives while seeking new tenders. This specific offence has an even broader scope of application as the said "*associated*" persons can be any person performing services for the benefit, or on behalf, of the company, regardless of his title. (22)

The French law of 9 December 2016, known as "Sapin 2" also provides for a similar compliance obligation with respect to the prevention of corruption. Article 17-I of the statute sets out an obligation for companies employing at least five hundred employees as well as their managers "*to take measures to prevent and detect the commission, in France or abroad, of acts of corruption or influence peddling*" within the company. (23) In this respect, companies must, *inter alia*, adopt a "*code de conduite*" ("code of conduct") that defines and illustrates the prescribed behaviours. They must also implement a "*dispositif d'alerte interne*" (an "internal alert

(19) Bribery Act, 2010 (UKBA).

(20) UKBA, Section 7: "*Failure of commercial organisations to prevent bribery.*"

(21) UKBA Section 7-1°: "*A relevant commercial organization ('C') is guilty of an offence under this section if a person ('A') associated with C bribes another person intending (a) to obtain or retain business for C, or (b) to obtain or retain an advantage in the conduct of business for C.*"

(22) UKBA, Section 8-1° and 8-2°.

(23) French law No. 2016-1691, 9 December 2016, Article 17, I°, free translation of: "*de prendre les mesures destinées à prévenir et à détecter la commission, en France ou à l'étranger, de faits de corruption ou de trafic d'influence.*" Article 17-I° applies more specifically to "*chairmen, chief executives and managers of a company with at least five hundred employees, or belonging to a group of companies whose parent company has its registered office in France and whose workforce includes at least five hundred employees, and whose sales or consolidated sales exceed 100 million euros*" (free translation of: "*présidents, directeurs généraux et gérants d'une société employant au moins cinq cents salariés, ou appartenant à un groupe de sociétés dont la société mère a son siège social en France et dont l'effectif comprend au moins cinq cents salariés, et dont le chiffre d'affaires ou le chiffre d'affaires consolidé est supérieur à 100 millions d'euros.*")

system") intended to collect reports from employees on acts committed in breach of said code. Companies must also establish a "*cartographie des risques*" ("risk map") to identify and prioritise the risks of exposure to corruption, while evaluating the risks associated with certain clients, suppliers or intermediaries. Moreover, companies must provide specific training for their most exposed managers. But above all, companies must set up a "*régime disciplinaire permettant de sanctionner les salariés de la société*" ("disciplinary system to sanction company employees") who are found guilty of corruption or money laundering. (24) Compliance with this system is monitored – and where necessary, sanctioned – by the *Agence française anticorruption – AFA* (French Anti-Corruption Agency – AFA).

In addition to actual textual sources, it is worth noting that compliance obligations may also arise from decisions or transactions imposed by administrative or judicial authorities. For example, the US Federal Foreign Corrupt Practices Act (FCPA) (25) does not expressly provide for a compliance obligation. However, it is common for companies to be required to accept, in the context of a transaction, to set up such program within. This is particularly the case with Deferred Prosecution Agreements (DPAs) entered into with the US Department of Justice (DOJ) or other prosecuting authorities, which generally contain two components. The first is financial in nature: it sets the amount of the settlement fine to be paid. (26) The second relates precisely to an obligation to implement an internal compliance program within the company.

Lastly, it is important to note that there is another possible source of compliance, namely the choice made by a company – and not forced upon it by a text – to set up a prevention program. Thus, as part of its advisory mission, the *AFA* has updated its anti-corruption guidelines in a notice published in the *Journal Officiel de la République Française – JORF*. (27) This text is akin to a *vade mecum* of what a legal entity can or must do in order to prevent and detect the acts of corruption, influence peddling, misappropriation of public funds and favouritism likely to occur within the course of its activities. It is intended to apply to legal entities required

---

(24) French law No. 2016-1691, 9 December 2016, Article 17, II°.

(25) US Foreign Corrupt Practices Act (FCPA), 1977, as amended, 15 U.S.C. paras. 78dd-1 *and seq*.

(26) L. D'Avout, "Sanctions négociées. La nouvelle discipline étatique des entreprises mondiales", *Droits*, 2016, No. 64, pp. 73-96.

(27) *Avis relatif aux recommandations de l'Agence française anticorruption destinées à aider les personnes morales de droit public et de droit privé à prévenir et à détecter les faits de corruption, de trafic d'influence, de concussion, de prise illégale d'intérêts, de détournement de fonds publics et de favoritisme, Journal Officiel de la République Française – JORF*, No. 10 of 12 January 2021.

by law to set up such program within their organisation, but also to other entities that nonetheless decide of their own initiative to subject themselves to it. (28)

Similarly, a manual from the United Nations Office on Drugs and Crime (UNODC), the World Bank and the OECD (29) brings together all the standards in the fight against corruption and provides practical tools for companies wishing to set up a compliance program.

Accordingly, when a breach of compliance is mentioned in the context of arbitration proceedings, one of these possible sources must necessarily be mobilised. As stated, there cannot be a compliance obligation imposed *per se* on a party to a dispute pending before the arbitrators. Only a standard – whether contractual, legal, or even judicial or administrative – can impose it, and it is only pursuant to this standard that the conduct of a party can be assessed by the arbitral tribunal.

II. BREACH OF A COMPLIANCE OBLIGATION

Should there be a source that may impose a compliance obligation upon a party to a dispute, it must be determined what the consequences of non-compliance with this obligation should be in the context of the arbitration proceedings. Specifically, the question is, on the one hand, whether and how such non-compliance could be sanctioned by an arbitral tribunal (A) and, on the other hand, what consequences could be drawn as to the reality of the criminally reprehensible conduct that compliance was intended to prevent (B).

A. Conformity with the arbitration mission

The identification of a source of a compliance obligation binding upon a party to the dispute does not necessarily imply that it is the task of the arbitral tribunal to sanction the breach of that obligation. Specifically, the power of the arbitral tribunal to sanction the breach of the compliance obligation depends, to a large extent, on the source of the compliance obligation.

(28) *Ibid.*, Article I.2) *Champ d'application*.

(29) UNODC, OECD, World Bank, "Anti-Corruption Ethics and Compliance Programme for Business: A Practical Guide", 2013.

In fact, if the source of said obligation is contractual – in the sense that it is the same contract that contains both the compliance commitments imposed on one party to the dispute, as well as the arbitration clause – there is no real difficulty. The arbitral tribunal will assess this breach of contract and deduce the consequences thereof in light of the *lex contractus*. If the breach is established, it may result in a finding of breach of contract. The arbitral tribunal may then grant compensation to the other party accordingly. In such case, the arbitral tribunal cannot be considered to exceed its mission, at least if the breach was invoked in the course of the proceedings.

The situation is more delicate, however, if the party is in breach of legal provisions imposing compliance obligations. It is conceivable that a party was subject to an obligation to prevent corruption as part of its internal processes, either pursuant to the UK Bribery Act or the French "Sapin 2" law for instance, but failed to do so.

In this respect, one may consider whether an arbitral tribunal confronted with such question would be able to rule that there was a breach of the relevant provisions. The difficulty lies in the fact that the domestic law imposing the compliance program, undoubtedly the *lex societatis* of the company concerned, may be distinct from the law applicable to the merits of the dispute, as defined in the contract subject of the dispute or in the terms of reference. The question then arises as to whether it is consistent with the mission of the arbitral tribunal to identify a breach by one of the parties of its *lex societatis* in this respect.

However, it is now generally accepted that arbitral tribunals may depart from the law applicable to the merits chosen by the parties in order to apply, in particular, mandatory rules, without exceeding their mission.(30) It is therefore quite natural to consider that a similar reasoning could be applied to important issues such as compliance and the prevention of serious offences that it entails.

(30) Y. Derains, "Les normes d'application immédiate dans la jurisprudence arbitrale internationale", *in Études Goldman*, Paris, Litec, 1992, p. 29; id., "L'ordre public et le droit applicable au fond du litige dans l'arbitrage international", *Rev. arb.*, 1986, 375; P. Mayer, "L'interférence des lois de police", *in L'apport de la jurisprudence arbitrale*, ICC, No. 440/1, 1986, p. 31; id., "La sentence contraire à l'ordre public au fond", *Rev. arb.*, 1994, p. 615; C. Séraglini, "Loi de police et justice arbitrale internationale", Paris, Dalloz, 2001, p. XI; B. Audit, "Du bon usage des lois de police", *in Mélanges en l'honneur du Professeur Pierre Mayer*, Paris, LGDJ, 2015, p. 25; L. G. Radicati di Brozolo, "Arbitrage commercial international et lois de police: considérations sur le conflit de juridictions dans le commerce international", *RCADI*, 2005, t. 315, p. 265.

The consideration by an arbitral tribunal of a national law other than the one applicable to the merits, in order to identify the rules binding on one party, does not appear to be problematic from the point of view of the arbitral tribunal's conformity with the terms of its mission. In contrast, the sanction that the arbitral tribunal may attach to the disregard of these legal rules could prove more problematic.

B. The sanction of non-compliance

Setting aside contractual compliance obligations and focusing instead on those that have a legal, administrative, judicial or even transactional source, *e.g.*, a DPA concluded with the US authorities, we observe that the issue of arbitral tribunals sanctioning non-compliances may prove to be problematic.

Indeed, the imposition of compliance obligations by certain national laws is usually accompanied by specific sanctions, usually of a criminal nature. Consequently, under the terms of Articles 17-III°, 17-IV° and 17-V° of the French "Sapin 2" law, if it cannot be demonstrated that adequate internal procedures for the prevention of corruption exist and are effective, the natural and legal persons concerned may be held criminally liable. The *Agence française anticorruption – AFA* (French Anti-Corruption Agencey – AFA)'s Sanctions Committee may, following an injunction of the judge heading the agency, impose a financial penalty of up to 200,000 euros for individuals and 1,000,000 euros for legal entities.(31) Additionally, and within the framework of the "*convention judiciaire d'intérêt public*" ("Judicial Public Interest Agreement") – a form of penal transaction for legal entities charges with offences of corruption, influence peddling, tax fraud or money laundering – the fine can reach "*30% of the average annual turnover calculated on the last three known annual turnovers at the date of observation of these breaches.*" (32)

Needless to say, Criminal Law is not arbitrable, and arbitrators may not implement such laws under any circumstances. However, they can draw consequences from the breach of a legal compliance obligation on the international trade dispute referred to them. Moreover, in the absence of

(31) French law No. 2016-1691, 9 December 2016, Article 17-III°, IV° and V°.

(32) *Ibid.*, free translation of: "*30 % du chiffre d'affaires moyen annuel calculé sur les trois derniers chiffres d'affaires annuels connus à la date du constat de ces manquements.*"

implementation of a similar program imposed by a judicial or administrative authority, or through a DPA for instance, the consequence could be the same: the arbitral tribunal may not implement the sanctions specifically provided for but could – here again – draw conclusions on the dispute subject to arbitration.

In such configuration, *i.e.*, where the compliance obligation is not imposed by the contract subject of the arbitration, but by another source – whether legal, administrative, judicial or transactional – the question of the absence of a prevention program within the company concerned is no longer at the centre of the debate. This means that arbitrators do not have to sanction this failure directly, nor do they have the means of doing so.

Nonetheless, it is possible for them to support their decision by reference to the said failure. At this stage of the reasoning, however, there is a slippage which may occur, and which should be avoided. When it is not the subject of a dedicated contractual provision, and even where a normative source external to the contract imposes the compliance obligation, the failure to implement a compliance program cannot *a priori* in and of itself lead to the nullity or termination of the contract. What can lead to such a result is the existence of behaviours such as corruption or money laundering that the compliance program, had it been implemented, could have prevented.

In other words, it is a sufficiently high degree of certainty as to the existence of corrupt practices, for example, in the case at hand that may lead the arbitral tribunal to declare the contract null and void. But a mere finding that a compliance program was not implemented would not be sufficient to nullify the contract. To put it differently, even where one party to the arbitration proceedings or the other was indeed subject to an obligation to implement a corruption prevention program within its company, pursuant to its *lex societatis* for example, and if this implementation obligation was breached, this does not mean that said party did engage in such practices. There is no necessary equation between the lack of compliance and the existence of corruption or money laundering practices.

By contrast, a breach of a compliance obligation is naturally likely to constitute one element – among others – that could lead to the arbitral tribunal's finding that a corruption offence, in particular, is attributable to one of the parties. In other words, it may be one of the warning signs or red flags on which the arbitral tribunal's conclusion is based.

The Basel Institute on Governance, in its practical guide to arbitrators for identifying bribery and money laundering practices, considers that a company's general attitude towards compliance may be an indication of illegal behaviour. (33) The guide specifies that "*the lack of code of conduct*" or "*certificates*" "*for example mentioning its compliance with the UK Bribery Act of 2010, the United States Foreign Corrupt Practices Act of 1997 or the French Sapin II regulation*" is an indication likely to arouse the arbitrator's suspicions. (34)

Arbitrators may also rely on the ICC Rules on Combating Bribery and the ICC Guidelines on Agents, Intermediaries and Other Third Parties – a self-regulatory code for companies to vet third parties with whom they deal and to prevent reputational damage – to check the facts vis-à-vis "*Red Flags.*" (35)

The first of these tools lists several anti-corruption rules and best practices for companies. It also promotes the implementation of a "*Corporate Compliance*" program designed to "*prevent and detect*" corruption. (36) Therefore, the understanding is that a failure to comply with these anti-bribery rules or best practices, or the lack of a prevention program in line with these best practices, could give arbitrators grounds for suspicion when allegations of bribery are submitted. More directly, the ICC Guidelines on Agents, Intermediaries and Other Third Parties state that failure by the third party, agent or intermediary to comply with anti-bribery or other applicable laws is a "*red flag,*" which is not in and of itself a violation of anti-bribery laws, but is a "*warning sign that need to be taken seriously and investigated*" by companies. (37)

Similarly, in the *Alstom* case, which is known for having introduced into French case law the method of warning signals for purposes of reviewing awards, the *cour d'appel de Paris* (Paris Court of Appeal) did not mention, in this respect, the breach of a compliance program. (38) Yet, nothing prevents that such finding, combined with others, constitutes a warning

(33) Basel Institute on Governance, *Corruption and Money Laundering in International Arbitration: A Toolkit for Arbitrators*, 2019.

(34) *Ibid.*, Tool 1.

(35) ICC Rules on Combating Corruption, 2011; ICC Guidelines on Agents, Intermediaries and Other Third Parties, 2011, Article VI.

(36) ICC Rules on Combating Corruption, 2011, Article 10.

(37) ICC Guidelines on Agents, Intermediaries and Other Third Parties, Article VI.

(38) Decision of the *cour d'appel de Paris* (Paris Court of Appeal), 10 April 2018, see *supra*.

signal. As a matter of fact, the lists proposed in this respect both by case law and by international soft law instruments are not exhaustive.

In this case, the breach of compliance does not come into play as such, but as one element amongst others likely to allow the arbitral tribunal to find for the existence of corruption or another illicit practice with a sufficiently high level of certainty. In light of this finding, the arbitral tribunal shall then be able to draw all the necessary consequences on the dispute at hand and in particular on the validity of the contract in question.

The objectives of compliance confronted with the actors of arbitration

Elie Kleiman*

Partner, Jones Day

When international arbitration and compliance meet, what happens? On account of the trend towards expansion of the field of compliance, the frequency of encounters between arbitration and compliance is likely to increase. However, these two great figures of globalisation do not only have common points. Arbitration (1) is a creature of contractual autonomy, laissez-faire and international trade relations. Compliance is characterised by mandatory prescriptions dictated by the public interest, *ex ante* control of the activities it embraces and the pursuit of "monumental goals."(2) Part of the answer seems to be implied in the topic from which one can guess that the confrontation envisaged augurs a clash of these titans of

---

* The opinions expressed herein are the sole responsibility of the author. These opinions can in no way be attributed to or equated with those of Jones Day, where he practices as a partner.

(1) This paper deals only with international arbitration and not with domestic arbitration or other forms of so-called professional, sectoral, technical arbitration, etc.

(2) Marie-Anne Frison-Roche defines "compliance" by reference to the "monumental goals" it intends to advance with efficiency, see M.-A. Frison-Roche, *Compliance and Regulation Law Bilingual Dictionary* (online): "Viewed from the point of view of Law, Compliance is a set of principles, rules, institutions and general or individual decisions, corpus of which the primary concern is efficiency, in space and in time. The purpose is to put into practice general interest goal targeted by these gathered techniques. The list of these goals, whether negative ('fighting': corruption, terrorism, embezzlement of public funds, drug trafficking, trafficking in human beings, organ trafficking, trafficking in poisonous and contagious goods - medicines, financial products, etc.) or positive ('fighting for': access to essential goods for everyone, preservation of the environment, fundamental human rights, education, peace, transmission of the planet to future generations) shows that these are political goals. These goals correspond to the political definition of the Regulatory Law. These political goals require means which exceed the forces of the States, which are also confined within their borders. These monumental goals have therefore been internalized by public authorities in global operators. The Compliance Law corresponds to a new structuring of these global operators. This explains why the new laws put in place not only objective but structural repressions, as in France the 'Sapin 2 Law' (2016) or the 'obligation of vigilance Law' (2017)." https://mafr.fr/en/glossaire-du-droit-de-la-regulation-et-de-la-compl/?letter=c.

Global Law. Does fulfilling the objectives of compliance necessarily imply a conflict with arbitration practice, its habits and customs, its mores? The author does not think so.

Undeniably, compliance has caught up with the actors of arbitration and this phenomenon can be seen everywhere: arbitration centres, arbitrators and courts responsible for judicial review of arbitral awards are regularly called upon to take into consideration rules of compliance. Arbitration institutions and arbitrators have spontaneously anticipated the expectations generated by compliance and are effectively self-regulating. But it is also in a more authoritarian form that compliance has entered arbitration in France: indeed, the *Cour d'appel de Paris* (Paris Court of Appeal), when exercising judicial review of arbitral awards issued in disputes involving allegations of bribery of foreign public officials, utilises evidentiary methods that it has borrowed from the book of compliance in order to determine whether enforcement in France violates international public policy. It is therefore undeniable that the objectives of compliance and the actors of arbitration intersect, meet and even jostle each other somewhat (I).

At the same time, the objectives and tools of compliance stimulate and nourish arbitration practice. Arbitral tribunals, when they are confronted with illicit behaviour, have the power to apply, or at least to take into consideration, the objectives of compliance in the resolution of disputes arising from international relations, in particular in order to protect their award from the impact that could result from subsequent criticism. On another plane, compliance as a legal market also presents the arbitration players with the opportunities that its expanding field is bringing. Arbitral tribunals are thus called upon to hear disputes arising from commercial relations that are related to compliance, such as services contracts relating to the implementation of anti-corruption and anti-money laundering measures or due diligence obligations, or contracts arising from operations relating to the reduction of the carbon footprint and climate change. (3) As a result, compliance can also be the subject-matter of arbitral activity, and as such its objectives can be achieved through the activity of arbitration actors (II).

(3) This is not an exhaustive list; new areas of human rights, for example, come to mind.

I. ARBITRATION AND ITS ACTORS ARE OVERTAKEN BY COMPLIANCE

A. The legitimacy of international arbitration as the preferred method of resolution of international trade disputes requires visible and effective self-regulation by its players, who operate in a globalised market

1. Arbitration as the preferred method for resolving international trade disputes

The international consensus in support of arbitration is very strong. The almost universal acceptance of this method for resolving disputes arising out of international trade is largely due to the New York Convention on the Recognition and Enforcement of Foreign Arbitral Awards of June 10, 1958. (4) Its 168 signatory States adhere to the recognition of the principle of contractual autonomy, which underlies the effectiveness of the arbitration clause, and to the uniform system of simplified recognition of awards, without review of the merits, which is provided for in this instrument. Many modern Arbitration Laws have since adopted legislation and case law favourable to arbitration, often drawing inspiration from the UNCITRAL Model Law on International Commercial Arbitration (which is the counterpart to the New York Convention) adopted in 1985 and amended in 2006. (5) In France, the *Cour de cassation* (French Court of cassation) has long adopted a favourable attitude towards international arbitration. (6) French Law of Arbitration is based on a principle of favour in support of arbitration and its efficiency is ensured through specific rules: (7) principle of validity and autonomy of the arbitration clause outside of any state law, priority jurisdiction of arbitrators to rule on disputes regarding their own jurisdiction, correlative lack of jurisdiction of the state courts except if the arbitration agreement is blatantly void or not applicable and availability of the supporting judge, limited curial review of awards, which excludes merits review. Moreover, the Court of cassation sees international arbitration

(4) https://www.newyorkconvention.org/

(5) https://uncitral.un.org/en/texts/arbitration/modellaw/commercial_arbitration

(6) E. Gaillard, "La jurisprudence de la Cour de cassation en matière d'arbitrage international", Conférence, 13 March 2007, *Rev. arb.*, 2007.709; also see: D. Hascher, "Table ronde 1 : L'apport et la place des textes et de la jurisprudence depuis le décret du 13 janvier 2011", in *Arbitrage, 10e anniversaire de la réforme du droit français de l'arbitrage*, Club des juristes, online conference of 13 January 2021, report, pp. 3-4, https://www.leclubdesjuristes.com/wp-content/uploads/2021/02/CR-conference-arbitrage-13-janvier-2021.pdf.

(7) E. Gaillard, "La jurisprudence de la Cour de cassation", *op. cit.*

as a delocalised form of justice, and arbitral awards as international judicial decisions. (8) The scope of arbitrability is very broad: it is widely accepted that almost all disputes arising from all economic activities can be submitted to arbitration. The application to the dispute of rules of public policy does not affect the arbitrability of the civil aspects of the dispute in respect to the contractual relations of the parties. (9) In short, arbitration is a fundamentally private activity, which is inseparable from contractual freedom and is dependent on sustained arbitration-friendliness.

Therefore, the relationship between arbitration and compliance is anything but obvious. Arbitration does not belong to the category of regulated activities, i.e. activities that involve public trust and are strongly tinged with general interest. While it is not denied that arbitrators are entrusted with a jurisdictional function, which involves public interest to a certain degree, the disputes and issues submitted to arbitration generally concern strictly private interests. (10) Arbitration practice is thus truly characterised by freedom, which is built on the foundation of a broad presumption of trust. The dimension of general interest which is concerned by arbitration is indeed sufficiently guarded by the parties' right to seek judicial review of the award, or the court order (*exequatur*) allowing its execution. The control of the activity of the actors of arbitration is thus conceivable

(8) Decision of the *Cour de cassation* (French Court of cassation), *Première Chambre civile* (First Civil Chamber), 29 June 2007, *Putrabali*, (2 esp.) *Rev. Arb.*, 2007.507, report J. P. Ancel, note E. Gaillard; *RJDA*, 2007, 883, note J.-P. Ancel; P.A., 2007, No. 192, p. 20, note M. de Boisséson; *D.*, 2007, *Actu. Jur.*, 1969, note X. Delpech; *JDI*, 2007, No. 4, note T. Clay; *Gaz. Pal.*, 21-22 November 2007, p. 14, note Ph. Pinsolle: "*Mais attendu que la sentence internationale, qui n'est rattachée à aucun ordre juridique étatique, est une décision de justice internationale dont la régularité est examinée au regard des règles applicables dans le pays où sa reconnaissance et son exécution sont demandées*" (free translation: "But whereas the international award, which is not attached to any State legal system, is an international legal decision whose legality is examined in the light of the rules applicable in the country where its recognition and enforcement are sought.")

(9) Decision of the *cour d'appel de Paris* (Paris Court of Appeal), 29 March 1991, *Ganz*, *Rev. arb.*, 1991, 478, note L. Idot: *le différend n'est pas inarbitrable "du seul fait qu'une réglementation d'ordre public soit applicable au rapport de droit litigieux"* (free translation: the dispute is not inarbitrable "merely because a regulation of public order is applicable to the legal relationship at issue"); see also, Court of cassation, First Civil Chamber, 22 October 2008, *Monster Cable*, *Bull. Civ.* I, No. 233; *JCP*, 2008, p. II-10187, note L. D'Avout; *D.*, 2009, chron., 684; *RCDIP*, 2009, 69, chron. D. Bureau and H. Muir Watt; Paris Court of Appeal, 19 May 1993, *Labinal*, *Rev. arb.*, 1993, 645, note C. Jarrosson; *JDI*, 1993, 957, note L. Idot: "*les arbitres peuvent tirer les conséquences civiles d'un comportement jugé illicite au regard des règles d'ordre public pouvant être directement appliquées aux relations des parties en cause*" (free translation: "arbitrators may draw the civil consequences of conduct found to be unlawful from the standpoint of the rules of public policy that may be directly applied to the relations of the parties involved."

(10) Even in investment arbitration where, in expropriation and fair and equitable treatment disputes, there is often a question of balance between the interests of an investor and those of a sovereign State (which, by hypothesis, has taken measures that it justifies in the name of the general interest), the arbitration most often settles only the dispute arising from the specific facts of the dispute, without the decision being intended to produce legal effects with regard to third parties, and in particular with regard to the State's citizens.

only *ex post*. To put it differently, any *ex ante* regulation of arbitration appears from the outset as a contradiction and an obstacle to the freedom and favour of arbitration that must prevail. But this is not to say that the actors of arbitration are unaware of the spirit and the expectations that inspire compliance, quite the contrary.

2. Spontaneous self-regulation in the global international arbitration market

It is a fact that international arbitration is self-regulating. The actors of arbitration are aware that they have to prove themselves worthy of the quasi-universal trust that this institution enjoys. As economic actors of an expert, freedom-based, jurisdictional and unregulated activity, the actors of arbitration know that they have to deserve this trust every day. The integrity and efficiency of the professional services provided by these "dealers in virtue"(11) therefore directly conditions the social acceptance of arbitration.

In arbitration, the feeling of trust is primarily nourished by the quality of the justice rendered.(12) However, in our interconnected world, it is not enough for one to do well; one must also be seen as doing and be known to do well. Over the last twenty years, arbitration has indeed become a truly global and highly competitive market. Both an instrument and a product of globalisation, international arbitration has experienced considerable growth, driven by the expansion of transnational disputes for which arbitrators are the natural judges. Arbitration and its actors have become specialised and professionalised, and they operate globally. Also, the leading financial centres compete with each other to attract the business of resolving the most important disputes. Likewise, information on the latest developments in global arbitration market circulates freely on the Internet and dematerialised means of communication, through a specialised press(13) and other information initiatives multiplied by social networks. Today, no one can ignore the availability, in direct and almost instantaneous access, of a wealth of information on arbitration and its actors.

(11) Y. Dezalay and B. G. Garth, *Dealing in Virtue, International commercial arbitration and the construction of a transnational legal order*, foreword P. Bourdieu, Chicago, The University of Chicago Press, 1996.

(12) One legitimately expects arbitral award to meet the following qualities: intelligible, pedagogical, rational and thorough reasoning in fact and Law, so each of the parties, regardless of the outcome, can feel that they have been heard impartially, fairly and rigorously, within a reasonable time and at a reasonable cost.

(13) For example, the aptly named *Global Arbitration Review* (https://globalarbitrationreview.com/).

Thus, arbitration operators, like all those whose activities are eminently based on trust, are constantly required to meet the expectations of transparency and ethical exemplarity that are dictated by the global and interconnected society in which they evolve. Stakeholders' ongoing trust in arbitration must be fuelled by the ability of the arbitration actors to live up to such expectations of honourable behaviour. Those stakeholders are of course the potential parties in arbitration, their counsel, who are likely to promote arbitration agreements and represent clients in arbitration when a dispute arises; they also include shareholders, investors, members of the civil society, and of course legislators, courts and enforcement agencies. How effectively the arbitration actors manage to self-regulate is therefore key in order to retain the users' trust in the whole system. This reason only justifies the important self-regulation to which the actors of the arbitration community readily submit. In short, it is in the interests of the actors of arbitration to impose on themselves a self-regulation that is both effective and perceived as such. The couple formed by self-regulation and transparency constitutes a form of spontaneous, self-imposed compliance.

3. The visibility and effectiveness of self-regulation in international arbitration

At the initiative of members of the arbitration community (gathered in associations, in particular within the International Bar Association ("IBA"), in congresses, in working groups sheltered by arbitration institutions, with the International Chamber of Commerce ("ICC") in the forefront), a set of recommendations and soft law standards has emerged, the purpose of which is to self-regulate the activity of players in the arbitration market.(14) Their field is vast and covers in particular: the prevention and control of conflicts of interest,(15) the control of arbitrators' availability and the respect of good practices in terms of time and cost management,(16) parity and diversity,(17) the representation of parties in

(14) Another, equally important, objective is the necessary harmonisation of practices among operators whose diverse backgrounds include different legal traditions and cultures.

(15) *IBA Guidelines on Conflicts of Interest in International Arbitration* https://www.ibanet.org/MediaHandler?id=e2fe5e72-eb14-4bba-b10d-d33dafee8918.

(16) *ICC Arbitration Commission Report on Techniques for Controlling Time and Costs in Arbitration* https://iccwbo.org/publication/icc-arbitration-commission-report-on-techniques-for-controlling-time-and-costs-in-arbitration/.

(17) http://www.arbitrationpledge.com/.

arbitration, (18) the use of third party funding, (19) the reduction of the carbon footprint... (20)

The *IBA Guidelines on Conflicts of Interest in International Arbitration* are a topical example of this movement. (21) The duties of independence and impartiality of arbitrators are at the heart of the perception of the integrity of the arbitral process, and any breach in that field is likely to snowball into a systemic attack on the legitimacy of arbitration. It was therefore natural that the actors of international arbitration should take up these questions, in order to provide answers that are adapted to the particularity of arbitration. Since 2004, the IBA guidelines, which were drafted by the international experts composing the IBA Arbitration Committee, have transformed the approach to the identification and assessment of arbitrators' conflicts of interest. By specifying the disclosure obligations with respect to the circumstances that may give rise to reasonable doubt, with the famous red, orange and green lists, the IBA rules were thus allowing the red flags method to set foot in the international arbitration world. These guidelines were revised in 2011 and updated in 2015. Despite their non-binding nature (or perhaps because of it), they are now almost universally accepted and their undeniable scope has even inspired the largest arbitration institutions, which have in turn issued recommendations on the subject, (22) the scope of which is now recognised as having a certain authority in case law. (23)

Other examples illustrate the self-regulating and transformative capacities of arbitration:

– statements of availability of arbitrators (24) as well as monitoring (and sanction) of award issuance deadlines;

---

(18) *IBA Guidelines on Party Representation in International Arbitration*, 2013 https://www.ibanet.org/MediaHandler?id=6F0C57D7-E7A0-43AF-B76E-714D9FE74D7F.

(19) *Report of the ICCA-Queen Mary Task Force on Third-Party Funding in International Arbitration* https://cdn.arbitration-icca.org/s3fs-public/document/media_document/Third-Party-Funding-Report%20.pdf.

(20) https://www.greenerarbitrations.com/.

(21) See footnote 16.

(22) To name but two: ICC, *Note to Parties and Arbitral Tribunals on the Conduct of Arbitration under the ICC Rules of Arbitration*, 1 January 2021, https://iccwbo.org/publication/note-parties-arbitral-tribunals-conduct-arbitration/; London Court of Arbitration, *Notes for Arbitrators*, https://www.lcia.org/adr-services/lcia-notes-for-arbitrators.aspx.

(23) See Paris Court of Appeal, 26 January 2021, pole 5, chamber 16, No. RG 19/10666, about the ICC *Guidance Note on conflict disclosures by arbitrators* (February 2016) now contained in the *Note to Parties and Arbitral Tribunals on the Conduct of Arbitration under the ICC Rules of Arbitration* (1 January 2021).

(24) https://iccwbo.org/publication/icc-arbitrator-statement-acceptance-availability-impartiality-independence-form/.

- publication of the reasons for decisions rendered by arbitration centres on requests to challenge arbitrators; (25)
- parity and diversity in the governance of arbitration institutions, as well as in the constitution of arbitral tribunals and more generally the composition of conference panels and other working groups; (26)
- reduction of the carbon footprint through dematerialised submissions and generalisation of virtual hearings. (27)

Self-regulation endeavours from arbitration actors go far beyond aspirational statements. These initiatives clearly state the values and objectives pursued, which are then expressed in objective and quantifiable data. (28) Arbitration institutions such as ICC also track this information and publish it regularly.

B. The corruption exception: compliance in the judicial review of the arbitral award's conformity with international public policy by the Paris Court of Appeal

1. The context: judicial review of arbitral awards for inconsistency with international public policy due to corruption risk

A more authoritarian form of compliance has also overtaken arbitration, at least in France. This observation is based on a recent series of decisions, widely commented on, (29) which the *Cour d'appel de Paris* (Paris

(25) Since 2018 the LCIA has made available online the content of decisions rendered since 2010 on challenges to arbitrators (https://www.lcia.org/challenge-decision-database.aspx); since 2015, the ICC has made available to the parties upon request the reasons for its decisions on requests for challenge and replacement of arbitrators, *ICC Rules of Arbitration*, Appendix II, Article 5).

(26) ICC: https://iccwbo.org/global-issues-trends/diversity/; LCIA, "Launch of the Report of the Cross-Institutional Task Force on Gender Diversity in Arbitral Appointments and Proceedings", https://www.lcia.org/News/report-of-the-cross-institutional-task-force-on-gender-diversity.aspx; See joint initiative (including ICC, LCIA, ICSID) and other arbitration players, *Cross-Institutional Task Force on Gender Diversity in Arbitral Appointments and Proceedings*, 28 July 2020 Report, International Council for Commercial Arbitration (ICCA) Reports Series, Vol. 8.

(27) Campaign for Greener Arbitrations https://www.greenerarbitrations.com/.

(28) "You get what you measure." attributed to Peter Drucker.

(29) *Cour d'appel de Paris* (Paris Court of Appeal), pole 1, chamber 1, 17 November 2020, No. 18/02568, *État de Libye v. SA Sté orléanaise d'électricité et de chauffage électrique* (*Libye v. Sorelec*), JurisData No. 2020-023089, note I. Fadlallah, *JDI*, No. 3, July 2021, comm. 20; Paris Court of Appeal, 10 April 2018, No. 16/11182 and Paris Court of Appeal, 28 May 2019 (decision overturned by the decision of the *Cour de cassation* (French Court of cassation), *Première Chambre civile* (First Civil Chamber), 29 September 2021, No. 19-19.769, *cf. chronique d'arbitrage* J. Jourdan-Marques, Dalloz, 19 novembre 2021), *Sté Alstom Transport SA and a. v. Alexander Brothers Ltd.* (*Alstom v. ABL*): *Rev. arb.*, 2018, p. 574, note. E. Gaillard; *RTD com.*, 2019, p. 42, note E. Loquin; *D.*, 2018, p. 1934, obs. L. d'Avout; *D.*, 2018, p. 2448, obs. Th. Clay; *D.*, 2019, p. 1956, esp. p. 1965, obs. S. Bollée; *Dalloz actualité*, 7 June 2019, obs. J. Jourdan-Marques; *D.*, 2019, p. 2435, obs. Th. Clay; *Gaz. Pal.*, 2 July 2019, p. 22,

Court of Appeal) issued in relation to consistency with international public policy of arbitral awards. The common feature of these cases was that the debtor of the award opposed its enforcement on grounds directly or indirectly related to suspicions of corruption, influence peddling, or money laundering. The issue frequently arises in the context of disputes between a consultant who had been retained to facilitate public tender contracts, and its client after the latter refused to pay the agreed fees on the ground of anticorruption laws. The issue also arises in Investment Law, since the "clean hands" doctrine deprives the investor of international protection against expropriation or sanctions. (30)

The Court of Appeal is indeed engaged in a genuine search for the facts that may constitute the basis of such an illegality. Quoting Emmanuel Gaillard: "Like all legal systems, the French legal system is reluctant to include any decision that offends its fundamental convictions. Any suspicion on this subject requires the judge, who cannot leave any ambiguity on such an important matter, to inquire into the reality of the situation." (31) This research is based on tools inspired by compliance methods that are specific to the prevention of corruption. This change in approach represents a revolution in the judicial review of awards in respect to consistency with international public policy.

In short, the Paris Court of Appeal has reversed its own case law, which previously subjected the review of consistency of an arbitral award with international public policy on the basis of the provisions of Article 1520-5°

obs. Bensaude; *Rev. arb.*, 2019, p. 850, note E. Gaillard, "La corruption saisie par le juge du contrôle de l'ordre public international"; *CAPJIA*, 2018, p. 465, note A. Pinna. K. Mejtiyeva, *Chronique de coopération judiciaire*; *JDI*, 2019, chron. 4, p. 581; *Rev. arb.*, 2020, p. 289, note L.-C. Delanoy and R. Dethomas; Paris Court of Appeal, 16 January 2018, No. 15/21703, *MK Group v. Onix*, JurisData No. 2018-002910; *Rev. arb.*, 2018, p. 401, note S. Lemaire; *JDI*, 2018, comm. 12, p. 883, note S. Bollée; *JDI*, 2018, comm. 13, p. 898, E. Gaillard; *D.*, 2018, p. 968, obs. S. Clavel. K. Mejtiyeva, *Chronique de coopération judiciaire*: *JDI*, 2019, chron. 4, p. 581); Paris Court of Appeal, 21 February 2017, No. 15/01650, *Rep. Kirghizistan v. Belokon* (about money laundering): *JDI*, 2017, comm. 20, p. 1361, note E. Gaillard; *Rev. arb.*, 2017, p. 915, note M. Audit and S. Bollée; *D.*, 2017, p. 2559 and 2570, obs. Th. Clay; *RDC*, 2017, p. 304, note X. Boucobza and Y.-M. Serinet; *Bull. ASA*, 2017, p. 552, note L.-C. Delanoy; Paris Court of Appeal, 27 September 2016, No. 15/12614: JurisData No. 2016-030302; *Rev. arb.*, 2017, p. 942; Court of cassation, First Civil Chamber, 13 September 2017, No. 16-25.657, *Bauche v. Indagro*: JurisData No. 2017-018502; *Rev. arb.*, 2017, p. 900; *JDI*, 2017, comm. 20, p. 1361, note E. Gaillard; *Rev. arb.*, 2017, p. 942; *Rev. arb.*, 2017, p. 900; *Procédures*, 2017, comm. 268, obs. L. Weiller; *JCP G*, 2017, 1326, obs. Ch. Seraglini; *D.* 2017, p. 2571, obs. Th. Clay; *JCP E*, 2018, 1188, obs. Ch. Seraglini; *JCP E*, 2018, 1282, obs. C. Nourissat; *Bull. ASA*, 2018, p. 31, obs. A.-M. Lacoste.

(30) See for example, E. Teynier, "L'office de l'arbitre d'investissement: le cas particulier de l'investissement illicite", *Revue de l'Arbitrage*, 2019, No. 1, pp. 117-172.

(31) E. Gaillard, "La corruption saisie par le juge du contrôle de l'ordre public international", *op. cit.*, free translation of: *"Comme tous les ordres juridiques, l'ordre juridique français répugne à insérer en son sein toute décision qui heurte ses convictions fondamentales. Toute suspicion à ce sujet commande au juge, qui ne saurait laisser planer une ambiguïté quelconque sur une matière aussi importante, de s'enquérir de la réalité de la situation."*

of the *Code de procedure civile* (French Civil Procedure Code) (32) to the triple test of a flagrant (and then manifest), effective and concrete violation. (33) Abandoning the requirement of flagrant or manifest violation with the series of decisions cited, (34) the Paris Court of Appeal now exercises an in-depth control in Law and in fact over any allegation that falls within the French conception of international public policy. Although narrow and demanding, there is no question that this conception includes criminal offences such as corruption or influence peddling (35) and money laundering, (36) which are generally condemned according an "international consensus." (37)

(32) "*La reconnaissance ou l'exécution de la sentence est contraire à l'ordre public international*" (free translation: "recognition or enforcement of the award is contrary to international public policy") (formerly article 1502-5°) This provision applies to annulment applications and appeals against execution orders (*exequatur*) (by reference of Article 1525 of the *Code de procedure civile* (French Civil Procedure Code)).

(33) Court of cassation, First Civil Chamber, 21 March 2000, *Verhoeft v. Moreau*, not published, *Rev. arb.*, 2001, 804 (3e esp.), chron.Y. Derains, esp. p. 817; Paris Court of Appeal, 18 November 2004, *SA Thalès Air Défense v. GIE Euromissile*, *JCP G*, 2005, p. II-10038, note approb. G. Chabot; *JDI*, 2005, p. 357, note A. Mourre, *Rev. Lamy Concurrence*, February/April 2005, p. 68, note crit. E. Barbier de la Serre and C. Nourissat; *RTD com.*, 2005.263, note crit. E. Loquin; *JCP G*, 2005, p. I-134, obs. crit. Ch. Seraglini and "L'affaire Thalès et le non-usage immodéré de l'exception d'ordre public (ou les dérèglements de la dérèglementation)", *Cah. arb.*, vol. III, p. 86; L. Radicati di Brozolo, "L'illicéité 'qui crève les yeux': critère de contrôle des sentences au regard de l'ordre public international (à propos de l'arrêt Thalès de la Cour d'appel de Paris)", *Rev. arb.*, 2005, 529; C. Lucas de Leyssac, "Arbitrage et concurrence: retour sur Ecoswiss", *Concurrences*, 2005/1, p. 1; Paris Court of Appeal, 23 March 2006, *Sté SNF SAS v. Sté Cytec Industries BV*, *Rev. arb.*, 2006.483 and 2007.97 (3e esp.), note S. Bollée; *D.*, 2006.3033, obs. T. Clay. See also L.-Ch. Delanoy, "Le contrôle de l'ordre public au fond par le juge de l'annulation: trois constats, trois propositions", *Rev. arb.*, 2007, 177.

(34) See footnote 30.

(35) Paris Court of Appeal, 28 May 2019, *Alstom v. ABL*, *op. cit.*: "*La prohibition de la corruption d'agents publics étrangers est au nombre des principes dont l'ordre juridique français ne saurait souffrir la violation même dans un contexte international. Elle relève par conséquent de l'ordre public international. La lutte contre la corruption est un objectif poursuivi, notamment, par la Convention de l'OCDE sur la lutte contre la corruption du 17 décembre 1997, entrée en vigueur le 15 février 1999, et par la Convention des Nations Unies contre la corruption faite à Merida le 9 décembre 2003, entrée en vigueur le 14 décembre 2005.*" (free translation: "The prohibition of bribery of foreign public officials is among the principles whose violation cannot be tolerated by the French legal system, even in an international context. It is therefore a matter of international public policy. The fight against corruption is an objective pursued, in particular, by the OECD Convention on Combating Bribery of December 17, 1997, which entered into force on February 15, 1999, and by the United Nations Convention against Corruption signed in Merida on December 9, 2003, which entered into force on December 14, 2005.")

(36) Paris Court of Appeal, 21 February 2017, *Rep. Kirghizistan v. Belokon*, *op. cit.*: "*la prohibition du blanchiment est au nombre des principes dont l'ordre juridique français ne saurait souffrir la violation même dans un contexte international; qu'elle relève, par conséquent de l'ordre public international; Considérant, en effet, que la lutte contre le blanchiment d'argent provenant d'activités délictueuses fait l'objet d'un consensus international exprimé notamment dans la Convention des Nations Unies contre la corruption faite à Mérida le 9 décembre 2003, signée par 140 Etats et entrée en vigueur le 14 décembre 2005*" (free translation: "the prohibition of money laundering is among the principles whose violation cannot be tolerated by the French legal system, even in an international context; that it is, therefore, a matter of international public policy; Considering, in fact, that the fight against the laundering of money derived from criminal activities is the subject of an international consensus expressed, in particular, in the United Nations Convention against Corruption made in Merida on December 9, 2003, which was signed by 140 States and entered into force on December 14, 2005").

(37) See, Paris Court of Appeal, 21 February 2017, *Rep. Kirghizistan v. Belokon*, *op. cit.*, and 28 May 2019, *Alstom v. ABL*, *op. cit.*

The Court of Appeal continues to require a demonstration of the actual and concrete nature of the alleged illegality, (38) but it accepts that the proof can be provided by "serious, precise and concordant indications that the award would have the effect of giving force to a contract obtained by corruption." (39) To this end, the Court allows the submission of new arguments and new evidence; moreover, it does not hesitate to request them from the parties. (40) Nor does the Court hesitate to raise, upon its own initiative (*sua sponte*), the point of consistency with international public policy. (41) Further, the Court allows litigants to raise the corruption defence even though they knowingly failed to raise it before the arbitrators; (42) indeed, the implied waiver provision, which is provided by Article 1466 of the French Civil Procedure Code, (43) does not apply where judicial review

(38) Paris Court of Appeal, pole 1, chamber 1, 27 March 2018, *Antrix*, No. 16/03596.

(39) Paris Court of Appeal, 16 May 2017, *Rep. Congo v. Tax and Customs*, *op. cit.*, free translation of: "*des indices graves, précis et concordants que la sentence aurait pour effet de donner force à un contrat obtenu par corruption*"; in Paris Court of Appeal, 10 April 2018, *Alstom v. ABL*, the Court mentioned and provided a list of relevant "*faisceau d'indices*" ("red flags"); in Paris Court of Appeal, 28 May 2019, *Alstom v. ABL*, the Court held "*il résulte de ces éléments des indices graves, précis et concordants de ce que les sommes versées [...] finançaient et rémunéraient des activités de corruption d'agents publics*" (free translation: "it follows from these elements that there is serious, precise and concordant evidence that the sums paid [...] financed and remunerated activities involving the corruption of public officials"); Paris Court of Appeal, 17 November 2020, *Libye v. Sorelec*: "*Il est ainsi démontré par un faisceau d'indices suffisamment graves, précis et concordants que le Protocole entre l'État de Libye et SORELEC a couvert des relations sous-jacentes entretenues entre cette dernière et M. O., permettant à SORELEC de retirer les bénéfices de ce Protocole obtenu de manière illicite*" (free translation: "It is thus demonstrated by a body of sufficiently serious, precise and concordant evidence that the Protocol between the State of Libya and SORELEC covered up the underlying relations maintained between the latter and Mr. O., enabling SORELEC to derive the benefits of this Protocol, which it had obtained in an illicit manner.") -- see also the decision of the Paris Court of Appeal, 21 February 2017, No. 15/01650, *Rep. Kirghizistan v. Belokon*, about money laundering, see also section I.B.2.

(40) In Paris Court of Appeal, 10 April 2018, *Alstom v. ABL*, the Court reopened the discussions and invited submissions on indications of potential influence peddling or corruption.

(41) First decision of the Paris Court of Appeal, 10 April 2018, *Alstom v. ABL*, *op. cit.*

(42) Paris Court of Appeal, 17 November 2020, *Libye v. Sorelec*, *op. cit.*: "*[l]e respect de la conception française de l'ordre public international implique que le juge étatique chargé du contrôle puisse apprécier le moyen tiré de la contrariété à l'ordre public international alors même qu'il n'a pas été invoqué devant les arbitres et que ceux-ci ne l'ont pas mis dans le débat*" (free translation: "the respect for the French concept of international public policy means that the state judge responsible for the review can assess the plea of conflict with international public policy even though it was not raised before the arbitrators and the arbitrators did not put it in the debate.") See also the decision of the Paris Court of Appeal, 2 April 2019, No. 16/24358, *Dalloz actualité*, 17 April 2019, obs. J. Jourdan-Marques; *Rev. arb.*, 2019.304: the Article 1466 "*ne vise pas les seules irrégularités procédurales, mais tous les griefs qui constituent des cas d'ouverture du recours en annulation des sentences, à l'exception des moyens fondés sur l'article 1520, 5°, du code de procédure civile*" (free translation: "does not refer solely to procedural irregularities, but to all the complaints that constitute grounds for an action to set aside an award, with the exception of pleas based on Article 1520, 5° of the French Civil Procedure Code.")

(43) Applicable in international arbitration by reference in Article 1506 of the French Civil Procedure Code.

of awards is based on contrariety with *substantive* international public policy. (44)

However, the control in fact and in Law that the Court undertakes to exercise remains, in principle, limited by the prohibition of review on the merits. (45) In the *Schneider* case, the *Cour de cassation* (French Court of cassation) held that "the judge in charge of the annulment is the judge of the award in order to admit or refuse its incorporation into the French legal system and not the judge of the case for which the parties have concluded an arbitration agreement." (46) The appeal was based on ground of inconsistency with international public policy (47) due to corruption, and on an argument that the award had erred in dismissing the illegality defence the respondent had raised to resist contract enforcement (in that case, the Court of Appeal had also denied the appeal against the exequatur order). (48) It is not easy to identify the point of balance that

(44) This is not the case for *procedural* public policy, which remains within the scope of the waiver provided for in Article 1466 of the French Civil Procedure Code (see the decision of the Paris Court of Appeal, October 12, 2021, RG No. 20/0230, "*Ce texte ne vise pas les seules irrégularités procédurales mais tous les griefs qui constituent des cas d'ouverture du recours en annulation des sentences, en ce compris le principe d'égalité des armes qui relève de l'ordre public international de protection, à l'exception des moyens tirés de ce que la reconnaissance ou l'exécution de la sentence violerait l'ordre public international de fond*" (free translation: "This text does not refer only to procedural irregularities, but to all the grievances that constitute grounds for annulment of the awards, including the principle of equality of arms, which is a matter of international public policy, with the exception of arguments based on the fact that the recognition or enforcement of the award would violate substantive international public policy.")

(45) In the words of I. Fadlallah: "*Le juge de l'annulation, qui est juge de la sentence et non de l'affaire, ne devrait connaître de la corruption qu'à travers la sentence, au titre de l'ordre public. Dans la conception dominante il y a peu, il ne peut soulever une question non soumise aux arbitres. Une telle prérogative relève de la révision de la sentence rendue, si les conditions en sont réunies. Il ne peut non plus modifier les faits ou les qualifications retenues par les arbitres, la révision au fond étant, en toutes circonstances, proscrite.*" (free translation: "The annulment judge, who is the judge of the award and not of the case, should only know about corruption through the award, as a matter of public policy. In the view prevailing not long ago, he cannot raise an issue not submitted to the arbitrators. Such a prerogative falls within the scope of the review of the award if the conditions are met. Nor may he modify the facts or the qualifications adopted by the arbitrators, revision of the merits being, in all circumstances, prohibited.") – see commentary of *Libye v. Sorelec op. cit.*, point 6; I Fadlallah also emphasises, in point 7, the disregard of the New York Convention. Indeed, its Article V contains an exhaustive list of cases of refusal of enforcement and is exclusive of any other grievance. E. Gaillard and G. Bermann have written in this regard: "*The grounds for refusal under article V do not include an erroneous decision in law or in fact by the arbitral tribunal. A court seized with an application for recognition and enforcement under the Convention may not review the merits of the arbitral tribunal's decision. This principle is unanimously confirmed in the case law and commentary on the New York Convention*", *UNCITRAL Secretariat Guide on the Convention on the Recognition and Enforcement of Foreign Arbitral Awards (New York, 1958)*, 2016.

(46) Decision of the Court of cassation, First Civil Chamber, 12 February 2014, No. 10-17.076, *Schneider*, free translation of: "le juge de l'annulation est juge de la sentence pour admettre ou refuser son insertion dans l'ordre juridique français et non juge de l'affaire pour laquelle les parties ont conclu une convention d'arbitrage."

(47) Article 1502-5° of the French Civil Procedure Code, now 1520-5°.

(48) Paris Court of Appeal, 10 September 2009, RG No. 08/11757.

allows the full control in fact and in Law to be confined to the perimeter of the award. (49) Eminent authors affirm, without it being possible to really contradict them, that the control is in fact an examination of the merits of the case. (50) Nevertheless, the Court of cassation has recently reminded the Court of Appeal that its assessment of the alleged illegality cannot contradict the factual elements that come from the arbitration proceedings: thus, in the case of *Alstom v. ABL*, the Court of cassation censured on 29 September 2021 the judgment of May 28, 2019 for distorting the minutes of the hearing of the witnesses heard by the arbitral tribunal, criticising the Court for having considered as established elements of fact that contradicted the testimony. (51) This call to order by the regulatory court highlights the great practical difficulty that the review judge faces, within the constrained framework of his or her office, in carrying out a factual and legal review of issues that often involve a very detailed enquiry into the facts. The fact that often no criminal prosecution has been initiated makes it even more complicated. If this factual enquiry in the allegations of corruption has already been carried out by the arbitrators, the Court must at least take it into account in order to compare it with the documents in the file and any new documents that may be filed in the appeal. When corruption has not been alleged before the arbitral tribunal (in *Alstom v. ABL*, the defence raised in arbitration was based on alleged breaches of contractual compliance obligations, which the Court

(49) The reasoning of the Court of Appeal in *Libya v. Sorelec* demonstrates the difficult dividing line between review of the award and review of the merits – see point 39: "*Au surplus, le contrôle du juge de l'annulation a une finalité propre et distincte de celui du tribunal arbitral auquel en l'espèce, le moyen tiré de ce que le Protocole serait entaché de corruption n'a pas été soumis. Le juge de l'annulation peut ainsi, dans le respect du principe de non révision de la sentence, rechercher dans l'ensemble des faits qui lui sont soumis, les indices de nature à caractériser l'illicéité du Protocole, en particulier en examinant si le contournement de procédures internes et des autorités de contrôle libyennes constitue un des indices de la corruption alléguée, nonobstant les motifs que le tribunal arbitral a retenus, en application du principe de l'estoppel et de la théorie de l'apparence, pour juger que SORELEC pouvait légitimement croire en l'apparente légitimité du ministre de la Justice du gouvernement provisoire émanant du Parlement.*" (free translation: "Moreover, the review by the annulment judge has its own purpose and is distinct from that of the arbitral tribunal to which, in this case, the plea that the Protocol is tainted by corruption was not submitted. The annulment judge may thus, in compliance with the principle of non-review of the award, seek in all the facts submitted to him, the indications that the Protocol is unlawful, in particular by examining whether the bypassing of internal procedures and Libyan control authorities constitutes one of the indications of the alleged corruption, notwithstanding the reasons given by the arbitral tribunal, in application of the principle of estoppel and the theory of appearance, for holding that SORELEC could legitimately believe in the apparent legitimacy of the Minister of Justice of the provisional government emanating from the Parliament.")

(50) See for example, I. Fadlallah, commentary of *Libye v. Sorelec op. cit.*; J. Ortscheidt, "Table ronde 3: Le contrôle étatique des sentences arbitrales", report, *in Arbitrage, 10e anniversaire de la réforme du droit français de l'arbitrage, op. cit.*, p. 13, https://www.leclubdesjuristes.com/wp-content/uploads/2021/02/CR-conference-arbitrage-13-janvier-2021.pdf.

(51) Court of cassation, First Civil Chamber, 29 September 2021, No. 19-19.769, see footnote 30.

does not review(52)), the Court must at least take into account the factual elements, and in particular the testimonies, if they are not contradicted (in particular, no criminal proceedings had been brought). This decision illustrates the danger of allowing retrospective review of the award on the occasion of late allegations of corruption that the arbitrators were not able to investigate or examine as such.

2. The tools borrowed from compliance: the evidentiary method known as *faisceau d'indices*(53)

As mentioned above,(54) the Paris Court of Appeal assesses whether the award is contrary to international public policy on the basis of "*indices graves, précis et concordants*" ("serious, specific and concordant indicators") that the effect of the award would give force to a contract obtained by corruption.(55) Such a conclusion may be drawn from an examination of the facts, even if they have not resulted in criminal prosecution.(56) From a methodological point of view, the Court borrowed from compliance regulation a list of indicators(57) (which Anglo-American supervisory authorities(58) commonly refer to as red flags). This means that, in order to assess whether a bribery offence is likely to have been committed, the supervisory judge applies the red flag criteria specific to compliance. For example, in the *Alstom v. ABL* case, the Court invited the parties to make submissions

(52) Paris Court of Appeal, pole 1, chamber 1, 10 April 2018, *Alstom v. ABL*, No. 16/11182.

(53) Literally, "*faisceau d'indices*" means bundle of clues, or bundle of indicators.

(54) See cases mentioned at footnote 30.

(55) For example, see Paris Court of Appeal, pole 1, chamber I, 16 May 2017, *Rep. Congo v. Customs and Tax Consultancy* and Paris Court of Appeal, pole 1, chamber 1, 10 April 2018, *Alstom v. ABL*.

(56) See the decisions *Alstom v. ABL* and *Libye v. Sorelec op. cit.* for examples of the indicators the Court considered. At point 38 of *Sorelec*: "*L'annulation de la sentence partielle en cause est encourue s'il est démontré par un faisceau d'indices suffisamment graves, précis et concordants qu'en homologuant le Protocole conclu entre l'État de Libye et SORELEC, elle couvrirait des faits de corruption, sans qu'il y ait lieu, eu égard au caractère occulte de cette activité, d'exiger que l'État de Libye ait engagé des poursuites pénales.*" (free translation: "The partial award in question may be annulled if it is shown by a body of sufficiently serious, precise and concordant evidence that, by approving the Protocol concluded between the State of Libya and SORELEC, it would cover up acts of corruption, without there being any reason, in view of the hidden nature of this activity, to require the State of Libya to have initiated criminal proceedings.")

(57) For a detailed list of these indicators in relation to consultancy contracts, see the decision *Alstom v. ABL* of 10 April 2018, *op. cit.*: absence or insufficiency of documents justifying diligence, insufficiency of material and human resources, proportionality of remuneration with regard to diligence, remuneration on a percentage basis, deficient or insincere accounting, award of the contract in spite of a bid that is less favourable than those of the competitors, notorious corruption (of the country, of the sector, of the client).

(58) E. Glucksmann, "Oppetit et l'illicite dans le commerce international", in Institut des hautes études internationales, *L'illicite*, coll. "Grandes pages du droit international", Paris, Pedone, Vol. 7, 2021, pp. 241-292, esp. p. 289; Ch. Dargham, J. Feigher, M. de Fontmichel, B. Siino, "Arbitrage et compliance: au cœur de la lutte contre la corruption en matière civile et commerciale", *Revue internationale de la compliance et de l'éthique des affaires*, No. 6, doss. 192, December 2019.

in respect to the identified red flags and requested the production of additional documents. As a result of this review, the Court of Appeal assesses whether, in the particular case, sufficiently serious, precise and concordant indicators must lead to a conclusion that the plea of illegality was justified, and that the arbitral award should not be given effect.

Conceptually, this approach is not dissimilar to that which would be adopted by arbitrators faced with the same problem. From a practical point of view, however, the means available to the Court are limited. In contrast, international arbitrators have the time, resources and experience to organise a very thorough evidentiary phase, involving a rigorous comparison of the allegations with the documentary reality of the case. The means of the Court of Appeal are not comparable. The assessment of the sufficiently serious, precise and concordant indicators, however, requires an immersion in the substantive file. Admittedly, neither arbitrators nor the Court of Appeal are held to the standard of proof that apply before criminal courts having to make a finding of criminal guilt. Yet, assessing the likelihood of allegations of corruption in order to draw civil consequences(59) is a very serious matter, and a rather fact-intensive one. Bearing in mind that *faisceau d'indices* lend themselves to approximations and presumptions, it is advisable to use utmost caution before drawing from red flags the conclusion that an unlawful act was committed.

Finally, when it comes to the investigation into facts that may fall under a penal qualification, the question of the standard of proof is absolutely central. When none of the indicators alone are sufficient to establish the conclusion that the offence has been committed, the application of the *faisceau d'indices* method should require a demonstration that it results from the indicators, considered as a whole, that only an act of corruption could explain that the contract in question was entered into. The Court of Appeal said the same thing when it concluded that the failure to comply with the rules of transparency in public procurement is an insufficient indication of corruption as such to justify the nullity of the contract concluded, in the absence of a demonstration of actual corruption.(60) The question arises in the same terms, if not with the same means, before the arbitrators and the judge reviewing the award. As it stands, the practice of the Paris Court of Appeal cannot be ignored by those involved in international arbitration, which will be the subject of further comments below.

---

(59) E. Glucksmann, "Oppetit et l'illicite dans le commerce international", *op. cit.*

(60) D. Chilstein, "Arbitrage et Droit Pénal", *Rev. arb.*, 2009, No. 3; Paris Court of Appeal, 16 May 2017, *Rep. Congo v. Customs and Tax Consultancy*, *op. cit.*

II. ARBITRATION TAKES OVER THE ADJUDICATION OF COMMERCIAL DISPUTES ARISING FROM COMPLIANCE

A. Compliance is as an arbitrable matter

1. The impact of French case law on consistency with international public policy

To the extent the Paris Court of Appeal (61) allows a review of points of fact and Law that underpin issues of international public policy, this case law prompts reflection on its impact on arbitration practice. Arbitrators sitting or anticipating award enforcement in France, ought to be mindful of the Paris court approach when considering facts that are likely to be relevant in respect to compliance and the criminal offences compliance seeks to prevent. (62)

We will first look at cases in which, despite the presence of compliance elements, the Court of Appeal does not exercise judicial review. Our focus will be on objections based on allegations of breach of compliance obligations arising from contractual sources and those arising from local regulations of public policy. In both cases, allegations of this nature are the arbitrator's reserved domain. Indeed, the Paris Court of Appeal's views any allegation that an arbitral tribunal disregarded compliance rules of contractual (63) or legal (64) sources as a point of substance that is extraneous to the scope of international public policy, and therefore outside the scope of its review.

(61) Not only that. See for example: "Corruption and Money Laundering in International Arbitration: A Toolkit for Arbitrators" (Basel Institute on Governance, 2019), an effort which presents arbitrators and counsel with methodological advice in toolbox format. Available at: https://baselgovernance.org/publications/corruption-and-money-laundering-international-arbitration-toolkit-arbitrators

(62) E. Gaillard, "La corruption saisie par les arbitres du commerce international", *Rev. arb.*, 2017, No. 3.

(63) Paris Court of Appeal, 10 April 2018, *Alstom v. ABL, op. cit.*

(64) Paris Court of Appeal, pole 1, chamber I, 16 May 2017, *Rép. Démocratique Congo v. Customs and Tax Consultancy, op. cit.*: "Considérant que si l'inobservation des règles de transparence dans la passation des marchés publics est un indice particulièrement significatif de telles infractions, elle ne saurait être sanctionnée pour elle-même, indépendamment d'une atteinte actuelle à l'objectif de lutte contre la corruption ; Considérant qu'en l'espèce, la RDC n'a pas allégué devant les arbitres que le contrat litigieux serait entaché de corruption ; qu'elle ne le fait pas davantage devant cette cour ;" (free translation: "Whereas if the non-observance of the rules of transparency in the awarding of public contracts is a particularly significant indicator of such offences, it cannot be sanctioned for its own sake, independently of an actual infringement of the objective of combating corruption Whereas in the present case, the DRC did not allege before the arbitrators that the disputed contract was tainted by corruption; whereas it did not do so before this Court either;").

The first issue arises from compliance-specific contractual clauses. One such stipulation is the "no-agent" clause. By requiring the non-intervention of an intermediary, this clause may obviate the need to enquire into the existence of bribery, as its breach alone may allow for a refusal of performance or termination. (65) General "compliance with the law" clauses may also lend themselves to this use, provided that their language is sufficiently clear and that it can be established that mandatory statutory provisions of the governing law have been disregarded. At the other end of the spectrum, however, unilateral voluntary pledges that companies make in the context of corporate social responsibility programs are generally aspirational declarations and for that reason often lack any specific binding content.

Moreover, arbitrators can be presented with alleged breaches of compliance obligations or procurement rules derived from mandatory statutory rules, whether they are contained in the governing law of the contract or in the law of a different country which may have connections with the dispute. This issue is not limited to corruption or money laundering. Indeed, it follows from the irresistible expansion of compliance in fields such as human rights, climate change and social responsibility that arbitration actors must be prepared for increasingly frequent and serious interactions with public policy.

In the above situations, the arbitrators are in principle free to decide how they wish to approach compliance-related issues, insofar as they are not confronted with indications suggesting that, beyond the compliance allegations, violations of the major infringements that compliance aims to prevent may be involved. However, when the circumstances of the case are susceptible to be relevant to the definition of international public policy as understood by the Paris Court of Appeal, arbitrators are expected to use their investigative powers to their full extent. This applies even if in fact the parties have not mentioned criminal misconduct or compliance violations.

---

(65) The issue arose in the Taiwan frigate case, where the no-agent clause allowed the buyer to deduct the commission or terminate the contract: the arbitrators upheld the allegation of contractual breach without having to deal with the issue of proof of corruption. See E. Gaillard, "La corruption saisie par les arbitres du commerce international", *op. cit.*

2. The powers of arbitration confronted with compliance and the violations it seeks to prevent

Arbitrators have significant freedom when dealing with those issues. They have discretion to administrate the proceedings as they see fit, and notably under French International Arbitration Law, arbitral tribunals are not required to stay the proceedings in the event of criminal prosecution or investigations by the regulatory authorities. (66) Freedom also characterises all issues relating to evidence, such as the burden, the means or the standard of proof. (67)

It is widely recognised that arbitrators have the power to raise on their own initiative (*sua sponte*) issues of corruption or money laundering on the ground of public policy. (68) Especially when arbitral tribunals suspect that the circumstances of the dispute are likely to give rise to issues that are relevant to the scope of review of substantive public policy by the Court of Appeal, they should not hesitate to raise this issue on their own initiative – and, of course, in such case arbitrators must be sure to give all parties a fair opportunity to be heard.

(66) In the event of criminal proceedings relating to facts also discussed in the arbitration, international arbitrators have the right but not the obligation to stay the proceedings (Article 4 of the *Code de procedure pénale* (French Criminal Procedure Code) applies only in domestic arbitration). The stay of proceedings is therefore a pragmatic consideration, as an arbitral tribunal may or may not consider it useful to wait for the outcome of the criminal investigation, for example if there is a serious risk that the effectiveness of the arbitral award will depend on the decision of the criminal court on the characterisation of the facts. See P. Mayer, "L'office de l'arbitre en arbitrage commercial", *Rev. arb.*, 2019, No.1.

(67) The Civil Law tradition relies on *intime conviction*. International arbitration practice is strongly inspired by the Common Law approach: a balance of probabilities will suffice for a purely commercial matter, but for an arbitrator's assessment of Criminal Law issues, it would not be shocking to require proof beyond a reasonable doubt.

(68) E. Gaillard, "La corruption saisie par les arbitres du commerce international", *Rev. arb.*, 2017, pp. 805-836; I. Fadlallah comment on the decision of the Paris Court of Appeal, pole 1, Chamber 1, 17 November 2020, No. 18/02568, *Lybie v. Sorelec*, *JDI*, No. 3, July 2021, comm. 20; S. Lemaire, "La preuve de la corruption", *Rev. arb.*, 2020, p. 185; *JDI*, 2017, comm. 20, p. 1361, note E. Gaillard on the decision of the Court of cassation, First Civil Chamber, 13 September 2017; J.-Y. Garaud, "L'office de l'arbitre en arbitrage commercial : caractérisation de l'illicéité et mise en œuvre des sanctions", *Rev. arb.*, 2019, p. 173; D. Baizeau, T. Hayes, "The Arbitral Tribunal's Duty and Power to Address Corruption Sua Sponte", ICCA Congress Services, Vol. 19, 2017, pp. 225-265; Ch. Seraglini, "Le contrôle par le juge de l'absence de contrariété de la sentence à l'ordre public international: le passé, le présent, le futur", *Rev. arb.*, 2020, p. 347; E. Gaillard, "The emergence of transnational responses to corruption in international arbitration", *Arbitration International* 2019; E. Teynier, "L'office de l'arbitre d'investissement : le cas particulier de l'investissement illicite", *Rev. arb.*, 2019, p. 117; M.-D. Veit, "Proving Legality instead of Corruption, in The Powers and Duties of an Arbitrator", *in* P. Shaughnessy and S. Tung (eds), *The Powers and Duties of an Arbitrator: Liber Amicorum Pierre A. Karrer*, Alphen aan den Rijn, Kluwer Law International, 2017, pp. 373-382; I. Fadlallah and D. Hascher, "Les grandes décisions du droit de l'arbitrage commercial", on the decisions Court of cassation, First Civil Chamber, 19 November 1991, No. 89-22.042, *Sté Grands Moulins de Strasbourg v. Sté Cie Continentale France*, and Court of cassation, Second Civil Chamber, 20 February 1991, *Sté SICA Veradour v. Éts Larroche*, No. 89-19.159, *D.*, 2019, pp. 292-312).

Whether arbitrators should consider raising on their own initiative an issue arising only from rules of compliance deriving from the contract or from local law may depend on circumstances. For example, it may be considered normal to raise *sua sponte* the application of a mandatory rule that belongs to the governing law, if the arbitrators' mission and the circumstances of the case so permit. The question may also arise in the case of a mandatory rule contained in the law of the debtor's place of residence, given the arbitrators' obligation to make an enforceable award. (69) If the mandatory rules come from the law of the seat of the arbitration, deciding to apply the rules of compliance may be a less obvious conclusion(even less so in view of the delocalised conception of arbitration in France). However, there is no doubt that arbitrators have the power to raise *sua sponte* such a question.

It is on this occasion that the use of the red flags method is fully justified because, in accordance with the arbitration agreement, the arbitral tribunal is in principle the only indisputable judge of the substance of the case. Indeed, arbitrators have the required experience to organise in-depth debates and hear witnesses and experts. They also have real investigative powers and the power to sanction an the uncooperative party by drawing negative presumptions. At the end of their examination, the arbitrators will be in a position to rule on the possible qualification of the allegations of corruption (or other major offence) and, if necessary, to draw all the civil consequences that are necessary in terms of unenforceability of the illicit agreement (or obtained through corruption). The arbitrators will also be able to rule on reparations and restitution, an area in which they have significant discretion. (70)

Is it also desirable to raise a question of compliance with a mandatory compliance rule on the arbitrators' own initiative? This is a different question: answering it presupposes, in particular, that the circumstances of the dispute give rise to suspicion of a serious risk of subsequent difficulty on the basis of a violation of international public policy. The answer will

(69) For example, in ICC arbitration see Article 42 "In all matters not expressly provided for in the Rules, the Court and the arbitral tribunal shall act in the spirit of the Rules and shall make every effort to make sure that the award is enforceable at law."

(70) However, care must be taken not to expose oneself to the criticism of giving effect, by equivalent, to the unlawful agreement. *A priori* in the case of corruption, the two parties being convinced of fraudulent concert, the adage "*in pari causa turpitudinis cessat repetitio*" comes into play. See on this point, J.-Y. Garaud, "L'office de l'arbitre en arbitrage commercial: caractérisation de l'illicéité et mise en œuvre des sanctions", *op. cit.*

also depend on the connection of the mandatory compliance rule to the circumstances of the dispute and to the arbitrator's mission.

B. Arbitration and disputes arising from the compliance market

1. Compliance, a new business for arbitration players

Arbitration players also see compliance as a new field of intervention. Indeed, as an industry compliance generates professional services which, in turn, are likely to produce potential disputes.

Numerous service contracts deal with the implementation of compliance measures, whether in terms of anti-corruption, anti-money laundering, due diligence or other future regulations. These services are very diverse: auditing, consulting, assistance, training and monitoring. They all lend themselves to arbitration.

Climate change, in the wake of the Kyoto Protocol and the Paris Agreement, is another example of the points of contact between compliance and arbitration. Public and private operators wishing to decarbonise their activities have recourse to contractual mechanisms, notably through emissions trading. These activities involve complex interactions between public regulations, international rules and commercial contracts. All this represents an emerging market for many legal actors, including arbitration actors. (71) Indeed, the characteristics of these activities make the resulting disputes particularly compatible with arbitration. Only arbitration allows to combine party-autonomy and flexibility in order to efficiently settle complex technical issues, in compliance with multiple legislations, in full confidentiality, without appeal and, if necessary, within the framework of an accelerated procedure leading to a decision that can be enforced throughout the world.

2. Transitioning from confrontation to collaboration

Regardless of the slightly ominous premise of a *confrontation* between the objectives of compliance and the actors of arbitration, this conclusion ends on a cautiously optimistic note. The author is in favour of freedom

(71) *ICC Commission report, Resolving Climate Change Related Disputes through Arbitration and ADR*, November 2019; available at https://iccwbo.org/publication/icc-arbitration-and-adr-commission-report-on-resolving-climate-change-related-disputes-through-arbitration-and-adr/.

for arbitration, but agrees that deserving such freedom requires accountability. It is up to the arbitrators to demonstrate their abilities to take into account the monumental goals that compliance seeks to achieve and to stay on top of the requirements of international public policy. Arbitrators concerned with the effectiveness of their award are bound by a real duty of vigilance and anticipation. They are also compliance actors when they come to suspect that the actual motive or the role of the contract in dispute could be related to corruption or money laundering. It is foreseeable that the growing demands of climate change and environmental mandatory laws will reinforce these duties. In turn, however, compliance requirements generate commercial activities, and with them come disputes, some of them complex, which arbitration can help resolving effectively. Thus, we have come full circle: while the objectives of compliance contribute to the perennial social acceptance of arbitration, arbitration contributes to the achievement of the objectives of compliance.

CHAPTER IV
THE JUDGE IN COMPLIANCE LAW

The Judge, the Compliance Obligation and the Company. The Compliance Evidence System*

Marie-Anne Frison-Roche

Agrégée des Facultés de droit

Professor of Regulatory and Compliance Law

Director of the *Journal of Regulation & Compliance (JoRC)*

Director of the *European School of Regulation and Compliance Law*

1. Introduction. The system of Evidence Law. In order to articulate the evidentiary system of Compliance Law, it must first be admitted that Evidence Law is a system in its own autonomy and perspective. (1) This could be difficult to accept, especially in Civil Law systems, as Evidence is most often considered either as an extension of the substantial branches of Law or as an extension of General Procedural Law. (2) This is undoubtedly why Evidence, deeply studied in British and American Law schools, is studied so little in other places and presented in a quite abstract way, whereas in practice everything depends on it and it is essential to identify its principles that apply regardless of the different concrete situations.

---

* This article is based on a bilingual working paper, along with additional developments, numerous technical references and hypertext links. It is accessible at the following address: https://mafr.fr/en/article/prolegomenes-pour-le-systeme-probatoire-de-la-comp/.

(1) J. Doak, C. Mcgourlay, M. Thomas, *Evidence: Law and Context*, Routledge, 2018.

(2) For a full account of the various positions on this subject, see E. Vergès, G. Vial and O. Leclerc, *Droit de la preuve*, "Thémis" Serie, 2nd ed, Paris, PUF, 2022, pp. 31 *et seq*.

It is therefore in the substantial branches of Law, in particular Competition Law (3) and Financial Regulatory Law, (4) that the question of an evidentiary system arises, undoubtedly because these branches of Law are more sensitive to factual situations and maybe because the American thinking is very influential in Economic Law, notably through Law & Economics.

However, the evidentiary system is based on what we might call an "evidentiary square" that operates regardless of the different concrete situations, a system whose very principles Compliance Law seems to reject. This increases what is more generally the difficulty of articulating compliance techniques and the classical fundamental legal principles. (5)

This difficulty becomes a clear contradiction when compliance is poorly defined as the obligation for companies to show (which is a matter of proof, since showing means proving) that they have complied with all the regulations applicable to them. On the other hand, in a State governed by the Rule of Law, the subjects of Law enjoy freedom of action, and are liable for breaches of the Law and infringements of the rights of others only *ex post*. So, if companies are obliged to show their effective respect of all regulations in *ex ante*, compliance is then an attack against the Rule of Law, maybe justified by the Security imperative, but an attack nevertheless...

Fortunately, however, Compliance does not have to be defined in this way. Compliance Law consists of all the principles, institutions, rules and decisions which, in an alliance between public authorities and crucial companies, are substantially aimed at achieving Monumental Systemic Goals: (6) as an *ex ante* branch of Law that protects systems and the human beings involved in them, Compliance Law aims to detect, prevent and build so that systems in the future are less exposed to disaster than they would be if nothing was done, or even so that these systems are better thanks to compliance mechanisms of detection and prevention.

(3) For a British and American perspective, D. Mantzari, *Courts, Regulators, and the scrutiny of Economic Evidence,* Oxford, Oxford University Press, 2022; for the European Union perspective, J.-F. Castillo de la Torre & E. Gippini Fournier, *Evidence, Proof and Judicial Review in EU Competition Law,* "Elgar Competition Law and Practice" Serie, Cheltenham, Edward Elgar Publishing, 2017; see also J.-Chr. Roda, "Le standard de preuve : réflexion à partir du droit de la concurrence", *D.* 2021. Chron., pp. 1297-1303.

(4) N. Ida, *La preuve devant l'Autorité des marchés financiers*, preface by H. Barbier, foreword D. Schmidt, Paris, Dalloz, 2022.

(5) On this fundamental issue, which is that compliance system cannot and must not be outside the Law, see M.-A. Frison-Roche, "Compliance Law", 2016, https://www.mafr.fr/en/article/le-droit-de-la-compliance/; "Reinforce the Judge and the Lawyer to impose Compliance Law as a characteristic of the Rule of Law", *this book*.

(6) *Ibid.*

The action required of companies in relation to precisely identified systemic goals – goals that are both more limited (it is not about all regulations) and more gigantic (eradicating corruption, establishing effective equality between human beings, curbing climate change, etc.), which require the implementation of permanent structures and a series of behaviours – requires a specific Evidence System to be attached to it, one that is both respectful of the General Evidence principles (7) and specific to this new branch of Law that is Compliance.

The evidentiary system of Compliance is made up, firstly, of specific objects of proof, attached, on the one hand, to Compliance Structures and, on the other hand, to Compliance Behaviours. Secondly, the great specificity of compliance, which is often criticised, lies in the burden of proof, the load of which rests on companies, even when they are defending themselves procedurally. This burden is justified by the position of companies, but also by the scope of the objects of proof, a scope that must therefore remain strictly defined, while the requirements of other branches of Law (such as Criminal Law and Repressive Administrative Law) must be integrated, because while Compliance Law is indeed a specific branch of Law justifying new evidentiary obligations, it cannot destroy the other branches of Law and must take account of the legal system in which it is deployed. Thirdly, the magnitude of the evidential stakes is such that the means of proof have multiplied, and even have to be constructed on purpose, according to the triptych of effectiveness, efficiency and efficacy expected from the compliance system itself with regard to the Monumental Goals (and not the regulations). Science and technology, derived from the systems involved in the Compliance Monumental Goals, play a major role in this. (8) Fourthly, because Compliance Law is an *ex ante* branch of Law and yet the Judge is at the centre of it, it is logical that all efforts should focus on the pre-construction of evidence, carried out by the company either by force or voluntarily.

(7) For a similar approach, see T. Kern, "Blockchain and intellectual property rights: blockchain anchoring, a ground-breaking means of proof to the rescue of creators?", *I.B.L.J.* 2021, 2, pp. 279-287.

(8) This puts into perspective what seems to be a *summa divisio* in the *Dictionnaire de l'Académie française* which, in defining what "*prouver*" ("to prove") is, distinguishes between what is the establishment of truth on the one hand and what would be "*preuve juridique*" ("legal proof") on the other: "*Prouver : Établir la vérité d'une proposition ou la réalité d'un fait, au moyen d'un raisonnement, d'une démonstration, d'un témoignage, etc. (Droit): Démontrer l'existence d'un fait ou d'un acte dans les formes admises par la loi, en fournir la preuve juridique.*" (free translation: "To prove: To establish the truth of a proposition or the reality of a fact, by means of reasoning, demonstration, testimony, etc. (Law): To demonstrate the existence of a fact or an act in the manner permitted by law, to provide legal proof thereof."), 9th ed., 2020. See generally N. Le Douarin & C. Puigelier (eds), *Science, éthique et droit*, Paris, Odile Jacob, 2007, especially the contribution on "Science et justice: des empreintes digitales aux empreintes génétiques: de la recherche de la preuve indiscutable", a hypothesis in which it is science (and no longer Law) that makes the allegation incontestable (p. 135 *et seq.*).

I. PRE-REQUISITE: SITUATING PROOF AND COMPLIANCE IN RELATION TO EACH OTHER

2. The clash between the Evidentiary System and what would be the Company's obligation to demonstrate its "conformity" with the applicable regulations. It is worth recalling the basic principles of the evidentiary system (A) in order to emphasise that, at first sight, Compliance Law, when wrongly defined by "conformity," would destroy them (B).

A. The basis: the Evidentiary Square

3. Evidence, the strategic heart of Law and of the trial to let the person become master of time. Quite unloved in the Continental legal education curriculum, Evidence is nonetheless at the heart of how the legal system works. (9) No one can allege a situation, which is a construction of facts, and claim to benefit from the legal effect that the legal system attaches to it without proving the existence of the facts involved. Because the legal system works for the benefit of the person, a person who cannot activate the evidentiary system is therefore in the same situation as a person who has no rights: *idem est non esse et non probari.* (10)

That person may have a right, but the system will not work for him or her. The evidentiary system is therefore "vital," in the sense that the legal system will only "come to life" through the operation of the evidentiary system which, like a fabric, covers the whole Law, enabling it to be activated for the benefit of persons, individuals and entities. This vitality operates at all times outside of confrontation: because the truth of the facts of each situation is usually established; because in practice, this truth is not contested; because, more often than not, this benefit, which we continually derive from the Law, a benefit crystallised in our subjective rights, (11) spontaneously gives rise to recognition by others, admission by all and more particularly by the debtor making payment on his or her own

(9) See, for example, F. Ferrand & G. Lardeux, *Preuve*, "Dalloz corpus" Serie, Paris, Dalloz, 2020.

(10) "What is not is the same and does not appear", i.e. it's the same thing to have no right or to have no proof of your right.

(11) H. Motulsky, *Principes d'une réalisation méthodique du droit privé. La théorie des éléments générateurs des droits subjectifs*, preface by P. Roubier, Paris, Sirey, 1948, republished with a foreword by M.-A. Frison-Roche, "Bibliothèque Dalloz" Serie, Paris, Dalloz, 1992, the foreword of M.-A. Frison-Roche, which summarises the substance of the book, is available in English at the following address: https://mafr.fr/en/article/avant-propos-a-la-reimpression-de-louvrage-dhenri-/.

accord. This is how, even without litigation, the legal system comes to life in practice, thanks to the evidentiary system, whose multiple mechanisms of presumption and dispensation from proof enable rights to be enforced and substantial rules to be applied.

It may happen that this quiet river of the legal order is disturbed by a contestation, taking the form of a claim, for example, against another person. The evidentiary system, which was only virtual, will appear in a more active form, since it is before a judge that the alleged facts will have to be proven in order for the related claim to be satisfied. The whole trial can be described as an evidentiary mechanism, both theatrical and scientific. Depending on the culture and the case, the trial will be more or less one or the other.

But because the Law is an order that unfolds over time, always unifying the past, the present and the future, the need to prove created by the dispute, the effectiveness of what were traditionally called subjective rights rendered "in a state of war" by legal action before the judge, justifies wise people having prepared for this prospect, even before the need for effective proof of the benefits derived from texts and the titularity of rights, at a time when no one disputed or claimed them: it is a wise practice to take evidence in advance, even when the legal system does not require it.

The evidentiary system therefore covers all segments of time, from the fury of *ex post* litigation to the wisdom of *ex ante* evidence, just in case. For those who are in the time of the trial, it is most often a question of finding facts from the past, but also of anticipating facts from the future; for those who are in the time of pre-constitution, for example contractual time, it is a question of constructing in advance a more or less indisputable account of facts in the event that allegations formulated in the future would concern them.

Compliance Law, this *ex ante* branch of Law, will develop this concern for the future more than any other branch of Law. This is why it will increase the techniques of proof, and even oblige companies to develop new means of proof, sometimes against themselves, and increase the burden of proof, specific features of compliance which must not, however, disregard the general system of proof in its guiding principles. The Law must ensure that compliance does not devour these principles, for example through the mechanical performance of algorithms.

But the more the Law worries about the future and wants to control it, with compliance expressing this "claim," the more the Evidence System will be called upon, in a form that is certainly more and more scientific, but also probably more and more theatrical.

The evidentiary system therefore entirely covers the legal system and enables people to control time as far as possible: to keep track of the past or to reconstruct it, to anticipate future difficulties, using all the techniques available to freeze it in advance. Those who neglect evidence, or who do not have access to its resources, reduce the benefits offered by the Law, or even exclude themselves from it. Enduring the "risk of proof," he will succumb to his claim, because this presupposes that the allegation is proven in the factual information it articulates, the "right to proof" existing only in specific cases covered by texts and not in a general way. At a time when everything is data, this is a considerable challenge. But this is not the sudden result of digital technology or of the information society: since Roman Law, and in every legal system, a square of evidence has been established.

4. The Evidence Square. In the vast field of Evidence Law,(12) let us briefly recall what can be called the evidentiary square on which all evidentiary systems operate, answering 4 questions: "*Who must prove? What to prove? How to prove? What are the conditions for proving?*" These questions relate to the burden of proof, the object of proof, the means of proof and the admissibility of evidence. The answers are rooted in all the substantive branches of Law and come under both General Procedural Law(13) and underlying Substantial Law since we are slow to give Evidence Law the autonomy it deserves.

Anyone who can answer the four questions, manipulate the four answers and use the answers to one question to change the way another question is formulated, as one does with a kaleidoscope, for example manipulating a means of proof to change the burden of proof, or even obtaining its division,(14) becomes the master of trials, particularly in preventing them and resolving them successfully.

(12) The reference works remain those of the *Centre de logique de Bruxelles: Centre national de recherche logique*, Ch. Perelman and P. Foriers (eds), *La preuve en droit*, Brussels, Bruylant, 1981. See also C. Puigelier (ed.), *La preuve*, "Études juridiques" Serie, Paris, Economica, 2004.

(13) M.-A. Frison-Roche, "Adjusting General Procedural Law to Compliance Law by the Nature of Things", *this book*.

(14) This can happen under specific legal provisions, for example to combat discrimination in companies: A. Danis-Fatôme, "Le dispositif propre à la charge de la preuve, frein ou outil de lutte contre les discriminations?", *Revue des droits de l'homme*, 2016.

5. The first vertex of the Evidence Square - the burden of proof. The burden of proof deserves its name: (15) it is a heavy load. This burden falls on the person making an allegation. The first person to make an allegation is the one who brings the matter before the court; therefore, Law usually places this burden on the plaintiff, but only because this plaintiff makes the first allegation, stating, for example, that the sum for which he or she is claiming payment (which constitutes his or her claim) is owed to him or her by the defendant (assertion which constitutes his allegation). Once the burden of proof has been satisfied, because the party to the lawsuit has provided proof of the factual elements that make up his or her allegation, either all of the objects of proof at stake in the dispute are proven and the judge can then rule, or the burden of proof begins to circulate and it is another party, usually his opponent, who will in turn have to bear the burden of proving, because he or she too will have made an allegation.

In this way, the trial is often an alternation of burdens of proof, as the parties meet them, by confronting each other in various allegations that contradict each other in a debate. In this way, a round of burdens of proof is created, because faced with the plaintiff in the proceedings, who was the first to make an allegation, the other parties do not remain inactive, formulating claims (if only the rejection of the claims of the others) and fuelling these claims by providing evidence, since the proceedings may involve many parties. But at some point, this roundabout process comes to an end: it is then the party that has not met his or her burden of proof that loses. The burden of proof thus contains the "risk of proof," a mortal risk since the cost is judicial defeat. For example, the person who demanded payment but was unable to prove that the sum was due bears the risk of proof correlated to the burden of proof and then loses. (16)

The more technical the case, the more difficult it is to prove the allegations. This is particularly true in Economic Law. If the fact is past, we often never know what happened; if the fact is future, it is often impossible for anyone to reliably reconstruct what will happen. Merger control is played

(15) In a strict legal pespective see N. Hoffschir, *La charge de la preuve en droit civil*, preface by S. Amrani-Mekki, "Nouvelle Bibliothèque de Thèses" Serie, Paris, Dalloz, Vol. 153, 2016. For a more economic analysis, see R. J. Allen, "Burdens of proof", *Law, Probability and Risk*, Vol. 13, Issue 3-4, September–December 2014, pp. 195–219.

(16) This is expressed, for example, in Article 9 of the *Code de procédure civile* (French Civil Procedure Code): "*Il incombe à chaque partie de prouver conformément à la loi les faits nécessaires au succès de sa prétention*" (free translation: "It is incumbent on each party to prove, in accordance with the law, the facts necessary for the success of its claim.").

out on the scaffolding of "tests," The evidentiary stakes are therefore above all the burdens of proof, in that they contain the risk of proof, and the parties' strategies aim to shift them onto the shoulders of another party, or even onto those of the judge.

However, the presumption of innocence has the considerable effect of placing the burden of proof on the accuser, which explains why this principle, which is political in nature, is given such importance in economic litigation, as it enables companies to place the risk of proof on the shoulders of the prosecuting authority, whether it be the regulatory or supervisory authority, the administration or the public prosecutor, even the company itself, and to interfere with the round of burdens of proof described above. (17)

6. The second vertex of the Evidentiary Square - the object of proof. The object of proof is what the person who bears the burden of proof must show. From the outset, Law grants a major dispensation: it is not up to the claimant to prove the existence of the legal rules applicable to the claim, (18) *jura novit curia.* (19) In the claim that the party develops, only the element that has a factual dimension is therefore object of proof: in the example given above, the existence of the sum owed to the claimant by another person. As a factual situation is like a painting with multiple points, not all the facts that make up the situation need to be proven: it is considered that the constant facts are exempt from proof and that only the contested points need be established. To continue with the example given, the nationality of the person in question will not be proven, but their status as debtor will be, because the evidentiary system anticipates that this status will be denied by the adversary.

The fact must also be "relevant," i.e. its demonstration or non-demonstration must have an effect on the outcome of the judicial dispute. In this example, the fact is relevant because if the plaintiff to the allegation (which in this case is the plaintiff to the proceedings) cannot show that the defendant summoned actually owes the sum, he or she will lose the case, since this quality of debtor was required to found its claim.

---

(17) On the question of internal investigations, see M.-A. Frison-Roche, "Reinforce the Judge and the Lawyer to impose Compliance Law as a characteristic of the Rule of Law", and "Adjusting General Procedural Law to Compliance Law by the Nature of Things", *this book*.

(18) We will see the extent to which this simple and yet fundamental rule is being challenged by Compliance Law. See *supra* No. 3.

(19) "The court knows the Law."

Finally, the fact must be apprehensible, i.e. it must be possible to grasp it. This is why the evidentiary system excludes the proof of negative facts,(20) because we cannot prove what is not, for example in principle what has not yet happened because it is a future event. This is a major issue which has been revived by Compliance Law, since Compliance Law is an *ex ante* branch of Law(21), the object of which is the future... Conversely, the fact that it is difficult for a party to obtain proof is not enough to remove his or her obligation to prove, but it does justify his or her being helped to do so. Such a difficulty arises, for example, because the fact is very complex, and the court may order an expert opinion, even *in futurum,* or because the evidence is in the hands of the opposing party, and the court may require it to be produced. However, for the moment there is no such thing as a "general subjective right to evidence," with texts granting it only in specific cases, notably in Labour Law.

7. The third vertex of the Evidentiary Square - the means of proof. To meet the burden of proving the relevant facts alleged, the plaintiff resorts to means of proof. This is where Law and Science meet since the purpose of the evidence is to establish the truth of the alleged facts. In principle, as in scientific matters, the person may use any means of evidence that he or she can gather: in principle, the evidence is free(22) and, as in scientific matters, the judge must then be convinced. The freedom to adduce evidence is matched by the judge's freedom to assess the evidence. In general presentations, Evidence Systems seems very different in Civil Law and Common Law systems. In Continental Law systems, the principle is the freedom of proof and the Judge is free to be convinced or not. On the contrary, in the Anglo-American Law systems, the standards of proofs are applied and, in Criminal Law, the prosecutor is obliged to prove "beyond the reasonable doubt,"(23) while, in non-criminal cases, the principle of "preponderance of evidence"(24) obliges the person who

(20) On the problem created by "compliance" defined as the non-violation of regulations, which constitutes a negative fact, see *infra* No. 11.

(21) This is an essential element in the development of Compliance Law, which as *ex ante* branch of Law is concerned precisely with the future.

(22) For instance, in French Law, Article 1358 of the *Code civil* (French Civil Code) states: "*Hors les cas où la loi en dispose autrement, la preuve peut être apportée par tout moyen*" (free translation: "Except where the law provides otherwise, proof may be provided by any means.")

(23) Cornell Law School, "beyond a reasonable doubt", *Legal Encyclopedia*, https://www.law.cornell.edu/wex/beyond_a_reasonable_doubt#:~:text=This%20means%20that%20the%20prosecution,to%20render%20a%20guilty%20verdict.

(24) Cornell Law School, "preponderance of the evidence", *Legal Encyclopedia*, https://www.law.cornell.edu/wex/preponderance_of_the_evidence and the case law mentioned: Superior Court of Pennsylvania, 11 Octobre 2005, *Karch v. Karch, 885 A.2d 535.*

bears the burden of proof to present means of proof convincing that the claim is true for at least a 50% chance.

But technically, in Civil Law systems, on the one hand, the segments in which the exception of "legal evidence" is adopted, in particular in favour of written evidence, are so vast, and on the other hand, the growing demand for the requisite of "standards of evidence," or even for a typology of evidence that is more reliable than others, according to the American methodology of the "standards of proof,"(25) may cast doubt on a so abrupt opposition between these two evidence cultures, especially in Economic Law which mixes the pure economic techniques, for instance the "test," with evidentiary methods.

On the contrary, in Common Law systems, even if the prosecutor must prove beyond the reasonable doubt, the technique of popular juries, particularly in class actions in civil liability cases, calls into question the scope of the required standards of proof.

The fact remains that if the person who bears the burden provides the means of what he or she has to prove, then he or she satisfies his or her burden, unless the defendant to his or her allegation in turn makes an allegation, which in an evidentiary turn will have to be proved by the defendant (for example, extinction of the obligation to pay as a result of the plaintiff's failure to perform his or her own obligation).

Evidence may take the form of testimony (testimony against oneself being an admission) in any form (oral, written, image, etc.), writing or reasoning. One of these forms of reasoning is the presumption. The more difficult the object is to prove, the more presumptions will be activated, because they consist in changing the object of proof. The presumption consists in shifting the object of proof: unable to prove the direct object of proof, the plaintiff proves another object of proof that is connected to the first by a logical link, in particular a causal link. For example, if the party cannot directly prove the presence of a person on the premises, he will prove the presence of an object belonging to that person, which allows that presence to be presumed. The presumption then reverses the burden of proof, as the party opposing the allegation may in turn allege, for example, that the person in question was present at the time in another place, a presence that he or she will in turn have to prove. Presumptions play a central role in Economic Law, because it is so difficult to prove directly...

(25) J.-Chr. Roda, "Les standards de preuve : réflexion à partir du droit de la concurrence", *op. cit.*

Therefore, Economic Law constitutes a natural field in which behaviour is often reconstructed on the basis of economic and financial rationality models. (26)

One of the difficulties encountered in laying the foundations of a Compliance Evidence System therefore lies in the lack of solidity of the evidentiary system itself, because, in order to design the special evidentiary system in harmony with the general evidentiary system, the latter would have to be solid. However, this is not the case on many essential points, such as whether it should be linked to General Procedural Law or Substantive Law, whether evidence is free in principle or not, what is the place of standards of proof, what the judge is bound by, etc. The same uncertainty about the foundations of the general system is found in the admissibility of evidence. (27)

As a result, each branch of Law is developing its own little system of evidence, with Economic Law seeming to stand apart and migrate towards the American system of evidence, which has little to do with classical Civil Law evidence system, since the latter lacks solid and clear foundations. This is highly prejudicial, since evidence is what gives life to Law and to rights, (28) i.e. to the legal system itself. The issue is that Compliance Law is certainly part of Economic Law, so impregnated by American legal culture thanks to Law & Economic influence, but it is growing through classical civil Tort Law, in application of classical Continental Evidence System.

It might be thought that compliance, in that it both creates a specific branch of Law (29) and gives new life to other branches of Law, (30) could remedy this.

8. The fourth vertex of the evidentiary square - the admissibility of evidence. Means of proof are more or less admissible. This is where legal evidence differs from scientific evidence, either below the latter since

(26) For example, proof of the relevant market, an essential element in any dispute concerning competitive markets, is established by a set of presumptions. The adoption of "Economic standards of proof" could imply, obliging those who judge to abandon their freedom of appreciation, even in Civil Law systems, and therefore, by reflex effect, the very principle of freedom of proof to the benefit of the party. The Court of Justice of the European Union aims to maintain the balance between these principles. See J.-F. Castillo de la Torre & E. Gippini Fournier, *Evidence, Proof and Judicial Review in EU Competition Law, op. cit.*

(27) See *infra* No. 8.

(28) See *supra* No. 1.

(29) On this specific issue, see M.-A. Frison-Roche, "Compliance Law", 2016, https://mafr.fr/en/article/le-droit-de-la-compliance/.

(30) On this more general perspective, see M.-A. Frison-Roche (ed.), *Compliance Monumental Goals*, "Compliance & Regulation" Serie, Brussels, Journal of Regulation & Compliance (JoRC)/Bruylant, 2023; M.-A. Frison-Roche (ed.), *Compliance Obligation*, to be published.

legal evidence, even if convincing, may not be admissible (for example, when it is not obtained faithfully), or above it if, even if unconvincing, it is binding on the judge (for example, in factual situations governed by the legal evidence system, for instance through an *acte authentique* (authentic *instrumentum*) which is an indisputable document). (31) First of all, this system known as "free evidence" does not always apply, as certain situations exclusively require pre-constituted written evidence (system known as "legal evidence," applicable in the case of legal acts relating to civil transactions for a rather large amount). (32) Evidence constituted in accordance with the rules of legal proof (authentic *instrumentum* / private *instrumentum*) has a different probative value, (33) with certain elements being indisputable. (34) In the same way, an oath is an evidentiary technique that binds the parties and the judge, and this powerful effect casts doubt on whether it is even evidence, since the link with the truth is so loose.

Anyway, the way in which the information is gathered must be fair, since fairness of evidence is considered to be a general principle of the evidentiary system, an application of the general standard of fairness that characterises States governed by the Rule of Law, to which only by exception, and therefore duly justified and confined, is the opposite admitted.

9. The interplay between the four corners of the Evidence Square. Based on these four interfering points summarised here, texts and case law have developed numerous rules to make the system heavier or lighter in favour of some or others. For example, the French Constitution has established the principle of the Presumption of Innocence in favour of a person threatened with a decision causing grievance to them, be it not only a penalty but every sort of sanction, Constitutional courts interpreting

(31) This incontestability is bearable only because the persons who draw up the authentic *instrumentum* verify the accuracy of the facts they mention and because the incontestability of the instrument as regards the facts is limited to those facts. See M.-A. Frison-Roche, "Acte authentique, acte de marché", *JCP N*, 2010, pp. 1290 *et seq*.

(32) On this complex system of legal evidence, see e.g. J. Wroblewski, "La preuve juridique : axiologie, logique et argumentation", *in* Ch. Perelman and P. Foriers (eds), *La preuve en droit*, *op. cit.*; on the excessive importance given to the distinction between legal evidence and free evidence, sometimes presented as the *summa divisio* of the evidentiary system, whereas it is only part of it, E. Vergès, G. Vial and O. Leclerc, *Droit de la preuve*, *op. cit.*, No. 39, pp. 38 *et seq*.

(33) It is only possible to prove against a written document by another written document.

(34) This is what makes authentic acts so valuable. See M.-A. Frison-Roche, "Acte authentique, acte de marché", *op. cit.* This can be combined with the technological power of blockchain, in its security of storage. See T. Kern, "Blockchain and intellectual property rights: blockchain anchoring, a ground-breaking means of proof to the rescue of creators?", *I.B.L.J.* 2021, 2, pp. 279-287.

this principle broadly: this places the burden of proof on the shoulders of the accuser, in particular the public prosecutor. Because it impedes what has been described here as the natural round of burdens of proof, (35) the presumption of innocence, attached to the prospect of sanction, has been described not as a rule of evidence but as a substantive rule, in particular because this presumption constitutes a political foundation of the social community. (36) However, it is presented by some as being very badly treated by Compliance Law… (37)

In the same way, the Freedom of Evidence principle allows for reasoning, including economic reasoning, as a means of proof. From this margin offered by the principle of freedom of evidence, Economic Law has made great use of, to the point of sometimes substituting what has been called "economic evidence," claiming greater objectivity and security, for what should no longer be called "legal evidence," in particular in that the latter still requires proof of an intention to act in order to punish a person, whereas "economic evidence" could reconstitute, on the basis of calculations, behaviour that is likely to be rational in order to impose remedies. (38)

However, this is often seen as a lack of understanding of the evidentiary system in Economic Law, particularly in its repressive dimension. In the same way, the proliferation of "rights to evidence" in litigation before regulatory authorities has been seen as inconsistent with traditional principles. This seems to be only one of the head-on clashes between Compliance and Evidence, but it appears as a confrontation only if we seek to define compliance as that which would give rise to an obligation on the part of legal subjects to show *ex ante* that they are "in conformity" with all the regulations applicable to them (B). But this is not the pertinent definition of Compliance Law (C).

(35) See *supra* No. 5.

(36) On the specificity of presumption, its difficulty in fitting into an evidentiary system that maintains its link with truth, L. Grozdanovski, "Le probable, le plausible et le vrai. Contribution à la théorie générale de la présomption en droit", *Revue internationale d'études juridiques* 2020/1, Vol. 84, pp. 39-72.

(37) This is not correct, see *infra*, No. 14 *et seq*.

(38) On the use made of it by the courts, see A.-L. Sibony, *Le juge et le raisonnement économique en droit de la concurrence*, foreword B. Vesterdorf, preface by G. Canivet, "Droit & Économie" Serie, Paris, LGDJ, 2008.

B. The head-on collision between Evidence principles and Compliance, defined as the obligation to demonstrate its conformity with all applicable regulations

10. The first clash between Compliance and Proof, generated by the definition of compliance as the company's obligation to prove its "conformity with the regulations applicable to it": the obligation to prove the Law? At first sight, the confrontation gets off to a bad start, because the first thing the evidentiary system does is dispense with the need to know the Law, as no one has to gather together the applicable legal rules in order to benefit from them.(39) In fact, the other rule, known as "*ignorantia juris non excusat,*" does not require knowledge of the Law but implies that ignorance of the Law cannot be used to avoid its application and a penalty for disregarding it: for instance, in the United Kingdom, "Ignorance of the law is no excuse," in France, "*nul n'est censé ignorer la loi.*"

But if Compliance is defined as a general obligation to spontaneously obey all applicable regulations and to make this obedience visible, it would be necessary for the subject of Law to effectively know all these "regulations" beforehand. All compliance departments explain that their first task, and a difficult one at that, is to collect all these "regulations." A gigantic task, for which only machines, algorithms and A.I. seem to be the solution, leading to what would be "automatic compliance."

Quite apart from the negation that this automatism represents in terms of what is the Rule of Law,(40) this would place a prior obligation on the company, as a subject of Law, to provide proof of all the regulations that apply to it, him, her. They could do it by using algorithms. But first of all, as everyone points out in practice, this is extremely difficult since the Law, which is then presented as a "regulatory fabric," is in flux and the company is unable, despite its technological investments, to know what it is. But since it is obliged to do so, because it has to know it in the first instance, in order to comply with it in the second, if it subsequently turns out that there was a rule that it did not know about, and which it therefore failed to show that it was actively conforming with, it would have to be penalised... The company therefore invests in technology, machine memory and the

(39) See *supra* No. 6.

(40) For an overview, see M.-A. Frison-Roche, "Reinforce the Judge and the Lawyer to impose Compliance Law as a characteristic of the Rule of Law", *this book*.

processing capacity of algorithms in order to get to know the regulations, which is a prerequisite for conforming with them. (41) The hope in deep learning, through machines that would be "intelligent" as humans are, could be a perspective, but is very disputed.

Secondly, however, this is totally contrary to the very principle of the Evidentiary System, since it is not up to the subjects of Law to demonstrate to the judge their knowledge of the legal rules because the evidentiary system exempts them from proving the applicable legal rules, or even from invoking any of them.

For Compliance Law not to destroy one of the foundations of the evidentiary system, the definition of Compliance Law must not be this *ex ante* demonstration of obedience to all applicable regulations, including the gathering of all of them, but rather the participation in the achievement of Monumental Goals. (42)

11. The second clash between Compliance and Proof, generated by the definition of Compliance as the company's obligation to prove negative facts: the non-violation of applicable regulations. Let us continue with this definition, which makes no sense whatsoever, requiring companies to prove to everyone that they are actively conforming with all applicable regulations at all times, in all places and through all the people for whom they are accountable. If Compliance Law was to be such a straitjacket, then not only would the burden of proof be colossal, since the company would have to demonstrate that it was indeed aware, through its machines, of all the applicable regulations, (43) but it would also be impossible to satisfy this burden of proof because it is a negative object: "non-violation."

In this conception, the proof of compliance is not a positive proof: it is a matter of proving that the company has not breached the applicable regulations in the past, is not breaching them now and will not breach them in the future. To "be conform" would mean to not violate the regulations. It is therefore a negative fact. However, as a matter of principle, negative facts cannot be proven (44) and it is totally exhausting, and ultimately

(41) See in this regard the article written by two in-house lawyers, B. Laroche and J. Boullu-Chataigner, "*Brave New Planes* ou la conformité juridique de grands groupes aéronautiques face aux défis de l'intelligence artificielle", *Dalloz IP/IT*, 2022, pp. 83 *et seq*.

(42) M.-A. Frison-Roche (ed.), *Compliance Monumental Goals*, "Compliance & Regulation" Serie, Brussels, Journal of Regulation & Compliance (JoRC)/Bruylant, 2023.

(43) See *supra* No. 10.

(44) See *supra* No. 6.

impossible, to demonstrate that nowhere in the past, and nowhere in the future, anyone has deviated, is deviating or will deviate from the rules. How can this be demonstrated? Other than by making statements such as "I am not corrupt, and no one for whom I am answerable is or will be corrupt," a statement which the public authorities have sometimes described as nothing more than a marketing process, but which is difficult to replace by anything in practice... In fact, the burden of proof in the face of such an object of proof is such that companies are led to make general commitments, conducts presented as "exemplary" and speeches, which the public authorities frequently analyse as nothing more than pretences. But it is the object itself that is not, in the technical sense of the term, "bearable."

This seemingly impossible link between the Evidentiary System and Compliance Law, in that the latter would disregard two essential principles, namely the non-necessity of proving regulations and the prohibition on requiring proof of negative facts, stems from this definition of compliance as an obligation on companies to "conform with all applicable regulations."

To overcome this aporia, one must either try to achieve this extraordinary compliance performance by dehumanising compliance through the use of software that would take care of everything (45), or not adhere to this definition of compliance as proof provided to everyone by the company of its conformity with all the regulations applicable to it. (46)

12. The temptation to replace human beings with machines in order to achieve compatibility between the Evidence System and Compliance, defined as the company's obligation to prove that it is not in breach of the applicable regulations. In the face of what appears to be an inhuman requirement, the solution seems to be to move away from human solutions and entrust everything to algorithms. Engineers are building computers to store the mass of information in the form of texts and decisions of all kinds and origins, while algorithms correlate the cases processed with each other, with the correlations gradually covering all past, present and future factual hypotheses. (47) This would have the radical effect, assuming that such compliance was obtained in this way, of proving that the company has always obeyed, is obeying, and will always obey the rules, legal and non-legal, which would exclude the judge from

(45) See *infra* No. 12.

(46) See *infra* No. 13.

(47) For a more detailed presentation of the mechanism, see M.-A. Frison-Roche, "Reinforce the Judge and the Lawyer to impose Compliance Law as a characteristic of the Rule of Law", *this book*.

the Compliance System since violation would be excluded. This would also exclude the Rule of Law, which always presupposes the presence of a Judge,(48) which may not seem insurmountable, and may even seem attractive to some.

13. It is preferable to define Compliance Law by its Monumental Goals in order to make it compatible with the Evidence System. But if the Rule of Law is to be valued and imperatively protected, another solution must be sought: this lies in defining Compliance Law substantially, in terms of its Monumental Goals.(49) It should be kept in mind that Compliance Law is defined teleologically in terms of the aims pursued by this branch of Law: the goal is to ensure that, through an alliance between the public authorities and Crucial economic Operators,(50) the future is changed in relation to the path mapped out for it by the present. In this systemic perspective, Negative Monumental Goals aim to block what would happen without immediate and constant action, such as an endemic disaster and/or the disappearance of systems. There may also be Positive Monumental Goals to ensure that these economic and social systems progress, for example through the principles of equality between human, probity and respect, and the new ecological balances.

This definition eliminates apparent contradictions. For example, if Compliance Law is defined in a substantive way by these Monumental Goals that are specific to it and that the crucial operators pursue, whether by force or by choice,(51) then the regulations applicable to the company no longer need to be stored by it in technological memories since it is not required to show that it is in conformity with them, the Law therefore not being an object of proof.

More generally, it is on the basis of the objects of proof that Compliance Law carves out its specificity, with regard to this definition, in order to define an Evidentiary System specific to Compliance, which is not inhuman and which transcribes the originality of Compliance Law: it is therefore not with the burden of proof that we must begin but with the objects of proof, because it is first and foremost through these that the specificity of this branch of Law is marked. Everything follows from there.

(48) M.-A. Frison-Roche, "Reinforce the Judge and the Lawyer to impose Compliance Law as a characteristic of the Rule of Law", *this book*.

(49) M.-A. Frison-Roche (ed.), *Compliance Monumental Goals, op. cit.*

(50) M.-A. Frison-Roche, "Proposal for a notion: the 'Crucial Operator'", 2006, https://mafr.fr/en/article/28-proposition-pour-une-notion-loperateur-crucial/.

(51) M.-A. Frison-Roche (ed.), *Compliance Monumental Goals, op. cit.*

II. OBJECTS OF PROOF SPECIFIC TO COMPLIANCE LAW: STRUCTURAL MECHANISMS AND BEST PRACTICES EXPECTED

14. The fundamental distinction between structural and behavioural measures. With regard to the goals pursued, whether it is the legal rules that require it or the company through what is then called ethics or societal responsibility, in documents which most often reproduce the letters of the Law, duplication leading to many difficulties because of this superimposition of sources of various kinds,(52) the company puts in place "Compliance Tools."(53)

As the goals are both negative (eradicating money laundering, eliminating corruption, suppressing market abuse, eliminating the expression of hatred and discrimination, etc.) and positive (protecting nature, promoting women, educating, etc.), companies need to put in place specific structures, thanks to which high-performance behaviours are obtained or increased and the Monumental Goals designated by the public authorities are better achieved.

Translated into the Evidentiary System, the crucial companies, which are the legal subjects of the Compliance System,(54) are faced with two objects of proof, drawn by the Monumental Goals: the implementation of the structural measures expressly required, by Law or by the company itself, and effectively organised (A) or the adoption of the relevant behaviours to achieve the Monumental Goals, behaviours which prove to be more or less effective (B).

A. Proving that the required structural organisations have been put in place to achieve the Monumental Goals

15. Setting up structures, an obligation to achieve results. Many of the Compliance Tools are structural. These include plans, mapping and training. It is quite another thing for these tools to produce the effects expected of them, i.e. the expected behaviours, for example, behaviours of prudence following risk mapping, or behaviours of responsibility following training.

---

(52) This is another subject, analysed in particular in *Compliance Monumental Goals, op. cit.*

(53) On the variation in these, see M.-A. Frison-Roche (ed.), *Compliance Tools*, "Compliance & Regulation" Serie, Brussels, Journal of Regulation & Compliance (JoRC)/Bruylant, 2021.

(54) On crucial companies, insofar as they are the legal subjects of compliance, see N. Borga, J.-Cl. Marin and J.-Chr. Roda, *Compliance : l'entreprise, le régulateur et le juge*, "Régulations & Compliance" Serie, Paris, Dalloz, 2018.

A person whose interest it is may therefore ask the company, which is the subject of Compliance Law, to show that it has put in place the compliance structures required by a legitimate source of compliance, for example a law, a judgment (as an additional compliance penalty or as a commitment), a judicial settlement such as a deferred prosecution agreement or a *convention judiciaire d'intérêt public* (Judicial Public Interest Agreement), or a contract. (55)

16. The only object of proof for compliance structures is their effectiveness. But the only object of proof is this implementation, not the effect produced by it. As soon as the company has put in place a plan, a map, monitoring and training mechanisms, the outline of the object of proof is correctly drawn, and the burden of proof arises from this and will be satisfied if the documents are communicated. What the compliance tools produce, their results, which are measured in consideration of the Monumental Goals, is another object of proof. It is true that this is not always clearly perceived, because of the language game, maybe the language trap, which consists of asserting that the "results" obtained thanks to the means of compliance are only obligations of "means," whereas the execution of the structural obligations is an obligation of "result." It's hard not to get lost... Especially if you entrust all this to algorithms, whose only skill lies in matching words.

17. A strict analysis of the object of proof, the shifting of the object of proof by presumption and the reversal of the burden of proof. Once a company has shown everyone the existence of the compliance structures it is required to put in place, because the Law, a court ruling or its own commitments have led it to do so, the company has met its burden of proof. The company does not have to prove the efficiency of the structures it puts in place. According to the "burden of proof round mechanism," (56) it is up to the party challenging the company's performance of its obligation to show that the company, in setting up its structure, knew or could not have failed to know that the compliance structure could not produce the minimum effect expected by Law. For example, a company that does not provide the person or the department in charge of compliance with any resources cannot claim to have fulfilled its compliance obligation, even if the company is free to decide how to do so. However,

(55) M.-A. Frison-Roche, "Compliance contract, Compliance clauses", 2022, https://mafr.fr/en/article/contrat-de-compliance-clauses-de-compliance/.

(56) See *supra* No. 5.

it is up to the person alleging this inadequacy, in this case the Regulatory Authority, to demonstrate this inadequacy, which is also structural, by showing, for example, that there were only one or two people to monitor many individuals and structures in many places. Initially, the effective implementation of structures presumes their effectiveness. (57) For example, a better ability on the part of individuals to resist corruption or detect money laundering in the future, or to combat harassment, is presumed by the setting up and running of training courses in this area. These are two separate items of evidence: the provision of training on the one hand, and the results of that training on the other. However, what is relevant for Compliance Law defined by Monumental Goals, a non-mechanical concept, is not the training courses but their results. But then the presumption comes into play, allowing the company bearing the burden of proof to move from the direct object of proof (the result of the training) to the indirect object (the implementation of the training), with the implementation and holding of the training presuming an effect. The burden of proof is then reversed: another party can break this presumption. It is possible for someone to allege that, despite this training on fighting corruption, money laundering, environmental destruction, climate imbalance, etc., no change in behaviour has been observed in the company, among those for whom it is accountable.

But this new object of proof, the unproductiveness of the Compliance Tools, creates a burden of proof that rests on the author of such an allegation, not on the company that has put in place the required tool. However, it would be prudent for the company to provide evidence of the efficiency of this tool, for instance a training, i.e. an increased awareness among the people for whom it is responsible of the need to prevent and combat corruption, or even to provide (58) evidence of the efficiency of this training, i.e. an observed reduction of corruption in the geographical area, industrial sector, etc., greater respect for others, or even the first signs of a cultural change. The need to gather evidence in advance (59) is emerging, anticipating this round of burden of proof. (60)

18. A possible burden of proof of the efficiency of the structures put in place. Furthermore, even if in any case it is always more prudent for companies not to confine themselves to the object of proof, which is

(57) See *supra* No. 17.
(58) On the pre-constitution of evidence, see *infra,* No. 22 and 44 *et seq*.
(59) *Ibid*.
(60) See *supra* No. 8.

only the effectiveness of the compliance structures put in place, it may happen that, because of the heavy burden of proof that Compliance Law places on companies, (61) legislation requires more than this and demands that companies provide ongoing proof of a link of efficiency between the structures and behaviours. This is the purpose of the specific obligation to "monitor," as the legislation refers to it, whereby companies must regularly report either internally or externally, in a targeted manner (to a monitor, public regulatory and/or supervisory authorities) or generally, on the effects produced by the structures put in place with regard to the Monumental Goals set.

With regard to such an object of proof, so that this does not lead to a *de plano* reversal of the burden of proof, in particular when a sanction is attached, which would contradict the presumption of innocence principle, this object of proof can only be that of *plausibility*: the company must, through monitoring that it puts in place itself, not prove the efficiency of its system on behaviours, but prove that this goal has *plausibly* been achieved. This is the purpose of compliance audits, (62) which are both a management tool and a proof tool.

B. Demonstrating the best efforts to achieve behaviours that concretise Monumental Goals

19. Achieving Compliance Behaviours is an obligation of means. If it is conceivable to express such a gradation between Compliance Structural Obligation and Compliance Behavioural Obligation, one could say that it is even more impossible to actually achieve the Monumental Goals than it is to be fully conform with all the regulations. Indeed, companies cannot root out all corruption, eliminate all money laundering, restore climate balance, replace war with peace, or insert probity and equality as full principles in all human societies, not only those in which they have their headquarters but also all those in which the people for whom they are accountable are. The extraterritorial effect of Compliance Law makes all this impossible and unbearable, in every sense of the word. This is also why companies protested so much against the adoption of the French

(61) See *supra* No. 13.

(62) On "compliance audits," see A. Gutierrez-Crespin, "Audit Of Compliance Systems", *in* M.-A. Frison-Roche (ed.), *Compliance Tools*, *op. cit.*, pp. 151-158.

"Vigilance" law of 2017, sometimes presenting it as unbearable,(63) the same protestation arose against the European directive on *Corporate Sustainability Due Diligence.*(64)

However, quite apart from the fact that this new Vigilance duty allows companies to obtain a great deal of information on other companies at the behest of the legislator,(65) the confusion has largely arisen over proof. While companies are required to put in place compliance structures, such as vigilance plans, they are not required to obtain from the persons for whom they are accountable the behaviour that constitutes the very purpose of the system: for example, stopping any wrongful damage to the environment or restoring effective respect for rights in countries where they have interests in the value chain.

The two types of evidence are cumulative and must not be confused. If they are confused, by transforming everything into obligations of result relating to behaviour and results, Compliance Law will become unbearable for companies. However, the *Conseil constitutionnel* (French Constitutional Council) confirmed in its decision of 23 March 2017, *Loi relative au devoir de vigilance des sociétés mères et des entreprises donneuses d'ordre*(66), that the so-called "Vigilance" law, which imposes what is admittedly a personal liability on companies in this respect, implements it in accordance with the ordinary Tort Law, which does not target an obligation of result, the obligation of means remaining the principle of any obligation and requires specific conditions.(67) If we confuse structural obligations with behavioural obligations, if we do not bear in mind what Compliance Law is all about, either by transforming everything into obligations of means, which would make the implementation of compliance structures almost optional (plans, monitoring, training), or by transforming everything into obligations of result, which would make Compliance Law unbearable, then nothing will be able to function. It is therefore essential to bear in

(63) For a more measured analysis, even from an economic perspective, of this law and, more generally, of the duty of vigilance, see M.-A. Frison-Roche, "Assessment of Whistleblowing and Vigilance Obligation with regard to International Competitiveness", *in* M.-A. Frison-Roche (ed.), *Compliance Monumental Goals, op. cit.*, pp. 401-429.

(64) M.-A. Frison-Roche, "Vigilance, a piece of the European puzzle", 2023, https://mafr.fr/en/article/la-vigilance-piece-dun-puzzle-europeen/.

(65) *Ibid.*

(66) *Conseil constitutionnel* (French Constitutional Council), 23 March 2017, No. 2017-750 DC, *Loi relative au devoir de vigilance des sociétés mères et des entreprises donneuses d'ordre.*

(67) M.-A. Frison-Roche, "Thinking and using Vigilance through its Compliance Monumental Goals", 2023, https://www.mafr.fr/en/article/vigilance-buts-monumentaux-de-la-compliance-et-soc/.

mind these two objects of proof, structures on the one hand (subject to obligations of result) and behaviours on the other (subject to obligations of means), their distinction and their addition.

20. The object of proof: the company's proportionate efforts to achieve Compliance Monumental Goals. The obligation of means triggers evidential obligations. Thus, the company, which bears the burden of proof, (68) must show that it has acted to ensure that the persons for whom it is accountable behave actively so that the Monumental Goals are achieved. For example, with regard to the imperative of fighting money laundering, the bank must have carried out checks on the financial flows of the customer whose account was functioning abnormally, and the information must have been promptly passed on to the public authorities. The judge must not, by looking back and knowing that a particular customer was a drug trafficker – information that the banker did not have – analyse the situation as if the obligation to know your customer (KYC), a well-known Compliance Obligation, had been an obligation of result: it must remain an obligation of means, with appropriate behaviour also coming under such an obligation.

The appropriate principle is that of Proportionality. (69) Compliance gives companies burdens, obligations and powers, for example to control others. By carrying out these controls, it diminishes the rights of others, for example the right to secrecy, right to privacy, right to be forgotten, which are the rights of the personal data holders. The company must make its "best efforts," which is a standard of behaviour *in abstracto* with regard to professional rules, but also *in concreto* with regard to the information in question. The efforts that the company must make to collect, analyse, transmit, preserve and transform Information must be proportionate to the Monumental Goal that gives meaning to all the obligations, rights and powers that punctuate Compliance Law. (70)

(68) See *infra* No. 25.

(69) On this subject, see Lucien Rapp's very enlightening demonstration, in which he makes the *Compliance Officer* the bearer of the principle of proportionality in the implementation of compliance mechanisms in corporate strategy: L. Rapp, "Compliance, Proportionality and Normativity", *in* M.-A. Frison-Roche (ed.), *Compliance Monumental Goals*, "Compliance & Regulation" Serie, Brussels, Journal of Regulation & Compliance (JoRC)/Bruylant, 2023, pp. 189-212.

(70) M.-A. Frison-Roche, "Definition of Proportionality and Definition of Compliance Law", *in* M.-A. Frison-Roche (ed.), *Compliance Monumental Goals*, *op. cit.*, pp. 259-288.

By its very nature, as soon as a company take action, this action must be presumed to be proportionate to the goals imposed by Law and for which it is acting. It is up to the party contesting this proportionality, for example the customer who alleges that by acting in this way, the right to the secrecy of his or her personal data has been infringed, which would render the action disproportionate from above, or the administrative authority or the public prosecutor who alleges that by acting in this way the information collected by the company was insufficient or too late, which would render the action disproportionate from below, to prove this.

21. The major issue is the distinction between the Effectiveness, Efficacy and Efficiency of Compliance Tools. Thus, the general assertion that Compliance Law works well with "effective, efficacious and efficient tools," i.e. tools that are first put in place (effectiveness), then produce the expected effects (efficacy) and finally achieve the goals for which they were designed (efficiency), can be broken down into as many evidentiary rules. Structural obligations are subject to obligations of result, but it is only a question of proving the effectiveness of their execution, unless the other parties can show that these structural tools were never able to produce the expected behaviour. Behavioural obligations are subject to an obligation of means, but the object of proof is that of efficacy with regard to the monumental goals that give meaning to the whole Compliance Law, with "best efforts" being demonstrated with regard to the principle of proportionality. As for the efficiency of the whole, since the actions of companies are inseparable from those of States, the population and what happens on the planet as a whole, the proof that can be adduced is more that of the goodwill of the company, thus reinforcing the proof of efficacy, than of the fulfilment of an obligation, since companies are no more obliged to save the world than they are legitimate to govern it.

22. Evidentiary wisdom: pre-constituting evidence not only of the Effectiveness but of the Efficacy and the Efficiency of the entire Compliance System, regardless of the burden of proof. Because Compliance Law is an *ex ante* branch of Law, companies must have the wisdom to pre-prove everything, even if it is not a legal obligation, the "evidentiary reflex" being undoubtedly the most important element in the overall "Compliance Culture" that needs to be disseminated. Borrowing from the British and American cultural way of thinking, the idea that one day a judge will get involved, and that the further away that day is, the more difficult the company's position will be, the company must gradually build up its own evidence system daily. As widely as possible, as early as possible, by all possible means.

Rather than using their strength to pass on the burden of proof to others, by contractual clauses for instance, companies should concentrate their strength, even in a system of evidence still governed by the principle of free proof, on pre-constituting evidence of their compliance diligence, because it is on them that the burden rests.

III. WHO BEARS THE BURDEN OF PROOF IN COMPLIANCE LAW?

23. The weight of the burden of proof, moderated by the other corners of the "evidential square." Whether we welcome it or complain about it, the burden of proof rests on companies, which are in a position to structure themselves and act to give concrete form to the monumental systemic goals that give meaning and coherence to Compliance Law. The compliance tool may be the obligation, which may be express, to "comply" with obligations, but because Evidence Law is a system, (71) the burden of proof is defined by the purpose of the evidence and the means of proof. Thus, the purpose of proof is not to show that a company is in conformity with all the applicable regulations and that it succeeds in enforcing them, but to prove that the company actually contributes to the achievement of the monumental systemic goals for which Compliance Law exists. Similarly, the means of proof are freely organised by the company and not by the public authorities. (72)

24. The weight of the burden of proof in Compliance Law, moderated by the principles of other branches of Law. That Compliance Law, itself an autonomous branch of Law, should develop its own Evidentiary System, is the very purpose of this article, which sets out the prolegomena and considers whether the evidentiary system is itself an autonomous branch of Law. But neither are autonomous from the legal order, that expresses a State governed by the Rule of Law, which by its very nature requires the Evidentiary System of Compliance to respect the guiding principles common to all branches of the legal order, such as the principle

(71) See *supra* No. 1.

(72) As the Sanctions Committee of the *Agence française anticorruption – AFA* (French Anti-Corruption Agency) had occasion to point out in its decision of 12 July 2019.

of loyalty and the principle of protection of persons in danger. It must therefore be stated that Compliance Law does, of course, place the burden of proof on the company (A), but interfere with all the other branches of Law (B).

A. The burden of proof on the Company in meeting its legal Compliance Obligations

25. The position of the Company "charged" of a Compliance Obligation, independently of its place in the proceedings, because of its "Compliance Obligations." It has been pointed out that in the Evidentiary System, the plaintiff in the proceedings bears the first burden of proof only by coincidence with the fact that he makes the first allegation in initiating the proceedings.(73) In principle, it is the party who makes the allegation who bears the burden of proof. But Compliance Law interferes with this general principle, unless it becomes a substantive rule – which is the case with the Presumption of Innocence(74) – because it creates a set of Compliance obligations for companies.

The compliance obligations imposed on companies by laws, contracts, voluntary commitments or compliance programmes ordered by public, regulatory, administrative or judicial authorities, whether structural or behavioural requirements, place the onus on companies to prove that they meet these various Compliance Obligations, which in turn give concrete form to the company's general Compliance Obligation.(75) In this respect, by their very existence, Compliance Obligations place the burden of proof on companies, even if they are defendants in the proceedings and even if they do not allege anything.

However, we must not leave it at that, as this does not mean that the company has to prove that it "is conforming" with all the applicable regulations (which is in fact impossible), that it is not in breach of any of them (which is *de jure* impossible),(76) or even that it has to prove its innocence (which is contrary to the Rule of Law).(77)

(73) See *supra* No. 5.

(74) See *supra* No. 9.

(75) For an example about international arbitration, see M. Audit, "The arbitrator's position on compliance", *this book*. On the very idea of a "Compliance Obligation", see M.-A. Frison-Roche (ed.), *Compliance Obligation*, to be published.

(76) On the prohibition on compelling proof of negative facts, see *supra* No. 11.

(77) See *supra* No. 9 and *infra* No. 38.

26. The burden remains on the other party to prove the existence of a Compliance Obligation, obligation placing the burden of proof on the company. In order for this burden of proof to be placed on the company regardless of its procedural position, even if, for example, it is a defendant, (78) the compliance obligation borne by the company must first be established since this is what interferes with the ordinary evidentiary principle. A distinction needs to be made between the sources of Compliance Obligations.

27. The scope of legal and regulatory Compliance Obligations and the burden of proof on the Company. If the compliance obligation arises from a legal or regulatory obligation, the person claiming its performance, the contractor for example, even if this legal obligation is included in a contractual clause, does not have to prove the existence of this compliance obligation, since *jura novit curia.* (79) For instance, the *Cour d'appel de Paris* (Paris Court of Appeal) had the occasion to reiterate this point in connection with the company's obligation to detect corruption in the companies for which it is accountable, an obligation included in an act of soft Law, the source of which the Court considered to be also of legal nature, and a matter of public policy, justifying the immediate and sudden termination of commercial relations with the supplier. (80)

In addition, the company may, before moving on to the other object of proof which is the actual performance of its Compliance Obligation, make an allegation which is a challenge to that obligation, in terms of its existence or enforceability, or the status or capacity of the person alleging it to demand performance, etc. In this case, the company shall then have to prove what it alleges, but the evidential debate will then remain solely on the object of the Compliance Obligation, in terms of its existence, and not already on its performance. Of course, the company will then have to prove what it is alleging, but the evidentiary debate will then remain solely on the topic of the Compliance Obligation, in its existence, and not already on its performance, which constitutes the next evidentiary stage.

28. The contours of contractual or soft Compliance Obligations blocking the burden of proof on the Company. The further one moves away from hard Law – treaties, the Constitution, laws and regulations – the

(78) On the effect of mechanisms from other branches of Law, see *infra* No. 36 *et seq*.

(79) See the technical explanation of this adage *supra* No. 6.

(80) *Cour d'appel de Paris* (Paris Court of Appeal), 5 May 2021, *Carrefour*, decision confirmed by *Cour de cassation* (French Court of cassation), *Chambre commerciale* (Commercial Chamber), 16 November 2022, No. 21-18.491.

more consistent the burden of proving the Compliance Obligation becomes for the other party who is seeking performance of its Compliance Obligation against the company.

If the source is not the law or a decree, the person who requires the Compliance Obligation to be fulfilled must provide proof of its existence, so that the company has to bear the burden of proving that the obligation has been fulfilled. For example, this person would have to produce the contract and show that the company is actually concerned by it, either under Contract Law, Company Law or Tort Law, since if we take the case of the duty of vigilance, the 2017 French law states that it is under Tort Law that the elements must be assessed (and therefore proven), whereas if we read what will become the European directive, it is rather under Company Law that the duty of vigilance must be assessed. (81)

This brings us to the oxymoron of the soft Compliance Obligation. In fact, it is in terms of "duty" that the texts, internal documents or simple statements are expressed, and the proof that this entails for the company, even if it is itself the author of this use, an obligation, is incumbent on the person requesting performance. Unless a natural obligation is brought into the evidentiary game, a very specific technical case which will prevent the company from requesting restitution for beneficial actions taken, which is legally justifiable, it is up to the party requesting enforcement of compliance promises to demonstrate that they give rise to obligations. (82) For the time being, the vagueness of the words, which can be avoided by combining them and stating that Compliance is the sum of Regulatory Law, Criminal Law, Contract Law, Tort Law and Ethics, can only be tolerated until the day when, for example, only ethics are at issue and someone nevertheless demands compliance, the compliance obligation then appearing as an autonomous object of proof, the question of its burden of proof becoming primary and essential.

29. The intensity of the burden of proof depending on the structural or behavioural Compliance Obligation incumbent on the Company. Finally, as the four vertices of the evidentiary square interact, the burden of proof is affected by the objects of proof. (83) Thus, struc-

(81) M.-A. Frison-Roche, "Vigilance, a piece of the European puzzle", 2023, https://mafr.fr/en/article/la-vigilance-piece-dun-puzzle-europeen/.

(82) M.-A. Frison-Roche, "Thinking and using Vigilance through its Compliance Monumental Goals", 2023, https://www.mafr.fr/en/article/vigilance-buts-monumentaux-de-la-compliance-et-soc/.

(83) As was demonstrated at greater length in relation to the object of proof, see *supra* No. 9.

tural compliance obligations (84) generate a heavy burden of proof since they constitute an obligation of result, whereas behavioural compliance obligations (85) generate a lighter burden since they only constitute an obligation of means.

30. Availability of the burden of proof by contract. Moreover, burdens of proof are not of public order, unless they interfere with substantive rules from other branches of Law. There can therefore be a kind of "contractual management of the burden of proof," and in principle contracts concerning proof are valid when they relate to rights which are freely available to the parties, more precisely it is accepted that the burden of proof can be contractually reorganised as long as the public order is not affected. This last point does not mean, moreover, that a contractual reorganisation is excluded, but requires that, if a contract reorganises, no rule of public policy must be affected. If we consider that in Compliance Law, a systemic branch of Law of a teleological nature whose normativity is located in the Monumental Goals, (86) which are most often of a political nature, public policy is very present, contracts may nevertheless reorganise burdens of proof, as long as the goals remain the intended objects and the means to achieve them remain deployed. It is then up to others than the company to prove that they have deviated from these aims through the contractual mechanism: the burden of proof will have been transferred by the contract. Specifically evidentiary contracts will have to be drafted to ensure that the shift in burden is not ambiguous and that the judge can take note of it.

31. Contractual transfer of the burden of proof by drawing up a "Compliance Contract." Thus, by contract, one company may transfer to another the burden of proving the performance of Compliance Obligations, or even of the "Compliance Obligation," if it is accepted that there is such a general obligation, of which the various specific obligations are merely the expression. (87) This may be the case, on an incidental basis, when a sort of "special contract" is drawn up with a service provider, the purpose of the contract being to entrust the latter with the task of ensuring that

(84) For an explanation of structural compliance obligations, see the discussion on the object of proof *supra* No. 15 *et seq*.

(85) For an explanation of behavioural compliance obligations, see the discussion of the object of proof *supra* No. 19 *et seq*.

(86) M.-A. Frison-Roche, "Compliance Monumental Goals, Beating Heart of Compliance Law", *Compliance Monumental Goals*, "Compliance & Regulation" Serie, Brussels, Journal of Regulation & Compliance (JoRC)/ Bruylant, 2023, pp. 33-58.

(87) M.-A. Frison-Roche (ed.), *Compliance Obligation*, to be published.

the company complies with a specific regulation, such as that relating to personal data, with the obligation then assumed by the co-contractor being accompanied by the evidentiary obligation transferred by the incidental obligation to prove that the obligation has been fulfilled. The recommended use of “trusted third parties” in many cases will increase the number of this type of contract. Indeed, in the event that a third party, whether a stakeholder, an authority or a judge, demands accountability from the company, the latter will be able to transfer this burden to its co-contractor because of this double transfer: the transfer of the burden of proof having had to be spelt out in a clear and unambiguous clause.

32. Contractual transfer of the burden of proof in a contract with a different economic purpose. The “compliance clause.” This may also be part of more general contractual relations and no longer in this special contract, which will be referred to here as a “Compliance Contract,”(88) but in a contract with a main purpose, for example a supply or sales contract or a subcontracting contract, the provisions of which include a possible transfer of compliance obligations incumbent on the company. This raises the question of whether or not the “compliance clause” constitutes a decisive element of the contract and of the obligations of the other party.

33. The difficulties arising from the overlap between the legal and contractual sources of the Compliance Obligation on the prospect of contractual management of the burden of proof of Compliance Obligations. This difficulty may arise in particular in the case of the “duty of vigilance” as formulated in the French law of 2017, because the legislator has attached personal liability to it, and even if the company, in order to fulfil this duty, has recourse to service providers who, in turn, may have to prove the performance of their services as part of their contractual obligations, this should be with regard to the company, which in turn will be able to rely on it regarding to the stakeholders, authorities and judges, without being authorised to claim to place the burden of proof solely on the shoulders of their service providers, the company being left to face the beneficiaries of the legal obligation.

34. Wisdom with regard to the burden of proof through pre-constitution of evidence, in supervision of the principle of freedom of evidence. Even if one refers to the distinction between the system of free evidence and the system of legal evidence, a distinction whose importance

(88) On the existence of a specific category of “compliance contract”, see M.-A. Frison-Roche, “Compliance contract, Compliance clauses”, 2022, https://mafr.fr/en/article/contrat-de-compliance-clauses-de-compliance/.

is, moreover, overestimated because the system of standards of proof being very common in Economic Law, (89) it does not matter that the pre-compilation of evidence would not be required, because of the burden of proof that rests on the company as a result of the Compliance Obligation that concerns it, requiring the company to pre-compile evidence of the fulfilment of its obligation. This is why the means of proof, freely devised, (90) must be the subject of every care by the company.

35. Evidentiary *continuum*, *continuum* of compliance tools. Example of "monitoring." We often oppose the *ex ante* nature of pre-constitution of evidence, for example the drawing up of a written document, with the *ex post* nature of free evidence. However, in Compliance Law, the proof provided by the company of the proper performance of its Compliance Obligation, in terms of results for its structural obligations and of means for its behavioural obligations, (91) is more of a *continuum*. Indeed, the notion of monitoring is essential, and it is in this way that the company can provide evidence that mechanisms were "effectively" put in place *ex ante*, and then subsequently produced "efficacy" effects, generating in an "efficient" manner the expected effects on the system. (92) To achieve this, the company must carry out evidence monitoring on an ongoing basis. The "monitoring" mechanism provided for in compliance programmes, whether adopted spontaneously or as a sanction, is an evidence tool, and as such constitutes a compliance tool. (93)

B. The Evidentiary Dialectic when the fact, which is the subject of evidence, may give rise to sanctions

36. Articulating Compliance Evidentiary System with the other principles of Law within the same legal system. Even if Compliance Law is an *ex ante* branch of Law, which justifies the fact that not only "regulation" but also the contract, which is also an *ex ante* instrument, are essential, sanctions are part of the system. In this respect, when the prospect of them being triggered arises or when their model of sanction is

(89) See *supra* No. 7.

(90) See *infra* No. 39 *et seq*.

(91) See *supra* No. *14 et seq*.

(92) On the identiary trilogy of "effectiveness – efficacy – efficiency", see *supra* No. 21.

(93) See M. Galland, "The Regulator's Inspection Of The Effectiveness Of The Compliance Tools Implemented By The Company", *in* M.-A. Frison-Roche (ed.), *Compliance Tools*, "Compliance & Regulation" Serie, Brussels, Journal of Regulation & Compliance (JoRC)/Bruylant, 2021, pp. 211-224.

borrowed, for example by the company itself,(94) in particular through internal investigations, or even through the disciplinary sanctions that may follow, other principles also impose themselves. Putting all this together is not easy.

37. Compliance's requirement that the burden of proof be placed on the company and Repressive Law's requirement that the burden of proof be placed on the authorities: the two blocks to the burden of proof, on opposite sides of the fence. Firstly, the opposition already observed between the General Evidentiary System and the Compliance System(95) is exacerbated here. Since Compliance Law is an Information system, it implies an "obligation to collaborate" on the part of the company, which is a manifestation of its compliance obligation to encourage the gathering of the information needed to combat efficaciously the systemic risk for which the authorities or the hierarchical superior are themselves responsible. But Repressive Law, which remains governed by the guiding principles of Criminal Law, which is expressed through Criminal Procedure Law, implies the fundamental subjective right of the person who is destined to suffer the legitimate violence of the sanction, not to collaborate, i.e. not to bear the burden of proof.

In this way, two fundamental rules – one based on information, the other on innocence – come into conflict, since the "round of the burdens of proof"(96) must be blocked.

38. The happy and fragile balance of European Union case law. However, the legal system is always readjusting antinomies. Thus, as described at greater length elsewhere,(97) the Court of Justice of the European Union, in its judgment of 2 February 2021, *DB v. Consob*,(98) dissociating the burden of plausibility from the burden of proof,(99) states that the internal or external authority (manager, or supervisory authority for example) may call to account the company or its employee or the third party for whom it is responsible. This reverses the burden of proof, but the

(94) See the entire first part of the book on "The Company established Prosecutor and Judge of itself by Compliance Law."

(95) See *supra* No. 1.

(96) On this concept, see *supra* No. 5.

(97) M.-A. Frison-Roche, "Adjusting General Procedural Law to Compliance Law by the Nature of Things", *this book*.

(98) CJEU, Grand Chamber, 2 February 2021, *DB v. Consob*, case C-481/19.

(99) On this concept, which is also dear to Perelman, see more generally L. Grozdanovski, "Le probable, le plausible et le vrai. Contribution à la théorie générale de la présomption en droit", *Revue internationale d'études juridiques* 2020/1, Vol. 84, pp. 39-72.

burden of proof which then falls on the company, the employee or the third party is transformed by the principle of Repressive Law: the onus is not on the employee to prove his innocence, which would be inadmissible, or even to cooperate fully. They must demonstrate the prospect of a penalty, a likelihood that triggers for them the rights of defence, a concept distinct from the adversarial principle, which gives them in particular the fundamental right to remain silent, producing *ex ante* the subjective right not to collaborate.

IV. RELEVANT MEANS OF PROOF IN COMPLIANCE LAW

39. Evidence of Compliance Obligations. Because the Law requires pre-established structures, such as plans, mapping, training, etc., it is essential to keep track of them since the company must show at all times that, not only is this established, but that the company also controls that it is established. Thus, the audit mechanisms for these "compliance structures" are both a management method and a method of proof for everyone. It is remarkable in this respect that American Law requires, but often limits, compliance, particularly in environmental and climate matters, more to Information Obligation on what the company is doing than to an Obligation to take Positive Action in environmental and climate matters. This is notably the position of the SEC. *However, designing Compliance Law around the obligation to provide Information means making Compliance Law primarily an Evidentiary System.* (100) The *continuum* between Regulatory Law and Compliance Law thus shows its full force, since Law can have a more or less restrictive conception of the obligation to "inform others."

40. The means required to prove the information is effective, fficacious, and Efficient. Law has moved on from the right to information to the obligation to inform, then to the obligation to make information understood, to the right to intelligibility. The structural tools of compliance must enable all those concerned to appreciate the risks and goals pursued by the Compliance Tools put in place, if only to participate in them. This *intelligibility*, which is at the heart of Data Law, must be organised structurally *ex ante*, in particular through the intelligibility of algorithms, which goes beyond their transparency, and which is fully part of Compliance Law.

(100) European Law is much more ambitious in this respect. See S. Pottier, "In Favour of European Compliance, a Vehicle of Economic and Political Assertion", *in* M.-A. Frison-Roche (ed.), *Compliance Monumental Goals*, *op. cit.*, pp. 459-468.

The burden of proving the intelligibility of algorithmic mechanisms, which makes it possible in particular to ensure that the mechanical "consent" procedures correspond to the expression of a "will," lies with the companies, supervised in this by the public authorities.

41. From Information to Training. Training as Compliance Proof. Even if there are no specific training obligations, which is rare nowadays,(101) the result for the company is that training provides information in the form of intelligibility of the standard that the company itself is responsible for, both internally and externally. In so doing, the company proves that it is doing its best to ensure that compliance requirements are understood, by spreading the "Compliance Culture" that the public authorities are looking for.

42. Does the obligation to prove give rise to an obligation to construct *ad hoc* means of proof? An open question is whether, in order to prove that the company is making its "best efforts,"(102) it should invent the technologies required. The question arises for monitoring by digital companies when the legislator obliges them to "effectively" monitor the age of Internet users accessing services available on their websites, for instance when these services are of a pornographic nature, because new technologies are needed to control the age of users without breaching their privacy right. This compliance obligation must therefore be fulfilled by them, and its proper fulfilment monitored by the supervisory authority, which may require the installation of technology to do so,(103) with failure being sanctioned by the courts.(104) Constituting a "systemic case,"(105) this sort of case law could require a judicial resolution by interregulation.(106)

---

(101) On the obligation to provide training, see M.-A. Frison-Roche, "Training: Content and Container of Compliance", *in* M.-A. Frison-Roche (ed.), *Compliance Tools*, *op. cit.*, pp. 245-264.

(102) This corresponds to the formulation of an obligation of means, see *supra* No. 20.

(103) On the effectiveness of this compliance obligation, see M.-A. Frison-Roche, "L'efficacité de la compliance illustrée par l'affaire *Youporn*" ("The Efficacy of Compliance illustrated by the *Youporn* case"), *Actu-Juridique*, 21 June 2022, https://mafr.fr/en/article/lefficacite-de-la-compliance-illustree-par-laffair/.

(104) M.-A. Frison-Roche, "*Youporn*. The question is: how to apply the texts? To achieve something rather than nothing", *Newsletter MAFR Law, Compliance, Regulation*, 30 September 2022, https://mafr.fr/en/article/youporn-la-question-estcomment-appliquer-les-texte/.

(105) On this notion, M.-A. Frison-Roche, "The hypothesis of the category of systemic cases brought before the judge", 2021, https://mafr.fr/en/article/lhypothese-des-causes-systemiques/.

(106) In this conception, *Tribunal judiciaire de Paris* (Paris First Instance Civil Court), 7 July 2023, No. RG 22/55687, *Arcom v. Orange and others*; M.-A. Frison-Roche, "Present and future of 'systemic cases': the case of porn websites (judgment of 7 July 2023)", *Newsletter MAFR Law, Compliance, Regulation*, 8 July 2023, https://www.mafr.fr/en/article/present-et-avenir-des-causes-systemiques-cas-des-s/.

43. The evidence of behaviour obtained from the perspective of Compliance Monumental Goals. However, even if structural obligations are subject to obligations of result, while behavioural obligations are subject only to obligations of means, it is nevertheless the behavioural obligations that are the most important, since through the structures it is behaviour that must be obtained: it is thanks to a "Compliance Culture" that systemically harmful actions are stopped and systemically beneficial actions spread. *Consequently, this evidence, i.e. the results obtained thanks to the tools put in place, is decisive in providing others, in particular employees, supervisors, regulators, stakeholders and judges, with proof that Compliance Culture is supported by the company in order to obtain the systemically proven behaviours.*

With this in mind, the company must gather all the evidence it can, daily and regardless of any prospect of litigation.

V. PRE-CONSTITUTION OF EVIDENCE, MIRROR OF THE *EX-ANTE* NATURE OF COMPLIANCE LAW

44. Pre-constitution of the Compliance Evidence System, in order to never be used. As in the case of Regulatory Law, the ideal Compliance Law is one that builds a system that never needs to be applied: for example, Banking Compliance that is so well designed and ensures the solidity of systemic banking operators and that none of them will get into difficulty, no resolution will need to be organised and the banking system will never be threatened. The triumph of Compliance Law lies in the absence of *ex post*. It assumes that there will never be any need for the company to have to account to a judge for the diligence it has accomplished, because no one will have the opportunity to allege liability since no damage will have occurred or no future damage is feared. So, evidence must be built up *ex ante*, even if, ideally, sanctions should never be imposed *ex post*.

Indeed, the proof that a company has fulfilled its Compliance Obligation must be reliable and available to all, to such an extent that the system itself is so strengthened that the risks affecting it do not materialise: *the pre-constitution of proof is therefore a reflection of the ex ante nature of Compliance Law and constitutes, through the trust it engenders and the permanent accountability it provides, a key element of Compliance Law itself.*

This is why companies need to ensure that their compliance tools are effective and efficient.

45. Pre-constituting the Effectiveness of Compliance Tools. The judge is only one of the recipients of this Compliance Evidence, as public opinion is sometimes the first recipient when the effect, positive or negative, on reputation is at stake. (107)

Pre-constitution of effectiveness is the simplest: it is necessary, but also sufficient, to keep archived proof that the required acts have been performed, and to keep a record of the content, dates, persons, etc. of the acts. If necessary, have the register kept by a third party. If a compliance contract is entered into, (108) this pre-constitution must be required: it must be specified that this evidence must be provided, being either portable or disposable for the benefit of the company, and possibly for the benefit of third parties, duly listed by the company, in a closed rather than open list. If information is contained, prior authorisation may be contractually required. These clauses must be drafted with great care.

46. Pre-constituting the Efficacy of Compliance Tools. The pre-constitution of the efficacy of compliance tools is more delicate. The aim is to show that the tools have achieved their purpose. This may involve preserving proof that the mapping had been "usefully" drawn up, that the training had been "assimilated" by its recipients, or even that they had made appropriate use of the knowledge assimilated. This can be invaluable pre-constituted evidence to show the company's goodwill, because, while good faith is presumed, goodwill is not, and this is one way of establishing the latter.

47. The pre-constitution of the Company's will to fulfil its Compliance Obligation by the desire to "progress" in the use of Compliance Tools. Evidence does not exist in isolation. Indeed, it is often by bringing them together that evidence against the company emerges, with the notion of a "body of consistent evidence" increasingly becoming a "standard of proof" in Economic Law. (109) But this also works to the company's advantage. The public authorities point out that the accumulation of compliance expenditure is not enough to establish compliance obligation satisfaction, suspecting that it may simply be a matter of buying

(107) S. Pottier, "In Favour of European Compliance, a Vehicle of Economic and Political Assertion", *op. cit.*

(108) On the concept of a "compliance contract", see *supra* No. 31.

(109) See *supra* No. 7.

impunity for an offence that Compliance Law seeks to detect or prevent, such as corruption, harassment or pollution. Conversely, a company that can prove that it has built on a failure or semi-success in using one compliance tool and replace it with another that remedies the shortcomings of the first, for example a new risk assessment method, additional training or a more appropriate determination of the people to whom the programmes are addressed, will have proved that it is effectively incorporating the "lessons" of compliance.

48. Proof of the Efficiency of structural and behavioural Compliance Tools. Efficiency relates to the effect produced on the system itself. For example, greater respect for minorities in companies through quota obligations in management bodies or through compliance tools that penetrate Labour Law. Companies are not legally obliged to measure the impact of compliance on economic and social systems, especially on a global scale. But if they measure it, modify their actions to achieve greater efficiency and can provide evidence to that effect, they increase the demonstration of their "good will." (110)

49. Proof of the Efficiency of the action of the crucial companies involved: a means and an object of proof without an underlying burden of proof. Although a company does not have the burden of proving that it has improved Society as a whole and humanity as a whole, nor can it claim to govern society, (111) it nonetheless benefits from providing proof of the benefit it brings by using compliance techniques. (112)

50. Conclusion. Building the Evidentiary Square specific to Compliance Law. This study, which lays down the prolegomena of the Compliance Evidence Law, has been written in order to build such an evidentiary square specific to Compliance Law, so that jurisdictional, contractual and soft Law practice may find common ground in the definitions, principles and reasoning, without ever sacrificing the Rule of Law.

(110) See for instance C. Peicuti & J. Beyssade, "Feminisation of Positions of Responsibility in the Workplace as a Goal of Compliance. Example of the Banking Sector", *in* M.-A. Frison-Roche (ed.), *Compliance Monumental Goals, op. cit.*, pp. 117-136.

(111) On the relationship between business and politics through Compliance Law, see M.-A. Frison-Roche, "Compliance Monumental Goals, Beating Heart of Compliance Law", *in* M.-A. Frison-Roche (ed.), *Compliance Monumental Goals, op. cit.*, pp. 33-58 and "Reinforce the Judge and the Lawyer to impose Compliance Law as a characteristic of the Rule of Law", *this book*.

(112) For concrete examples, see *in* M.-A. Frison-Roche (ed.), *Compliance Monumental Goals, op. cit.*, C. Peicuti & J. Beyssade, "Feminisation of Positions of Responsibility in the Workplace as a Goal of Compliance. Example of the Banking Sector", pp. 117-136, and A. Le Goff, "Monumental Goals Perceived by the Firm: Serene Business or Business under Pressure?", pp. 83-90.

The application of compliance standards by European Union judges

Juliette Morel-Maroger*

Professor at Paris-Dauphine PSL University, CR2D

Intended to pursue the attainment of general interest objectives – or "monumental goals"(1) – the purpose of compliance standards is in principle to modify and guide the behaviour of economic operators. Compliance standards are therefore characterised by their goals, the techniques and procedures for achieving them. As pointed out, this is as much an organisational phenomenon as a legal one.(2) In order to achieve these objectives, compliance uses the full range of normativity. Although it may in some cases take the form of hard Law, compliance standards are in principle there to explain, encourage and change the behaviour of operators and thus ensure the effectiveness of these monumental goals, but without necessarily creating rights and obligations directly. Compliance is therefore a natural choice for "soft law."(3) Recommendations, guidance, statements, recitals, opinions, pronouncements, guidelines, etc. The European soft Law acts(4) participating in this movement are very diverse. Compliance standards have particularly varied names and are resistant to any form of classification.

---

* This contribution is the result of a presentation given within the framework of the conference "*Quels juges pour la compliance?*" ("Which judges for Compliance Law?") held at the University of Paris-Dauphine with the *Journal of Regulation & Compliance (JoRC)*, on 23 September 2021.

(1) M.-A. Frison Roche, "Le droit de la compliance", *D.*, 2016, p. 1891; M.-A. Frison Roche, "*Legal Approach to Compliance Tools: Building by Law the Unity of Compliance Tools from the Definition of Compliance Law by its 'Monumental Goals'*", *in* M.-A. Frison Roche (ed.), *Compliance Tools*, Brussels, Bruylant, 2021, p. 35.

(2) A. Gaudemet, "Introduction", *in* A. Gaudemet (ed.), *La Compliance, un monde nouveau ?*, Paris, Éditions Panthéon Assas, 2016, p. 11.

(3) Study of the *Conseil d'État* (French Council of State), *Le droit souple*, 2013.

(4) D. Guinard, "À propos du Soft Law en droit de l'Union européenne, analyses théorique et pratique", *Rev. UE*, 2013, p. 609.

Compliance, in its dual preventive and punitive dimensions, also encompasses very broad areas. Competition, anti-corruption, vigilance, personal data protection, environmental protection... The list is long. But when it comes to analysing the application of compliance standards by European Union judges, two areas are particularly concerned today: Competition Law, which has been affected for a long time already, (5) and, more recently, Banking and Financial Law, (6) because the deployment of the Banking Union has considerably renewed the regulation and supervision of the financial sector. (7) Why are these sectors more concerned than others? This is mainly due to the fact that the European Authorities have powers in these areas – sometimes prescriptive – and can also directly sanction operators. This is not the case in other areas of compliance, however, such as the fight against corruption or the duty of care, (8) which are still largely in the hands of Member State authorities and judges. Although the European level is undoubtedly much more effective than the national level in ensuring the effectiveness of compliance objectives in these areas, the construction of a European Compliance Law still has to deal with the difficulties inherent in taking collective decisions within the European Union. But things could change in the future with the entry into operation of the European Public Prosecutor's Office on 1 June 2021 and the progress of European work on the duty of care.

What is and what should be the role of the European Union judges in view of the development of these compliance standards? The proliferation of standards from a wide variety of sources of which the scope remains uncertain undoubtedly raises serious questions. As the European Parliament recalled on 4 September 2007, the excessive use of soft Law standards risks "flouting the principles of democracy and the rule of law",

(5) E. Claudel, "Les sources vives du droit de la concurrence, Étude de droit européen et français des pratiques anticoncurrentielles", *in* G. Parleani (ed.), *Mélanges C. Lucas de Leyssac*, Paris, LexisNexis, 2018, pp. 57 *et seq.*; C. Vincent,"La force normative des communications et lignes directrices en droit européen de la concurrence", *in* C. Thibierge (ed.), *La force normative, naissance d'un concept*, Paris, LGDJ, 2009, p. 691.

(6) T. Bonneau, "Compliance et secteur bancaire et financier en Europe", *in* M.-A. Frison Roche (ed.), *Pour une Europe de la compliance*, Paris, Dalloz, 2019, p. 79.

(7) The personal data protection sector, in which compliance has a considerable role, but which, unlike the competition sector and the banking and financial sectors, does not (yet) have a European authority with direct sanctioning powers, might also be included. See A. Debet, "Les nouveaux instruments de conformité", *Dalloz IP/IT*, 2016, p. 592; L. Pailler, "Technological Tools, *Compliance by Design* and the GDPR:Data Protection by Design", *in* M.-A. Frison-Roche (ed.), *Compliance Tools*, *op. cit.*, p. 299; I. Falque-Pierrotin, "L'Europe des données ou l'individu au cœur d'un système de compliance", *in* M.-A. Frison-Roche (ed.), *Régulation, Supervision, Compliance*, Paris, Dalloz, 2017, p. 29.

(8) B. Lecourt, "Vers une directive sur le devoir de vigilance des sociétés. Résolution du Parlement européen du 10 mars 2021 contenant des recommandations à la Commission sur le devoir de vigilance et la responsabilité des entreprises, P9_TA-PROV (2021) 0073, (2020/2129[INL])", *Revue des sociétés*, 2021, p. 335.

as well as principles specific to European Union Law, namely the principles of subsidiarity and proportionality. Sometimes described as legal UFOs, or even recently by an Advocate General of the Court of Justice of the European Union as "crypto-legislation,"(9) adherence to compliance standards, an essential dimension of their effectiveness and efficiency, also presupposes the recognition of their legitimacy. And to establish this legitimacy, the role of judges is essential.

In French domestic Law, the *Conseil d'État* (French Council of State) has adapted and taken over the control of these new standards since the *Fairvesta* (10) judgement and has since issued some fifteen judgements aimed at assessing the legality of soft Law acts issued by administrative authorities. (11)

The questions put to the French Council of State and the courts of the European Union are similar, but nonetheless differ due to European legal specificities. How are compliance standards applied by European judges? As in domestic Law, the very legality of the compliance standards drawn up by the regulatory authorities is contested. It will therefore be necessary to analyse the control exercised by the European judges over them (I). But while the success of compliance presupposes above all the adherence of economic operators to its methods and objectives, taking into account or applying compliance standards by judges also plays a role in this (II).

I. CHALLENGING THE VALIDITY OF COMPLIANCE STANDARDS BEFORE THE EUROPEAN JUDGES

The issue of judicial review of compliance is not entirely new, but it is now gaining momentum in the European courts, particularly in the context of the implementation of the Banking Union. (12) This can be

(9) See Concl. Adv. Gen. Bobek, of 15 April 2021, case C-911/19, *adde*, T. Bonneau, "Le juge, l'ABE, la 'crypto législation' et l'État de droit", *RDBF*, July 2021, marker 4.

(10) Judgment of the *Conseil d'État* (French Council of State), Ass., 21 March 2016, *Fairvesta*, No. 368082, *D.*, 2016, 715, obs. M.-C. de Montecler; *AJDA*, 2016, 572, and 717, chron. L. Dutheillet de Lamothe and G. Odinet; *AJCA*, 2016, 302, obs. S. Pelé; *Rev. Sociétés*, 2016, 608, note O. Dexant de Bailliencourt; *RFDA*, 2016, 497, concl. S. von Coester; *RTD civ.*, 2016, 571, obs. P. Deumier; *RTD com.*, 2016, 298, obs. N. Rontchevsky, and 711, obs. F. Lombard; *adde*, B. Stirn, "Le juge administratif et la compliance", *in* N. Borga, J.-Cl. Marin and J.-Chr. Roda (eds), *Compliance: l'entreprise, le régulateur et le juge*, Paris, Dalloz, 2018, p. 193.

(11) L. Calandri, "Autorités administratives indépendantes - La justiciabilité variable des actes de Soft Law des autorités de régulation: retour sur une jurisprudence en construction", *Dr. adm.*, January 2020, No. 1, study 2.

(12) T. Bonneau, "Le TUE et la CJUE, des acteurs essentiels pour le secteur bancaire et financier", *RDBF*, January 2019, point 1.

explained quite naturally: the banking and financial sector has been a breeding ground for compliance for a long time now and this is reflected in the proliferation of soft Law acts. The advent of the Banking Union and the important powers granted to the European Authorities in this context – in particular to the ECB or the European Supervisory Authorities – have given rise to a large amount of litigation aimed at challenging the acts adopted in this context, which has given the European General Court and the Court of Justice the opportunity to rule on the admissibility of appeals with regard to "soft law" acts.

The judgement delivered by the Court of Justice on 15 July 2021 (13) issued by the European Banking Authority (EBA) in a case challenging guidelines provides a particularly interesting illustration of how European Union judges understand these soft Law standards. In principle, the EBA has the power to encourage and persuade national authorities and financial institutions. The EBA has been very active in banking regulation in recent years and, on 22 March 2016, published guidance on the governance and supervision of retail banking products. On 8 September 2017, the *Autorité de Contrôle Prudentiel et de Résolution – ACPR* (French Banking Supervisory Authority) published an opinion in which it declared that it complied with the said guidelines. This opinion was challenged by the *Fédération bancaire française* (French Banking Federation) by way of an action for misuse of power before the French Council of State. The Council of State then referred questions to the Court of Justice of the European Union for a preliminary ruling on the remedies available for challenging these guidelines. (14) This case highlights the fact that compliance standards can be challenged by means of an action for annulment based on Article 263 of the *Treaty on the Functioning of the European Union* (TFEU) on the one hand (A), and exceptionally by means of a preliminary ruling based on Article 267 of the TFEU on the other (B).

---

(13) CJEU, 15 July 2021, *FBF v. ACPR*, *Banque et Dr.*, case C-911/19, September 2021, note J. Morel-Maroger, *RDBF*, 2021, comm. 122 note T. Samin and S. Torck; *D.*, 2021, p. 1956, note A.-C. Rouaud; *D.*, 2021, p. 1890, obs.

(14) Council of State, 9th and 10th ch. combined, 4 December 2019, No. 415550, *BJB*, 2020, No. 11, p. 9, note Th. Bonneau; *RDBF*, 2020, comm. 13, note M. Gillouard and A. Gourio. See also M. Gillouard and A. Gourio, note under Concl. Adv. Gen. Bobek; *RDBF*, 2021, comm. 80.

A. The action for annulment

Can recommendations, guidance, opinions, press releases or any other manifestation of soft Law adopted by a European authority be the basis of actions for annulment under Article 263 of the TFEU?

In principle, the answer is no. Only acts of EU bodies or agencies intended to produce legal effects *vis-à-vis* third parties may be challenged. But, as in domestic Law, the EU judges do not stop at the form of the act alone. If an act produces legally binding effects (thus constituting a "false" instrument of soft Law), an appeal is possible. In order to determine whether the contested act produces legally binding effects, the Court of Justice states that it is necessary to focus on the substance of the act and to assess its effects in the light of objective criteria, such as the content of the act itself, taking into account, where appropriate, the context in which it was adopted and the powers of the institution that created it. (15) This analytical grid, which focuses on the act and its author, does not take into account the perception of those to whom it is addressed – be it the national authorities or the regulated institutions. Thus, unlike the Council of State, the European Union judges refuse to rely in part on the perception of the addressees of the act in order to determine whether the latter may be the subject of an action for annulment. However, this perception seems to be essential for determining the binding nature of an act. (16)

The admissibility of the action for annulment is thus rarely admitted, and undoubtedly feeds a certain mistrust of the European regulatory authorities. Admittedly, determining the precise boundaries of binding and non-binding acts is delicate, and completely eliminating the "grey areas" between hard and soft Law is undoubtedly illusory. However, following the example of the Council of State, it would undoubtedly be useful for the perception of the addressees of the act to be included as an element in the assessment of the binding scope of the acts, which would make it possible to ensure closer monitoring of the practice of regulators, which consists of compelling in fact and pretending in law to limit itself to recommending. (17)

(15) CJEU, 20 February 2018, *Belgium v. Commission*; case C-16/16, CJEU, 26 March 2019, *Commission v. Italy*, case C-621/16.

(16) In favour of taking into account the perception of the addressee of the act, Concl. Bobek, *op. cit.*

(17) H. Synvet, Chron. "Droit bancaire", *D.*, 2016, p. 2305.

Any change in the criteria for admissibility of an action for annulment would undoubtedly open the door to new challenges, but would it not also encourage greater acceptance of these standards, which is in principle at the very heart of the approach taken by compliance promoters? Opponents of any such development might argue that operators are not deprived of any action, since the preliminary ruling is much more widely available than the action for annulment.

B. The preliminary ruling

Is it possible to bring an action by way of exception by a preliminary ruling based on Article 267 of the TFEU? At first sight, it might seem surprising or even incomprehensible that an act which is considered non-binding and does not have binding effect within the meaning of Article 263 of the TFEU can be the basis for a reference for a preliminary ruling. However, these two remedies must be separated, particularly where non-binding measures of EU Law are at issue. Article 267 of the TFEU gives the Court of Justice jurisdiction to give preliminary rulings on the validity and interpretation of acts adopted by the EU institutions, without any exception and therefore without distinction according to the normative scope of the contested act. This explains why the Court of Justice, since the *Grimaldi* judgement,(18) has accepted that an act, even a non-binding one, can always be the subject of a reference for a preliminary ruling. The admissibility of a reference for a preliminary ruling is thus completely independent of the assessment of the binding scope of the act. This dissociation is useful, as there seems to be a lack of clarity today when it comes to ruling on the delicate question of the binding scope of acts of soft Law. This means that litigants always have a means of challenging acts adopted by the European authorities, without having to worry about the extraordinary complexity resulting from the overlapping of competences and the considerable growth of soft Law acts as tools of economic regulation.

In practice, however, although the admissibility of references for preliminary rulings is largely open, it will not always be possible to challenge compliance standards, for at least two reasons. On the one hand, the national courts refer questions to the Court of Justice of the European Union for preliminary rulings: referral to the Court of Justice

(18) ECJ, 13 December 1989, *Grimaldi*, case C-322/88.

thus presupposes that the validity of compliance standards resulting from European acts is directly at issue before the national courts, for example when actions are brought concerning the actions of national regulatory authorities that have expressed their willingness to comply with compliance standards adopted by European authorities. On the other hand, the intensity of the control exercised by the Court of Justice on the occasion of these preliminary rulings raises certain questions. If we take as an example the judgement delivered by the Court of Justice on 15 July 2021 on the EBA guidelines, the control exercised by the Court seems to have been particularly "soft" and the conclusions it reached have been unanimously criticised by the commentators of the decision. (19) Is or should the control exercised by the European judges be more limited with regard to compliance standards? Can the European courts modulate the intensity of the control of legality (20) exercised according to whether the acts in question are soft, the adoption of which is expressly provided for by the European treaties or regulations, (21) or, on the contrary, acts that are not included in the nomenclature? It will undoubtedly be necessary to strike a fair balance between the effectiveness and legitimacy of these norms and, in the future, to better circumscribe the intensity of the jurisdictional control that must be exercised over them.

Although the questions raised by challenging compliance standards before EU judges are far from being resolved, the latter are also potentially important actors in their implementation.

II. THE ROLE OF THE EU JUDGE IN THE APPLICATION OF COMPLIANCE STANDARDS

In addition to monitoring the legality of compliance standards exercised by EU judges, (22) the latter also contribute to their application. Of course, the effectiveness of compliance depends above all on the support of those to whom it is addressed, and economic operators are undoubtedly the primary actors in its success. The European Union judges, who are

(19) See notes above.

(20) See the findings of Advocate General Bobek, cited above, para. 76 *et seq.*

(21) Which is the case of the EBA guidelines, the adoption of which is provided for by Article 16 of Regulation (EU) No. 1093/2010 of the European Parliament and of the Council of 24 November 2010.

(22) K. Lenaerts, "Le juge de l'Union européenne dans une Europe de la compliance", *in* M.-A. Frison-Roche (ed.), *Pour une Europe de la compliance*, *op. cit.*, p. 1.

competent to settle disputes relating to the application of European Union Law between the Member States, the European institutions and individual claimants, may have to ensure the effectiveness of European compliance standards (A) and interpret them (B).

A. The application of compliance standards by EU judges

While national courts remain the ordinary judges of the EU, the courts of the European Union, within the limits of the texts that allow them to be seized, can play an important role in ensuring the implementation of compliance standards. Regardless of the type of action on which the jurisdiction of the EU courts is based, these may provide them with an opportunity to participate in the effectiveness of compliance standards.

Firstly, the Court of Justice could sanction the inertia of the Member States, or why not of the European institutions, in the implementation of European texts aimed at imposing compliance standards. The Court could, for example, in an action against a State for failure to fulfil obligations based on Articles 258 to 260 of the TFEU, sanction a failure to transpose – or an incomplete transposition of – a directive, of which the main purpose would be to create new compliance obligations. Such a scenario could be imagined, for example, if a directive on the duty of care was to be issued.

But the effectiveness of these standards is also ensured by their possible invocation by litigants before the European Union courts. Particularly noteworthy examples of this are provided by European Competition Law, which has long been imbued with the logic of compliance.(23) Thus, the prescriptions contained in certain guidelines or notices may justify the position of judges in disputes between Member States and companies. The Court of Justice has ruled, for example, that a notice may constitute a normative basis enabling a company to avoid an infringement.(24) It is also possible for litigants to challenge compliance standards against the European authorities that adopted them. This is what the Court of Justice ruled on 28 June 2005(25) in relation to the Commission's guidelines on the calculation of fines in competition matters.

(23) K. Lenaerts, "Le juge de l'Union européenne dans une Europe de la compliance", *op. cit.*

(24) ECJ, 16 December 1975, *Coöperatieve Vereniging "Suiker Unie" UA*, case 114/73, *European Court Reports* 1663: an undertaking which relies on a notice to reach an agreement cannot be fined if the agreement is in fact covered by the notice.

(25) ECJ, 28 June 2005, joint cases C-189/02, C-202/02, C-205/02 to C-208/02 and C-213/02, *Dansk Rørindustri A/S*, ECR I-5425, esp. pts 209 *et seq.*; *RSC*, 2006, 155, obs. L. Idot; *RTD eur.*, 2006, 477, chron.

Finally, EU judges contribute to the application of compliance standards by allowing litigants to invoke them before national courts, even when they originate from soft Law instruments. Once again, an interesting illustration is provided by a recent judgement of the Court of Justice on EBA guidelines. (26) The Court held that, even if recommendations do not produce legally-binding effects, national courts must "*take them into account,*" in particular when they are intended to supplement binding provisions of European Union Law. Thus, a litigant who has been harmed by an infringement of EU Law must be able to rely on the recommendation in order to establish the responsibility of the Member State concerned. The invocable nature of soft Law acts by individuals could therefore be extended to other sectors of activity.

All the types of action provided for by the European Treaties before the courts of the European Union can thus be mobilised by these courts in order to participate in the effectiveness of compliance standards, and it is likely that their role will be extended in the future to other sectors in which compliance methods and tools are deployed.

B. The interpretation of compliance standards by European Union judges

The courts of the European Union do not limit themselves to ensuring compliance with – and thus the effectiveness of – compliance standards. They can also help to consolidate or even construct them by interpreting them.

The vast majority of judgements delivered by the Court of Justice of the European Union are based on references for preliminary rulings from national courts under Article 267 of the TFEU. The interpretation given by the Court of Justice to a rule of EU Law in the exercise of its jurisdiction to give a preliminary ruling clarifies and specifies, where necessary, the meaning and scope of that rule as it should be or should have been understood and applied from the time when it came into force.

J.-B. Blaise, where the Court considers that, "in adopting such rules of conduct and announcing by publishing them that they will henceforth apply to the cases to which they relate, the institution in question imposes a limit on the exercise of its discretion and cannot depart from those rules under pain of being found, where appropriate, to be in breach of the general principles of law, such as equal treatment or the protection of legitimate expectations. It cannot therefore be precluded that, on certain conditions and depending on their content, such rules of conduct, which are of general application, may produce legal effects."

(26) CJEU, 25 March 2021, *BT v. Bulgarska Narodna Banka*, case C-501/18, *Europe*, 2021 comm. 148, obs. D. Simon; *D.*, 2021, p. 1890, obs. H. Synvet.

However, the interpretation of compliance standards may also result from decisions delivered by the European courts when examining actions for annulment on the basis of Article 263 TFEU. Indeed, while the annulment procedure is largely closed to litigants wishing to challenge acts of soft Law, it is the preferred legal route for opposing sanction decisions issued by the European authorities. By confirming or, on the contrary, by censuring the sanctions pronounced by the European authorities (ECB and European Commission in particular), the European Union judges still participate in the interpretation of compliance standards, in Competition Law (27) or in banking matters. (28)

Regardless of the type of action that leads to referral to the European Union courts, the very detailed reasons given for the decisions delivered by the European courts, informed by the conclusions of the Advocates General, also contribute to a better understanding of the rules and decision-making processes of European Union Law, which are sometimes particularly complex.

The judges of the European Union thus have the task of clarifying the obligations that are at the heart of compliance, whether in terms of the goals to be achieved or the procedures for achieving them.

By contributing to the interpretation, understanding and implementation of compliance standards, European Union judges are essential players in the construction of a Compliance Law. (29) Their decisions have the added advantage of being absolutely *res judicata* and are binding on national judges and authorities. If the developments already taking place in the banking and financial sector, where European judges are constantly called upon to clarify the obligations of institutions, (30) are anything to go by, the role of the EU courts could become central in interpreting compliance standards as they develop in ever more varied areas.

(27) E. Claudel, "Les sources vives du droit de la concurrence, Étude de droit européen et français des pratiques anticoncurrentielles", *op. cit.*

(28) J. Morel-Maroger, "Premiers contrôles juridictionnels des décisions de la BCE infligeant des sanctions pécuniaires en tant que superviseur bancaire", note on the judgement of the General Court of 8 July 2020, *Crédit Agricole SA v. ECB*, case. T-576/16, *Crédit agricole Corporate and Investment Bank v. ECB*, case T-577/18 and *CA Consumer Finance v. ECB*, case T-578/18 *VQ v. ECB*, case T-203/18, *Banque et Droit*, September-October 2020, No. 193, p. 68.

(29) See in the banking and financial areas, T. Bonneau, "Le TUE et la CJUE, des acteurs essentiels pour le secteur bancaire et financier", *RDBF*, January 2019, marker 1; and in Competition Law, E. Claudel, "Les sources vives du droit de la concurrence, Étude de droit européen et français des pratiques anticoncurrentielles", *in* G. Parleani (ed.), *Mélanges C. Lucas de Leyssac*, Paris, LexisNexis, 2018, pp. 57 *et seq.*

(30) T. Bonneau, "Compliance et secteur bancaire et financier en Europe", *in* M.-A. Frison-Roche (ed.), *Pour une Europe de la compliance*, Paris, Dalloz, 2019, p. 79.

The judges of the European Union thus play a role in constructing a jurisdictional regime for Compliance Law and are emerging as key players, responsible for both the litigation of challenges to compliance standards and for ensuring their effectiveness and uniform interpretation within the European Union.

But it is also possible to envisage in the future the EU judges, but perhaps even more so the European Public Prosecutor's Office – in particular if its powers were to be strengthened (31) – becoming even more important and becoming the real driving force behind the development of a European Compliance Law.

(31) See in particular the proposals made in the report of the *Club des juristes*, B. Cazeneuve and A. Gaudemet (eds), *Pour un droit européen de la compliance*, November 2020, available at www.leclubdesjuristes.com; J.-Cl. Marin, "Quels outils pour la construction du droit de la compliance en Europe", *in* M.-A. Frison-Roche (ed.), *Pour une Europe de la compliance*, *op. cit.*, p. 67.

A single judge in the event of an international breach of compliance obligations?

Sophie Schiller

Professor at Paris-Dauphine PSL University

Director of the Dauphine Law School

Summary: Given the very international nature of the subjects dealt with, the actors involved and therefore the compliance disputes, it is essential to know if a person can be implicated before several judges, attached to different states or even if they can be convicted by several jurisdictions. The answer is given by the non bis in idem *principle, which is the subject of an abundant case law on the basis of Article 4 of Protocol No. 7 of the ECHR, clearly inapplicable for jurisdictions from different States.*

To assess whether breaches of compliance obligations may be subject to multiple sanctions in different states, it will first be necessary to ascertain whether there is a textual basis to be invoked.

At European level, Article 50 of the Charter of Fundamental Rights of the European Union now allows the principle of ne bis in idem *to be invoked. Applicable to all areas of compliance, it provides a very strong protection which covers both convictions and prosecutions. Like its effects, the scope of Article 50 is very broad. The proceedings concerned are those which have a repressive nature, beyond those pronounced by criminal courts in the strict sense, which makes it possible to cover the convictions pronounced by one of the many regulatory authorities competent in matters of compliance.*

Internationally, the situation is less clear. Article 14-7 of the International Covenant on Civil and Political Rights may be invoked if several obstacles are overcome, including the decision of 2 November 1987 of the Human Rights

Committee, which restricted it to the domestic context, i.e. the assumption of double jeopardy by the same State.

Even if the grounds are applicable, two specificities of compliance situations might hamper their application: the first related to the applicable procedural rules, in particular the rules of jurisdiction, and the second related to the specificities of the situation.

The application of the non bis in idem *principle is formally accepted only with regard to universal jurisdiction and personal jurisdiction, i.e. extraterritorial jurisdiction, which is only part of the jurisdiction. The* Cour de cassation *(French Court of cassation) confirmed this in the famous so-called "Oil for food" decision of 14 March 2018. The refusal to recognise this principle as universal, regardless of the jurisdiction rule in question, deprives French companies of a mean of defence. Moreover, the repression of breaches of compliance rules is increasingly resolved through transactional mechanisms. The latter will not always fall within the scope of European and international rules laying down the* non bis in idem *principle as they are sometimes qualified as "final" under the terms of Article 50 of the Charter of Fundamental Rights of the European Union and Article 14-7 of the International Covenant on Civil and Political Rights.*

Compliance breaches are often based on multiple acts. This results in statutes of limitations whose starting point is delayed to the last event and in a facilitated jurisdiction for French courts when only one of the constitutive facts is found in France. In terms of compliance, the non bis in idem *principle therefore generally does not protect companies and does not prevent them from being sued before the courts of two different countries for the same case. It nevertheless grants them other protections by obliging them to take foreign decisions into account in determining the amount of the penalty. The sanction against Airbus SE in the* convention judiciaire d'intérêt public – CJIP *(Judicial Public Interest Agreement) of 29 January 2020 perfectly illustrates this.*

*
* *

One of the particularities of compliance, whatever the field, is the very international nature of the subjects dealt with, the players involved and therefore the disputes. A case almost always has a cross-border dimension, either because of the presence of an activity in several countries or because of the multinational nature of the people involved. In the financial field and in Competition Law, the assumption is commonly made that 80% of cases have an international dimension. The latest applications of compliance, namely to fight against corruption and against human rights or environmental violations, follow the same logic. Most of the cases involve Western companies that are accused of acts outside their borders. A question then seems essential: can a person be a defendant before several judges, each attached to a different state? Following this logic, can a person be convicted by several courts?

There is a wealth of case law on this topic, known as *non bis in idem*, prohibiting the same person from being prosecuted and punished twice for the same acts. This principle is inherited from a procedural rule of Roman Law in order to put an end to judicial debates and protect the institution from its contradictions. It is found in Canon Law and in particular in the famous formula of Gilles de Noyers in the 16th century, according to which "one should not make two penances of one sin."(1) Although it was taken over in the 18th century by the philosophy of the Enlightenment as a guarantee of the individual against the arbitrariness of repression, France twice refused to give it a very broad constitutional value.(2) It first excluded this principle from the 1958 Constitution, whereas it was found in the 1791 and Year III constitutions, relegating it to the *Code de procedure pénale* (French Criminal Procedure Code). It then formulated a reservation to the accession to the Additional Protocol No. 7 to the European Convention on Human Rights (ECHR) which enshrines it. This principle has often been invoked and is the subject of an abundant case law, on the basis of Article 4 of Protocol No. 7 to the ECHR, which states that "No one shall be liable to be tried or punished again in criminal proceedings under the jurisdiction of the same State for an offence for which he has already been finally acquitted or convicted in accordance with the law and penal procedure of that State." The European and French courts have deduced from it the framework for the cumulation of prosecutions tending to a cumulation of sanctions by a repeatedly quoted formula: "The principle of the necessity of offences and punishments does not prevent the same acts committed by the same person from being subject to different

(1) Free translation of: "*on ne doit pas faire d'un péché deux pénitences*"; on the history of the principle, J.P. Carton, comm. on the 7th Additional Protocole to the Convention, Article 4, *in* M. Cliquennois (ed.), *La convention européenne des droits de l'homme et le juge français*, Paris, L'Harmattan, 1997, p. 286.

(2) F. Drummond, "La décision de la CEDH du 4 mars 2014 et la décision du Conseil constitutionnel du 18 mars 2015 et leurs conséquences", *BJB*, March 2017, p. 162.

prosecutions for the purposes of sanctions in accordance with distinct bodies of rules."(3) Nevertheless, the wording of Article 4 of Protocol No. 7 clearly excludes any application to jurisdictions from different States.

In order to assess whether breaches of compliance obligations may be subject to multiple sanctions in different states, it will be necessary to determine whether any textual grounds can be invoked (I) and then to verify their effectiveness (II).

I. POSSIBLE GROUNDS

There are textual grounds, both in European (A) and international (B) matters, whereby their application to these situations must be verified.

A. European text

The Schengen Agreement of 14 June 1985, in setting up a European area without borders, modified the rules of territoriality and stipulated that "A person whose trial has been finally disposed of in one Contracting Party may not be prosecuted in another Contracting Party for the same acts provided that, if a penalty has been imposed, it has been enforced, is actually in the process of being enforced or can no longer be enforced under the laws of the sentencing Contracting Party." (Article 54). The rule has been subject to numerous limitations in application, in particular because of the restrictions imposed by France.(4) It is therefore Article 50 of the Charter of Fundamental Rights of the European Union that will now allow for better protection of the *non bis in idem* principle at the European level. It states that "No one shall be liable to be tried or punished again in criminal proceedings for an offence for which he or she has already been finally acquitted or convicted within the Union in accordance with the law." The principle applies only in the context of the implementation of EU Law in accordance with Article 51 of the Charter. This exclusion of areas that do not fall within the competence of the European Union is not problematic to avoid double jeopardy in terms of compliance. Indeed, not

(3) Formula taken up and freely translated from the decision of the *Conseil constitutionnel* (French Constitutional Council), 26 March 2021, No. 2021-892 QPC, para. 19, "*Le principe de nécessité des délits et des peines ne fait pas obstacle à ce que les mêmes faits commis par une même personne puissent faire l'objet de poursuites différentes aux fins de sanctions de nature différente en application de corps de règles distincts.*"

(4) D. Rebut, *Droit pénal international*, 3rd ed., Paris, Dalloz, 2019, No. 94 *et seq.*

only are several areas expressly covered by Article 83 of the TFEU (money laundering, corruption, trafficking in human beings, etc.), but the others are included in those covered by Article 50 on the grounds that they prove "essential to ensure the effective implementation of a Union policy in an area which has been subject to harmonisation measures" (Article 83-2 TFEU). It is in the name of this interpretation that stock exchange, financial, competition and data protection compliance rules will be concerned.

Article 50 is applicable to all areas of compliance and provides very strong protection. Unlike Article 4 of Protocol No. 7, it has not been the subject of any French reservations, according to which "only offences falling under French law within the jurisdiction of the courts ruling on criminal matters are to be regarded as offences within the meaning of articles 2 to 4." It does not limit the application of the *ne bis in idem* principle only to convictions, but also to prosecutions. A State must therefore not only refrain from convicting a person a second time; it must also refrain from prosecuting the person if he or she has already been tried for the same acts by another Member State. The solution has been described as "daring, if not avant-garde, which stems from the idea that a prosecution before the criminal courts is part of the repression in the same way as the sanctions that follow."(5) This logic is particularly true in the area of compliance, where defendants are almost exclusively legal entities that are very sensitive to the reputational damage suffered as soon as they are prosecuted. Moreover, the article ignores the condition of the sentence being served or not being able to be served and therefore does not make the application of the *ne bis in idem* principle conditional on any completion of the sanction previously imposed. This implies, on the contrary, that a failure to serve the sentence, such as an acquittal or a conviction, is an obstacle to a second prosecution and conviction.

Like its effects, the scope of Article 50 is very broad. In view of the conception adopted by the European Court of Human Rights, the proceedings concerned are those of a repressive nature, beyond those pronounced by criminal courts strictly speaking. This is the case of convictions delivered by one of the numerous regulatory authorities competent in the area of compliance, be it the *Autorité des marches financiers – AMF* (French Financial Markets Authority), the *Autorité de la concurrence – ADLC* (French Competition Authority), the *Commission nationale de l'informatique et des*

(5) *Ibid.*, No. 100, free translation of: "*audacieuse sinon avant-gardiste, laquelle procède de l'idée qu'une poursuite devant les juridictions pénales participe de la répression au même titre que les sanctions qui ont suivi.*"

libertés – CNIL (French data protection authority), etc. Whether or not they have imposed a sanction, their previous referral in another Member State will prevent prosecution in France, and vice versa.

Given the close proximity of the wording of the two provisions, the solution found for Article 4 § 1 of Protocol No.7 to the ECHR can be applied to define the application of Article 50 of the Charter of Fundamental Rights. Four conditions must be met to prevent cumulation. The facts potentially prosecuted must be identical, the proceedings must have the same purpose, i.e. they must protect the same social interests, the nature of the sanctions must be equivalent in severity and the orders of jurisdiction must be identical. There are countless procedures applicable to compliance that meet these criteria, even if some remain excluded. (6) Thus, in its decision of 4 August 2021, the *AMF* Enforcement Committee refused to apply the *non bis in idem* principle. (7) One of the respondents had been sanctioned on 18 October 2016 by the sanctions committee of Eurex, a German platform that deals in derivatives. The Enforcement Committee considered that "It follows from the sworn translation of the Eurex Enforcement Committee's decision of 18 October 2016, which refers to the German Civil Code, that the sanction imposed on Mr. Vignon qualifies as a civil fine. Furthermore, the rules whose violation was sanctioned were laid down by Eurex, a German private-sector company operating as a market undertaking, and are only binding on market members permitted to trade on that market. As in French Law, which provides, in Article L. 421-18 of the Monetary and Financial Code, that relations between a market undertaking and the members of the regulated market it manages are contractual in nature, it should be noted that the rules set forth by Eurex, which organise the operation of the market and relations between its members, do not have a repressive purpose. This is further evidenced by the sanctions incurred before the Eurex Sanctions Committee, which can impose a reprimand, an exclusion from the market for a maximum of thirty days of trading and a civil fine of up to 250,000 euros, which is disproportionate to the pecuniary sanction of up to 100 million euros or ten times the amount of the benefit obtained incurred before the Sanctions Committee

---

(6) For example, complementary prosecutions, ECHR, 15 November 2016, *A. and B. v. Norway*, No. 24130/11, *D.*, 2017, 128, obs. J.-F. Renucci; or the combination of disciplinary and criminal proceedings, ECHR, 29 September 2020, *Faller and Steinmetz v. France*, No. 59389/16 and 59392/16.

(7) *AMF* Enforcement Committee, 4 August 2021, SAN-2021-14.

for price manipulation."(8) Despite the constraints of its application, the *non bis in idem* principle effectively protects against double jeopardy or prosecution for breach of compliance obligations in different EU Member States. It should be ascertained whether this effectiveness is also present when jurisdictions in non-European countries are involved.

B. International text

Article 14-7 of the International Covenant on Civil and Political Rights [ICCPR] states that "no one shall be liable to be tried or punished again for an offence for which he has already been finally acquitted or convicted in accordance with the law and penal procedure of each country." The wording is very unclear. Contrary to Article 50 of the Charter of Fundamental Rights, it is very different from Article 4 § 1 of the Protocol No. 7 to the ECHR, which will limit the transposition of the interpretations that have been made about it. Nevertheless, both texts use the adjective "penal," one in relation to the judgement and the other in relation to the procedure, and the expression "in accordance with the law." There is therefore no reason why the broad application to the decisions of so many administrative authorities in compliance matters cannot be retained for the International Covenant on Civil and Political Rights. It is true that the *Jammet* opinion of the *Conseil d'État* (French Council of State) limits the application of Article 14-7 to dual prosecutions "*devant une juridiction répressive*" ("before a criminal court"),(9) but it is difficult to draw definitive conclusions from this response for several reasons. Firstly, it concerned the very specific situation of a combination of surcharges provided for by the *Code général des impôts – CGI* (French General Tax Code) and the

(8) Free translation of: "*il résulte de la traduction assermentée de la décision du comité des sanctions d'Eurex du 18 octobre 2016, qui se réfère au Code civil allemand, que la sanction infligée à M. Vignon est qualifiée d'amende civile. En outre, les règles dont la violation a été sanctionnée ont été édictées par Eurex, société de droit privé allemande ayant une activité d'entreprise de marché et ne lient que les membres de marché admis à négocier sur ce marché. À l'instar du droit français qui prévoit, à l'article L. 421-18 du code monétaire et financier, que les relations entre une entreprise de marché et les membres du marché réglementé qu'elle gère sont de nature contractuelle, il y a lieu de retenir que les règles édictées par Eurex, qui organisent le fonctionnement de marché et les relations entre ses membres, n'ont pas de finalité répressive. En attestent encore les sanctions encourues devant le comité des sanctions d'Eurex qui peut infliger un blâme, une exclusion du marché pendant une durée maximale de trente jours de négociation boursière et une amende civile pouvant aller jusqu'à 250 000 euros, sans commune mesure avec la sanction pécuniaire d'un montant maximum de 100 millions d'euros ou du décuple du montant de l'avantage retiré encourue devant la commission des sanctions pour des faits de manipulation de cours.*"

(9) Council of State, opinion, 4 April 1997, No. 183658, *Jammet*, *Dr. Fisc.*, 1997, No. 24, comm. 660, concl. F. Loloum.

reminder of duties imposed on a taxpayer convicted of a criminal penalty for tax fraud. Secondly, the opinion dates back to 1997 and has not been confirmed since then and, thirdly, it concerns an "organic condition not laid down by the Covenant."(10)

If the application to the various criminal decisions were retained, the text could help avoid a person being prosecuted even for a breach of a compliance obligation when he or she has already been acquitted or convicted by a final judgement, i.e. one that has not been appealed. Such an application would imply ignoring the decision of the Human Rights Committee of 2 November 1987, which restricted the recognition of *res judicata* to the domestic context, i.e. to the case of dual jeopardy by the same State.(11) Subsequently, in 1997, the Committee "recalled" in its own words, "that article 14, paragraph 7, of the Covenant does not guarantee the *ne bis in idem* principle with respect to the national jurisdictions of two or more states – this provision prohibits double jeopardy only with regard to an offence adjudicated in a given State" (§ 6.4).(12) Although the interpretation of the Covenant is one of the missions of this committee, its decisions remain non-binding and there is no obligation to follow them. The same committee considered on 10 August 2014 that the plenary assembly of the *Cour de cassation* (French Court of cassation) had disregarded the fundamental rights recognised by the International Covenant on Civil and Political Rights in the *Baby Loup* case.(13) The First President of the Court of cassation reacted by recalling its lack of "binding force" and by underlining the "new destabilising factor of the jurisprudence which disturbs, in the eyes of the trial judges, the unifying role of our Court, which is moreover at the highest level of its plenary assembly."(14) The reaction reminds us of the place that should be given to appreciation. It is therefore permitted to consider the application of the ICCPR and the *non bis in idem* principle it contains when proceedings are initiated in different countries of the world. This basis would complement Article 50

(10) M. Cliquennois, "Fraude fiscale: cumul des sanctions fiscales et pénales", *JCP G*,1998, II, 10087, free translation of: "*condition organique pourtant non posée par le Pacte.*"

(11) "The Committee observes that this provision prohibits double jeopardy only with regard to an office adjudicated in a given State" (*A.P. v. Italy*, communication No. 2074/1986, UN Doc., HRC, CCPR/C/31/D/204/1986).

(12) *A.R.J. v. Australia*, communication No. 692/1996 HRC, UN DOC. CCPR/C/60/D/692/1996.

(13) Decision of the *Cour de cassation* (French Court of cassation), *Assemblée plénière* (Plenary Assembly), 25 June 2014, No.13-28.369, *JCP G*, 2014, 903, note D. Corrignan-Carsin.

(14) *JCP G*, 2018, 970, free translations of: "*force contraignante*" and "*acteur nouveau de déstabilisation de la jurisprudence qui vient perturber, aux yeux des juges du fond, le rôle unificateur de notre Cour, qui plus est au niveau le plus élevé de son assemblée plénière.*"

of the Charter of Fundamental Rights applicable in the case of proceedings in European countries. Nevertheless, the specificities of compliance situations may deprive these applicable foundations of their effectiveness.

II. DIFFICULTIES OF APPLICATION IN COMPLIANCE

Two types of difficulties are likely to hamper the use of these foundations in compliance matters, some linked to the applicable general procedural rules, in particular the rules of jurisdiction (A), and others linked to the specificities of situations (B).

A. General procedural rules

The application of Criminal Law in space is governed by four principles: territoriality, personality, reality and universality. Each principle has a corresponding jurisdiction. However, they do not all have the same value or the same regime. Some can be identified as constituting ordinary Law. (15) Such is the case of territorial jurisdiction and of personal jurisdiction, whether passive or active. Others, on the contrary, can be likened to special regimes. The actual jurisdiction is referred to as a special jurisdiction for specific offences. (16) It is based on Article 113-2 of the *Code pénal* (French Criminal Code), according to which "the applicable criminal law is that of the place of arrest of the offender." (17) The derogatory nature of universal jurisdiction is not in doubt since it can only be applied to certain offences (*Code de procedure pénale* (French Criminal Procedure Code), Article 689-1 *et seq.*) and the case law has chosen it in case of conflict of laws in space in application of the rule *lex specialis derogat legi generali.* (18) One author deduced that "universal jurisdiction is a sum of derogatory regimes." (19) However, the application of the *non bis in idem* rule is formally admitted only with regard to universal jurisdiction

(15) D. Chilstein, *Droit pénal international et lois de police. Essai sur l'application dans l'espace du droit pénal accessoire*, foreword by P. Mayer, "Nouvelle bibliothèque de thèses" Serie, Paris, Dalloz, 2003, pp. 18 *et seq.*

(16) D. Rebut, *Droit pénal international*, *op. cit.*, p. 81.

(17) Free translation of: *"la loi pénale applicable est celle du lieu d'arrestation de l'auteur de l'infraction."*

(18) See Court of cassation, Criminal Chamber, 21 January 2009, No. 07-88-330, *Bull. crim.*, 2009, No. 22; *Rev. sc. crim.*, 2009, p. 829, obs. Y. Mayaud; *D.*, 2009, p. 634; *AJP*, 2009, p. 184, obs. J. Lasserre Capdeville.

(19) O. Beauvallet, "L'univers intérieur. À propos de l'arrêt de la chambre criminelle du 21 janvier 2009", *Dr. pénal*, 2009, study 7, free translation of: *"la compétence universelle est une somme de régimes dérogatoires"*.

and personal jurisdiction, i.e. extraterritorial jurisdiction. (20) The Court of cassation confirmed this in the famous "Oil for Food" case, adding "that the provisions of Article 4 of Protocol No. 7 to the European Convention on Human Rights (ECHR Convention) and Article 14-7 of the International Covenant on Civil and Political Rights (ICCPR), which preclude double prosecution for a single act, are applicable only when the two proceedings have been initiated in the territory of the same State." (21) The solution was considered "consistent but questionable," (22) given the difference in wording between the ICCPR and the Charter of Fundamental Rights, as well as the purpose of the principle. "Indeed, it is an elementary rule of justice. For the beneficiary of the rule, it does not matter whether the new proceedings are initiated in the same state or in a different state. Secondly, we regret the lack of ambition of our Court of cassation in the implementation of this principle: it shows itself to be more respectful of the sovereignty of States than of fundamental rights." (23) In this corruption case, the French courts accepted jurisdiction even though a conviction had already been delivered for the same acts by an American court. In terms of compliance, the texts aimed at sanctioning illicit behaviour by economic operators with extraterritorial effect have developed considerably. Many claim that these various provisions have created a real economic war, allowing States to sanction foreign companies as a matter of priority, according to some. Refusing to recognise the *non bis in idem* principle as universal, regardless of the jurisdictional rule at issue, will deprive our companies of a defence.

In addition, the repression of breaches of compliance rules has the additional characteristic of being increasingly settled by different transactional mechanisms: penal composition, penal mediation or settlement in a wide variety of forms. In order to apply the European and international

---

(20) E. Dreyer, "Corruption active d'agents publics étrangers: difficile d'appliquer la loi sans la corrompre", note on the decision of the Court of cassation, Criminal Chamber, 14 March 2018, No.16-82.117, *JCP E*, 2018, 1363, esp. p. 44.

(21) Court of cassation, Criminal Chamber, 14 March 2018, No.16-82.117, *op. cit.*, free translation of: "*que les dispositions des articles 4 du Protocole no 7 à la Convention européenne des droits de l'homme [convention EDH] et 14-7 du Pacte international relatif aux droits civils et politiques [Pacte IDCP], qui font obstacle à des doubles poursuites pour des faits uniques, ne trouvent à s'appliquer que dans le cas où les deux procédures ont été engagées sur le territoire du même État.*"

(22) E. Dreyer, "Corruption active d'agents publics étrangers: difficile d'appliquer la loi sans la corrompre", *op. cit.*, free translation of: "*constante mais contestable.*"

(23) *Ibid.*, free translation of: "*En effet, il s'agit d'une règle de justice élémentaire. Pour le bénéficiaire de la règle, il importe peu que les nouvelles poursuites soient engagées dans le même État ou dans un État différent. Ensuite, on regrettera le manque d'ambition de notre Cour de cassation dans la mise en œuvre de ce principe : elle se montre à son tour plus respectueuse de la souveraineté des États que des droits fondamentaux.*"

rules laying down the *non bis in idem* principle, settlements should be qualified as a "final judgment" according to the terms of Article 50 of the Charter of Fundamental Rights and Article 14-7 of the International Covenant on Civil and Political Rights. Some of these mechanisms can easily be assimilated to judgements. This is the case, for example, of the *comparution sur reconnaissance préalable de culpabilité – CRPC* (guilty plea procedure) under French Law, which is still not widely used in matters of business crime, and which presupposes a double condition: prior recognition of guilt and a confirmation order which is equivalent to a conviction. (24) Restricting application of the *non bis in idem* principle to this double condition would undoubtedly contribute to rendering the principle of its interest partially meaningless in an international context. (25) Indeed, if we look at the sanctions imposed in the United States, which are now the most numerous and the most spectacular, they are often based on a collaborative approach that largely escapes the control of the judge and does not always involve recognition of guilt. This is the case, for example, with sanctions imposed in the area of corruption in the form of a DPA (Deferred Prosecution Agreement), whereby a company agrees to pay a financial penalty, to acknowledge the facts and to adopt monitoring and prevention measures. But this is also the case, for example in France, of the *accords de composition administrative* (administrative composition agreements) before the *AMF*, which do not require any recognition of guilt either. Thus, in order to guarantee a real scope to the application of the *non bis in idem* principle in an international context, it would undoubtedly be appropriate to extend its application to all alternative procedures to traditional criminal or repressive procedures. Only a flexible interpretation of this principle would make it possible to make it an effective tool for fair repression in an international context and for the protection of litigants. (26)

(24) The *comparution sur reconnaissance préalable de culpabilité – CRPC* (French guilty plea procedure) was nevertheless used to complete a *convention judiciaire d'intérêt public – CJIP* (Judicial Public Interest Agreement) in the *Bolloré* case and the *tribunal correctionnel de Paris* (Paris First Instance Criminal Court) refused to approve it on 26 February 2021, https://www.dalloz-actualite.fr/node/l-affaire-ibollorei-ou-limites-d-une-justice-penale-negociee#.YaSt8lPjL0o.

(25) J. Morel-Maroger, "Les difficultés posées par la mise en œuvre du principe non bis in idem dans un contexte international", *JCP E*, 2015, 1397, esp. para. 15.

(26) *Ibid.*, para. 16.

B. Characteristics of the situations in question

In addition to their international nature, compliance violations are often based on multiple acts. In order to commit a trading violation or a breach of competition, personal data protection, corruption prevention or human rights protection rules, a single act can rarely be sufficient, especially as the decision is distinct from the execution. There is thus a succession of material acts over time and in different spaces with a constant guilty intent. Such a violation is treated in Criminal Law as a continuing offence, which is subject to a special regime. The starting point of the limitation period is set at the moment when the offence ends, and this type of offence is an exception to the *ne bis in idem* rule, since it allows a new conviction when it persists and gives jurisdiction to all the courts in whose jurisdiction the offence was committed.(27) The objective of the rule is to facilitate repression,(28) even if it means sacrificing the protection of the respondent.

According to Article 113-2 of the *Code pénal* (French Criminal Code), "The offence is deemed to have been committed on the territory of the Republic as soon as one of its constitutive acts has taken place in this territory."(29) Faced with these multiple facts that have succeeded one another, it is sufficient for a piece of materiality, however small, to be carried out on our territory for the French courts to intervene. This is what the judges recognised in the "Oil for Food" case.(30) The Court of Appeal had noted that one of the beneficiaries of the oil grants was domiciled in France where his company had an account with a Parisian bank through which its margins transited, so that he "*avait son centre d'intérêt économique à Paris*" ("had his centre of economic interest in Paris."). The Court of cassation considered that it had thus characterised enough "*faits constitutifs*" ("facts constituting an offence") in France to justify the application of French law to all the facts before the criminal courts of that country.

In terms of compliance, the *non bis in idem* principle therefore generally does not protect companies from being sued in the courts of two different countries for the same case. It nevertheless grants them other

(27) Court of cassation, Criminal Chamber, 31 August 1992, *Bull. Crim.*, No. 304.

(28) M. Bouchet, "Coup de projecteur sur le recul silencieux de l'infraction continue en droit pénal", *RSC*, 2020, p. 871.

(29) Free translation of: "*L'infraction est réputée commise sur le territoire de la République dès lors qu'un de ses faits constitutifs a eu lieu sur ce territoire.*"

(30) Court of cassation, Criminal Chamber, 14 March 2018, No.16-82.117, *op. cit.*

protection by making it compulsory to take foreign decisions into account in determining the amount of the sentence. Thus, sentences delivered abroad must be taken into account. The obligation stems from the principle of the necessity of penalties, which prohibits a person from being punished by a penalty that exceeds the maximum penalty provided for under French Criminal Law for the offence of which he or she is guilty. (31) The Court of cassation has therefore affirmed that the total amount of the sanctions imposed cannot exceed the highest amount of one of the sanctions incurred. (32) This analysis was retained by the Council of State for actual jurisdiction and can be applied to territorial jurisdiction. (33) These solutions led the Court of cassation to reject a *question prioritaire de constitutionnalité – QPC* (application for a priority preliminary ruling on the issue of constitutionality) which argued that the possibility of new prosecutions in France was contrary to the principles of *non bis in idem* and the necessity of penalties. (34) It considered that new prosecutions "are not likely to infringe the principle of strict necessity of penalties in that, in the event of a conviction, on the one hand, the total amount of any penalties imposed may not exceed the highest amount of one of the penalties incurred, and, on the other hand, when a possible custodial sentence imposed in France is executed on national territory, the time spent in detention abroad for the offences judged in France will be deducted in full from the duration of the sentence." (35)

This was the logic followed in determining the sanction against Airbus SE in the *convention judiciaire d'intérêt public – CJIP* (Judicial Public Interest Agreement) of 29 January 2020. (36) After highly coordinated investigations, the agreement stated that "this agreement is concluded in coordination with two other *Deferred Prosecution Agreements* (DPAs) which Airbus SE had concluded separately with the SFO and DOJ. (…) The total amount of fines imposed on Airbus SE appears proportionate to the benefits derived

(31) D. Rebut, *Droit pénal international*, *op. cit.*, No. 87.

(32) Court of cassation, Criminal Chamber, 15 April 2015, No.15-90.001, *Dr. penal*, 2015, comm. 119, obs. E. Bonis-Garçon.

(33) Council of State, *Assemblée générale* (General Assembly), opinion, 29 February 1996, No. 358-597.

(34) Court of cassation, Criminal Chamber, 15 April 2015, No.15-90.001, *op. cit.*

(35) Free translation of: "*ne risquent pas de porter atteinte au principe de stricte nécessité des peines en ce que, en cas de condamnation, d'une part, le montant global des sanctions éventuellement prononcées ne peut dépasser le montant le plus élevé de l'une des sanctions encourues, et, d'autre part, lors de l'exécution sur le territoire national d'une éventuelle peine privative de liberté prononcée en France, sera déduite intégralement de sa durée la détention subie à l'étranger pour les faits jugés en France.*"

(36) https://www.agence-francaise-anticorruption.gouv.fr/files/files/20200129%20CJIP%20AIRBUS%20sign%C3%A9e.pdf

from the wrongdoing."(37) In order to respond effectively to the compliance violations found, the Judicial Public Interest Agreement provided for the implementation of a compliance programme. Here again, coordination between various prosecutions was very strong. Airbus SE undertook to submit to audits conducted by the *Agence française anticorruption – AFA* (French Anti-Corruption Agency – AFA) for a period of three years to ensure the completeness and deployment of the compliance programme, and it was stipulated that "The AFA will report at least once a year to the French National Financial Prosecutor's Office on the performance of this obligation. The French National Financial Prosecutor's Office will inform SFO and DOJ of the same."(38) A model to follow in answering the question of Which Judge for Compliance…

(37) Free translation of: "*la présente convention est conclue en coordination avec deux autres accords de* Deferred Prosecution Agreement *(DPA) conclus séparément par Airbus SE avec le SFO et le DOJ. [...] Le montant total des amendes mises à la charge d'Airbus SE apparaît proportionné aux avantages tirés des manquements constatés.*"

(38) Free translation of: "*L'AFA rendra compte au moins annuellement au PNF de l'exécution de cette obligation. Le PNF informera le SFO et le DOJ du déroulement de cette mesure.*"

Compliance and Judge of the Law

Olivier Douvreleur

Avocat général à la Cour de cassation
(Advocate-General at the French Court of cassation)

Compliance has with the judge – and even more so with the judge of the Law, who, in principle, does not deal with the facts and leaves them to the sovereign appreciation of the judges of the merits – a relationship that is not easy to discover. However, it is on this discovery that we will focus here, by trying to understand the role that this judge of the Law – the *Cour de cassation* (French Court of cassation, highest court in the French judiciary) in the judicial order – plays in the implementation of compliance, to appreciate its scope and to consider its future developments. This research starts from an observation that could be discouraging: at first glance, everything tends to distance the judge from Compliance Law, both in terms of its substance and its implementation.

On its substance, compliance is eminently factual in nature, like Regulation Law of which it is an extension and from which it borrows "violence, radicalism, even archaism," (1) so that the judge of the Law is, by definition, kept at bay. In the same way, the absence of any general compliance mechanism can be noted, both at the levels of legislations and regulations. Compliance could only be glimpsed "in the interstices of Law" (2)

(1) M.-A. Frison-Roche, "Le droit de la compliance au-delà du droit de la régulation", *D.*, 2018, 1561, free translation of: "*la violence, la radicalité, voire l'archaïsme*" of Compliance Law; see also, in English, the Working Paper underlying this article, M.-A. Frison-Roche, *Compliance Law loses the ties of Regulation Law but retains its principles: consequences for companies*, 2018, https://mafr.fr/en/article/le-droit-de-la-compliance-lache-les-amarres-du-dro/.

(2) A. de La Cotardière and E. Hannezo, "Le rôle de l'avocat en matière de compliance", *in* M.-A. Frison Roche (ed.), *Régulation, Supervision, Compliance*, "Thèmes & Commentaires – Régulations & Compliance" Serie, Paris, Dalloz, 2017, pp. 117-140, free translation of: "*dans les interstices du droit.*"

and is only the subject of scattered provisions appearing, for the most part, in the *Code monétaire et financier* (French Monetary and Financial Code), the *Code de commerce* (French Commercial Code), the *Code pénal* (French Criminal Code), or the French so-called "Vigilance" law of 27 March 2017. (3) Moreover, the "monumental goals" pursued by compliance reveal a strong moral and ethical dimension in that they are linked to the "societal responsibility" of companies in the areas of prevention of corruption, the protection of environment, human rights or personal data. Some people therefore conclude that compliance is "an a-legal concept," or even that it is "the enemy of the Law," (4) thus relegating the judge of cassation out of its scope of application.

On its implementation, compliance is marked by a double shift, on the one hand, from *ex post* to *ex ante* and, on the other hand and correlatively, from the judge and the regulator to the companies: it is towards the latter that compliance mechanisms "outsource" the *ex ante* achievement of objectives, by means, for example, of vigilance plans, risk mapping, codes of conduct and internal alert mechanisms required by the French so-called "Sapin 2" and "Vigilance" laws. (5)

These objectives, which were the "prerogative of the State," (6) are no longer the sole matter of the judge's *ex post* intervention but, to a large extent, are devolved to the company, which is entrusted with "a policing mission over those with whom it is in contact at all levels." (7) It has therefore been observed that in the compliance system, "the conformity with the rules in force, rather than being imposed from the outside, is increasingly internalised by the economic actors who seek to show, through transparent processes, that they respect not only the economic rules specific to

(3) French law No.2017-399 of 27 March 2017 *relative au devoir de vigilance des sociétés mères et des entreprises donneuses d'ordre* (on the duty of vigilance of parent companies and ordering companies), so-called "Vigilance law."

(4) See, M.-A. Frison-Roche who observes that, according to other sources, compliance is on the contrary "a notion so legal that it would be useless" (free translation of: "*une notion si juridique qu'elle en deviendrait inutile*"), M.-A. Frison-Roche, "Le droit de la compliance", *D.*, 2016, 1871.

(5) French law No. 2016-1691 of 9 December 2016, *relative à la transparence, à la lutte contre la corruption et à la modernisation de la vie économique* (on transparency, fight against corruption and modernisation of economic life), so-called "Sapin 2" law.

(6) T. Amico, "Compliance or the passage from *ex post* to *ex ante*: a copernican revolution for the criminal lawyer?", *in* M.-A. Frison-Roche (ed.), *Compliance Tools*, "Compliance & Regulation" Serie, Brussels, Journal of Regulation & Compliance (JoRC)/Bruylant, 2021, pp. 165-172.

(7) A. de La Cotardière and E. Hannezo, "Le rôle de l'avocat en matière de compliance", *op. cit.*, free translation of: "*une mission de police sur ceux avec lesquels elle est en contact à tout niveau.*"

their sector, but also the imperative rules which are not directly economic in nature." (8)

Moreover, the control that the judge of the Law normally exercises over the courts which belong to its jurisdictional order is sometimes expressly excluded. In France, this is the case with the *convention judiciaire d'intérêt public – CJIP* (French Judicial Public Interest Agreement), an instrument of negotiated justice and compliance introduced in 2016 to combat corruption, influence peddling and tax fraud, (9) and extended in 2021 to the offences provided for in the *Code de l'environnement* (French Environmental Code). (10)

Proposed and negotiated by the public prosecutor's office, this agreement may provide for the payment of a fine and the implementation by the offending company of a compliance programme based on the compliance tools listed in the Article 131-39-2 of the French Criminal Code and which consist of codes of conduct, internal alert systems, risk mapping, evaluation procedures, etc.

In order to come into force, the agreement must be validated by the president of the First Instance Civil Court, who must ensure, that it is properly implemented, that the amount of the fine complies with legal limits and that "the measures provided for are proportionate to the benefits derived from the breaches." (11) However, the law expressly provides that the decision of this magistrate, in charge of the case for the purpose of validation, "is not subject to appeal" (12) and therefore, in principle, escapes the final control of the judge of cassation. A recent news item provides an example of this: in the context of the same case which implied Judicial Public Interest Agreement concluded with an industrial group and an agreement of *comparution sur reconnaissance préalable de culpabilité – CRPC* (French guilty plea procedure) concluded with three of its executives,

(8) J.-M. Sauvé, "Compliance, droit public et juge administratif", *in* M.-A. Frison Roche (ed.), *Régulation, Supervision, Compliance, op. cit.*, p. 47, free translation of: "*la conformité aux règles en vigueur, plutôt que d'être imposée de l'extérieur, est de plus en plus internalisée par les acteurs économiques qui cherchent à montrer, par des processus transparents, qu'ils respectent non seulement les règles économiques propres à leur secteur, mais aussi des règles impératives qui ne sont pas directement de nature économique.*"

(9) French law of 9 December 2016, *op. cit.*

(10) French law No. 2021-1104 of 22 August 2021 *portant lutte contre le dérèglement climatique et renforcement de la résilience face à ses effets* (on the fight against climate change and the reinforcment of resilience to its effects).

(11) Free translation of: "*la proportionnalité des mesures prévues aux avantages tirés des manquements.*"

(12) Free translation of: "*n'est pas susceptible de recours.*"

the magistrate delegated by the president of the court only validated the Judicial Public Interest Agreement. The public prosecutor considered that, in doing so, the magistrate had exceeded his powers, in particular by mentioning in his order that the group's executives had admitted their guilt in the context of the *CRPC*. He therefore relied on the classic principles according to which the absence of an appeal expressly provided for by the law leaves open the possibility of an appeal on the grounds of abuse of power, and referred the matter to the French Court of cassation. However, the *Chambre criminelle* (Criminal Chamber of the French Court of cassation) did not follow this analysis and rejected the legal recourse against the validation order. (13)

However, it cannot be deduced from these specific characteristics of compliance that the judge, and even more so the judge of the Law, is destined to play only a marginal role. On the contrary, it has been argued that the judge, "the one to whom everyone returns," (14) is destined to play "an essential role," (15) and the origins of this are described as follows: the judge is a "refuge" from the rigour of the sanctions imposed by the regulators; he or she prints his or her form and procedural requirements to compliance and its regulators; finally, compliance takes the form of liability, which "always leads back to the judge." (16) This observation can only encourage further research into the role of the judge of the Law in the implementation of compliance; moreover, current legal developments themselves suggest a similar approach.

The French Court of cassation had to examine one of the most recent *ex ante* compliance tools, the "vigilance plan", which has been in place since 2017 (17) to identify and prevent serious violations of human rights and fundamental freedoms, human health and safety and the environment, likely to result from the activities of companies and their "sphere of influence" (subsidiaries, subcontractors, suppliers, etc.), when they exceed certain thresholds. (18) In this case, the vigilance plan adopted by the

(13) See *Le Monde*, 7 May 2021.

(14) Free translation of: "*celui auquel chacun revient.*"

(15) Free translation of: "*un rôle essentiel.*"

(16) M.-A. Frison-Roche, "Le droit de la compliance", *op. cit.*, free translation of: "*ramène toujours devant le juge*".

(17) French law No. 2017-399 of 27 March 2017, *op. cit.*, the provisions of which are codified in the Article L. 225-102-4 of the French Commercial Code.

(18) The vigilance plan must be drawn up when the company and its direct and indirect subsidiaries employ, at the closing of two consecutive financial years, more than 5.000 employees in France or more than 10.000 employees in France and abroad (Article L. 225-102-4 of the French Commercial Code).

Total group was called into question, as several NGOs and a trade union considered that it was insufficient with regard to the activity that the group carried out in Uganda through one of its subsidiaries, which consisted, on the one hand, in the exploitation of several oil fields and, on the other hand, in the construction of an oil pipeline. These organisations used the prerogatives that the law now gives them, as well as "any person with an interest in the case," (19) sent a formal notice to the Total group and then applied to the *juge des référés du Tribunal judiciaire de Nanterre* (the judge of the emergency of Nanterre First Instance Civil Court) for the group to be ordered comply with its obligations. (20)

The merits of this action, however, have not been examined by this judge, as he considered that the case did not fall within his jurisdiction and referred the parties back to the *Tribunal de commerce* (French First Instance Commercial Court). This decision was confirmed by the Court of Appeal, which, having seen a "direct link" (21) between the drawing up and implementation of the vigilance plan and the "management of the company," (22) considered that what was at issue was a "dispute relating to a trade company" (23) within the meaning of Article L. 721-3 of the French Commercial Code, and therefore falling within the jurisdiction of the First Instance Commercial Court even though the plaintiffs were not merchants. This led to contrasting reactions from legal doctrine who, while noting that "the prevention of infringements of human rights and fundamental freedoms is an essential aspect of a company's commercial decisions and of the responsibilities assumed by its governing bodies," (24) nevertheless

(19) Article L. 225-102-4 II of the French Commercial Code, free translation of: "*toute personne justifiant d'un intérêt à agir.*"

(20) Article L. 225-102-4 II of the French Commercial Code: "*II. – Lorsqu'une société mise en demeure de respecter les obligations prévues au I n'y satisfait pas dans un délai de trois mois à compter de la mise en demeure, la juridiction compétente peut, à la demande de toute personne justifiant d'un intérêt à agir, lui enjoindre, le cas échéant sous astreinte, de les respecter. Le président du tribunal, statuant en référé, peut être saisi aux mêmes fins.*" (free translation: "II. - If a company which has been given formal notice to comply with the obligations set out in the I fails to do so within three months from the date of the formal notice, the competent court may, at the request of any person with an interest in bringing proceedings, enjoin the company to comply with these obligations, if needed with a penalty. The president of the court, ruling in summary proceedings, may be requested for the same purpose.")

(21) Free translation of: "*lien direct.*"

(22) Free translation of: "*gestion de la société.*"

(23) Free translation of: "*contestation relative à une société.*"

(24) N. Lenoir, "La cour d'appel de Versailles confirme la compétence du tribunal de commerce pour connaître des contestations relatives au plan de vigilance des sociétés commerciales", *D.*, 2021, 515, free translation of: " la prévention des atteintes aux droits humains et libertés fondamentales est une dimension essentielle des décisions commerciales de l'entreprise et des responsabilités assumées par ses organes."

stressed that "by confining the dispute to commercial matters"(25) this decision could lead to a "risk of seeing the spirit of the French law of 27 March 2017 distorted since, by including human rights and environmental protection in the scope of the vigilance plan, the legislator precisely wanted to oblige the company to leave its commercial fortress in order to live in the City and be part of society."(26)

Whatever its relevance, this fear is no longer valid. For the record, the French Court of Cassation has overruled the decision of the Court of Appeal and ruled in favour of the plaintiffs who argued that, since they were not merchants, they could not be required to take action before the French First Instance Commercial Court. It deemed that if the vigilance plan, which does not constitute an "*acte de commerce*" ("commercial act"), has a direct link with the management of the company, justifying the jurisdiction of the First Instance Commercial Court, the non-trading plaintiff had the choice of bringing the case before the Civil Court or the Commercial Court.(27) Since then, however, the French legislator has intervened and has chosen the jurisdiction of the Paris First Instance Civil Court for actions relating to the duty of vigilance.

In the same way, other case-law precedents illustrate the role of the judge of cassation in matters of compliance, as in the case of the confrontation between American compliance requirements and French Law, and the need to resolve the resulting conflict.

This was the case when, in a 2019 ruling,(28) the French Court of cassation had to combine the American compliance rules with the rules of the French Commercial Code on the sudden break of economic relations. In this case, a French company, a business agent for the French subsidiary of an American group, refused to adhere to the anti-corruption measures imposed on the latter by the American authorities under a so-called "deferred prosecution agreement."(29) The American group argued that

(25) Free translation of: "*en enfermant le litige dans la commercialité.*"

(26) P. Abadie, "Les enseignements de la procédure sur la nature du devoir de vigilance: entre contestation relative aux sociétés commerciales et contestation relative à la responsabilité sociale", *D.*, 2021, 614, free translation of: "*risque de voir dénaturé l'esprit de la loi du 27 mars 2017, dès lors qu'en incluant les droits humains et la protection de l'environnement dans le périmètre du plan de vigilance, le législateur a précisément voulu obliger l'entreprise à sortir de sa forteresse marchande pour habiter la Cité et faire Société.*"

(27) French Court of cassation, Commercial Chamber, 15 December 2021, No. F 21-11.957 and No. Z 21-11.882.

(28) French Court of cassation, Commercial Chamber, 20 November 2019, No. D 18-12.817, see J.-Chr. Roda, "Quand la compliance américaine s'invite dans le contentieux contractuel français", *D.*, 2020, 913.

(29) The decision of the French Court of cassation points out that the Court of Appeal noted that the American group "*était soumis aux États-Unis aux règles, issues du 'United States Foreign Corrupt Practices Act',*

this refusal could result in its own liability towards the American authorities and, to avoid this risk, it terminated its contract with the French company. The French company then brought the matter before the courts, arguing that by abruptly terminating its established business relationship with the American group, it had incurred liability towards the French company, as provided for in Article L. 442-6 of the French Commercial Code. Agreeing with the trial judges, the Court of cassation gave precedence to the compliance requirements imposed on the American group, holding that, "considering the rules laid down by the compliance programme and the agreement concluded [with the American authorities]," (30) the French company's refusal to comply with them constituted a "breach [...] of its contractual obligations [...] sufficiently serious to justify termination of the economic relationship without advance notice." (31)

The French Court of cassation has also had to deal with American compliance obligations imposed on a French company on the grounds that it was listed in the United States, and to assess them in the light of the French Labour Law. (32) In this case, the French company, *Dassault Systèmes*, had been required, under the Sarbanes-Oxley Act of 30 July 2002, to adopt a "Code of Business Conduct" which aimed, in particular, at facilitating the triggering of alerts to prevent embezzlement and corruption and, to this end, restricted the ability of employees to disseminate information relating to the company by providing, especially, for prior authorisation for their disclosure. The *Confédération générale du travail – CGT* (a French trade union) challenged this code before the courts, arguing firstly that

---

interdisant aux sociétés visées de commettre des actes de corruption d'agents publics étrangers et qu'il avait, le 26 mars 2012, conclu avec les autorités américaines un accord dit de poursuites différées (APD), afin de mettre un terme aux enquêtes du Department of Justice and Securities and Exchange Commission, à la condition de mettre en place, pendant une durée de trois ans pouvant être prorogée d'un an, une coopération substantielle de ses employés, distributeurs et agents commerciaux avec les professionnels de santé" (free translation: "was subject in the United States to the rules of the Foreign Corrupt Practices Act, which prohibits companies from committing acts of bribery of foreign public officials, and that on 26 March 2012 it entered into a deferred prosecution agreement (DPA) with the US authorities, in order to put an end to the investigations by the Department of Justice and the Securities and Exchange Commission, on condition that, for a period of three years, which may be extended by one year, it establishes substantial cooperation of its employees, distributors and sales agents with the healthcare professionals.")

(30) Free translation of: "*compte tenu des règles fixées par le programme de 'compliance' et de l'accord conclu [avec les autorités américaines.]*"

(31) Free translation of: "*manquement* [...] *à ses obligations contractuelles* [...] *suffisamment grave pour justifier la rupture de la relation commerciale sans préavis.*"

(32) French Court of cassation, Social Chamber, 8 December 2009, No. 08-17.191; *D.*, 2010, 96, obs. L. Perrin; 574, note I. Desbarats and 672, obs. O. Leclerc; R. de Quenaudon, "Codes de conduite et dispositifs d'alerte. Les réponses de la Cour de cassation", *RTD*, 2010, 171; F. Barrière, "Le whistleblowing. À propos de l'arrêt du 8 décembre 2009 de la chambre sociale de la Cour de cassation", *Rev. sociétés*, 2010, 483.

it infringed the fundamental freedoms of employees protected by the *Code du travail* (French Labour Code) and secondly that the whistleblowing mechanism it introduced did not comply with the "single authorisation" (33) given by the *Commission nationale de l'informatique et des libertés* – CNIL (French Data Protection Authority) and should have been the subject of a new authorisation by the latter. In its ruling, the *Chambre sociale* (Labour Chamber of the French Court of cassation), after giving the code of business conduct a full legal scope by refusing to see it as merely an instrument of soft law, considered these criticisms to be well-founded and ruled that it violated employees' freedom of expression in breach of Articles L. 1121-1 and 2281-1 of the French Labour Code, and the French *loi informatique et libertés* of 6 January 1978.

Lastly, the prospects opened up by the control of proportionality used by the French Court of Cassation could be an important area for developing its role in compliance. As we know, following the report submitted in April 2017 (34) by the Reflection Commission set up at the initiative of its *Premier president* (First President), the Court of cassation has identified, among the avenues for development, the gradual construction of a doctrine and practice of proportionality review. However, this development could push back one of the limits of the judge of the Law control over compliance: the fundamentally factual nature of compliance, as mentioned above, would consequently escape his control. Indeed, some observers have taken the view that proportionality review "erases" (35) the distinction between fact and Law in that, "breaking the prohibition on which its institution is based," (36) it leads the Court of cassation to take the facts into account, and to incorporate them into its reasoning, in order to weigh them up against the applicable rights and rules. (37)

These prospects must undoubtedly be viewed with caution, and we must not conclude from them that the Court of cassation will soon become a "judge of the facts" in the same way as the lower courts. While the development of proportionality review can only accentuate the Court's understanding of the facts, it is as they are "frozen" by the trial judges, without

(33) Free translation of: "*autorisation unique.*"

(34) *Commission de réflexion de la Cour de cassation* (Reflection Commission of the French Court of cassation), *Rapport de la Commission de réflexion sur la réforme de la Cour de cassation*, April 2017.

(35) Free translation of "*efface.*"

(36) Free translation of: "*brisant l'interdit qui fonde son institution.*"

(37) F. Zenati-Castaing, "La juridictionnalisation de la Cour de cassation", *RTD civ.*, 2016, 511.

being able, for example, to call into question their materiality or establish new facts. (38) In any event, the scope of proportionality review may be extended. To date, it has essentially been used to protect the rights and guarantees enshrined in the European Convention for the Protection of Human Rights and Fundamental Freedoms, and is therefore a review of conventionality. The future will tell whether, and to what extent, this same proportionality review will be used to achieve the "Monumental Goals" of compliance.

(38) V. Vigneau, "Libres propos d'un juge sur le contrôle de proportionnalité", *D.*, 2017, 123.

The Administrative Judge and Compliance

Fabien Raynaud

Conseiller d'État

The administrative judge may appear to be far removed from the issue of compliance. In two respects: on the one hand, because, generally, compliance is based on the idea that the players concerned should internalise the standard, precisely in order to avoid litigation; on the other hand, because the judicial judge appears to be the most natural judge of compliance, which primarily concerns private players.

But this assumption needs to be qualified.

The case law that the *Conseil d'État* (French Council of State) has developed over the last few years concerning what is known as "soft law" makes the administrative judge the guardian of the legality of the acts on which compliance is largely based, at least, of course, when these acts emanate from French authorities. Compliance is generally based on respect by the economic players concerned of guidelines, opinions, positions and recommendations formulated for their attention by public regulators. These acts are not formally legally binding norms, but they play an essential role insofar as they often form the basis of compliance.

It is true that, in principle, administrative courts can only be called upon and apply acts that are characterised by their normativity, i.e. acts that modify the legal system or, at the very least, restate it or provide an interpretation of it (circulars).

In principle, therefore, the situation was binary: either an act was prescriptive and could be challenged before the courts; or it was not prescriptive and could not be referred to the administrative judge (the annulment judge).

But, with the development of regulation and then compliance, this classical "French garden" has become more baroque.

Between normative and non-normative acts, an intermediate category of acts has developed which do not, strictly speaking, have binding legal force, but which, because of the authority of their author, in particular his ability to impose sanctions, have a very clear incentive effect.

These acts have developed particularly in the economic and financial fields, but they have gradually spread to other sectors such as health, communications, etc.

In its 2013 study on soft law, (1) the *Conseil d'État* acknowledged the existence and development of these instruments and their growing importance for the players concerned. It emphasised their place in the legal landscape, not to mention the normative order…

It is true that since the early 2010s, the *Conseil d'État*, ruling in contentious cases, had begun, in small steps, to open its courtroom to appeals lodged against acts whose strictly normative nature was uncertain or even doubtful… This was the case in 2011 for recommendations of good practice from the *Haute Autorité de Santé – HAS* (French National Authority for Health), "in view of the ethical obligation" incumbent on professionals, (2) or in 2015 for an opinion from the *Autorité de régulation des transports ferroviaires* (French Railway Transport Regulatory Authority) the content of which determines the decision to be taken by the organising authority (*Région PACA*, 2015).

However, the decisive turning point came in 2016 with the decisions in the *Fairvesta* and *Numéricable* cases, which concerned, respectively, a simple press release issued by the *Autorité des Marchés Financiers – AMF* (French Financial Markets Authority) and a simple "position" adopted by the *Autorité de la concurrence – ADLC* (French Competition Authority). (3)

With these decisions, the *Conseil d'État* affirms that the annulment judge has jurisdiction to hear appeals against "opinions, recommendations,

(1) *Conseil d'État* (French Council of State), *Le droit souple*, Étude annuelle 2013, Paris, La documentation française, 2013.

(2) *Conseil d'État*, 27 April 2011, *Association pour une formation médicale indépendante (FORMINDEP)*, No. 334396, p. 168, free translation of: *"eu égard à l'obligation déontologique."*

(3) *Conseil d'État*, *Assemblée* (Assembly), 21 March 2016, *Société Fairvesta International GmbH et autres*, Nos. 368082 368083 368084, p. 76; *Conseil d'État*, Assembly, 21 March 2016, *Société NC Numericable*, No. 390023, p. 88.

warnings and positions adopted by the regulatory authorities in the performance of their duties" (4) in two situations:

- when these acts are of a general and mandatory nature – which is obvious – or – which is more innovative – when they set out individual prescriptions which these authorities could subsequently censure if they are not complied with;
- when they are likely to produce "significant effects," particularly of an economic nature, or are intended to have a significant influence on the behaviour of the persons to whom they are addressed: this second hypothesis is obviously the most interesting, both in terms of the extension of the control of the judge and in terms of issues of compliance.

However, the *Conseil d'État* is cautious and restrained about the nature of the review it intends to exercise over such acts. As the decisions of the *Assemblée du contentieux* (Administrative Jurisdiction Division) expressly state, when the annulment judge hears an appeal against such acts, it confines itself to examining the defects likely to affect their legality, taking into account, on the one hand, their nature and characteristics and, on the other hand, the discretionary power of the regulatory authority that adopted them. In other words, the annulment judge carries out a relatively distanced review.

These 2016 decisions are obviously very important insofar as they clearly demonstrate the *Conseil d'État*'s willingness to hear appeals against acts of regulatory authorities which, although not formally legally binding, have in reality a very strong prescriptive force for the players concerned, due to the will and the nature of their authors.

The *Conseil d'État* applied this grid to guidelines issued by the *Autorité de la concurrence* (French Competition Authority) on mergers, (5) to a "position" issued by the *Autorité de Contrôle Prudentiel et de Résolution – ACPR* (French Banking Supervisory Authority) (6) or to best practice recommendations issued by this authority, (7) as well as to a joint press release issued by

(4) Free translation of: "*les avis, recommandations, mises en garde et prises de position adoptés par les autorités de régulation dans l'exercice des missions dont elles sont investies.*"

(5) *Conseil d'État*, 25 May 2018, *Société OCEA*, No. 404382, T., pp. 508-589.

(6) *Conseil d'État*, 30 June 2016, *Crédit agricole SA et autres*, No. 383822.

(7) *Conseil d'État*, 20 June 2016, *Fédération française des sociétés d'assurances*, No. 384297, T., pp. 653-862.

this authority and the *AMF*, (8) a deliberation of the *Commission de régulation de l'énergie – CRE* (French Energy Regulatory Commission), (9) guidelines of the *Autorité de régulation des communications électroniques, des postes et de la distribution de la presse – Arcep* (France's Electronic Communications, Postal and Print media distribution Regulatory Authority), (10) a position of the *Autorité de régulation des jeux en ligne – ARJEL* (French Online Gambling Regulatory Authority), (11) guidelines of the *Autorité de régulation des activités ferroviaires et routières* (French Rail and Road Activities Regulatory Authority). (12) It has also applied it to a decision by the *Conseil Supérieur de l'Audiovisuel – CSA* (French Broadcasting Regulator) on whether or not a television advert should be used for advertising purposes, (13) to a position taken by the *Commission nationale de l'informatique et des libertés – CNIL* (French data protection authority) (14) or, in the health sector, to a sheet on the proper use of a medicine published on the *HAS* website (15) or to a recommendation by the *Agence nationale de sécurité des médicaments – ANSM* (French National Agency for Medecines and Health Products Safety) on the name and packaging of medicines. (16)

It has gone beyond the simple application of this grid by agreeing to hear appeals against acts of soft law that do not emanate from a regulatory authority in the strict sense. This is the case for the assessment by the *Haute Autorité pour la transparence de la vie publique – HATVP* (High Authority for Transparency in Public Life). (17)

These decisions reflect the *Conseil d'État*'s concern to be realistic and to open its courtroom to appeals lodged by persons whose interests may be adversely affected by an act of soft law, i.e. an act which, although not legally binding, has "significant effects" on their rights or situation.

When faced with appeals against acts of soft law, the *Conseil d'État* has not hesitated to make use of its usual prerogatives.

(8) *Conseil d'État*, 2 April 2021, *Société Blockchain et autres*, No. 448415.
(9) *Conseil d'État*, Section, 13 July 2016, *Société GDF Suez*, No. 388150, p. 384.
(10) *Conseil d'État*, 13 December 2017, *Société Bouygues Télécom et autres*, No. 401799, p. 356.
(11) *Conseil d'État*, 24 March 2021, *Association française du jeu en ligne*, No. 431786, à mentionner aux T.
(12) *Conseil d'État*, 20 March 2017, *Région Aquitaine-Limousin-Poitou-Charentes*, No. 401751, p. 99.
(13) *Conseil d'État*, 10 November 2016, *Mme Marcihacy et autres*, No. 384691, *Rec.*, p. 509.
(14) *Conseil d'État*, 16 October 2019, *La Quadrature du net et Caliopen*, No. 433069, p. 358.
(15) *Conseil d'État*, 19 July 2017, *Sté Menarini France et autre*, No. 399766, T., pp. 427, 716-718, 809-818.
(16) *Conseil d'État*, 21 October 2019, *AFIPAR*, No. 419996, *Rec.*, p. 374.
(17) *Conseil d'État*, Assembly, 19 July 2019, *Mme Le Pen*, No. 426389, p. 326.

It has thus gone so far as to censure some of the acts of soft law referred to it, such as:

- guidelines issued by the *CNIL* (the *Conseil d'État* annulled the contested act on the grounds that the *CNIL* had exceeded what it could legally do under an instrument of soft law) (18);
- the deliberation in which the *CRE* gave its interpretation of the scope of the suspension clause on grounds of force majeure in the framework agreements concluded with *EDF* under the regulated access to historical nuclear electricity (ARENH) mechanism provided for in Article L. 336-1 of the *Code de l'énergie* (French Energy Code). (19)

When necessary, particularly when the soft law interprets an act of European Law, the *Conseil d'État* has not hesitated to stay proceedings and refer a preliminary question to the Court of Justice of the European Union (CJEU).

In an interesting case, the *Conseil d'État*, seized by the *Fédération bancaire française* (French Banking Federation) against a notice issued by the *ACPR* to the financial institutions subject to its supervision, in which it stated that it complied with the guidelines issued by the European Banking Authority, decided to stay proceedings in order to ask questions to the Court of Justice of the European Union on the justiciability of an act of soft law issued by a European authority in order to determine whether such acts could be directly challenged before the European courts and, if not, whether they could nevertheless be the subject of a question by the national courts as to their validity. (20) In a judgment of 15 July 2021, the CJEU replied that acts of soft law issued by a European authority could not be directly challenged before the European courts, but that they could be the subject of a request for an assessment of their validity from the national courts to the European courts (it ruled that, in this case, the EBA's guidelines were valid, which led the *Conseil d'État* to dismiss the French Banking Federation's appeal). (21)

Through its jurisprudence on the justiciability of acts of soft law, the *Conseil d'État* is asserting its role as a player in the compliance field by allowing entities targeted by these acts and subject to a compliance

(18) *Conseil d'État*, 16 October 2019, *La Quadrature du net et Caliopen*.
(19) *Conseil d'État*, 10 December 2021, *SAS Hydroption*, No. 439944, à mentionner aux T.
(20) *Conseil d'État*, 4 December 2019, *Fédération bancaire française*, No. 415550.
(21) *Conseil d'État*, 21 December 2021, No. 415550.

obligation to be able to bring an action for annulment of these acts before the administrative judge, so that they can be subject to a legality review and, where appropriate, be annulled.

It is true that the practical scope of this case law will depend on how it is applied by the courts, of course, but also, and perhaps above all, on how it is appropriated by those involved in compliance, because the judge can only give a ruling if a case is brought before him. The best, most sophisticated and most subtle judicial control will remain purely theoretical if it does not find an opportunity to be exercised.

Furthermore, it should be emphasised that other questions will inevitably arise concerning the relationship between the administrative judge and these acts of soft law, in particular concerning the application of these acts of soft law by this judge itself, espacially in the context of litigation concerning disciplinary sanctions taken by the regulators (for the moment, the question has not really arisen and has not given rise to any decisions of principle). Similarly, the question of any liability litigation that might arise as a result of an unlawful act of soft law causing damage to a particular undertaking will no doubt arise one day, even if it has not at this stage.

To conclude this all-too-brief presentation, it is worth pointing out that the logic of compliance is now tending to extend to new areas, which may lead the administrative courts, particularly the *Conseil d'État*, to explore new territories. The issue of climate change springs to mind.

In fact, the obligations to reduce greenhouse gas emissions by 2030 set by national and European Union legislators for the implementation of the United Nations Framework Convention on Climate Change (UNFCCC) of 9 May 1992 and the agreements reached in Paris on 12 December 2015 within this framework can be seen as a form of compliance obligation that the State imposes on itself. When the Grande-Synthe municipality appealed against the State's refusal to take any measures to reduce these emissions, the *Conseil d'État*, basing its decision on the quantified target set for 2030 and on the "*stratégie bas carbone*" ("low-carbon strategy") and "*budgets carbone*" ("carbon budgets") set out in Articles L. 100-4 of the French Energy Code and L. 222-1 A and B and D. 222-1 A and B of the *Code de l'environnement* (French Environmental Code), examines the compatibility of this refusal with compliance with the path set by decree for achieving the 2030 target. (22) In this case, it acts as the judge of the State's

(22) *Conseil d'État*, 19 November 2020 and 1st July2021, *Commune de Grande-Synthe e.a.*, No. 427301, *Rec.*

own compliance with the objectives set for it by the French legislator and the European Union for reducing greenhouse gas emissions by 2030.

This is certainly an innovation, which stems from the logic of the system put in place by the legislator and the regulatory authorities to implement the Paris agreements, which are based on a global compliance approach, with each signatory State undertaking to do what is necessary to achieve a common objective by a given date and with the onus on each to organise itself to achieve it. In the absence of an international judge capable of verifying compliance with these commitments, the national judge would seem the most natural to agree to verify, when a dispute is referred to him, that these commitments do not remain a dead letter.

Some Reflections on Compliance and the European Court of Human Rights*

Erik Wennerström
Judge
European Court of Human Rights

I. INTRODUCTION

In her pioneering paper "Definition of Proportionality and Definition of Compliance Law," Professor Marie-Anne Frison-Roche demonstrates how compliance as a legal concept evolves from a simple measurement of hermitical effectiveness within a normative system, towards a process – even more effective than its more static origins – and in that sense a procedure anchored in the rule of law. (1)

Over the years, the European Court of Human Rights (the Court, in the following) has delivered a large number of judgments which have dramatically advanced the protection of human rights in Europe, attracted good levels of compliance and thereby contributed to European political integration. Indications of its success includes the sharp increase of Contracting States subject to its jurisdiction over the last decades, the move from optional to compulsory jurisdiction, (2) attempts by other regional

* The author expresses his gratitude to Amanda Wallin, LL.M. (Leiden), for assistance with research for this article.

(1) See M.-A. Frison-Roche, *Definition of Proportionality and Definition of Compliance Law*, Working Paper, July 2021, https://mafr.fr/en/article/proportionnalite-et-conformite-in-compliance-et-pr/, and the article *in* M.-A. Frison-Roche (ed.), *Compliance Monumental Goals*, "Compliance & Regulation" Serie, Brussels, Journal of Regulation & Compliance (JoRC)/Bruylant, 2023, pp. 259-288.

(2) Through Protocol 11 to the ECHR.

organisations to emulate the Court's structure, as well as the inclination of domestic courts to rely heavily on its jurisprudence. (3)

In the context of the European Convention on Human Rights (ECHR), compliance predominantly refers to traditional, international law-type compliance, as we are accustomed to from the practices described in the Vienna Convention on the Law on Treaties (notably Articles 18, 26, 27 and 31). (4) The development of compliance as something different from legality presumably springs from the situation companies and other non-State entities find themselves in when operating in a globalised economy. They are not only faced with one set of norms from a singular, sovereign legislator, but several different, to some extent converging sets of legislative requirements or requirements condoned by a legislator actively (i.e. by referring in legislation to a standard found in the best practices of a professional sector, e.g. accountants, legal or medical professionals) or passively (i.e. the tacit acceptance of the development of complex regulatory and normative systems outside the control of any sovereign legislator, such as those found within different forms of international sports). (5) The systems' various compliance procedures aim to distribute different rights and sanction violations, while still maintaining respect for the system(s) as a whole.

The system under the ECHR is no different from any other system created under a constitution or an agreement or by a treaty, in that it requires general compliance under its constitutional treaty by its States Parties. This principle of loyalty or compliance is underlined in Article 1 ECHR: "The High Contracting Parties shall secure to everyone within their jurisdiction the rights and freedoms defined in Section I of this Convention."

The Court interprets the obligations arising from the Convention as threefold: "to cease the breach, to make reparation for it and ensure non-repetition of similar violations in the future." (6) The compliance with this depends on several factors, such as good governance, rule of law and political will. (7)

(3) See R. Mackenzie, C.P.R. Romano, Y. Shany and P. Sands, *The Manual on International Courts and Tribunals*, 2nd ed., pp. 356-357.

(4) See United Nations. 1969. "Vienna Convention on the Law of Treaties." Treaty Series 1155 (May): 331.

(5) See e.g. J. Mont, "What the Sports World Can Teach About Compliance", in *Compliance Week*, at https://www.complianceweek.com/what-the-sports-world-can-teach-about-compliance/4177.article.

(6) See *Scozzari and Giunta v. Italy* [GC] (39221/98 and 41963/98), para. 249.

(7) See A. Nussberger, *The European Court of Human Rights*, Oxford, OUP, 2020, p. 182, and for an enhanced analysis of the close relationship between the ECHR and the rule of law, see R. Spano, "The rule of law as the lodestar of the European Convention on Human Rights: The Strasbourg Court and the independence of the judiciary", in *European Law Journal*, 2021/02/01 10.1111/eulj.12377.

II. COMPLIANCE AND THE ECHR

Protocol 15 entered into force on 1 August 2021 and adds the concepts of subsidiarity and margin of appreciation – both concepts well-developed in the Court's case-law – into the sixth recital of the Preamble of the ECHR. (8) It reads: "Affirming that the High Contracting Parties, in accordance with the principle of subsidiarity, have the primary responsibility to secure the rights and freedoms defined in this Convention and the Protocols thereto and that in doing so they enjoy a margin of appreciation, subject to the supervisory jurisdiction of the European Court of Human Rights established by this Convention." (9)

According to the Explanatory Report on Protocol No. 15:

> "The jurisprudence of the Court makes clear that the States Parties enjoy a margin of appreciation in how they apply and implement the Convention, depending on the circumstances of the case and the rights and freedoms engaged. This reflects that the Convention system is subsidiary to the safeguarding of human rights at national level and that national authorities are in principle better placed than an international court to evaluate local needs and conditions. The margin of appreciation goes hand in hand with supervision under the Convention system. In this respect, the role of the Court is to review whether decisions taken by national authorities are compatible with the Convention, having due regard to the State's margin of appreciation." (10)

The concept of margin of appreciation has been thoroughly developed through the Court's case-law and "goes hand in hand with European supervision" (11) and "the final evaluation as to whether the reasons cited for the interference are relevant and sufficient remains subject to review by the Court for conformity with the requirements of the Convention." (12)

(8) See R. Spano, "Universality and Diversity of Human Rights? Strasbourg in the Age of Subsidiarity", *Hum. Rts L. Rev.*, 2014, Vol. 14, No. 3, p. 487, and W.A. Schabas, *The European Convention on Human Rights: A Commentary*, Oxford, OUP, 2015, p. 58.

(9) See Protocol No. 15 amending the Convention for the Protection of Human Rights and Fundamental Freedoms, Council of Europe Treaty Series - No. 213.

(10) See Explanatory Report on Protocol No. 15, para. 9.

(11) See *The Sunday Times v. the United Kingdom* (No. 2) (13166/87), paras. 50-51; *Vogt v. Germany* (17851/91), para. 52; *Perna v. Italy* [GC] (48898/99), para. 39; *Schwabe and M.G. v. Germany* (8080/08 and 8577/08), para. 113.

(12) See *Szuluk v. the United Kingdom* (36936/05), para. 45.

The Court regularly restricts its scope of examination, when assessing the proportionality of alleged violations, by granting domestic courts a "margin of appreciation." The Court highlights "that the machinery of protection established by the Convention is subsidiary to the national systems safeguarding human rights." (13) It also acknowledges that domestic "authorities are in principle in a better position than the international judge to give an opinion on the exact content of… the 'necessity' of a 'restriction' or 'penalty' intended to meet them." (14)

The margin may be broad or narrow depending on several factors, encompassing the nature or importance of the right implicated, the interest in justifying the restriction of rights, the technicality of the subject matter and the degree of consensus in national policies. (15)

The concept of subsidiarity allocates the main responsibility for enforcing the obligations arising from the Convention clearly with the States Parties. Only when they have failed to implement the obligations does the ECHR system and its Court intervene in the process. (16) Subsidiarity presents two different aspects:

1) a *procedural* aspect, requiring individuals to exhaust domestic remedies before seizing the Court, and

2) a *substantive* aspect, namely the presumption that States are generally in a better position to assess the necessity and proportionality of acts that may have interfered with specific rights. (17) (This may be described as a shared responsibility between the national authorities and the Court.) (18)

The Court has stressed "the Convention's special character as a treaty for the collective enforcement of human rights and fundamental freedoms." (19) Thus, it is said that "[u]nlike international treaties of the classic kind, the Convention comprises more than mere reciprocal engagements

(13) See *Handyside v. the United Kingdom* (REF), para 48. See also *Osmanoğlu and Kocabaş v. Switzerland* (29086/12), paras. 64 and 95 *et seq*.

(14) See *Handyside v. the United Kingdom* (5493/72), para 48.

(15) See D. Shelton, *The Oxford Handbook of International Human Rights Law*, Oxford, OUP, 2013, p. 375.

(16) See *Maaouia v. France* [GC] (39652/98), para. 36.

(17) See *Protocol No. 15 amending the Convention for the Protection of Human Rights and Fundamental Freedoms*, Council of Europe Treaty Series - No. 213.

(18) See R. Spano, *The significance of the ECHR at the national level*, text of speech held at Stockholm, 28 October 2021, p. 5.

(19) See recital 5 of Preamble to ECHR; *Nada v. Switzerland* [GC] (10593/08), para. 198; *Loizidou v. Turkey* (15318/89), para. 48.

between Contracting States. It creates, over and above a network of mutual, bilateral undertakings, objective obligations which, in the words of the Preamble benefit from a 'collective enforcement.'" (20) The reference to collective enforcement in the Preamble has also been linked to the requirement that the Convention "be interpreted and applied so as to make its safeguards practical and effective." (21)

III. OVERSIGHT, EXECUTION AND COMPLIANCE

Throughout its existence, the ECHR system has mainly relied on *ex post*-verification of system-compliance through the Court's adjudication and the subsequent execution of its judgments carried out by procedures of the Council of Europe Committee of Ministers (CM). On 1 August 2018, Protocol No. 16 to the ECHR came into force in respect of the 10 member States that had signed and ratified it. (22) Through the amendments of Protocol No. 16, the ECHR system enables the highest national courts and tribunals, as designated by the member States concerned, to request the Court to give advisory opinions on questions of principles relating to the interpretation or application of the rights and freedoms defined in the Convention or the Protocols thereto. The advisory opinions, which will be delivered by the Grand Chamber, will contain reasons and will not be binding. Requests for advisory opinions will be made in the context of cases pending before the national court or tribunal concerned. The Court will have discretion to accept or reject a request.

The preparatory works of the Convention shows the initial vision of a treaty with an essentially moral force, relying on the political pressure of civil society within State Parties to enforce judgments of the Court. As such, Article 46(2) enshrines the supervisory role of CM with regard to the enforcement of judgments. (23)

---

(20) See *Ireland v. the United Kingdom* (5310/71), para. 239. See also *Loizidou v. Turkey* (preliminary objections) (15318/89), para. 70; *Mamatkulov and Askarov v. Turkey* [GC] (46827/99 and 46951/99), para. 100; *Paladi v. Moldova* [GC] (39806/05), para. 84; *Knaags and Khachik v. the United Kingdom* (46559/06 and 22921/06), para. 199.

(21) See *Biç and Others v. Turkey* (55955/00) para. 18; *Shamayev and Others v. Georgia and Russia* (36378/02), para. 302; *Direkçi and Direkçi v. Turkey* (47826/99); *Sanles Sanles v. Spain* (48335/99); *İlhan v. Turkey* [GC] (22277/93), para. 51; *Yaşa v. Turkey* (22495/93), para. 64.

(22) At the time they were Albania, Armenia, Estonia, Finland, France, Georgia, Lithuania, San Marino, Slovenia and Ukraine. See Press Release ECHR 276 (2018), 1 August 2018.

(23) See W.A. Schabas, *The European Convention on Human Rights: A Commentary*, *op. cit.*, p. 871.

CM has adopted rules according to which the respondent States have to inform CM of the steps it has taken to comply with a judgment. (24) If the required steps have not been taken, the issue of the execution of the judgement in question is automatically put on CM's agenda for its consideration six months henceforth. (25) The Committee has a wide range of measures to assist execution, such as grouping the execution of a series of similar cases, qualifying execution as "enhanced," requiring information on the measures envisaged to remedy the issues, and adopting interim resolutions specifying measures to be taken. (26) (27)

The execution under the ECHR system portrays a trilateral relationship between the Court, the Committee of Ministers and national authorities, where execution measures are detailed in the judgment first and the supervision of the execution measures by the national authorities is subsequently carried out by CM. (28)

IV. COMPLIANCE AND CASE-LAW DEVELOPMENTS IN RELEVANT AREAS

An example of compliance-related review by the Court can be seen in the way the case-law from the *Bosphorus* case relates to States Parties to the ECHR that are also members of the EU. The *Bosphorus* presumption or doctrine evolves from the judgment in *Bosphorus v. Ireland*, (29) where the Court established that ECHR States Parties that also have membership obligations to the EU (or another international organisation) are fully liable under ECHR for "acts and omissions of its organs regardless of whether the act or omission in question was a consequence" of the obligations stemming from, in this case, EU membership. (30) While reiterating full ECHR liability, the Court also stressed the "need to secure the proper functioning

(24) See *Rules of the Committee of Ministers for the supervision of the execution of judgments and of the terms of friendly settlements*, Rule 6.

(25) See D. Shelton, *Remedies in International Human Rights Law*, Oxford, OUP, 2006, pp. 436-437.

(26) See A. Nussberger, *The European Court of Human Rights*, *op. cit.*, p. 157.

(27) The ultimate sanction available to the Council of Europe is the expulsion of a State in accordance with Article 8 of its Statute. In the case *Ilaşcu and others v. Moldova and the Russian Federation*, the CM's fourth interim resolution reminded the parties that "the obligation to abide by the judgments of the Court is unconditional and is a requirement for membership of the Council of Europe". Res. D.H. (2006) 26 of 10 May 2006; see D. Shelton, *Remedies in International Human Rights Law*, *op. cit.*, p. 438.

(28) See D. Shelton, *The Oxford Handbook of International Human Rights Law*, p. 911.

(29) See *Bosphorus Hava Yollari Turizm Ve Ticaret Anonim Şirketi v. Ireland* (45036/98).

(30) *Ibid.*, para. 153.

of international organisations" (31) and it is the consequence of these two statements that the Court outlines in paragraphs 155 and 156 of the judgment and that has since been referred to as the *Bosphorus* presumption.

> "155. In the Court's view, State action taken in compliance with such legal obligations is justified as long as the relevant organisation is considered to protect fundamental rights, as regards both the substantive guarantees offered and the mechanisms controlling their observance, in a manner which can be considered at least equivalent to that for which the Convention provides [...]. By 'equivalent' the Court means 'comparable'; any requirement that the organisation's protection be 'identical' could run counter to the interest of international cooperation pursued [...]. However, any such finding of equivalence could not be final and would be susceptible to review in the light of any relevant change in fundamental rights protection.
>
> 156. If such equivalent protection is considered to be provided by the organisation, the presumption will be that a State has not departed from the requirements of the Convention when it does no more than implement legal obligations flowing from its membership of the organisation.
>
> However, any such presumption can be rebutted if, in the circumstances of a particular case, it is considered that the protection of Convention rights was manifestly deficient."

Circumstances in an individual case may obviously rebut the presumption of compliance, but in the absence of such circumstances, the Court presumes compliance with ECHR norms of obligations of EU membership. This can be described as an assumption of compliance, when reviewing the way obligations under e.g. EU law, that somehow approaches the rights under ECHR, have been implemented. As with assumptions in general, it remains in place throughout the review, and if nothing in the review suggests otherwise, it will be assumed throughout.

It is also worth noting that the applicants in several cases of jurisprudential significance are companies or shareholders of companies, that no doubt have had reason to consider not only their own compliance with relevant regulation, but also the compliance of the relevant State and its authorities with international obligations, including the ECHR. In *Dubus S.A. v. France,* (32) the applicant was an investment company that was investigated and later disciplinary sanctioned by the French Banking Commission. The Banking Commission carried out supervisory functions, including administrative, and simultaneously disciplinary functions, and

(31) *Bosphorus Hava Yollari Turizm Ve Ticaret Anonim Şirketi v. Ireland* (45036/98), para. 150.
(32) See *Dubus S.A. v. France* (5242/04).

the applicant complained over the alleged absence of impartiality of the Commission when subjecting the company to both forms of functions. The Court found that there had been a lack of clear distinction between the authority's prosecutorial, investigative and judicial functions, and a violation of the applicant's right, under Article 6 § 1, to an independent and impartial tribunal.

In the Grand Chamber Case of *Albert v. Hungary*, (33) the applicants were individual shareholders in a number of banks, claiming that they had been individually affected by legislation putting the banks under central supervising authorities which resulted in significant loss of their operational autonomy. The Court drew a distinction between complaints brought by shareholders about measures affecting their rights as shareholders and measures and acts affecting companies as such. The Court furthermore did not consider shareholders as victims, in the legal sense stipulated in Article 34, of public acts affecting their companies unless there is close identity between shareholder and company (e.g. one shareholder only) and if "exceptional circumstances" preclude the affected companies from bringing the cases to the Court on their own behalf. The applicants were not closely identified with their banks and the Court found no weighty or convincing reasons demonstrating exceptional circumstances for allowing shareholders to bring complaints on banks' behalf.

The case *Xero Flor v. Poland* (34) concerned the failed attempts by the applicant company to get compensation from the State for damage to one of its products (turf) by game. The company had lodged a constitutional complaint that the Constitutional Court had declared inadmissible in 2017. The bench that heard that case had contained a judge, whose appointment was allegedly unconstitutional. (The judge had been elected by the new parliament despite his seat having already been filled by the previous parliament.) The Court found that the domestic courts had failed to answer the applicant's arguments that the law applied had been incompatible with the Constitution and, consequently, had failed in their duty under Article 6 § 1 ECHR to provide reasoned decisions, denying the applicant company a fair trial. The Court also found that the appointment procedure meant that the panel that had tried the case had not been a "tribunal established by law," Article 6, para. 1, ECHR. (35)

(33) See *Albert and Others v. Hungary* [GC] (5294/14).
(34) See *Xero Flor w Polsce sp. z o.o. v. Poland* (4907/18).
(35) See Press release ECHR 138 (2021), 7 May 2021.

There is, in addition, several examples in the Court's case-law where the Court identifies a standard, to be observed in specific circumstances, outside domestic legislation and rather in the realm of professional standards in a given area of activity. Cases that feature such cross-references to professional standards include *Kurt v. Austria*, referring to "criminological research and best practices in domestic violence cases,"(36) *Lopes de Sousa Fernandes v. Portugal*, where reference is made to the obligation of the State to "make regulations compelling hospitals, whether private or public, to adopt appropriate measures for the protection of patients' lives,"(37) as well as *Salikhov v. Russia*, where one fault was found with an investigative procedure that "deviated from the established best practice in the field of forensic medicine."(38)

The Court's case-law suggests that the Court applies the concept of subsidiarity with more intensity when the authorities in a State Party have demonstrated in preceding cases that they are taking their Convention obligations seriously.(39) It is through their acts, especially the reasoning provided by the courts of the jurisdiction in question, that States demonstrate the degree of adherence to the concept of subsidiarity.(40) States must therefore demonstrate structural capability of effectively securing the ECHR obligations and respect for the rule of law in domestic procedures in order to benefit from the advantages of the process-based review.(41)

A significant degree of incorporation of the ECHR in domestic law naturally improves the prospects for compliance, as it enables national authorities and courts to uphold ECHR rights and obligations through upholding domestic rather than international law. Successful integration of the Convention into domestic law permits the Court to focus on reviewing the relevant domestic decision-making. Court President Robert Spano has termed this a "process-based review," where the Court examines whether:

(i) the Convention principles have been adequately embedded in the legal order, and

(ii) whether certain material elements allow it to grant deference to national authorities.

---

(36) See *Kurt v. Austria* [GC] (62903/15), para. 171.

(37) See *Lopes de Sousa Fernandes v. Portugal* [GC] (56080/13), para. 166. In its turn referring to *Oyal v. Turkey* (4864/05) para. 54, and *Lambert and Others v. France* [GC] (46043/14), para. 140.

(38) See *Salikhov v. Russia* (23880/05), para. 79.

(39) See R. Spano, "The Future of the European Court of Human Rights – Subsidiarity, Process-Based Review and the Rule of Law", *Human Rights Law Review*, 2018, Vol. 18, No. 3, p. 481.

(40) *Ibid.*, p. 492.

(41) *Ibid.*, p. 473.

The process-based review, which is mainly limited to qualified rights and not to core or absolute rights and which should not be perceived as pertaining only to procedural issues, analyses if an issue has been examined through the domestic procedures in conformity with the States' obligations to secure the Convention rights to all within their jurisdictions, regardless of whether this is done through incorporation or transposition. It would be appropriate to say that the process-based review is the mechanism through which the Court gives practical effect to the concept of subsidiarity. (42)

V. CONCLUDING REMARKS

Through these reflections and references, I have tried to show, in the same spirit as Koen Lenaerts, President of the Court of Justice of the European Union, (43) that the ECHR system is not unaware of the development of compliance as such, and that it is, in its own fashion, contributing to it. Why do we see compliance-enhancing measures multiplying and expanding, notably through big leaps, such as Protocols 14, 15, and 16, but also through developments in case-law and procedural reasoning? It is naturally not just the prospect of future procedural benefits that such a prospective, *ex ante*-emphasising trend can be observed at least over the last decade.

Subsidiarity and the margin of appreciation have both emerged in order to enhance the effectiveness of ECHR compliance, for the benefit of all individuals on the territories of States Parties to the ECHR. The history of the ECHR system clearly demonstrates the risks of relying exclusively on extensive *ex post*-verification of compliance, which is what led to the need for the reforms heralded in the Interlaken Declaration 2010, (44) in turn leading to the adoption of Protocol 14. Embeddedness and incorporation of Convention obligations in domestic legal systems should also be mentioned in these circumstances. In States where the internalisation of the Convention has been successful, one possible feature of the future

(42) R. Spano, "The Future of the European Court of Human Rights – Subsidiarity, Process-Based Review and the Rule of Law", *op. cit.*, p. 481.

(43) See K. Lenaerts, "Le juge de l'Union européenne dans une Europe de la Compliance", in M.-A. Frison-Roche (ed.), *Pour une Europe de la Compliance*, "Régulations & Compliance" Serie, Paris, Dalloz, 2019, p. 1.

(44) See High Level Conference on the Future of the European Court of Human Rights, *Interlaken Declaration*, 19 February 2010.

dialogue is what the Court President has termed the process-based review, a more framework-oriented review of domestic decision-making in relation to qualified rights, ensuring a high degree of trust and subsidiarity.

The ECHR system is still mainly designed to verify *ex post* system compliance by the States Parties to the Convention, but there are more features today that make the ECHR system relevant also from a general compliance perspective:

- the development of rules of presumption through the Court's own jurisprudence, e.g. the Bosphorus doctrine, but likewise the process-based review, which rewards demonstrated compliance with procedural trust;
- the codification of the margin of appreciation and subsidiarity, two concepts derived from the Court's case-law, both demonstrate the necessity of the Court not engaging where States Parties to the ECHR are already complying fully at national level;
- the creation by the States Parties of new and prospective Convention mechanisms, notably the possibility for domestic courts to request advisory opinions from the ECHR, prior to the conclusion of a national procedure that potentially transcends the ECHR;
- the jurisprudential development opening the Convention rights more visibly to objects of general compliance, as can be seen in cases where the applicants were legal rather than natural persons (such as the case referred to above).

The examples above serve to demonstrate certain aspects of how the ECHR-system operates, cognisant of the correlating and variable requirements of compliance applicable on legal subjects within its jurisdiction. The ECHR-system strives, in its own logic, towards ever higher degrees of integration of its own imperatives among its subjects, in a way that strongly resembles other normative systems that encourages or requires compliance.

Contents